Bernfried Nugel, Jer

Aldous Hux
Volume 19 (2019)

Aldous Huxley Annual

A Journal of Twentieth-Century Thought and Beyond

edited by

Professor Jerome Meckier
Department of English,
University of Kentucky

and

Professor Bernfried Nugel
Englisches Seminar
der Westfälischen Wilhelms-Universität Münster

Volume 19

LIT

Bernfried Nugel, Jerome Meckier (eds.)

Aldous Huxley Annual

A Journal of
Twentieth-Century Thought and Beyond

Volume 19 (2019)

LIT

Cover design: Erwin J. Löhr

This book is printed on acid-free paper.

Bibliographic information published by the Deutsche Nationalbibliothek
The Deutsche Nationalbibliothek lists this publication in the Deutsche Nationalbibliografie; detailed bibliographic data are available in the Internet at http://dnb.dnb.de.

ISBN 978-3-643-91250-3 (pb)
ISBN 978-3-643-96250-8 (PDF)

A catalogue record for this book is available from the British Library.

Flössergasse 10
CH-8001 Zürich
Tel. +41 (0) 76-632 84 35
E-Mail: zuerich@lit-verlag.ch http://www.lit-verlag.ch
Distribution:
In the UK: Global Book Marketing, e-mail: mo@centralbooks.com
In North America: Independent Publishers Group, e-mail: orders@ipgbook.com
In Germany: LIT Verlag Fresnostr. 2, D-48159 Münster
Tel. +49 (0) 2 51-620 32 22, Fax +49 (0) 2 51-922 60 99, e-mail: vertrieb@lit-verlag.de
e-books are available at www.litwebshop.de

To the memory of Lothar Fietz

ALDOUS HUXLEY ANNUAL

A Journal of Twentieth-Century Thought and Beyond

Volume 19 (2019)

Contents

Editors' Preface

Aldous Huxley Annual (*AHA*) is founded on the conviction that Aldous Huxley's writings have important things to say to the twenty-first century.

We predict increased admiration for his thought and artistry.

In the new century, this poignant prophet will come fully into his own as novelist, essayist, philosopher and holy man.

This is the century in which many of the problems Huxley helped to identify and define will come to a head. The solutions he suggested remain pertinent, worthy of additional consideration. How to preserve the environment? How to stem overpopulation? How to improve education, prevent war, defuse nationalism, protect language, predict a future in which art, drugs, religion and their ilk combine to actualize human potentialities?

AHA is especially interested in publishing new Huxley materials: uncollected poems, letters, essays, one's personal encounters with Huxley, etc. It also hopes to feature studies of his poetry and prose that will strengthen his reputation as a major modern.

Volume 19 is dedicated to the memory of Prof Lothar Fietz (University of Tübingen) in appreciation of his merits as an outstanding Huxley scholar, as a Founding Member and Curator of the Aldous Huxley Society and as a true friend (see the In Memoriam below). The volume opens with a sequence of hitherto unpublished Huxley writings, starting with the three extant versions from 1949 of his dramatization of *Ape and Essence* (1948), thematically linked with two texts treating the physical survival of mankind and three contrasting texts discussing the question of spiritual survival. This section is followed by Huxley's draft for an introduction of Edna St. Vincent Millay at one of her poetry readings in 1938 and an autograph letter to Seabury Edwardes that he wrote shortly after the publication of *The Doors of Perception* (1954). The volume closes with several critical articles on Huxley's relationship with D. T. Suzuki, his Sanary period and his view and practice of literary utopias.

The Editors invite submissions for the fourth Peter Edgerly Firchow Memorial Essay Prize (see the special announcement below).

Prof Bernfried Nugel wishes to thank Uwe Rasch, M.A., for his assistance with formatting and proofreading this issue. For digitizing and proofreading profound thanks are due to Dr Gerhard Wagner and Matthias Kreimann, M.A.

Jerome Meckier   Bernfried Nugel

The Peter Edgerly Firchow Memorial Essay Prize in Aldous Huxley Studies

In appreciation of Peter Edgerly Firchow's merits as an outstanding Huxley scholar and also as a Founding Member and Curator of the International Aldous Huxley Society, the AHS Executive Committee has established the above prize in order to further research on Aldous Huxley. It invites contributions from scholars concerned, the award being subject to the following specifications:

(1) The prize is to be awarded periodically for the best journal-length essay in Aldous Huxley Studies submitted to *Aldous Huxley Annual* by an untenured Huxley scholar.

(2) The prize is endowed with $400.

(3) A jury of three alternating AHS specialists chooses the best essay out of the pertinent submissions to *AHA*.

(4) The essay chosen is published in the subsequent issue of *AHA*.

(5) The deadline for submissions for the fourth award is 31 July 2020.

AHS Executive Committee

In Memoriam Lothar Fietz

No man is an *Iland*, intire of it selfe; every man is a peece of the *Continent*…
If a *Clod* bee washed away by the *Sea*, *Europe* is the lesse…
Any mans *death* diminishes *me*, because I am involved in *Mankinde*;
And therefore never send to know for whom the *bell* tolls.

John Donne / Ernest Hemingway

The Aldous Huxley Society mourns the death of its Founding Member and Curator Prof. Dr. Lothar Fietz, who passed away on 15 December 2019 at the age of 86. He was Professor of English Philology and Modern Literature at the University of Tübingen, where he taught literature as well as literary theory and carried out research from 1981 to 1999. A singularly erudite scholar of German and international acclaim, he also was, among various other achievements, the first German Huxley critic to write a book-length study of Huxley's novels, entitled *Menschenbild und Romanstruktur in Aldous Huxleys Ideenromanen* (1969) ['Concept of Man and Fictional Structure in Aldous Huxley's Novels of Ideas']. This book laid the foundation for a kind of elective affinity with Huxley throughout his career.

In his self-chosen epitaph from John Donne quoted above, Lothar Fietz encapsulated what was particularly dear to him in the history of human thought: the idea of a community of fully human beings reaching out beyond frontiers, a community in which all individuals *idealiter* share their lives with those of other individuals and thus constitute their own intrinsic value. The subtitle of his ground-breaking book *Fragmentarisches Existieren* ['Fragmentary Existence'] (1994) aptly characterizes his lifelong search for the ideal of wholeness in philosophy, theology and literature: *Wandlungen des Mythos von der verlorenen Ganzheit in der Geschichte philosophischer, theologischer und literarischer Menschenbilder* ['Transformations of the Myth of Lost Wholeness in the History of Philosophical, Theological and Literary Concepts of Man']. Quite appropriately, he devoted a whole chapter of his book to Huxley's place in the framework of intellectual history from antiquity to the twentieth century. In the same vein he not only presented in-depth analyses of Huxley's work but also compared Huxley with other literary luminaries, as is amply documented in his volume of collected essays *Aldous Huxley – Prätexte und Kontexte* (2005) ['Aldous Huxley—Pretexts and Contexts']. This volume also contains a comprehensive bibliography of Lothar Fietz' writings. In addition, his several articles in *Aldous Huxley Annual* display the impressive range of his Huxley-centred scholarship.

As regards the publications of the Aldous Huxley Society, he served on the editorial board of *Aldous Huxley Annual* since its beginning and was co-founder and co-editor of the monograph series "Human Potentialities" published by LIT Verlag Münster, Wien, Zürich.

For his constant active support of the Huxley cause the Aldous Huxley Society owes him immense thanks, and in appreciation of his merits the editors of *Aldous Huxley Annual* have decided to dedicate the present issue to his memory.

In variation of Donne's pronouncement we may well say that Lothar's death diminishes all of us, in the global context as well as on the personal plane, where we have to take leave of an exceptional human being and friend. The Aldous Huxley Society has lost a mastermind and will never be the same again!

Bernfried Nugel
(Chairman of the Aldous Huxley Society)

In Memoriam Pierre Vitoux

Prof Pierre Vitoux, Curator and longstanding member of the Aldous Huxley Society, passed away on 14 June 2018. He had taught at the Université Paul-Valéry Montpellier since 1961 and had been an internationally acclaimed Huxley scholar of the early phase of Huxley criticism, doing for instance spadework in the Huxley holdings of the Harry Ransom Humanities Research Center, where he compiled a checklist of Huxley manuscripts and thus laid the foundation for subsequent Huxley research (see *Library Chronicle of the University of Texas*, 9 [1978]). He also studied the relationship between Huxley and D. H. Lawrence and gave a perceptive lecture on this topic at the Aldous Huxley Centenary Symposium in Münster 1994. His lifelong dedication to the work of Huxley can be seen in his French Huxley biography *Aldous Huxley: Romancier et critique de la modernité* (2002), which paved the way for a better understanding of Huxley in France.

Pierre Vitoux always supported the work of the Aldous Huxley Society to the best of his ability. He was a member of the editorial board of *Aldous Huxley Annual* since its beginning and gave solid advice on particular developments within the Society. In his last years, regrettably, he wished to retire from its activities, but nonetheless his devotion to the Huxley cause will always be gratefully acknowledged.

The Aldous Huxley Society mourns the loss of a great Huxley scholar and friend and will forever honour his memory.

Bernfried Nugel
(Chairman of the Aldous Huxley Society)

IN MEMORIAM VALERY RABINOVITCH

Prof Valery Rabinovitch of the Urals Federal University (Russia), member of the Aldous Huxley Society since 2004, passed away on 23 September 2019 at the age of 54. From 1989, he had taught literature at the Specialized Educational Center for Gifted Children, the school associated with Urals State University, where he began his life-long career of an educator as a regular teacher, later holding the positions of senior instructor and associate professor. In 1999 he had founded the Department of Philology of the Lyceum and served as its chair until 2005. He is the author of more than a dozen manuals for high school students: one of them, *Западная литература: История духовных исканий* ('Western Literature: The History of Spiritual Quests'), was awarded a Soros grant. For some years he was a director of Soros's educational project "The Dialogue of Times and Cultures." He became an equally popular educator when he began to teach at the Urals Federal University in 1994 and was appointed as full-time faculty member in 2005.

The research of Aldous Huxley and, generally, English literature of the first half of the twentieth century became his major field of studies. Both his PhD dissertation and his 'habilitation' (postdoctoral) thesis were devoted to the work and philosophy of Aldous Huxley. He is the author of many essays and the first Russian monography on Aldous Huxley: *Олдос Хаксли: Эволюция творчества* ('Aldous Huxley: The Evolution of His Art') [Ekaterinburg, 2001], which covered the writer's whole career. Since 2004, he attended three Aldous Huxley Symposia (in Riga, Los Angeles, and Almería) and contributed four articles to *Aldous Huxley Annual* and the monograph series "Human Potentialities," among which his essay on the Russian reception of Huxley (*AHA* 5) may well be considered his most important one. Besides, he published a collection of critical and biographical essays *Наедине с собой и людьми* ('Face to Face with Myself and Other People') [Moscow, 2012].

He will always be remembered as a dedicated scholar as well as a prominent and devoted educator.

On behalf of the Aldous Huxley Society,

Irina Golovacheva

Bernfried Nugel
(Chairman of the Aldous Huxley Society

James Sexton & Bernfried Nugel
(University of British Columbia & University of Münster)

Aldous Huxley's Unpublished Dramatization of *Ape and Essence*

The genesis of the play

"Plays are obviously the things one must pay attention to. Imprimis, they are the only literary essays out of which a lot of money can be made; and I am determined to make writing pay."[1] The young author Aldous Huxley wrote these words to his brother Julian in 1918, but his ambition to strike gold with a successful play was something of a will-o'-the wisp that he pursued on and off until only a few days before he died.[2] Reading through his letters, one is struck by the number of references to his time-consuming play-writing projects, almost all of which came to nothing—except for his one real stage success, the dramatic adaptation of his short story "The Gioconda Smile," directed by Jack De Leon, which in March 1948 began a nine-month run of 296 performances in London.[3] Moreover, Huxley's brother-in-law, the well-known French cinéaste and playwright Georges Neveux (1900–1982), had adapted this play for the French stage; it premiered in February 1949 as *Le sourire de la Joconde* in Paris,[4] and the foreword to the play, published in the journal *Réalités littéraires*, states that "la pièce de Huxley que Georges Neveux a admirablement adaptée pour la scène française, avait remporté à Londres un immense succès avant de triompher au théâtre de l'Œuvre avec Raymond Rouleau."[5] So understandably, Huxley must have jumped at De Leon's suggestion that he follow up that success by adapting his novel *Ape and Essence* for the stage.[6]

Huxley quickly went to work. In early January 1949, he had already completed a first draft, as he reported in a letter to Victoria Ocampo, dated 9 January 1949: "I have just finished a dramatization of my phantasy about the future, *Ape and Essence*" (*Letters*, 589). On 14 February he told Anita Loos that he had been preparing additional scenes for a second draft, asking her to return the copy of the first draft that he had sent her:

> [These are] scenes which will, I think, have the double advantage of increasing the playing time and heightening the drama and comedy. These are now nearly finished, and I am anxious to incorporate them into the script. Would you, therefore, be very kind and return the copy I sent you? I have only the rough draft here and would like to have a fair copy with all the additions.[7]

For some reason or other, Huxley no longer possessed a clean copy of the first draft and apparently wanted to use the copy he had sent to Anita Loos in order to insert into it the additional scenes he had composed in the meantime. On 24 February 1949, i.e., only ten days after his letter to Loos, he sent a letter to Neveux, in which he enclosed his more-or-less literal French translation of the play, implying that this was a more advanced version since he mentioned that De Leon had already seen a previous version, viz. presumably the first draft. He entitled the French play *Le vice du vase*, a phrase he had found in Montaigne's essay "Du pédantisme" (see below, 5 and note 11).

This course of revision is clearly reflected in the three extant drafts, i.e., the English draft with additional scenes, the French draft sent to Georges Neveux, and the "fair copy with all the additions" that Huxley wanted to have produced, as he wrote to Anita Loos (for further details, see the section "Editors' Note on the Text," below, 13).

In his letter to Neveux Huxley also made it perfectly clear that he had not yet arrived at a definitive version and at the same time provided much detail regarding his plans for style and staging:

> 'Dear Georges,[8]
>
> Here is the translation of the play—a bit rough but accurate. The present version is not definitive, and I would be grateful for any criticisms and suggestions.
>
> [Jack] De Leon, who saw a previous version, wanted to suppress the Narrator, about which I think he is wrong. The play must be non-realistic, and the Narrator contributes to this end. From another man of the theatre, I had some advice which seems to me better.' (*SL*, 402)

This man of the theatre was probably Albert B. Taylor, who was a literary agent in the New York office of the William Morris Agency, the firm Huxley employed. A specialist in dramatic and musical properties, Taylor later produced the hit musical *Damn Yankees* (1955). In his letter to Anita Loos, mentioned above, Huxley had referred to Taylor saying "that he liked the first version and hoped to sell it as a piece with incidental music and ballet. Which may be a good idea" (*SL*, 400).

Several days later, in his letter to Neveux, he enlarged on Taylor's advice that the play should employ ballet elements:

> '[His idea is] to show the ceremonies of the second act in ballet form (through a background wall of gauze), which would have the advantage of accentuating the non-realism of the play, letting the spectators see things which are now merely written and heard, as well as to cut the length of the discussions between Poole and the Arch-Vicar—too long in the present version.

> A ballet with appropriate music could be very beautiful. What do you think?
>
> At the beginning of the act [Act 3], I intend to add a scene between Loola and Flossie before Poole's arrival. Flossie will leave, and later, it will be because of her that the Arch-Vicar returns to surprise the lovers.
>
> They say it won't work at the end to lock the lead actor into a closet; so he will be tied to a chair and will be present, cursing, as the lovers exit.
>
> De Leon wants to divide Acts 2 and 3 into two separate scenes each, separated by a curtain, but I don't see the need. What do you think?' (*SL*, 402)

Huxley apparently overruled De Leon, since the narrator continues to play a key role in the fair copy. Whatever his final intentions, the draft as it comes down to us contains no stage directions suggesting ballet elements or music, although presumably these would have been added later.[9] And despite his admission that the exchanges between Poole and the Arch-Vicar were too long, similar to those in his previous play projects such as *Now More Than Ever*, Huxley's tendency to produce overly-talky dialogue remained a problem. Nor did he make good on his announced intention of adding a short scene between Flossie and Loola. Rather, Act 3 begins with conflict between Poole and Flossie. Lastly, the concluding cupboard scene remained—so, clearly, as of 24 February 1949, he intended to write in more changes.

Interestingly, Huxley carried on with his project for another three months or so and even congratulated himself on having won Neveux over to work together on the French version of the play. In his letter of 2 June 1949, he also mentioned De Leon again:

> 'Thank you for your letter; I take pleasure in the thought that you are once again to become my collaborator. If you think that changes (other than cuts) are necessary, please indicate them for me. [Jack] De Leon, who has written to me several times within a few weeks, wants me at all costs to add scenes "with human interest"—that is, scenes in which Poole and Loola's romance would be treated with much greater unction and other scenes in which the incentives for their elopement would become more "idealistic." In a word, De Leon wants me to underscore the "positive" side of the play, to proclaim more clearly its spiritual message etc. I have replied to him that I hesitate to take his advice, for I am finding that a bigger dose of "human interest" could destroy the plausibility of the phantasy as a whole—that in trying too hard to reassure the public, one risks spoiling the play. On the other hand maybe he is right in wishing to mitigate a little what you call the atomic-bomb impression that the play gives. But I believe that this mitigation can be produced by means of judicious cuts and the introduction of the spectacle and music. Tell me very

> frankly what you think of this question of "human interest" and the "positive" and "spiritual" side. If it seems to you necessary to bear down a little on the love affair of Poole and Loola, bear down without hesitation by adding what seems good to you. Not knowing very well what I've written, I am not attached to it and I can envisage no matter what surgical intervention with complete sang froid.' (*Letters*, 598–99)

Apparently, Huxley had tried hard to come to a consensus with De Leon, but was uncertain how far he should comply with the prospective producer's ideas of "underscor[ing] the 'positive' side of the play." On the other hand, he was willing to tone down what both De Leon and Neveux had objected to as "the atomic-bomb impression," a phrase which presumably refers to the overriding tendency of the play to shatter any belief in human values. All in all, he admits that he is at a loss and would welcome sound advice from Neveux. Unfortunately, no more letters either to De Leon or to Neveux seem to have survived.

From novel to play

Whatever Neveux's thoughts were, the fair copy reproduced below appears to be the last one that Huxley completed, and Huxley and Neveux must have soon dropped their plan to repeat the success of *Gioconda* by producing English and French stage versions of *Ape and Essence*. That the play remained unproduced should surprise no one. Ironically, the problems Huxley mentions in his 1920 review of Israel Zangwill's drama of ideas, *The Melting Point*, remained just as insurmountable in 1949:

> The drama is a form in which it is almost impossible to convey ideas of any complexity. To be understood at a first hearing by a mixed crowd of several hundred people an idea must be extraordinarily simple. [...] The difficulty of conveying an idea dramatically is so great, and the range of ideas that can be conveyed so limited, that one wonders why people who are interested in theories go to the trouble of writing a play when their notions could be far more subtly, accurately, and truly expressed in a novel or an essay.[10]

That Huxley was aware of the necessity to reduce the complexity of his novel to a simpler level in the play can be seen from what he cut as compared with his fictional model. He not only dispensed with the frame story set in Hollywood and the Mojave Desert but also left out the ape sequences and the filmic features in the script, such as camera shots and sound track, and only kept the Belial part and the Poole/Loola storyline as well as a number of pertinent Narrator passages. But even in this part he apparently felt the need for concentration: he omitted, for instance, Poole's mother complex and his relationship with Ethel Hook, and cut the scene in front of the Los Angeles Philharmonic Auditorium, transposing Poole's appropriation of the duodecimo Shelley to the scene in which dinner is being prepared for the Arch-Vicar.

Thus, Huxley generally seems to have been compelled by the dramatic format to focus on what really matters in terms of action and ideas, which may even be an advantage as far as public appeal is concerned. Still, he may have adopted too much dialogue and too many interventions by the Narrator from the novel as well as have given too much space to the deliberations of the Arch-Vicar. He may also have been too far ahead of his time inasmuch as he appears willing to ride roughshod over audience sensibilities. Even in a satire whose tone resembles that of Swift, the onstage depiction during the Purification Ceremony in Act 2 of babies having their throats cut and of mothers being flagellated for bringing these deformed babies into the world must have seemed—at least to Huxley's contemporaries—indefensible. Such material might have been acceptable in an essay such as *A Modest Proposal*, but not in a play. But in fairness, perhaps Huxley had anticipated this problem, and his intention was, as indicated in his February letter to Neveux quoted above, to interpose a thin sheet of gauze between the audience and the actors, thereby diminishing the goriness of the "Purification Ceremonies" by means of a shadowy depiction of the violence.

However, whatever weaknesses remained, he at least devised an effective surprise ending by having the lovers elope while the Arch-Vicar is left behind trapped in a closet and yelling in despair.

Huxley's monstrous play and the "dream of reason"

That Huxley chose *Le vice du vase* as the title for his French version of the *Ape and Essence* play, is thematically instructive for the English version as well. John Florio (1553–1625), the Anglo-Italian translator of Montaigne's "Du pédantisme" (1580)—Huxley's source—nicely rendered the sense of the phrase *le vice du vase* into English: "Knowledge is an excellent drug, but no drug is sufficiently strong to preserve it selfe without alteration or corruption, according to the *fault of the vessell* [i.e., *le vice du vase*] that containes it."[11] For central to Huxley's purpose in both the novel and play versions is his desire to retell the myth of Pandora's Box and the account of the Fall of Humankind—to warn against pride—the flaw or fault in the human 'vessel' (in Biblical language)—as demonstrated by homo sapiens' too-confident and too-slavish adherence to the empiricist project of controlling nature, perhaps most clearly announced by the scientific projector at Solomon's House in Francis Bacon's utopian work *New Atlantis*: "'The end of our foundation is the knowledge of causes, and secret motions of things; and the enlarging of the bounds of human *empire*, to the effecting of all things possible.'"[12]

In 1949, Huxley's attitude to the Enlightenment agenda was very similar to that described by Theodor W. Adorno and Max Horkheimer in *Dialectic of Enlightenment*, published in English in 1947. Huxley's Narrator states that the miserable regime of post-World War III Los Angeles is the end result of the Enlightenment project. As Robert Baker notes, Adorno and Horkheimer (like Huxley) argue that

> the history of the European Enlightenment of the late seventeenth and the eighteenth centuries was driven by an encompassing desire […] for intellectual autonomy [which] manifested itself in the mastery of nature, both external and human. The result was a technocratic ideology that reduced everything to technique, to efficiency and standardized measurement and that eventually was responsible for the release of something more uncomfortable and unknowable.[13]

That which was released was the nuclear bomb, biological warfare, and environmental disaster.

Huxley was fond of the maxim attributed to Chateaubriand: "*Les forêts précèdent les peuples, et les déserts les suivent*" ('Forests precede civilizations, and deserts follow them').[14] This chilling observation could serve as an epigraph to the play, whose theme reflects Huxley's belief that humanity must either control its proud empirical project to dominate nature and flaunt Natural Law, or else perish.

Huxley's play is set in Chateaubriand's desert phase. The Arch-Vicar's role resembles that of Mustapha Mond in *Brave New World*. Like Mond, he is not just an apologist for the current regime, he is also its historian, having been careful, like Mond, to retain many key books for posterity. However, unlike Mond's rationalized, controlled and science-worshipping regime, the Arch-Vicar's is not one that uses science to dominate nature. The Arch-Vicar despairs of progress, science and technology, blaming it for the devastating nuclear and biological war that resulted in near-universal scarcity. Unlike the survivors of the brave new world's Nine Years' War, the survivors of "the Thing" (24–25)[15] reject science, and instead try to propitiate the devil as they brace themselves for whatever final punishment Belial has in store for them. Meanwhile Church and State preserve a semblance of order through sadistic and fascistic exploitation of those healthy enough to scavenge for food and the other necessities of life.

Huxley begins his play with the Narrator's statement that misguided use of science and technology was the means by which the ancestors of the pathetic survivors in Los Angeles destroyed themselves (20). At roughly the same time that he was working on the *Ape and Essence* play, he was writing about Goya's *Caprichos*, in particular his etching "*El sueño de la razon produce monstruos*" ('the dream of reason produces monsters'), and in his play the symbolic monster-babies produced by the effects of gamma-rays are all-too-visible in post-apocalyptic Los Angeles. Huxley offers two interpretations of Goya's phrase, the second of which seems particularly congruent with the theme of this play:

> The moral of it all is summed up in the central plate of the *Caprichos*, in which we see Goya himself, his head on his arms, sprawled across his desk and fitfully sleeping, while the air above is peopled with the bats and owls of necromancy and just behind his chair lies an enormous witch's cat, [...] staring at the sleeper with baleful eyes. On the side of the desk are traced the words, 'The dream of reason produces monsters.' It is a caption that admits of more than one interpretation. When Reason sleeps, the absurd and loathsome creatures of superstition wake and are active, goading their victim to an ignoble frenzy. But this is not all. *Reason may also dream without sleeping; may intoxicate itself, as it did during the French Revolution, with the day-dreams of inevitable progress, of liberty, equality and fraternity imposed by violence, of human self-sufficiency and the ending of sorrow, not by the all too arduous method which alone offers any prospect of success, but by political re-arrangements and a better technology.*[16]

Structurally and thematically, however, the monster symbolism is counterpointed by another symbol—the volume of Percy Shelley's *Complete Poetry*. Poole and Loola will have a chance at salvation if they reject what Huxley called in his earlier California work, *After Many a Summer*, "the human level of time and craving"[17] and try to transcend temporal existence. From the moment Poole rescues Shelley's poems from the flames, Huxley injects mystical quotations that serve as a transcendental counterpoint to "the human level of time and craving." The first is from Shelley's "The Woodman and the Nightingale": "The world is full of woodmen who expel / Love's gentle dryads from the trees of life / And vex the nightingales in every dell" (47). The line, ironically, is read by the Arch-Vicar, who, of course, opposes the romantic love that Poole is beginning to feel for Loola. This excerpt is the first of several quotations from Shelley, which, with the introduction of a series of lines from *Epipsychidion*, and later from *Adonais*, effectively set up the motif of a movement from earthly to Divine love as outlined in Plato's *Symposium.* Poole speaks of Loola, just as Shelley described Emily: "See where she stands, a mortal shape indued / With love and life and light and deity […] / An image of some bright Eternity" (74). The next step on the ladder of ascent is suggested by Poole's implicitly Platonic idea of removed bandages from the eyes (see 76) as he realizes that "[w]hat's going on here isn't the last word. The last word is what you begin to understand when you're listening to Mozart," or as Loola responds, "Or when you love somebody." Poole recognizes that what Shelley referred to as "the image of some bright eternity […] breaks through and transfigures time, delivering it from evil. I suppose that's the whole point and purpose of being a human being" (76).[18]

Interestingly, in the play version, Huxley refers to Poole as having Quaker roots (not Congregationalist, as in the novel[19])—perhaps in an attempt to strengthen his link to the seventeenth-century Cambridge Platonist and Quaker sympathizer Peter Sterry (1613–1672), to whom Huxley refers in *Themes and Variations* as "another who lived in that world" (*TV*, 141)—"that transfigured other-world, which is yet our world" (*TV*, 140)—and whose mystical writings buttress the many Platonic quotations from Shelley. Speaking of the way to salvation, Huxley cites Sterry:

> "Didst thou […] ever descry a glorious eternity in a winged moment of time? Didst thou ever see a bright infinity in the narrow point of an object? Then thou knowest what Spirit is—the spire-top whither all things ascend harmoniously, where they meet and sit contented in an unfathomed Depth of Life." Such, then, is the mystical conception of true and complete salvation. (*TV*, 141)

And as Poole and Loola are about to try to make their escape, Huxley's Narrator reinforces the play's emerging transcendental theme, prefacing those exact lines from Sterry that Huxley used in *Themes and Variations* with a reference to "the [mystical] reality that underlies appearances" (84).

According to the "Chronology" at the beginning of Grover Smith's edition of Huxley's letters (see *Letters*, 17), Huxley wintered in Palm Desert from November 1948 until February 1949, devoting December 1948 to his stage adaptation of *Ape and Essence.* The desert environment is highly relevant to his abortive play as well as to his abortive scenario written in 1956 as the basis for a documentary for the NBC television program *Omnibus*, which details the terrible "things that happen when men do not collaborate with Nature, but try to exploit Nature. Such are the consequences of extractive agriculture."[20] Interestingly, the Arch-Vicar singles out "extractive agriculture" as one of the ruinously exploitative practices that led to the dystopia they now inhabit (55).

Huxley had earlier used this phrase in an essay published while he was at work in Palm Desert on his play—in November and December 1948. Its title is "The Double Crisis,"[21] and it reads like a prophetic preamble to the dystopian scenario of *Ape and Essence*:

> Man is his own Martian, at war against himself. Overbreeding and *extractive agriculture* are his weapons, and, though he may not know it, his war aims are the ravaging of the planet, the destruction of his civilization, and the degradation of his species. (*TV*, 239; editors' emphasis)

There are only two direct references to 'desert' in the play: the first is an entirely negative one, but later we see that Poole plans his escape to the north via the Mojave Desert see 85). To Huxley, the desert was the place where death/evil plays itself out—"[a]fter which the Order of Things comes to the surface again" (87)—just as he had witnessed in 1948 and 1953 when the cicadas and the Madonna lilies came to the surface after a lengthy period of hibernation, but emerged with a burst of extravagant life. Huxley's theme here develops this "triumph of life" (to use another phrase from Shelley): Huxley's dystopia, in the end, turns to utopian possibility—Poole and Loola, together with the northern group in Fresno, are the 'saving remnant' —so common in dystopias from Zamyatin, through Orwell's proles, and now those people in Fresno, who oppose the Satanic majority in the southern part of the state.

Poole, before he sets out on his escape journey, tells the Arch-Vicar:

> "The land goes back to nature and after a few hundred years it'll almost be fit for us to colonize. And [...] the same goes on in the spiritual world. Fear and hatred and anger and envy—[...] they wear themselves out, they tend to their own annihilation. That's why hell can't be everlasting. It finally makes a clean sweep of itself and then the Other One rushes in to fill the vacuum." (87)

Huxley dramatizes here the same victory that he describes in his three desert essays. The dystopian *Ape and Essence* drama is a scenic representation of the triumph of life over death as described in "Consider the Lilies" (travel essay and short story), "The Desert" and "Ozymandias"—that trilogy of California desert essays that were nearly contemporaneous with this play.

Perhaps Huxley's final word on what the desert meant to him[22] can be found in the above-mentioned travel essay that he published in early 1953, but whose thesis parallels that of a description of his desert trip in May 1948:

> "Consider the lilies of the field..." They, certainly, are marvelous enough. But even more wonderful are the lilies of the desert. These grow in the nakedest, the most utterly barren regions of the

> Borrego and Colorado deserts. Buried two feet underground, their bulbs can live through the most ferocious summers, can weather the longest droughts. Then, at last, comes the rain. And suddenly the sands are islanded with straggling tufts of grey-green leaves, and from the center of each tuft rises a tall stem surmounted by a pyramid of blossoms, white like the flowers of the Madonna lily, but with a blue vein at the back of each curving petal. They stand there in the desolation, and the poet would say, no doubt, that they were wasting their sweetness on the desert air.[23] But the poet would be wrong. The sweetness is not wasted, even for us. For as long as the desert lilies continue to make their appearance, as long as these denizens of the world of space remain capable of repeating their miracle, all is not lost even in our dismal universe of history.
>
> In the teeth of our most determined efforts at self-destruction, life may be trusted to save us from ourselves.[24]

Poole and Loola, who demonstrate miraculous resilience, are the human equivalents of those desert lilies.

---

[1] *Letters of Aldous Huxley*, ed. Grover Smith (New York and London, 1969), 157. Hereafter, *Letters.*

[2] Even with regard to *Ape and Essence* a similar statement can be found in his letters, when, in 1956, he speaks of Ralph Rose's play version of *After Many a Summer* (*Letters*, 789–90): "Rose is also working on the dramatization I did of *Ape and Essence*—a dramatization which was much too short for practical purposes and which he is re-shaping in the form of a music drama with ballets. Quite a good idea, I think. I count no chickens, but hope none the less that some of these eggs may hatch out. It would be very nice to get something without having to do any work, for a change!" Incredibly, on 17 November 1963, only a few days before he died, and too weak to hold a pen, Huxley dictated his last known letter to his agent in London: "A new interest in a theatrical production of *After Many a Summer* has recently manifested itself. I will let you know whatever progress is made over here" (*Letters*, 964). Several other examples of abortive plans for further adaptations appear throughout Huxley's correspondence, including a fruitless collaboration from March 1961 until April 1962 with Peggy Lamson on a dramatic adaptation of his short story "Voices," which Huxley had published in *The Atlantic Monthly* in July 1955.

[3] Jack De Leon (1902–1956). Theatrical manager and impresario. According to J. P. Wearing's *The London Stage, 1940–1949* (Lanham, MD, 1991), *The Gioconda Smile* premiered at the New Theatre on 6 March 1948 and ran there until 18 September 1948; then it transferred to Wyndham Theatre, Hammersmith, from 21 September 1948 until 19 February 1949. In a letter dated 9 January 1949, Huxley proudly mentions the play's nine-month run (see *Letters*, 589).

[4] See *Letters*, "Chronology," 17.

[5] *Réalités Littéraires*, 21 (1949), *Le sourire de la Joconde*, 2. ('Huxley's play, admirably adapted for the French stage by Georges Neveux, enjoyed great success in

London before its triumph in Paris at the Théâtre de l'Œuvre, with Raymond Rouleau' [Translation: James Sexton]). The full text was published on pp. 3–48 of this number. The Paris production was directed by Belgian director Raymond Rouleau (1904–1981), who also acted in the lead role of Henry Hutton.

6 In a letter to Harold Raymond, dated 16 December 1948, Huxley writes: "I am working for the moment on a dramatization of *Ape and Essence*, which several people, including De Leon, have advised me to attempt" (*AHA*, 15 [2015], 159).

7 *Selected Letters of Aldous Huxley*, ed. James Sexton (Chicago, 2007) [hereafter, *SL*], 400.

8 For the original French version of the letter, see *SL*, 401–02.

9 As can be seen from his letter quoted in note 2, Huxley was still convinced in 1956 that *Ape and Essence* would work well as "a music drama with ballets."

10 Aldous Huxley's review of *The Melting Point*, *Westminster Gazette* (9 December 1920), 6.

11 *The Essays of Montaigne*, trans. John Florio, with an introduction by George Saintsbury (reprinted London, 1892 [[1]1603]), Book I, Ch. xxiv: "Of Pedantisme," 144 (editors' emphasis).

12 Francis Bacon, *New Atlantis*, ed. Gerard B. Wegemer (Center for Thomas More Studies, 2003; <www.thomasmorestudies.org>), 31 (editors' emphasis).

13 Robert Baker, "The Nightmare of the Frankfurt School: The Marquis de Sade and the Problem of Modernity in Aldous Huxley's Dystopian Narrative," *Now More Than Ever: Proceedings of the Aldous Huxley Centenary Symposium Münster 1994*, ed. Bernfried Nugel (Frankfurt a. M., 1995), 247.

14 He uses this quotation twice in 1959—see "Man and His Planet" in *The Human Situation*, ed. Piero Ferrucci (New York, 1977), 21, and also his preface to Alvah W. Sulloway's book *Birth Control and Catholic Doctrine* (Boston, 1959), xii–xiii.

15 Page numbers in parentheses refer to the edition of the play, below.

16 Aldous Huxley, *Themes and Variations* (London, 1950), 215–16 (editors' emphasis). Hereafter, *TV*. For a detailed discussion of Goya's phrase in the context of misguided ideals, see Katja Reinecke, "The Order of Folly or the Folly of Order: Aldous Huxley's Critique of Ideals Based on Goya's "El sueño," *Aldous Huxley, Man of Letters: Thinker, Critic and Artist—Proceedings of the Third International Aldous Huxley Symposium Riga 2004*, ed. Bernfried Nugel, Uwe Rasch, Gerhard Wagner, "Human Potentialities," 9 (Berlin, 2007), 205–12.

17 *After Many a Summer* (London, 1939), 119.

18 Apart from Huxley's direct use of positive Shelley quotations as a counterpoint to the dehumanized world of Belial, it should be noted that he also employs Shelley for satirical purposes, for instance, by applying Shelley's antiphonal Semichorus pattern (see Act 2), occurring in Act IV of his lyrical drama *Prometheus Unbound* (1820), to the "Purification Ceremonies" celebrated in honour of Belial. Whereas Shelley presents Man's aspiration towards love and creativeness in the ancient mythological framework of the Prometheus story, which, incidentally, is just another manifestation of the 'proud man' motif

occurring in *Ape and Essence*, Huxley shows the Belial State perverting the Christian liturgical practice of singing antiphones, thus turning human values into utter depravity. More so than in the novel, Huxley's use of this device in his play appears geared to produce an immediate dramatic effect, reinforced by the fact that it originally comes from another drama.

[19] See *Ape and Essence* (London, 1949), 52; interestingly, the reference to "Congregationalist" is still present on the original pages 7 and 8 of the English draft: "Dr. Poole: No, sir. I am a liberal Congregationalist" (7) and "Dr. Poole: A liberal Congregationalist. Inclining, I must admit, to agnosticism. Definitely not a priest"(8). See below, 24.

[20] Unpublished and untitled 7-page typescript Huxley wrote on the dangers of overpopulation and environmental mismanagement. This first draft of the documentary, from which the citation above is taken (3), must have been written before 21 August 1956, as an autograph inscription on the first page of the typescript reads "sent by mail Aug 21 / 56 from Hollywood." The second draft, dated 15 March 1957, does not contain the passage quoted above. Both typescripts are housed in the Margaret Herrick Library, Academy of Motion Picture Arts and Sciences. For the full reprint of the second draft of this documentary, see below, 97–103.

[21] "The Double Crisis," *World Review* (November 1948), 9–14, and *World Review* (December 1948), 33–38. It was later included as the last essay in *Themes and Variations.*

[22] For a detailed discussion of this question, see Gerhard Wagner, "Aldous Huxley and the Desert," *AHA*, 8 (2008), 91–107.

[23] Compare Thomas Gray, "Elegy Written in a Country Churchyard," ll. 55–56: "Full many a flower is born to blush unseen, / And waste its sweetness on the desert air."

[24] "Consider the Lilies," *Lincoln-Mercury Times*, 5.1 (January–February 1953), 16–19. This essay should not to be confused with his short story with the same title, which was published in *The London Magazine*, 1.10 (November 1954), 17–43. The essay also appeared with the title "Out of Time Into Space" *The Ford Times Guide to Travel in the U.S.A.* (New York, 1962), 97–100. It was reprinted in *AHA*, 4 (2004), 33–35, and in *Consider the Lilies and Other Short Fiction*, ed. James Sexton (Victoria, 2010), 167–70. (The above passage is quoted according to the *AHA* reprint, 35.) For an interpretation of the corresponding central passage of the short story in the context of Huxley's critique of Goethe, see Bernfried Nugel, "'The Silliest Line in Goethe': Aldous Huxley's Emendation of 'Alles Vergängliche ist nur ein Gleichnis,'" *AHA*, 17/18 (2017/2018), 287–88; for an introduction to the short story, see James Sexton, "The Problems of Love: Three Little-Known Stories by Aldous Huxley: 'Over the Telephone'—'Nine A.M.'—'Consider the Lilies,'" *AHA*, 8 (2008), 33–36.

Editors' Note on the Text

Huxley's dramatization of *Ape and Essence* has survived in the form of three texts, which, fortunately, appear to bear out the points that Huxley discussed in his letters to Anita Loos and Georges Neveux (see above, 1–2). These extant drafts comprise the sporadically corrected English draft with additional scenes (hereafter, ED), the French draft, entitled *Le vice du vase*, which largely represents a translation of the same stage of revision (hereafter, FD), and the English fair copy, which does not go significantly beyond these two drafts (hereafter, FC). The two English versions are housed in the Aldous and Laura Huxley papers of the Charles E. Young Research Library (UCLA), Box 2, and the French translation is kept among the Georges Neveux papers (Fonds Georges Neveux, Archives) at the Société des Auteurs et Compositeurs Dramatiques (SACD, Paris). These three texts can be briefly characterized as follows:

(1) ED is a paginated typed draft (Act I: 1–33; Act II: 34–61; Act III: 61[1]–84) with paginated sheets inserted replacing original sheets. These added sheets doubtless render the additional passages mentioned by Huxley in his letters to Loos and Neveux.

(2) FC is a paginated script (Act I: 1–38; Act II: 1–38; Act III: 1–31); it contains only two major revisions (see below, 20, notes 4 and 5, and 85, note 34) beside several minor corrections.

(3) FD is a paginated typed draft (Acte I: 1–42; Acte II: 1–39; Acte III: 1–40) with numerous minor corrections.

Since FC incorporates almost all corrections of ED, it clearly represents a later state of the text. This can, for instance, be seen in the beginning of the play (see below, 19, note 2) and the first scene of Act II in FD (see below, 42, note 16), where corrections in Huxley's hand have been adopted in FC (see the facsimiles of the pertinent pages, below, 14 and 17). Therefore, FC clearly qualifies for the role of copy-text, which, however, has to be checked against variants in ED and FD. In the textual notes, variants as well as editorial emendations are enclosed in curly brackets. As a rule, the accidentals of FC, such as punctuation, spelling, word division, indentation etc., are adopted, and typing errors or mistakes of punctuation are silently corrected.

APE AND ESSENCE

ACT I

The Personality Cemetery: A cemetery in Los Angeles. Ruined skyscrapers in the background. A marble plaque is affixed to the wall inscribed with the words, "HOLLYWOOD PANTHEON". Two bearded men and two girls dressed in dirty, ragged homespun, are excavating a grave. On top of a mausoleum dedicated to "HEDDA BODDY, Public Sweetheart Number One," and with the inscription "hitch your wagon to a star" sits the Chief, in a mid-twenthieth century business suit and an Admiral's cap.

The Narrator sits in front, and to one side, in deep shadow except for his face. When the curtain rises he starts to speak, while the man and girls dig and the Chief refreshes himself from a bottle and gnaws at a beef bone.

NARRATOR

The sea with its clouds, the mountains of grey gold,
The valleys full of indigo darkness,
The drought of lion-coloured plains,
The rivers of pebbles and white sand,
And in the midst of them theCity of the Angels,
Los Angeles.
Half a million houses,
Five thousand miles of streets,
Fifteen hundred thousand motor vehicles,
Twenty-two thousand Beauty Parlours,
And more rubber than Akron,
More celluloid than the Soviets,
More deodrants than Denmark,
More Nylons than the Netherlands,
More oranges than anywhere,
With bigger and better girls,
Bigger and better girls --
The great Metrollopis of the West
But the great Metrollopis is now a ghost town. What was
once the world's largest oasis is now its most stupendous
collection of ruins in a wasteland. Nothing moves in the
streets. Dunes of sand have drifted across the concrete.
Only a few savages remain to grub and scrabble
among the relics of the technology, by means of which their
ancestors destroyed themselves.
Could it have been otherwise? One has one's doubts.
For man, proud man,
Dressed in a little brief authority, ---
Most ignorant of what he is most assured,
His glassy essence --- like an angry ape,
Plays such fantastic tricks before high heaven
As make the angels weep.

First page of Huxley's draft (ED) of *Ape and Essence—A Play*

ACT ONE

A cemetery in Los Angeles. Ruined skyscrapers in the background. A marble plaque is affixed to the wall inscribed with the words, "HOLLYWOOD PANTHEON, THE PERSONALITY CEMETERY." Two bearded men and two girls dressed in dirty, ragged homespun, are excavating a grave. On top of a mausoleum dedicated to "HEDDA BODDY, Public Sweetheart Number One," and with the inscription "hitch your wagon to a star" sits the Chief, in a mid-twentieth century business suit and an Admiral's cap.

The NARRATOR sits in front, and to one side, in deep shadow except for his face. When the curtain rises HE starts to speak, while the men and girls dig and the CHIEF refreshes himself from a bottle and gnaws at a beef bone.

NARRATOR

The sea with its clouds, the mountains of grey gold,
The valleys full of indigo darkness,
The drought of lion-coloured plains,
The rivers of pebbles and white sand,
And in the midst of them the City of the Angels,
Los Angeles.
Half a million houses,
Five thousand miles of streets,
Fifteen hundred thousand motor vehicles,
Twenty-two thousand Beauty Parlours,
And more rubber than Akron,
More celluloid than the Soviets,
More deodrants than Denmark,
More Nylons than the Netherlands,
More oranges than anywhere,
With bigger and better girls,
Bigger and better girls --
The great Metropolis of the West
But the great Metropolis is now a ghost town. What was once the world's largest oasis is now its most stupendous collection of ruins in a wasteland. Nothing moves in the streets. Dunes of sand have drifted across the concrete.

First page of the fair (carbon) copy (FC) of *Ape and Essence—A Play*

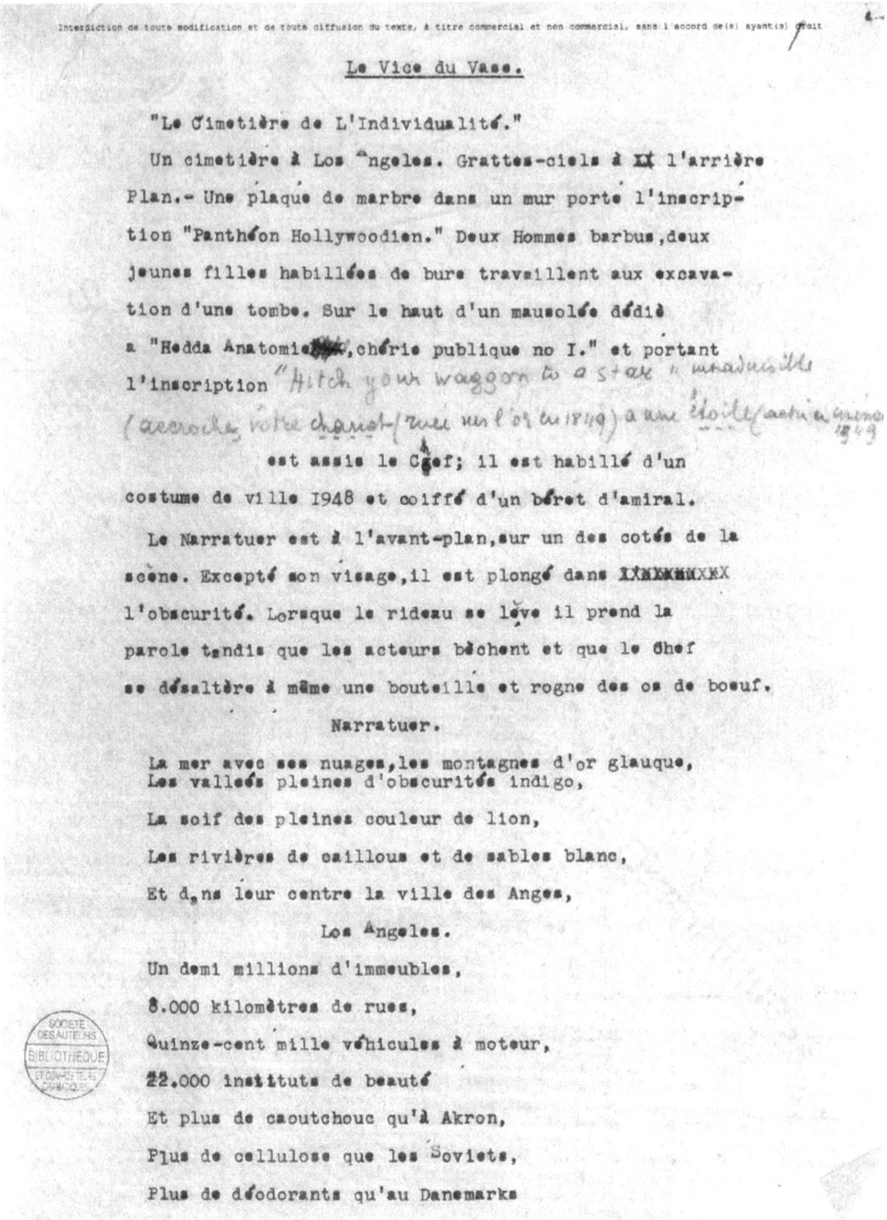

Le Vice du Vase.

"Le Cimetière de L'Individualité."

Un cimetière à Los Angeles. Grattes-ciels à XX l'arrière Plan.- Une plaque de marbre dans un mur porte l'inscription "Panthéon Hollywoodien." Deux Hommes barbus, deux jeunes filles habillées de bure travaillent aux excavation d'une tombe. Sur le haut d'un mausolée dédiè a "Hedda Anatomie, chérie publique no I." et portant l'inscription "Hitch your waggon to a star" inadmissible (accrochez votre chariot (ruée vers l'or en 1849) à une étoile (actrice cinéma 1849)

est assis le Chef; il est habillé d'un costume de ville 1948 et coiffé d'un béret d'amiral.

Le Narratuer est à l'avant-plan, sur un des cotés de la scène. Excepté son visage, il est plongé dans XXXXXXXX l'obscurité. Lorsque le rideau se lève il prend la parole tandis que les acteurs bèchent et que le Chef se désaltère à même une bouteille et rogne des os de boeuf.

Narratuer.

La mer avec ses nuages, les montagnes d'or glauque,
Les vallées pleines d'obscurités indigo,
La soif des pleines couleur de lion,
Les rivières de caillous et de sables blanc,
Et dans leur centre la ville des Anges,
Los Angeles.
Un demi millions d'immeubles,
8.000 kilomètres de rues,
Quinze-cent mille véhicules à moteur,
22.000 instituts de beauté
Et plus de caoutchouc qu'à Akron,
Plus de cellulose que les Soviets,
Plus de déodorants qu'au Danemarks

The first page of Huxley's typescript (FD) of *Le vice du vase*

2 I

141

Acte II

(Le soir du même jour. Chapelle de l'Esprit Maudit située dans l'arène d'un des stades de Los Angeles. Un autel s'élève contre le fond de la scène. Il est orné ~~de~~ d'ossements humains et de têtes de mort, arrangés d'une façon fantastique. Sur l'autel est posée une immense bougie entre deux cornes dorées, A gauche, sur le devant de la scène, une porte s'ouvre sur le stade où les Cérémonies de la Purification seront célébrées. Plus loin, du même coté se trouve une fenêtre non vitrée et fermée par un lourd volet en bois. De chaque coté de l'autel, sur le mur de fond, il y a un placard; l'un est grand et la porte arrive jusqu'au bas du sol; l'autre est plus petit et la porte ne s'ouvre qu'à 3 ou 4 pieds du sol. Au fond de la scène à droite, il y a un poele cylindrique fentôle au devant duquel un arc donne accès à une petite pièce intérieure. Lorsque le rideau se lève, la scène est illuminée par une seule bougie dans un candélabre accroché au mur de droite. ~~Elle éclaire~~ Un ~~des~~ prêtres ~~vu dans l'acte précédent~~. Il cuisine sur le poele . L'~~autre prêtre arrive de la pièce extérieure portant une queue-de-rat (allumoir). Il monte à l'autel et allume la grande bougie qui s'y trouve~~)

Narrateur (Consulter Ezéchiel)

" Et il me déposa dans la vallée couverte d'ossements; et en ~~vérité ils~~ vérité ceux-ci étaient très desséchés." Les ossements desséchés de ceux qui mourrurent dans le courant de ces trois beaux jours d'été qui, pour vous, là bas, sont encore dans l'avenir. Mourrurent déchiquetés; mourrurent rôtis; mourrurent étouffés et couverts d'ampoules; mourrurent plus lentement de (maladie infectieuses connus ~~par exemple de l'antrax "nglais fièvre tachetée.)~~

The beginning of Act Two of *Le vice du vase*

Ape and Essence—A Play[1]

ACT ONE

A cemetery in Los Angeles. Ruined skyscrapers in the background. A marble plaque is affixed to the wall inscribed with the words "HOLLYWOOD PANTHEON, THE PERSONALITY CEMETERY."[2] *Two bearded men and two girls, dressed in dirty, ragged homespun, are excavating a grave. On top of a mausoleum dedicated to "HEDDA BODDY, Public Sweetheart Number One," and with the inscription "hitch your wagon to a star"*[3] *sits the* CHIEF, *in a mid-twentieth century business suit and an Admiral's cap.*

The NARRATOR *sits in front, and to one side, in deep shadow except for his face. When the curtain rises he starts to speak, while the men and girls dig and the* CHIEF *refreshes himself from a bottle and gnaws at a beef bone.*

NARRATOR:

The sea with its clouds, the mountains of grey gold,
The valley full of indigo darkness,
The drought of lion-coloured plains,
The rivers of pebbles and white sand,
And in the midst of them the City of the Angels,
Los Angeles.
Half a million houses,
Five thousand miles of streets,
Fifteen hundred thousand motor vehicles,
Twenty-two thousand Beauty Parlours,
And more rubber than Akron,
More celluloid than the Soviets,
More deodorants than Denmark,
More Nylons than the Netherlands,
More oranges than anywhere,
With bigger and better girls,

---

[1] The Editors wish to thank the Aldous and Laura Huxley Literary Trust for permission to publish the following text and also wish to acknowledge the assistance of UCLA and SACD in providing scans of ED, FC and FD (see above, "Editors' Note on the Text," 13).

[2] ED:{"THE PERSONALITY CEMETERY":} put in parentheses and moved by a black line from the beginning of the paragraph to the present position. (For a facsimile of the pertinent page, see above, 14.)

[3] FD: Pencilled note on the margin, most probably in Maria Huxley's hand, who no doubt helped Huxley with the translation {intraduisible (accrochez votre chariot (ruée sur l'or en 1849) à une étoile (actrice cinéma [en] 1949)} ['untranslatable (fix your cart (goldrush in 1849) to a star (cinema actress [in] 1949)']. (For a facsimile of this page, see above, 16.)

Bigger and better girls—
The great Metropolis of the West.[4]

But the great Metropolis[5] is now a ghost town. What was once the world's largest oasis is now its most stupendous collection of ruins in a wasteland. Nothing moves in the streets. Dunes of sand have drifted across the concrete. Only a few savages remain to grub and scrabble among the relics of the technology, by means of which their ancestors destroyed themselves.

Could it have been otherwise? One has one's doubts.

For man, proud man,
Dressed in a little brief authority—
Most ignorant of what he is most assured,
His glassy essence—like an angry ape,
Plays such fantastic tricks before high heaven
As make the angels weep.[6]

Yes, most ignorant of what he is most assured, the glassy essence that is his spirit and the spirit of the world. And I need hardly add that what we call knowledge is merely another form of ignorance—highly organized, of course, and eminently scientific, but for that very reason all the more complete, all the more productive of angry apes. When ignorance was unmitigated by applied science, we were the equivalents of lemurs,[7] marmosets and howler monkeys. Today, thanks to the Higher Ignorance which is our knowledge, man's stature has increased to such an extent that the least among us is now a baboon, the greatest an orangutan or even, if he takes rank as a national hero or a Saviour of Society, a true Gorilla.

(*He is interrupted by a babel of excited voices from the open grave.*)

ALL: There she is... Chief, Chief, we've struck the pay dirt... Whoopee... Let me get out of here... Look out! Clumsy...

(*All scramble out except one man,* JOE. *As the girls emerge we see that they are wearing aprons on which the word "NO" is embroidered, very large, in crimson wool.*)

---

[4] ED: {Metrollopis}; FC: {ollopis} erased, {opolis} freshly typed over it. (For a facsimile of the pertinent pages, see above, 14 and 15.)

[5] ED: {Metrollopis}; FC: {ollopis} erased, {opolis} freshly typed over it. (For a facsimile of this page, see above, 14 and 15.)

[6] Compare William Shakespeare, *Measure for Measure*, 2:2.146–51: "*But* man, proud man [...]" (editors' emphasis).

[7] ED: Autograph insertion {of} in {equivalents lemurs}; FC: {equivalent of lemurs}.

JOE (*angrily*): Where's that rope?

(*All these people speak to one another in tones of irritation, suspicion or malignity.*)

FLOSSIE: OK, OK.

(*She throws down the rope. It hits* JOE *on the head.*)

JOE: What the hell do you think you're doing?

FLOSSIE (*laughing*): Serve you right.

CHIEF: What's the casket like?

JOE: Silver handles.

LOOLA: Oh, Boy!

CHIEF: Hurry up, you lazy swine!

(JOE *gets out of the grave.*[8] *The men and girls pull at the rope and hoist a coffin to the surface.*)

JOE (*as they pull*): Now all together. One, two, three. Here she comes.

CHIEF: Break it open.

JOE: OK, Chief.

(*He forces up the lid with a jimmy.*)

CHIEF: Is it a dame?

JOE: No, it's a man. Kind of fat.

CHIEF: Spill him out.

JOE: OK, Chief.

(*They tilt the coffin and roll the corpse out onto the sand.*)

LOOLA: Look at the watch chain, look at the rings!

(BILL, *the elder of the men, kneels down and starts to relieve the corpse of its jewelry.*)

NARRATOR: More than a hundred years have passed since the Managing Director of the Golden Rule Distillery Corporation had his final stroke. But thanks to the dry climate and the embalmer's art, what remains of him looks as though it had been buried only yesterday.

FLOSSIE (*pointing accusingly at* BILL): What are you doing with that ring?

CHIEF: What's that?

FLOSSIE: He's stolen the ring.

BILL: That's a lie.

FLOSSIE: No, it isn't. I saw him.

CHIEF: Give back the ring.

BILL: I don't know what you're talking about.

CHIEF: Well, we'll soon find out. (*He picks up a whip.*) What about it?

---

8 ED and FC: {out of grave}.

BILL: No, no please. I'll give it back. Please.

(He produces the ring.)

FLOSSIE: Didn't I tell you?

CHIEF: Put it there with the other things. *(The man obeys.)* Twenty-five lashes—that's what *you're* going to get this evening.

FLOSSIE: Serve you right.

(All laugh.)

BILL: Please, Chief, please.

CHIEF: Be quiet.

BILL: I'm an old man, I've worked hard all my life, I've never been in trouble before.

CHIEF: What does the Law say? Everything belongs to the Proletariat—isn't that right?

BILL: Yes, Chief.

CHIEF: And the Proletariat means the People's State. And what's the People's State?

BILL: The Chief.

CHIEF: Correct. And what's the penalty for robbing the People's State? *(The man looks up at him in speechless misery.)* What's the penalty?

BILL *(almost inaudibly)*: Twenty-five lashes.

CHIEF: Good. That settles that. What are the clothes like?

FLOSSIE *(fingering the corpse's double-breasted black jacket)*: Nice stuff. No stains. He hasn't leaked or anything.

CHIEF: I'll try on the jacket.

(The man and girls divest the corpse of its jacket—a rather difficult proceeding. While they are thus engaged, the NARRATOR *speaks.)*

NARRATOR: Put yourselves in their place. You may not know it, but a complete scribbler, or first card-engine, consists of a breast, or small swift, and two swifts, with the accompanying workers, strippers, fancies, dollies, etc. And if you don't have any carding machinery or power looms, if you don't have any electric motors to run them, or any dynamos to generate the electricity, or any turbines to turn the dynamos, or any coal to raise steam, or any blast furnaces to make steel—why, then obviously you must depend for your fine cloth on the cemeteries of those who once enjoyed these advantages, back in the twentieth century.

JOE: Here you are, Chief.

(He hands up the coat. The CHIEF *tries it on. The arms are too short, the waist line much too large.)*

CHIEF: What's it like?
JOE: I told you he was kind of fat.
FLOSSIE: Maybe we could let the arms out a bit.
LOOLA: And take it in around the middle.
VOICES OFFSTAGE: Long live the Chief.

(*All look in the direction from which the voices come. Two bearded men enter driving* DR. ALFRED POOLE, *who is gagged and has his hands tied in front of him.* DR. POOLE *is about twenty-eight, clean shaven, wears tweeds and carries a botanist's tin collecting box over his shoulder. He is very weary. When he lags or stumbles, his captors goad him forward with a sharp-pointed yucca leaf.*)

CHIEF (*in astonishment*): What in Belial's name? (*The newcomers halt at the foot of the mausoleum. The bearded men bow.*) Who's this?

(*He points at* DR. POOLE.)

FIRST MAN: We caught him. Near Culver City.
SECOND MAN: There was a big ship off Redondo Beach.
FIRST MAN: A tremenjus great ship.
SECOND MAN: Boy, what a ship!
FIRST MAN: Hundreds of feet high. Boy, what sails!
SECOND MAN: And then there was a little boat. A bunch of them landed.
CHIEF: How many?
SECOND MAN: Maybe ten, maybe twelve.
FIRST MAN: No, no, more than that. Fifteen, I'd say.
CHIEF: Where did they go?
FIRST MAN: Up the hill to them old oil wells. But this one he keeps wandering about by himself.
SECOND MAN: Picking flowers and digging things with a teeny little spade.

(*He holds up a trowel.*)

FIRST MAN: He was digging when we jumped on him.
SECOND MAN: Gagged him before he could yell.
FIRST MAN: Drug him down into a gully and tied him up.
CHIEF: Did the others see what happened?
FIRST MAN: No, we was too smart.
SECOND MAN: We fooled them.

(*Both laugh.*)[9]

---

[9] ED: The following text on pp. 7–8 is partly struck out in red pencil and replaced with sheets 7 (I) and 7 (II), connecting to "Steam? Do you mean to say you still have steamers?" on p. 9; see below, 24.

CHIEF: Take that thing out of his mouth. (*The men remove* DR. POOLE*'s gag.*) You—do you speak English?

DR. POOLE: Yes, I speak English.

CHIEF: Are you a priest?

DR. POOLE: A priest? No, sir.

CHIEF: Then why don't you have a beard?

DR. POOLE: I… I shave.

CHIEF: Oh, you haven't been… (*He scrutinizes* DR. POOLE *closely.*) You're not lying, are you?

DR. POOLE: No, I assure you. I'm not a priest. I'm not even a Catholic. My people were all Quakers.

CHIEF: What's that?

DR. POOLE: You know—Silent worship, The Inner Light.

CHIEF: Inner Light? I don't know what you're talking about. Where are you from?

DR. POOLE: New Zealand.

CHIEF: Never heard of it.

DR. POOLE: Well, I'm not surprised. It's a long way off.

CHIEF: What made you come here? Do you people think you can conquer us?

DR. POOLE: No, no, I assure you, our intentions are entirely peaceable.

CHIEF: They'd better be. We've got an army here. And there's the Grand Inquisitor and his security police.

DR. POOLE: We're just a group of scientists, that's all. The New Zealand Re-Discovery expedition to North America—That's our official title. If you'll let me go, I'll arrange a conference between you and Professor Craigie—he's the leader of our expedition. A most remarkable man. You'd enjoy meeting him.

CHIEF: When I've got a hostage, I don't let him go.

DR. POOLE: I'll come back. I give you my word of honour.

CHIEF: Honour—do you think that ever bound anybody? Give me a good stout rope. That and a dog whip.

DR. POOLE: But, Chief…

CHIEF: That's enough. Now, answer my questions. What sort of a ship did you come in?

DR. POOLE: A four-masted schooner.

CHIEF: That's a kind of sailing ship, isn't it?

DR. POOLE: There's no place to re-fuel here. We couldn't use steam.

CHIEF: Steam? Do you mean to say you still have steamers?

DR. POOLE: For all our coastwise traffic.

CHIEF: Then you didn't have the Thing?

DR. POOLE: I… I don't quite get your meaning.

CHIEF: The Thing.

DR. POOLE: What thing?

CHIEF: *The* Thing. You know—when He took over.

(*Raising his hands to his forehead, he makes the sign of the horns with his forefingers. His subjects follow suit.*)

DR. POOLE: You mean, the Devil?

CHIEF: Belial.

DR. POOLE: But… I mean… Well, *really*…

CHIEF: You must have heard of it. He won the battle, He took over completely. That was when people did all this… (*He indicates the distant ruins.*) Knocked everything to bits.[10]

DR. POOLE: Oh, I see. You mean the Third[11] World War. No, we were lucky. New Zealand was of no strategic importance to either side. We got off without a scratch. No bacterial warfare, no gases, no botulism, no atomic bombing.

CHIEF: Nothing destroyed?

DR. POOLE: Not a single casualty.

CHIEF: Then you've still got trains?

DR. POOLE: Yes, we've got trains.

CHIEF: And the engines really work?

DR. POOLE: Of course they work.

CHIEF: Belial, this is wonderful. (*To his followers*) Do you realize what this means? He can help us to get it all going again. Like in the old days, before the Thing. We'll have trains. Just think of it—*trains*. Dining cars, club cars, Pullmans. And there'll be toilets in them. Real toilets with water that goes wh-sh, when you press the pedal. And great big locomotives. And armoured cars and siege guns and…

DR. POOLE: But, listen, I'm not an engineer.

CHIEF: What's that?

DR. POOLE: I'm not an engineer. I'm a botanist.

CHIEF: A botanist?

DR. POOLE: That's a man who knows about plants.

CHIEF: War plants? We could do with some war plants.

---

10 Emendation: {bits}; ED and FC: {bite}.

11 Emendation: {Third}; ED and FC: {Fourth}.

DR. POOLE: No, no, just plants. You know, things with leaves and stalks and flowers—though of course we mustn't forget the cryptogams. New Zealand, I may add, is particularly rich in cryptogams.

CHIEF: But what about the engines?

DR. POOLE: Frankly, I hardly know the difference between a steam turbine and a diesel.

CHIEF: Does that mean you can't do anything to get the trains running again?

DR. POOLE: Not a thing.

(*A long silence. Then the* CHIEF *turns to his followers.*)

CHIEF: Bury him.

(*He points to the open grave.*)

DR. POOLE: Chief!

CHIEF: Bury him.

FLOSSIE: Alive or dead?

CHIEF: I don't care. Do what you want.

FLOSSIE: Goody goody! Come on, boys, let's have some fun.

(*They close in on* DR. POOLE *and seize him.*)

DR. POOLE: Don't, don't. For God's sake. (*They lower him feet first into the grave.*) For God's sake. (*The men start shovelling earth into the grave.*) For God's sake.

JOE (*striking him across the mouth*): Stop that!

FLOSSIE (*to* LOOLA): Hold his hands while I shovel some earth on him.

LOOLA: No, I don't want to.

FLOSSIE: Don't be a fool!

DR. POOLE (*to* LOOLA): Don't let them—Please.

LOOLA: Chief! Chief! Tell them to stop.

CHIEF: You keep your mouth shut!

LOOLA: After all, he hasn't done anything.

CHIEF: I'll teach you to talk back. (*He picks up his whip. She dodges away.*) You wait. (*To the others*) Hurry up. You're wasting my time. I've got to see about having those foreigners chased back to their ship. Get it over with. No fooling around. (*While they shovel earth into the pit, the* CHIEF *collects his belongings and climbs down from his perch on the mausoleum.*) Stand back. I can't see. (*They obey. The* CHIEF *approaches the grave and looks down at* DR. POOLE, *derisively.*) You know all about plants. Why don't you grow some roots down there? (*All laugh, except* LOOLA.) Why don't you put out some nice little pink flowers?

(*More laughter*)

DR. POOLE: Mercy, Mercy.

(FLOSSIE *pulls a half-gnawed mutton chop out of her pocket and holds it in front of* DR. POOLE*'s nose.*)

FLOSSIE: Ask for it! (*She withdraws the bone and brings it close again.*) Bow wow. Ask! (*She repeats the game.*) Good dog—ask! (*To the others*) Belial, this is fun! (*To* DR. POOLE) Ask!

DR. POOLE: Mercy.

CHIEF: It's your own fault. You ought to have known about engines.

DR. POOLE: Listen, I could be useful to you. I could show you how to get better crops. You'd have more to eat.

CHIEF: More to eat?

DR. POOLE: Yes, really!

CHIEF: You're lying!

DR. POOLE: I'm not. I swear by Almighty God.

(*There is dead silence. All make the sign of the horns.*)

CHIEF: He maybe almighty in New Zealand. But not in Southern California. Not since the Thing happened.

DR. POOLE: But I know I can help you. I know it.

(*The* CHIEF *takes a coin out of his pocket, spins it, catches it, looks at the face which has turned up.*)

CHIEF: Tails it is. Dig him up.

FLOSSIE: Oh, Chief, that isn't fair. We were having such fun—

CHIEF (*savagely yelling*): Dig him up!

ALL: OK, OK.

(*They coil the rope under* DR. POOLE*'s arms and pull him out.*)

CHIEF: Look lively there.

LOOLA: I'm afraid we might hurt him.

CHIEF: Who cares? Hurry up. (*Addressing* DR. POOLE) And you there, let this be a lesson to you. Do what you've said you'd do. If you don't—Well, you know what'll happen. (*They hoist* DR. POOLE *to the surface as he speaks. He staggers and falls down in a faint.* LOOLA *catches him.*) What's the matter with the fellow?

LOOLA: He's fainted.[12]

CHIEF (*handing her his bottle of wine*): Give him some of this. And when he can walk, bring him back to Headquarters.

LOOLA: OK, Chief.

FIRST MAN: Would you like me to stay here with her, Chief? Just in case he tries any funny business?

---

12 ED: The following text on p. 15 is struck out in red pencil and replaced with sheets 16, 16 (I), 16 (II), 16 (3), 16 (4), 16 (5) and 16 (6), connecting to "Dr. Poole: Thank God!" on p.17, see below, 30.

CHIEF: No, she can take care of him. I need you for running errands. Need you all. One man to go to the Arch-Vicar, another for the Grand Inquisitor, another for the Cavalry Barracks. And you and she (*pointing to* JOE *and* FLOSSIE) can come along with me. (*He turns to* LOOLA.) Now, remember, you're responsible for him. You know what'll happen if he gets away.

LOOLA: Yes, Chief.

CHIEF: Keep his hands tied. And if he should start anything… (*He takes a large butcher's knife from his belt and hands it to her.*) Don't hesitate.

LOOLA: OK, Chief.

CHIEF: Now, come on. Quick march.

(*He goes out, followed by the men.*)

FLOSSIE (*to* JOE): I'll catch up with you in a minute. (*She goes and squats besides* LOOLA, *who is supporting* DR. POOLE*'s head on her lap.*) Try pulling his hair. (*She pulls it.*) Wake up, wake up!

LOOLA: No, don't. You'll hurt him.

FLOSSIE: Do you suppose it's true, what he said about not being a priest? (*She runs her fingers over* DR. POOLE*'s face.*) Yes, I guess it is. Gee, it's nice and smooth! Almost like a girl's face.

LOOLA: And none of that soup and mutton fat they get into their whiskers. He's so clean—that's what I like. Look, even his ears are clean.

FLOSSIE (*looks at* DR. POOLE*'s ears, then picks up one of his limp hands*): Even his nails. (*She rubs the palm of his hand against her cheek.*) And soft. Feel that.

(*She passes the hand to* LOOLA, *who fingers it.*)

LOOLA: I guess he never had to do any digging.

FLOSSIE: He must be a big shot where he comes from. (*She bends down and sniffs* DR. POOLE*'s hair.*) Doesn't he smell good!

LOOLA: Like violets. What are you doing?

FLOSSIE (*who has opened a button of* DR. POOLE*'s shirt and is looking at his chest*): Not one flea-bite. I never saw anything like it.

LOOLA: Let's see if we can give him some more of this.

(*She raises* DR. POOLE*'s head and puts the bottle to his lips.*)

FLOSSIE: Give that to me. (*She takes the bottle.*) You hold his head.

(*She pours.*)

LOOLA: Careful, careful, you're spilling it. (*To* DR. POOLE) Wake up, honey, wake up! (*To* FLOSSIE) He's like a baby. You know the way they sleep—so relaxed. It seems a shame to wake him.

FLOSSIE: He must be awfully heavy. Why don't you give him to me for a bit? Here, let me take him.

(*She tries to pull* DR. POOLE *away from* LOOLA, *who holds on to him firmly.*)

LOOLA: No, no. I'm alright. Leave him alone.

FLOSSIE: Why don't you go with the Chief?

LOOLA: Because he told me to stay here.

FLOSSIE: He won't mind—so long as one of us stays. It'll be much more fun to be with the Chief.

LOOLA: If it's such fun, why don't you go?

FLOSSIE: I just wanted to do something for you.

LOOLA: You liar! I know what you want.

FLOSSIE: Liar yourself! I don't want it.

LOOLA: Yes, you do.

FLOSSIE: I don't. And anyhow I don't know what you're talking about.

LOOLA: Yes, you do.

FLOSSIE: I don't.

LOOLA: You can't wait—that's what's wrong with you. What does it say on your apron?

FLOSSIE: The same thing it says on yours. And if you think you can get away with being alone in a cemetery with a man, you're mistaken. I'll report you. I'll tell them about his ears, and the way his hair smells so good, and no flea-bites on his body. *They*'ll know what to think. And when they give you your whipping I'll be in the front row, laughing my head off.

LOOLA: I'm not listening to you.

FLOSSIE: Ha ha ha—and you'll be yelling like a pig that's having its throat cut.

LOOLA: I think you're unethical and lousy. (DR. POOLE *stirs.*) Look, he's waking up.

DR. POOLE (*faintly*): Where am I?

LOOLA: You're quite safe, honey. Drink some of this. (*She gives him some more wine.*) My name's Loola. What's yours?

DR. POOLE: Poole—Alfred Poole.

LOOLA: I shall call you Alfie.

FLOSSIE (*patting* DR. POOLE *on the arm*): Hya, Alfie!

DR. POOLE (shrinking away in alarm): Oh!

LOOLA: It's all right, honey. She won't do anything to you.

FLOSSIE: You mustn't be mad at me just because I wanted to bury you.

DR. POOLE (*nervously*): No, no, of course not. I'm not a bit mad.

FLOSSIE: I just wanted a laugh—that's all.

DR. POOLE: Quite, quite.

FLOSSIE: People look so screamingly funny when they're being buried.

DR. POOLE: Screamingly… (*to* LOOLA) I think I'll take a little more of that wine.

(*She raises the bottle to his lips and he drinks.*)

FLOSSIE: Isn't he cute? Here, would you like a bite of this?

(*From her knapsack she takes the gnawed mutton chop which she offered him while he was being buried. An expression of horror appears on* DR. POOLE*'s face.*)

DR. POOLE: No, thanks.

FLOSSIE: Don't be bashful, honey. It's good.

(*She takes a bite herself, then offers it again to* DR. POOLE.)

DR. POOLE: Really not.

LOOLA: Flossie, you'd better hurry.

FLOSSIE (*ignoring her*): Wouldn't you like me to stay here and look after you?

DR. POOLE: Please don't trouble.

FLOSSIE: I've got some oranges here. Look at them. Real beauties. Loola doesn't have anything like that.

(*A horn is blown in the distance.*)

LOOLA: Listen! That's the Chief.

FLOSSIE: Alfie wants *you* to go. Don't you, honey? Say you want her to go.

(DR. POOLE *shakes his head and refuses to take the oranges. The horn is blown again, a succession of short notes.*)

LOOLA: He's getting mad. He's cursing, he's grinding his teeth. Boy, what a whipping you are going to get. (*The horn sounds again, more impatiently than ever.* FLOSSIE *turns and rushes out.* LOOLA *laughs triumphantly.*) Well, that's the end of her.

DR. POOLE: Thank God!

LOOLA (*shocked*): Alfie!

(*She makes the sign of the horns.*)

DR. POOLE: What's wrong?

LOOLA: Such language!

DR. POOLE: Sorry, I forgot.

LOOLA: He might strike you dead.

DR. POOLE: I'll try not to do it again. (*He takes her hand between his two bound hands.*) Listen, Loola, I want to tell you how grateful I am.

LOOLA: I… I don't quite understand.

DR. POOLE: I want to thank you for what you did.

LOOLA: To thank me? Is that what people do where you come from?
DR. POOLE: It's what they're supposed to do.
LOOLA: You mean, they don't *have* to be mean to you?
DR. POOLE: No.
LOOLA: That must be wonderful!
DR. POOLE: You were the only one who tried to help me, the only one who showed a trace of human feeling.
LOOLA: I'll tell you something, Alfie; only you must promise not to repeat it.
DR. POOLE: I promise.
LOOLA: Well, I'm not like the others. I don't get a kick out of seeing people whipped or buried. In fact I really hate it.
DR. POOLE: Thank Goodness… I mean, you know…
LOOLA: But it's against His will. I'm scared. And just imagine if the priests were to find out! It would be terrible. That's why I wouldn't dare tell anybody from here.
Dr. POOLE: You mean, they might report you?
LOOLA: Of course.
DR. POOLE: Even your friends?
LOOLA: We don't have any friends.
DR. POOLE: No friends?
LOOLA: They're against the Law of Belial.
DR. POOLE: Yes, I can see they would be.
LOOLA: As a matter of fact I do have one girl friend. We daren't show that we like one another. But sometimes we manage to have a talk when nobody's around. She's swell.
DR. POOLE: You don't mean Flossie, I hope?
LOOLA: No, no. Flossie hates me. This is somebody quite different. She's called Polly.
DR. POOLE: Would you like *me* to be your friend?
LOOLA (*looking at him in astonishment*): You?
DR. POOLE: Yes, me.

(*He takes her hand and kisses it.*)

LOOLA: Oh!

(*She pulls her hand away.*)

DR. POOLE: I'm sorry.
LOOLA (*hesitates, then smiles at him*): It just gave me a start, that's all. (*She gives him her hand once more.*) Do it again. (*He kisses it. She shuts her eyes rapturously.*) Oh, Alfie… (*He stops to look up at her.*) Why do you stop?

(*He continues to kiss her. She sighs and at last opens her eyes.*) Now let me do that to you. (*She kisses his hand.*) Will you really be my friend?

DR. POOLE: Really and truly.

LOOLA: Think of it—having a friend, a real friend. Oh, Alfie, I'm so happy.

(*She leans her head against his shoulder.* DR. POOLE *looks rather apprehensive.*)

DR. POOLE: Do you mind if I ask you a personal question?

LOOLA: Anything you like.

DR. POOLE: That ring you're wearing—is it an engagement ring?

LOOLA: A *what* ring?

DR. POOLE: I mean, was it given to you by one of those young men who were here?

LOOLA: No, I found it. Rummaging through the skeletons in the Biltmore Theatre. The place is just packed with them. I took a candle and spent a whole day there last summer. Came back with seven diamond bracelets and sixteen rings. They allowed me to keep this one. (*She holds up her hand with the ring.*) Pretty, isn't it?

DR. POOLE: Charming. And those young men have nothing to do with it?

LOOLA: Catch *them* giving me anything!

DR. POOLE: So you're not thinking of getting married?

LOOLA: Getting married? What's that?

DR. POOLE: Well, your mother was married to your father.

LOOLA: She didn't know who my father was.

DR. POOLE: Didn't know?

LOOLA: How could she? It might have been almost anybody.

DR. POOLE: But, my dear girl…

LOOLA: Did *your* mother think she knew?

DR. POOLE: My late father was the Professor of Moral Science in the University of Wellington.

LOOLA: That's what *she* says. But how on earth can she be sure?

DR. POOLE: Loola!

LOOLA: What's the matter? Have I said something wrong?

DR. Poole: Don't you know what you've been saying?

LOOLA: I thought it was just common sense.

DR. POOLE (*after a pause*): Well, I suppose things are rather different here from what they are in New Zealand.

LOOLA: Alfie, you're still my friend, aren't you?

DR. POOLE: Of course, I am. (*She takes his hands and kisses them, then suddenly looks about her with an expression of terror.*) What's the matter?

LOOLA: I thought I heard something.

DR. POOLE: Well, what of it?

LOOLA: They might see us. (*She shudders.*) I can't help thinking of that poor girl.

DR. POOLE: Which girl?

LOOLA: They brought her into Headquarters yesterday evening. We all had to look on while they gave her forty lashes.

DR. POOLE: What for?

LOOLA: She'd forgotten her apron.

DR. POOLE: Forgotten her apron?

LOOLA: Don't you know how to read?

(*She points to the NO embroidered on her apron.*)

DR. POOLE: Oh, I see. You mean, she… Quite, quite, I must say, the punishment seems rather severe. Especially after what you were saying about people not knowing who their fathers are.

LOOLA: It's because it's the wrong season. Two days later, and it would have been perfectly legal. But of course that isn't any excuse. They're strict to the very last moment. It's the will of Belial. He *wants* us to be miserable. And He sees that everything happens in such a way that we always *are* miserable.

(*She covers her face with her hands.* DR. POOLE *looks at her solicitously.*)

DR. POOLE: Loola. You mustn't cry. What's the matter?

LOOLA: You don't know how terrible it is.

DR. POOLE: What's terrible?

LOOLA: Everything. You don't want to think about these things; but you're one of the unlucky ones—you can't help thinking about them. And you almost go crazy. Wanting to have a friend, wanting to have somebody who'll always be there, who'll always love you. And then seeing somebody look at you, and wondering if he feels the same way, and thinking how wonderful it would be if you and he could be happy together. But all the time, you know you mustn't. You're scared to death of what they'd do to you if they found out. Bury you, whip you to death. And you clench your fists and hold yourself in, and it's like being torn to pieces. And then suddenly, after all that suffering, there's another kind of misery.

DR. POOLE: What do you mean?

LOOLA: You know—when Belial starts to take possession of people. For weeks He makes them think about those things—and it's against the

Law, they're punished if they do anything, like that poor girl yesterday. The men get so mad they start hitting you and calling you names, the way the priests do.

DR. POOLE: What names?

LOOLA: Vessel, and things like that.

DR. POOLE: Vessel?

LOOLA: Vessel of the Unholy Spirit.

DR. POOLE: Oh, I see.

LOOLA: And then comes the change of season, and overnight it's all perfectly legal. Everybody's free, free to go mad, free to be a wild beast. That's all they live for—three weeks of being crazy animals. But if you're one of the unlucky ones, you suddenly wake up and see how awful it is. Oh, I've been so ashamed! (*She covers her face with her hands.*) And afterwards, if there's a baby, the chances are they'll kill it next Belial Day.

DR. POOLE: Kill it?

LOOLA: If it's deformed… They get rid of all the deformed ones at the Purification Ceremonies.

DR. POOLE (*after a silence*): Are there many deformed babies born here?

LOOLA (*nodding*): Ever since the Thing, ever since He won the battle. (*She makes the sign of the horns.*)

DR. POOLE: But this is very interesting, very interesting indeed. Did anyone ever talk to you about gamma rays?

LOOLA: No. What are they?

DR. POOLE: They're the reason for all those deformed children. The belligerents released enormous amounts of them during the Third[13] World War.

LOOLA: What happened then?

DR. POOLE: Well, people were either killed, or sterilized, or saddled with some harmful mutations. Of course it's a little difficult to explain to anyone who isn't familiar with nuclear physics and the mechanism of heredity. But I'll do my best. Let's begin with the chromosomes.

(*While he is talking, another young girl enters furtively, carrying a baby. This is* POLLY. *She wears the standard homespun shirt and trousers. Her hair has been cropped short. At the sight of* LOOLA *and* DR. POOLE, *she hides behind a monument. Then, looking out, she recognizes* LOOLA *and calls.*)

POLLY: Loola!

---

13 Emendation: {Third}; ED and FC: {Fourth}.

LOOLA (*starts, looks around, runs to her friend*): Polly! (*She puts her arms round* POLLY*, who sobs on her shoulder.*) Oh, your poor hair!

DR. POOLE (*approaching*): What's happened to it?

LOOLA: They do it to all the girls whose babies are going to be liquidated.

DR. POOLE: But why?

LOOLA: Just to remind them that He's the enemy. (*To* POLLY) Darling… What happened? Did they let you go?

POLLY: I ran away.

LOOLA: Ran away?

POLLY: They sent us along with the Arch-Vicar and his escort. Twenty or thirty of us with our babies. There were some young priests with us. They kept sharpening their knives and making jokes about the Purification Ceremonies. It was awful.

(*She shudders.*)

LOOLA: How on earth did you get away?

POLLY: They stopped for a rest at the corner of Hollywood and Vine. I managed to slip away between the sand dunes.

LOOLA: But you know what'll happen if they find you?

POLLY: I don't care. I can't let him be killed. I can't. (*She clasps the baby more closely to her breast.*) I love him so.

LOOLA: Here, sit down. You need a rest. Let me take him. (*She takes the child from* POLLY, *who sits down.* LOOLA *talks to the baby.*) There, there. Poor little thing.

(DR. POOLE *approaches and looks down at the child. An expression of horror appears on his face.*)

DR. POOLE: Goodness! Are there many born like this?

LOOLA: Hundreds and hundreds. And lots of them are much worse than this. Some don't have any eyes. And sometimes you see one that has little stumps instead of arms. It's awful. I tell you, He wants us to be miserable.

(*She goes and sits down beside* POLLY, *hands her the baby, opens the knapsack which is swung over her shoulder and hands her friend a piece of bread.*)

NARRATOR: "To put it," as Professor Schroedinger has said, "to put it drastically, though perhaps a little naïvely, the injuriousness of a marriage between first cousins might very well be increased by the fact that their grandmother had served for a long period as an X-ray nurse. It is not a point that need worry any individual personally. But any possibility of gradually infecting the human race with unwanted latent mutations ought to be a matter of concern to the community."[14] It ought to be. But, needless to say, it isn't Oakridge is working three shifts a day; an atomic power plant is going up on the coast of Cumberland; and on the other side of the ideological fence the same progressive science is preparing the same surprises for Marxist bodies and the vile carcasses of Social Democrats and Capitalists. And it is not a matter only of war. This squalid disintegration of the very substance of the species, this gruesome and infinitely unheroic death-in-birth, could as well be the product of atomic industry as of atomic war. In a world powered by nuclear fission everybody's grandmother would have been an X-ray technician. And not only everybody's grandmother—everybody's grandfather and father and mother as well. Everybody's ancestors back to the third and fourth generation of them that hate, saith the Lord. And how they hate Me! And, hating Me, how malignantly they have to hate themselves! How unforgivingly they must act as their own executioners.

(*Suddenly a whistle blows in the distance. Another answers closer at hand.* POLLY *jumps up in terror.*)

POLLY: It's them.

(*She snatches the child from* LOOLA *and starts to run towards one of the exits. There is another whistle and a shrill voice shouting.*)

VOICE: There she is.

(*She dashes to another exit. More whistles. From three sides simultaneously appear three* PRIESTS OF BELIAL, *dressed in goat-skin cassocks and wearing head-dresses adorned with one, two or three horns. They are all plump, beardless, greasy-skinned, and have shrill voices.*)

FIRST PRIEST: Got you!

SECOND PRIEST: Look out! Don't let her go.

THIRD PRIEST: No, you don't.

(POLLY *is seized by two of the* PRIESTS. *She screams.*)

POLLY: No, no.

FIRST PRIEST: You dirty little Vessel!

THIRD PRIEST: Thought you'd give us the slip.

(*They strike at her.* POLLY *tries to protect the child.*)

POLLY: Look out. Don't hurt him. Oh, please.

SECOND PRIEST: Look at her—clinging to the filth she's spawned.

FIRST PRIEST: Loathsome.

---

14 Erwin Schrödinger, *What Is Life? The Physical Aspect of the Living Cell* (Cambridge, 1944), 45.

THIRD PRIEST: Disgusting.

POLLY: Help!

LOOLA (*running to her assistance and trying to prevent the* PRIESTS *from striking her*): Don't, don't. You mustn't.

FIRST PRIEST: Another of them!

SECOND PRIEST: How dare you?

THIRD PRIEST: Vessel of Unholiness.

(*They strike at* LOOLA. DR. POOLE *emerges from behind the tomb where he has been standing and intervenes.*)

DR. POOLE: Stop it.

(*With his bound hands he pushes them away.*)

FIRST PRIEST: Belial!

THIRD PRIEST: What in Belial's[15] name?

SECOND PRIEST: No beard? (*Stroking* DR. POOLE*'s chin*) He's an imposter. Trying to pretend he's one of us.

FIRST PRIEST: Who are you?

(*As they speak, the* ARCH-VICAR *enters leaning on the arm of an* ACOLYTE. *He is dressed in a piebald goatskin cassock and wears a four-horned tiara on his head.*)

LOOLA: There's His Eminence.

(*She makes the sign of the horns and curtsies. The* PRIESTS *turn round and bow.*)

ARCH-VICAR: Good! I see you've caught your runaway. (*To* POLLY) What made you try to leave us, little vessel?

POLLY: I… I loved him. I couldn't bear to think…

(*Her voice breaks.*)

ARCH-VICAR (*playfully pinching her ear*): Charming little ear! It seems a shame we shall have to cut it off.

POLLY: Oh, Your Eminence…

ARCH-VICAR (*suddenly raising his voice to a shrill scream*): Silence! (*He catches sight of* DR. POOLE.) Who's this?

THIRD PRIEST: Your Eminence, we found him here in charge of this young vessel.

LOOLA: He's a prisoner, Your Eminence. The Chief told me to take him back to Headquarters.

DR. POOLE: Allow me to introduce myself, Your Eminence. Alfred Poole, Doctor of Science. Instructor of Botany in the University of Auckland.

---

15 Emendation: {What in Belial's name?}; ED and FC: {What in [empty space] name?}.

ARCH-VICAR: Oh, you're one of those foreigners. I've just had a report about you people from the Inquisitor. This is very interesting. (*He sits down on a tomb and beckons to* DR. POOLE *to sit down beside him.*) Come and sit here. (*Turning to the* ACOLYTE, *he holds out his hand without speaking. The young man produces a bottle and a horn drinking vessel, which he fills and hands to the* ARCH-VICAR, *who sips as he talks to* DR. POOLE.) Auckland, Auckland. That's in New Zealand, isn't it?

DR. POOLE: Yes, Your Eminence.

ARCH-VICAR: And you weren't affected by the Thing?

Dr. POOLE: Not at all.

ARCH-VICAR: Well, Belial must have had his reasons for sparing you. Have you had any revolutions since the Thing?

DR. POOLE: None, Your Eminence.

ARCH-VICAR: And civil wars?

DR. POOLE: No.

ARCH-VICAR: No fights between the North Island and the South Island? (DR. POOLE *shakes his head.*) That astonishes me. Well, it'll come—it'll come. Trust Belial for that. Unless, of course, He means to get you in some other way. A really good epidemic, for example. Or some brand new religion that would start burning and torturing people. Have you had anything of that sort?

DR. POOLE: Not yet.

ARCH-VICAR: Too bad. Well, we mustn't question His Providence. (*Changing his tone*) So you've already met my colleague on the secular side.

DR. POOLE: Yes, I've had this privilege.

ARCH-VICAR: I hope he treated you with all the consideration you deserve.

DR. POOLE: Well… As a matter of fact, he wanted to bury me.

ARCH-VICAR: What?

DR. POOLE (*pointing to the open grave*): In there.

LOOLA: He got mad because Alfie didn't know anything about engines.

ARCH-VICAR: Engines! You'd think he was five years old. Well, so he is, for all practical purposes. But that's between you and me and the doorpost.

DR. POOLE: Fortunately I was able to persuade him that I could be of help in the matter of food production.

ARCH-VICAR: And even if you couldn't help us, Dr. Poole, you'd still be an asset.

DR. POOLE: I'd be much more of an asset if Your Eminence would let me go and talk to the head of our expedition. We could do an enormous amount for your people.

ARCH-VICAR: A bird in the hand, Dr. Poole, is worth a whole expedition in the bush.

DR. POOLE: But I can assure Your Eminence …

ARCH-VICAR (*raising his voice again*): Silence!

DR. POOLE: I… I beg your pardon.

ARCH-VICAR (*resuming his genial manner*): Well, as I was saying, Dr. Poole, whatever you do or don't do, you're still an asset. Think of it. A man of science, a visitor from a country that never had the Thing… it's like suddenly finding yourself contemporary with ancient history, it's like shaking hands with Einstein or Queen Victoria. But of course, that's something you couldn't expect the Chief to understand. No culture, no education. Outside religious circles, the most anybody can read is the NO on a vessel's apron. (*He laughs contemptuously and drinks.*) Talking of vessels, I take it that in New Zealand you still have something you call 'love'?

DR. POOLE: We certainly do.

ARCH-VICAR: Do you still write novels about it?

DR. POOLE: We do more than write about it. We fall in it, we make it, we marry for it.

ARCH-VICAR: "Till death do us part"—isn't that the formula?

DR. POOLE: That's the formula.

ARCH-VICAR: Too quaint! Well, all that's been changed over here. Love's against the Law of Belial. It makes too much sense of life, it's too human. That's one of the reasons why He engineered the Thing. It wasn't enough to exterminate the human race. You could have done that with bacteria, or poison gas, or even butcher's knives. No—He wanted to *degrade* it. He wanted to make sure that the survivors wouldn't be human any more. For that he had to get at the germplasm. Gamma-rays, that's what He needed for his purposes. All the gamma-rays that science would provide. (*He beckons to the* PRIESTS.) Bring that vessel here… (*They lead* POLLY *to him.*) Give me the spawn. (*They take the baby from* POLLY, *who makes a movement of resistance, for which she is cuffed, and hand it to the* ARCH-VICAR. *The latter shows it to* DR. POOLE.) Pretty, isn't it?

DR. POOLE: I'd looked at it before you came.

ARCH-VICAR: Bah, it smells. Take it away. (*The* PRIESTS *take the child and give it back to* POLLY.) Too disgusting. (*He wipes his hands on his cassock.*)

Well, that's only one of the hereditary changes He brought about. (*He beckons to* LOOLA.) You there, the other vessel. (LOOLA *approaches.*) Did you have one of those things this season?

LOOLA: No, Your Eminence.

ARCH-VICAR: Have you ever had one of them?

LOOLA: No, Your Eminence.

ARCH-VICAR: *(to* Dr. Poole): There, you see. Sterile. Twenty percent of them are that way. And of the remaining eighty percent, more than half produce monsters, and even *that* isn't the whole story. (*To* Loola) You there, I want to hear how well you remember your Catechism.

LOOLA: Yes, Your Eminence.

ARCH-VICAR: To what fate is Man predestined?

LOOLA (*in a Sunday-school gabble*): Belial has, out of his mere good pleasure, from all eternity elected all now living to everlasting perdition.

ARCH-VICAR: And why do you deserve everlasting perdition?

LOOLA: Belial has perverted and corrupted us in all the parts of our being, therefore we are, merely on account of the corruption of our germplasm, deservedly condemned by Belial forever and ever, Amen.

ARCH-VICAR: Excellent. Now, tell me, what is the nature of Woman?

LOOLA: Woman is the vessel of the Unholy Spirit, the source of all deformity, the… the…

ARCH-VICAR (*prompting*): …the enemy.

LOOLA: Oh, yes… the enemy of the species, punished by Belial and calling down punishment on all those who succumb to Belial in her.

ARCH-VICAR: Precisely. And how has Belial divided the year?

LOOLA: Belial in His inscrutable wisdom has divided the year into two seasons, a season of cold lasting forty-nine weeks, a season of heat lasting three weeks.

ARCH-VICAR (*to* Dr. Poole): Sterility instead of parenthood. Monstrosity instead of normality. And finally a mating season instead of love. That's the third of the great changes He brought about.

(*He counts them off on his fingers.*)

DR. POOLE: And did that also happen after the Thing?

ARCH-VICAR: Within three generations.

DR. POOLE: Only three generations? Good God! Oh, I beg your pardon.

(*All make the sign of the horns.*)

ARCH-VICAR: Granted, granted.

DR. POOLE: And don't they—don't they feel attracted towards one another at any other season?

ARCH-VICAR: Just for those six weeks, that's all.

DR. POOLE: Six weeks? I thought she said three?

ARCH-VICAR: They're actually in heat for six weeks. But we don't allow any mating till after the Purification Ceremonies. And then only for twenty-one days.

DR. POOLE: Why?

ARCH-VICAR: On general principles. They have to be punished for having been punished. It's the Law of Belial. (*He points at the girls' aprons.*) Hence those aprons. NO NO NO. It's absolute hell for everybody. And if they break the rules—well, we really give them the works. (*Turning to the* PRIESTS) Isn't that so?

(*They nod affirmatively, chuckle with sadistic relish and crack their dog whips.*)

DR. POOLE: Quite, quite…

ARCH-VICAR: And then there are the people who throw back to the old-style mating patterns. We call them the unlucky ones. They feel like mating all the year round. Like you people in New Zealand. Why, I've actually heard some of them talk about being in love. In *love*! (*He laughs, empties his drinking-horn, hands it to the* ACOLYTE, *rises and takes* DR. POOLE*'s arm.*) Well, we mustn't be late for the Purification Ceremonies.

DR. POOLE: Are there many of those… those unlucky ones?

ARCH-VICAR: Here, in Southern California, it's between five and ten per cent of the population. But up north, near Fresno, there's a community where it runs to nearly thirty per cent. They actually tolerate them there—even allow them to marry.

DR. POOLE: Do you approve of that?

ARCH-VICAR: Approve? (*To the* ACOLYTE) Tell the doctor what we do when we catch any of those birds.

ACOLYTE: Beat the hell out of them.

ARCH-VICAR (*to* LOOLA): Did you hear that? (*In high good humor he gives her a playful pat on the behind.*) You be careful, little vessel, you be careful!

(*He starts to walk out.*)

CURTAIN

ACT TWO

TIME: *The evening of the same day.*
PLACE: *A chapel of the Unholy Spirit in the arena of one of the Los Angeles stadiums. There is an altar against the back wall. It is ornamented by human bones and skulls, arranged in fantastic patterns, and upon it stands a vast candle between two gilded horns. To the left, near the front of the stage, is a door giving on to the stadium, in which the Purification Ceremonies are about to take place. Further back, on the same side, is a glassless window closed by a heavy wooden shutter. On either side of the altar, in the back wall, are closets, one large, with a door going down to the floor, the other small, with its door opening three of four feet from the ground. Backstage, on the right, stands a cylindrical iron stove, and further forward is an archway, giving access to an inner chamber.*

When the curtain rises, the stage is illumined by a single candle stuck in a sconce on the right-hand wall. A PRIEST *is cooking something on the stove.*[16]

NARRATOR: "And he set me down in the valley that was full of bones; and lo, they were very dry."[17] The dry bones of some of those who died, in the course of those three bright summer days that, for you there, are still in the future. Died blown to pieces, died roasted, died choking and blistered, died more slowly and agonizingly of improved spotted fever and scientifically perfected glanders, of galloping leukemia and man-made cancers. Died by thousands, died by millions. "And he said unto me, 'Son of man, can these bones live?'"[18] The answer, I replied, is in the negative.[19]

---

16 ED: Revised passage, with the latter part struck out in red pencil: {When the curtain rises, the stage is illumined by a single candle stuck in a sconce on the right hand wall. ~~By its light one of the two priests seen in the preceding act is cooking something on the stove. The other priest enters from the inner room carrying a taper, goes to the altar and lights the big candle that stands on it.~~}; FD: {Lorsque le rideau se lève, la scène est illuminée par une seule bougie dans un candélabre accroché au mur de droite. ~~Elle éclaire~~ Un ~~des~~ Prètres* ~~vu dans l'acte précédent. Il~~ cuisine sur le poêle. ~~L'autre prètre arrive de la pièce extrérieure portant une queue-de-rat (allumeir). Il monte à l'autel et allume la grande bougie qui s'y trouve.~~} [*autograph correction of {un des prètres}]. For a facsimile of the pertinent page, see above, 17.

17 Compare Ezekiel 37:1–2.

18 Compare Ezekiel 37:3.

19 ED: The following text on p. 34 is struck out in red pencil and replaced with sheets 35, 35 (I), 35 (II), 35 (III), 35 (IIII), 35 (5), 35 (6), 35 (7) and 35 (8), connecting to "First Priest / Very nearly, Your Eminence" on p. -35- (see below, 46).

(*The door on the left is opened and the* FIRST PRIEST *enters, followed by* DR. POOLE, POLLY *and* LOOLA. POLLY *is on the verge of collapse and has to be supported by* DR. POOLE, *while* LOOLA *carries the baby.*)

SECOND PRIEST: Isn't His Eminence with you?

FIRST PRIEST: His Eminence stopped for a word with the Patriarch. He'll be here in a minute or two. (*To* POLLY) Come on, you. None of your malingering.

DR. POOLE: She isn't malingering. The poor girl's at the end of her strength.

FIRST PRIEST: Listen, Poole, if I say anything, it's true. Do you understand?

DR. POOLE: All I understand is that you've got the whip and I haven't. (*He lowers* POLLY *to the ground near the altar.* LOOLA *sits down beside her and supports her.*) I'd like to give her some water. Can you get me some?

FIRST PRIEST: No, I can't.

DR. POOLE: Well, can I get it?

FIRST PRIEST: No. Get back there.

(DR. POOLE *hesitates a moment, then goes and rejoins the two girls.*)

SECOND PRIEST: What's that young vessel doing here?

FIRST PRIEST: She's waiting for the Executioner.

SECOND PRIEST: Strangling?

FIRST PRIEST: No, just the ears—that's all. (*He approaches the stove and sniffs the food.*) Smells good. I'm hungry.

SECOND PRIEST: Let me see, you don't eat cabbage—isn't that right?

FIRST PRIEST: No. It's one of the things that gives me gas.

SECOND PRIEST: Too bad.

FIRST PRIEST: It's the will of Belial. (*He makes the sign of the horns.*) Well, I must get on with my work. (*He picks up a feather whisk and dusts the skulls and bones on the altar.*) Do you have much trouble with perspiring feet?

SECOND PRIEST: Quite a bit.

FIRST PRIEST: I find talcum powder very helpful. I'll give you a can of it.

SECOND PRIEST: Thank you. Are you sure you can spare it?

FIRST PRIEST: I've got six cans.

SECOND PRIEST: Where did you find them?

FIRST PRIEST: In a little old drugstore on Alvarado Street. The ceiling had fallen in; but when you scratched in the rubble there was all kinds of stuff.

SECOND PRIEST: You don't say so!

FIRST PRIEST (*to* POLLY): What are you blubbering about? Nothing's happened to you—not yet. Wait till the Executioner comes. Then you'll have some reason to blubber.

(*He goes out through the door on the right.*)

LOOLA: Darling, darling…

DR. POOLE: Listen, Polly. You mustn't cry like that. You're only making things worse for yourself. That's what they want you to do; you're just playing their game. Try to be brave. I know it's horribly difficult—I'm not brave myself. But try. Try.

SECOND PRIEST (*turning towards them, his saucepan in one hand, his spoon in the other*): That's no way to talk to a vessel that's going to have her ears cut off. Tell her how much it's going to hurt. Tell her how Belial's going to punish her for the punishment she's already had. On earth as it is in hell. And then in hell as it is on earth, only much more so.

(*While he is speaking, the* FIRST PRIEST *re-enters carrying a taper, with which he lights the candles on the altar.*)

FIRST PRIEST: In hell the whips are made of wire, and anyone who's had fifty lashes here, gets fifty thousand when he comes there.

SECOND PRIEST: Fifty thousand, and then another fifty thousand, and then another and another.

FIRST PRIEST: And if you've had your ears cut off, they'll be cut off again. Over and over again. Every night they'll grow back, and every morning you'll hear the footsteps of the Executioner coming up the stairs. You'll hear a knock, you'll see the door opening, you'll feel a hand on your shoulder. And then there'll be a hot stinking breath on your cheek and a gentle little whisper in your ear: "Your turn next, little vessel. Kindly step this way."

(*At this moment the door on the left opens noisily, and the* ARCH-VICAR *enters accompanied by the* EXECUTIONER, *a priest in black fur, carrying a small black bag.* POLLY *utters a piercing scream.*)

ARCH-VICAR: What's the matter?

DR. POOLE: Your Eminence, they're torturing this poor girl—they're frightening her out of her mind.

ARCH-VICAR (*sitting down*): My dear sir, that's what they're there for. (*To the* SECOND PRIEST) Is supper ready?

SECOND PRIEST: Very nearly, your Eminence.

ARCH-VICAR: Well, hurry up, hurry up. (*To* DR. POOLE) And meanwhile, if you're so concerned, why don't you try some of *your* religion on her?

DR. POOLE: If I had the strength or the faith, I would. But… well, I haven't got them. I've drifted away from it all.

ARCH-VICAR: That's a shame. I'd have loved to hear you tell her that God's in his heaven and all's right with the world.

DR. POOLE: Oddly enough, I think I may come to believe it, if I stay here long enough.

ARCH-VICAR (*chuckling*): What do you think of that, Brother Asmodeus?

FIRST PRIEST: A, it's blasphemous; B, it's imbecile. How could any sane man believe such a thing—in the teeth of all the evidence to the contrary?

DR. POOLE: I don't quite know myself. Perhaps it's just because darkness implies light.

ARCH-VICAR: Of course it implies light. But we take very good care that the light shan't break through. If they're in despair, we go out of our way to discourage them still further. If they show any sign of love, we punish them, if they're malicious, they get a prize. We've reduced it to a science; it's infallible.

EXECUTIONER (*stepping forward*): Excuse me, Your Eminence.

ARCH-VICAR: What is it?

EXECUTIONER: I have another job to do this evening. Would you mind if I got to work on this immediately?

ARCH-VICAR: Go ahead, go ahead. I'm sorry I kept you waiting.

(*The* EXECUTIONER *bows to the* ARCH-VICAR, *then turns to* POLLY.)

EXECUTIONER: Get up. (POLLY *huddles in terror against* LOOLA.) Get up!

(*She rises slowly to her feet, helped by* LOOLA.)

DR. POOLE: Your Eminence, I beg you. Be merciful.

ARCH-VICAR: My dear sir, Belial is never merciful. (*To the* FIRST PRIEST) Let me have some wine.

DR. POOLE: She doesn't deserve to be punished like this.

ARCH-VICAR: That's the beauty of it.

DR. POOLE: It's sheer cruelty.

ARCH-VICAR: Of course it is.

DR. POOLE: She can't stand it.

ARCH-VICAR: That's her lookout. She shouldn't have run away.

DR. POOLE: If somebody's got to suffer, I'd rather it were me.

(*There is a silence. The* EXECUTIONER, *who during the preceding conversation has been engaged in strapping* POLLY's *hands to her side and taking his instruments out of the black bag, stares at* DR. POOLE, *then shakes his head and taps his forehead.*)

FIRST PRIEST (*bringing a bottle and drinking-horn to the* ARCH-VICAR): I told you he wasn't quite right in the head.

(*He uncorks the bottle.*)

EXECUTIONER: Excuse me; but is there a light in the other room?

FIRST PRIEST: Yes.

EXECUTIONER: Good. I'll take her there. I don't want to make a mess on your nice clean floor.

(*He takes* POLLY*'s arm and leads her towards the door on the right.* DR. POOLE *bars their passage.*)

DR. POOLE: Stop! (*To the* ARCH-VICAR) Your Eminence, I'm not mad. I mean what I said. Every word of it.

ARCH-VICAR (*takes a pair of spectacles out of his pocket, puts them on and looks intently at* DR. POOLE): Remarkable, most remarkable!

EXECUTIONER: Listen, this is my busy day.

(*He pushes* DR. POOLE *aside, but the latter hangs on to his arm.*)

DR. POOLE: No, no. Your Eminence…

ARCH-VICAR (*empties the glass, which the* FIRST PRIEST *has filled for him*): I've changed my mind, Brother Azazal. Take the straps off.

(*The* EXECUTIONER *bows and releases* POLLY.)

DR. POOLE: Thank you.

EXECUTIONER (*pointing to* DR. POOLE*'s ears*): What about these? Do you wish me to operate, Your Eminence?

ARCH-VICAR: No, don't bother.

FIRST PRIEST (*shocked*): Your Eminence…

ARCH-VICAR: After all it isn't every day we have a visitor from New Zealand. (*Turning to the two girls*) Still here? Out with you. Get out!

(*They hurry towards the door on the left and go out.*)

EXECUTIONER (*closing his black bag*): May I be excused, Your Eminence?

ARCH-VICAR: Of course, of course. (*The* EXECUTIONER *goes out left.*) All's well that ends well, Dr. Poole. Not, of course, that anything ever does end well; but sometimes one has the momentary illusion that it might. (*To the* SECOND PRIEST) What about supper?

FIRST PRIEST: Very nearly, Your Eminence. (*To the* SECOND PRIEST) I need some more fuel.

(The SECOND PRIEST *goes out right.*)

ARCH-VICAR (*to* DR. POOLE, *who is looking at the altar*): Tasteful, isn't it? It was designed by one of our young vessels. What a talent! But unfortunately she kept on forgetting her apron. I overlooked it two or three times. But in the end we had to act… (*He shakes his head, clicks his tongue, and sighs.*) It was a great loss to art!

(*The* SECOND PRIEST *re-enters, carrying a basket full of books, and sets it down near the stove. The* FIRST PRIEST *opens the door of the stove, which emits a red glow, and his colleague throws books in.* DR. POOLE *looks at them with an expression of horror.*)

DR. POOLE: But this is frightful! What are they doing?

ARCH-VICAR: In goes *The Phenomenology of Spirit*, out comes the corned beef hash.

DR. POOLE: But there might be something really valuable. (*He approaches the two* PRIESTS *and looks down at the basket. The* SECOND PRIEST *picks up another handful of books and tosses them into the stove.*) No, no, not that one. Please. (*The* PRIEST *ignores his plea and throws it in.* DR. POOLE *thrusts his hand into the stove and pulls out the volume.*) Ouch!

(*He shakes his burned fingers, then puts them in his mouth.*)

SECOND PRIEST: Put that book back where it belongs!

DR. POOLE: No, I beg you.

FIRST PRIEST: Put it back!

ARCH-VICAR: Leave him alone.

FIRST PRIEST: But, Your Eminence…

ARCH-VICAR (*raising his voice to a shrill yell*): Hurry up with that supper!

BOTH PRIESTS: Yes, Your Eminence.

(*They bow, and get on with their work.* DR. POOLE *walks back to where the* ARCH-VICAR *is sitting.*)

ARCH-VICAR: What was it? Something worth burning your fingers for? (DR. POOLE *hands him the book. The* ARCH-VICAR *reads the title.*) "*Poetical Works of Shelley*." Really, Dr. Poole, really! (*He opens at random and reads.*)

"The world is full of woodmen who expel
Love's gentle dryads from the trees of life
And vex the nightingales in every dell."[20]

Vex the nightingales… That's rather nice. And do we vex them! Here—catch! (*He tosses the book to* DR. POOLE, *who catches it and slips it into his pocket.*) Before the Thing they had some pretty good libraries hereabouts. The Huntington out at Pasadena. The Los Angeles Public Library, the libraries of the two universities and Occidental College and the California Institute of Technology. Most of them are pretty well mined out now. In future we shall have to go further afield

---

[20] Percy Bysshe Shelley, "The Woodman and the Nightingale" (1818), ll.68–70.

for our fuel. But meanwhile we've done our cooking and I've managed to save eight or nine thousand volumes for our Seminary. (*The* FIRST PRIEST *approaches with a bottle and a plate of hash, which he sets down on a table in front of the* ARCH-VICAR.) Ah! (*He throws himself upon the food and eats noisily, with concentrated greed.*)

(*From outside comes the muffled sound of a strange music of flutes and xylophones, accompanied by chanting.*)

DR. POOLE: What's that?

ARCH-VICAR (*with his mouth full*): They're getting ready to begin. (*He waves his hand towards the window.*) Take a look. It's quite interesting, if you haven't seen it before.

(DR. POOLE *goes to the window, opens the wooden shutter and looks out. The sounds from outside increase in volume and become more distinct.*)

SEMICHORUS I:
Glory to Belial,
SEMICHORUS II:
To Belial in the lowest.
SEMICHORUS I:
Belial, Belial.
SEMICHORUS II:
Belial, Belial.

(*The chanting ceases, but the instrumental music continues.*)

DR. POOLE: What a crowd! The stadium's almost full.

NARRATOR: By the smoky and intermittent light of torches he sees them—tier above tier, like serried gargoyles, spouting the groundless faith, the subhuman excitement, the collective imbecility that are the products of mass religion; spouting them from black eye-holes, from quivering nostrils and parted lips, while the horned priests blow their thigh-bone flutes and bang their xylophones and chant the praise of triumphant Evil.

SEMICHORUS I:
Glory to Belial,
SEMICHORUS II:
To Belial in the lowest.

NARRATOR: At the centre of the arena stands the High Altar, with its glittering horns, its candles, its whips and consecrated knives, its bowl of burnished copper for the blood. In the sand, at the foot of the altar steps, the women are waiting on their knees. Hundreds of women, dark-skinned, fair-skinned, some slender, some matronly, but all of them abject, shaven, terrified; and in her arms each of them clasps the latest bequest of applied science, a tiny monster.

(There is a pause. Then the music changes. The chanting begins again on a new rhythm.)

SEMICHORUS I:
It is a terrible thing,
SEMICHORUS II:
Terrible, terrible,
SEMICHORUS I:
To fall into the hands,
SEMICHORUS II:
The huge hands and the hairy,
SEMICHORUS I:
Of the living Evil—
SEMICHORUS II:
Hallelujah!
SEMICHORUS I:
Into the hands of the Enemy of Man,
SEMICHORUS II:
Of the Rebel against the Order of Things,
SEMICHORUS I:
Of the Great Blowfly, who is the Lord of Flies,
SEMICHORUS II:
Crawling in the heart, crawling in the heart;
SEMICHORUS I:
Of the Prince of the Powers of the Air,
SEMICHORUS II:
Spitfire and Stuka, Beelzebub and Azazel;
SEMICHORUS I:
Of the Lord of this world,
SEMICHORUS II:
And its defiler, its destroyer;
SEMICHORUS I:
Of the great Lord Moloch,
SEMICHORUS II:
Patron of all nations;
SEMICHORUS I:
Of Mammon our master,
SEMICHORUS II:

The omnipresent;
SEMICHORUS I:
Of Lucifer incarnate
SEMICHORUS II:
In State, in Party;
SEMICHORUS I:
Of Belial transcendent,
SEMICHORUS II:
But oh, how inward!
ALL TOGETHER:
Belial, Belial, Belial.

NARRATOR: And now a pair of one-horned Presbyters descend, seize the nearest of the shaven women and lead her up, dumb with terror, to where, at the head of the altar steps, the Patriarch of Pasadena stands whetting the blade of his consecrated knife. One of the Presbyters takes the child out of its mother's arms and holds it up—blind, handless, hare-lipped—before the Patriarch.

SEMICHORUS I:
I show you the sign of Belial's enmity.
SEMICHORUS II:
Foul, foul!
SEMICHORUS I:
I show you the fruit of Belial's grace—
SEMICHORUS II:
Horror infused in filth.
SEMICHORUS I:
I show you the penalty for obedience to His will,
SEMICHORUS II:
On earth as it is in hell.
SEMICHORUS I:
Who is the breeder of all deformities?
SEMICHORUS II:
Mother.
SEMICHORUS I:
Who is the chosen vessel of Unholiness?
SEMICHORUS II:
Mother.
SEMICHORUS I:
Who carries the curse that is on our race?

SEMICHORUS II:
Mother.
SEMICHORUS I:
Belial possesses her,
SEMICHORUS II:
The blowfly in her blood;
SEMICHORUS I:
Stinging and goading,
SEMICHORUS II:
He drives her irresistibly,
SEMICHORUS I:
Human no longer, like a frenzied beast,
SEMICHORUS II:
Down a steep place
SEMICHORUS I:
Into filth unutterable,
SEMICHORUS II:
To bear this monstrous
SEMICHORUS I:
Mockery of a man.
SEMICHORUS II:
Mockery of a man.

NARRATOR: Hare-lipped, without hands, and the eyes are atrophied.
(*A pause. Again the music changes its character.*)

SEMICHORUS I:
How shall there be atonement?
SEMICHORUS II:
By blood.
SEMICHORUS I:
How shall misfortune be punished?
SEMICHORUS II:
By blood.
SEMICHORUS I:
How shall Belial be propitiated?
SEMICHORUS II:
Only by blood.

NARRATOR: Beyond the altar, tier above tier, the pallid gargoyles stare down in hungry anticipation. And suddenly the faces open their black mouths and start to chant in unison.

(*The chorus of spectators begins hesitantly, then continues with growing confidence and an ever greater volume of sound.*)

CHORUS:

Blood, blood, blood,
The blood, the blood,
Blood, blood,
The blood.
Blood, blood, blood, blood,
The blood, the blood, the blood.

(*The chanting goes on diminuendo to form a monotonous accompaniment to the words of the* NARRATOR.)

NARRATOR: And now the Patriarch hands his whetstone to one of the attendant Archimandrites. Stretching out his left hand, he takes the deformed child by the neck. The consecrated butcher's knife flashes in the candle-light.

(*There is a little bleating cry, and at once the monotonous chanting of the crowd swells in savage triumph.*)

Dr. POOLE: Good God!
CHORUS:

Blood, blood, blood,
The blood, the blood,
Blood, blood,
The blood.

(*And so on, diminuendo once more*)

NARRATOR: The patriarch turns and, withdrawing the knife, allows some blood to drain into the basin on the altar, then tosses the tiny corpse into the darkness beyond.

CHORUS (*crescendo*):

Blood, blood,
The blood, the blood, the blood,
(*diminuendo*)
Blood, blood, blood, blood.

PATRIARCH'S VOICE: Drive her away!

SEMICHORUS I:
Drive her, beat her.
SEMICHORUS II:
Beat her, beat her.
(*The sound of whips on flesh, followed by the piercing screams of a woman*)
(*From the congregation comes a great roar.*)
DR. POOLE: But this is too horrible!
(*He slams the window shut and walks back in a state of great agitation to the* ARCH-VICAR, *who laughs and pats him on the back.*)
ARCH-VICAR: Cheer up. You'll soon get used to this kind of thing.
DR. POOLE: Never!
ARCH-VICAR: "Never!" That's what they were saying at the end of the nineteenth century. The bad old days were over. Never again. Never. Fifty years later what had happened? Slavery was back, torture was back, public executions were back, forced migrations were back, wholesale massacre was back. And, apart from those that were actually suffering, nobody turned a hair or lost an hour's sleep about it. They were used to it, they took it all for granted. And that's what you'll do in a week or two. (*Shouting to the* PRIESTS) Bring another plate of hash for Dr. Poole.
DR. POOLE: No, really. I don't feel like eating anything.
ARCH-VICAR: Nonsense, man, nonsense! It'll settle your stomach. (*Shouting again to the* PRIESTS) And bring another bottle. Bring two more bottles. (*He empties the last of his own bottle into his drinking-horn.*) Are you familiar with world history?
DR. POOLE: As a dilettante. It's not my subject, of course.
ARCH-VICAR: But you know the main outlines? (DR. POOLE *nods.*) Good. I give a course every year at the Seminary. "Belial in History." It's part of the students' training in dogmatic diabology. One doesn't like to boast; but I think I can truthfully say that nobody has heard my course without experiencing a notable deepening and strengthening of his faith.
(*He makes the sign of the horns. There is a silence. The* FIRST PRIEST *comes and sets a plate and a bottle on the table in front of* DR. POOLE.)
DR. POOLE: Thank you.
(*He pours out a little wine and takes a sip, then raises a mouthful of food to his lips, changes his mind and pushes the plate away.*)
ARCH-VICAR: Ours, my dear sir, is essentially a rational religion. We have good reasons for believing as we do. Our faith is buttressed by evidence. Consider world history. What is it, my friend, what is it but

the record of Man pitting himself against Nature, of the Ego setting itself up against the Order of Things, of Belial indomitably struggling with—with the Other One. For a hundred thousand years the battle's entirely indecisive. Then, three centuries ago, the tide starts to run uninterruptedly in one direction. Belial inaugurates His triumphal march across a world of which He will soon become the undisputed master.

(*As he speaks the last words, the* FIRST PRIEST *goes to the window, opens and looks out. We hear the noises from outside.*)

CHORUS (*crescendo*):

Blood, blood,
The blood, the blood, the blood…

(*Whips thud on flesh, a woman screams.*)

ARCH-VICAR (*raising his voice in shrill anger*): Shut that window!

FIRST PRIEST (*hastily obeying*): Yes, Your Eminence.

ARCH-VICAR (*grumbling*): One can't hear oneself speak with this racket going on. Don't let it happen again.

FIRST PRIEST: No, Your Eminence.

ARCH-VICAR: If you want to see the Ceremonies, go outside.

FIRST PRIEST: Thank you, Your Eminence.

(*He bows and goes out through the door on the left.*)

ARCH-VICAR (*turning back to* DR. POOLE): I apologize for the interruption. Let me see, where was I?

DR. POOLE: You were just speaking about Belial's triumphal march across the world.

ARCH-VICAR: Of course, of course. Now, listen. It began with the first modern machines and the first grain ships from the New World. Food for the hungry and a burden lifted from men's shoulders. (*He chuckles.*) But, they forgot; nobody ever gets anything for nothing. Every blessing has its price, and Belial always makes sure that it's exorbitant. Take those wonderful new machines, for example. Belial knew perfectly well what they'd do to us. In finding a little alleviation from toil, man's flesh would be subordinated to iron and brass. And in producing more wealth, more efficiently, man's mind would become the slave of lifeless automats. He knew that, if a machine is fool-proof, it must also be skill-proof, talent-proof, inspiration-proof. Your money back if the product is faulty, and double your money back if you can find in it the slightest trace of genius or personality. No wonder that life came to seem more and more pointless! No wonder the incidence of neuroses and psychoses and psycho-somatic diseases went up and up and up. Faster and faster with every successive year. They kept on building more mental hospitals; but the lunatics were always two or three jumps ahead of the asylums. Which was exactly what Belial had been working for—a civilization that, as it advanced, would drive more and more people to take refuge in alcohol or schizophrenia or a nervous breakdown. When I read the morbidity statistics for the second half of the twentieth century, I can only bow my head in reverent admiration. (*He makes the sign of the horns.*) Only Supreme Malevolence could have achieved so frightful an end by means apparently so admirable…

(*He pauses to take a drink of wine.*)

DR. POOLE: One can see now, looking backwards, that they just didn't have time to make the necessary changes.

ARCH-VICAR: Of course they didn't. Belial never gave them the time. That was part of His strategy. Look at the way He handled population pressures. It began at the same time as the Industrial Revolution. Those food ships from the New World. Bread for everybody. No more famines. But Belial could see into the future. He knew that feeding means breeding. In the old days, when people married, they merely raised the infantile mortality rate and lowered the expectation of life. Then came the food ships; and the children no longer died of undernourishment, the parents lived ten years longer and produced yet more children. What blessings! Everybody was enchanted—including Belial. How He must have chuckled! Within five generations there were countries with six hundred, eight hundred, up to three thousand people to the square mile of productive land. Of course they didn't have time to work out any intelligent policy. They were too busy breeding. And the more they bred, the more food they needed. The more food they needed, the worse they had to treat the land. The worse they treated the land, the less food they had. The less food they had, the more they listened to the Communists and the Fascists and the Militarists. And the more wars and revolutions they indulged in, the less they could do to help themselves and the more they were tempted, as a way out of their difficulties, to ruin their environment. "Extractive agriculture"—isn't that the phrase?

DR. POOLE: Yes, that's it.

ARCH-VICAR: And of course you know what it meant. More and more erosion, less and less fertility. And each year there were twenty million more of them to be fed—sixty-five thousand new mouths every day of the week. Including Sundays. And Belial had foreseen it all. He'd planned the whole process step by step. First there's the old, primitive, immemorial hunger. Then you get improved communications and food from the New World. Imported food leads to booming populations. Booming populations lead to ruin of the soil. And ruin of the soil leads back again to hunger. Only this time it's the new hunger, the higher hunger, the hunger of industrialized proletariats, the hunger of city dwellers with money and cars and radios and all the gadgets. The typical twentieth-century hunger that was the cause of all those wars and revolutions—which in their turn, of course, were the cause of yet more hunger. I tell you, it's sublime, it's awe-inspiring. And that wasn't all. Just look at what Belial managed to make those maniacs believe. There they were, like a great horde of prurient and destructive apes, fouling the rivers, destroying the forests, washing the topsoil into the sea, turning pastures and ploughlands into deserts, burning up oceans of petroleum, squandering the minerals that it had taken the whole of geological time to deposit. An orgy of criminal imbecility. And He persuaded them to call it Progress. Progress!

DR. POOLE: It certainly seems pretty funny now.

ARCH-VICAR: Funny? Listen! Can you hear it?

DR. POOLE: What?

ARCH-VICAR: That noise. That enormous noise of laughing.

DR. POOLE: I don't hear anything.

ARCH-VICAR: No, you wouldn't. I hear it all the time, wherever I go. The laughter of Belial, the laughter of Moloch and Azazel, of Mammon and Beelzebub.

(*He makes the sign of the horns, then raises his head and utters a loud shrill peal of malignant and mirthless laughter.*)

DR. POOLE (*after a silence*): I've often discussed this matter with my colleagues. My own view is that, even after the Second World War, they might have saved the situation.

ARCH-VICAR: How?

DR. POOLE: If the governments could have admitted that the real problem wasn't political or economic, but cosmic—that it wasn't a question of who should have power, but of how the planet and its inhabitants could be saved from destruction. On that basis—and on that basis alone—they might have come to an agreement, they might have worked together to repair the damage that had been done, to reduce population, to conserve and increase resources, to discover how humanitarian ideals could be reconciled with biological reality.

ARCH-VICAR: But as a matter of historical fact they didn't do anything of the kind.

DR. POOLE: Unfortunately they didn't.

ARCH-VICAR: And why didn't they?

DR. POOLE (*shrugging his shoulders*): They preferred to go on cutting one another's throats.

ARCH-VICAR: But why did they prefer it? I'll tell you. Because their political thinking was inspired.

DR. POOLE: Inspired?

ARCH-VICAR: By the Great Blowfly crawling in the heart. You can see it at every turn. Think of Marx's phrase about Force being the midwife of Progress. Think of Hitler's Thousand-Year Reich. Direct and plenary inspiration.

DR. POOLE: That's easy to assert. How do you prove it?

ARCH-VICAR: The proof is history, the proof is what actually happened. Unlike God, who has always been interested in intentions, Belial is concerned exclusively with results. Look at the results of any action and, if they're evil, you'll know who inspired it. For example, what happened when Belial injected the idea of Progress into politics? Up came the Communists and the Fascists. All history, they proclaimed, is a progress towards the earthly paradise, and the destination is so gorgeous that it's our duty to murder everybody who gets in the way. So they made their wars and revolutions and the result, very naturally, was universal misery, culminating in the Thing. Exactly as Belial had always foreseen and intended.

DR. POOLE: But what about all the people who weren't Communists and Fascists?

ARCH-VICAR: Don't worry. Belial had given them Nationalism. It's the theory that every sovereign state is divine—that there isn't one God in heaven, but fifty-seven varieties of gods on earth. People still called themselves Christians and Jews and Buddhists and all the rest. But in actual practice they were all devout nation-worshippers. Look at the way Buddhism was used as the instrument of Japanese nationalism; the way Judaism was used as an instrument of Israeli nationalism; the way the Russians used Greek Orthodox Christianity as an instrument of Slav nationalism; the way Protestantism and Catholicism were used as instruments of the nationalisms of the West. It's remarkable, really remarkable.

DR. POOLE: And you think the whole thing was engineered by Belial?

ARCH-VICAR: Obviously. You've only got to look at the results. Pure, unmitigated evil. Nationalism and Progress—to my mind, they're the two most conclusive proofs of Belial's existence.

DR. POOLE: I'm sorry; but I'm a man of science. You can't expect me to swallow that.

ARCH-VICAR: As a man of science, you're bound to accept the hypothesis which explains the facts most plausibly and most economically. Well, what are the facts? The first is a fact of psychology; men don't like being killed, or hurt, or degraded. The second is a fact about the theories of Nationalism and Progress: they're both intrinsically absurd and it's perfectly obvious that both lead straight to mass slaughter and universal misery. And the third fact is a fact of history: at a certain moment of time the majority of human beings decided to adopt these fatal theories as their guides to political and economic conduct. Did they *want* to be butchered or turned into animals? No. The only plausible explanation for their actions is that they were possessed by some alien consciousness, some malignant power that willed their undoing and willed it more strongly than they were able to will their own happiness or even their own survival.

DR. POOLE: Of course, these facts could be accounted for in other ways.

ARCH-VICAR: But not so plausibly, not nearly so simply… And the really astounding thing is that Belial achieved all His purposes without ever resorting to a miracle. By purely natural means, using human folly and human science as his instruments, He created an entirely new race of men, with deformity in their blood, with squalor all around them and ahead, in the future, no prospects but of more squalor, worse deformity and, finally, of complete extinction. Yes, it's a terrible thing to fall into the hands of the living Evil.[21]

DR. POOLE: Then why do you go on worshipping Him?

ARCH-VICAR: Why do you throw food to a growling tiger? To buy yourself a breathing space. To put off the horror of the inevitable, if only for a few minutes. On earth as it is in Hell—but at least one's still on earth. (*A silence.* DR. POOLE *rises and walks up and down. The*

21 Compare "Hebrews," 10:31 (*New Living Translation*): "It is a terrible thing to fall into the hands of the living God." See also John Donne, who expounds this Bible quotation in his Sermon 76 (preached at Sion, ca. 1622): "[W]hen God's hand is bent to strike, [*i*]*t is a fearful thing to fall into the hands of the living God*; but to fall out of the hands of the living God is a horror beyond our expression, beyond our imagination."

FIRST PRIEST *re-enters through the door on the left, approaches the* ARCH-VICAR *and bows.*) What is it?

FIRST PRIEST: There's a messenger just come in from the Grand Inquisitor. He and his men caught those foreigners in an ambush. Killed two of them. The rest got back to the ship with the wounded.

ARCH-VICAR: Good, good. I don't think we shall be bothered by *them* any more. Don't mention it to him.

(*He indicates* DR. POOLE.)

FIRST PRIEST: Very good, Your Eminence.

ARCH-VICAR: How are the Ceremonies going?

FIRST PRIEST: The crowd's begun to get pretty hot.

ARCH-VICAR: Already? (*He gets up, assisted by the* FIRST PRIEST.) Put some more books on the fire. It's getting chilly. (*The* FIRST PRIEST *goes and does as he is told. The* ARCH-VICAR *moves over to* DR. POOLE.) Open the window, please.

(DR. POOLE *opens the window, while the* ARCH-VICAR *goes to the larger of the two cupboards in the wall near the altar and rummages about in it, looking for something.*)

DR. POOLE (*excitedly*): Your Eminence, something's happening. The people are leaving their seats.

ARCH-VICAR: They're warming up. It's the blood that does it. That and, of course, the whipping.

DR. POOLE: They're jumping down into the arena. They're running after one another. What on earth…? No, *really*…

ARCH-VICAR: What's the matter?

DR. POOLE: There *are* limits.

ARCH-VICAR: That's where you're wrong. There are no limits. Everybody's capable of anything—but *anything*.

DR. POOLE: It's monstrous. It's absolutely revolting.

ARCH-VICAR (*who has found what he was looking for and now approaches* DR. POOLE *with a pair of binoculars, which he hands to him*): Try these. Night glasses. Standard Navy equipment before the Thing. You'll see everything. (DR. POOLE *hesitates.*) Go ahead, man. Look! You've never seen anything like this in New Zealand.

DR. POOLE: I certainly have not.

ARCH-VICAR: Take them.

DR. POOLE: Very well, if you insist.

(*He takes the glasses and raises them to his eyes.*)

NARRATOR: It is a scene of Satyrs and Nymphs, of flights and pursuits and captures, of provocative resistances followed by the surrender, almost aggressive in its enthusiasm, of lips to bearded lips, of panting bosoms to the impatience of rough hands.

(*The muffled sound of shouting, squealing and shrill laughter rises in a wild crescendo.*)

ARCH-VICAR (*with disgust*): Like cats. Only cats have the decency not to be gregarious in their mating. And you still have doubts about Belial—even after this?

NARRATOR: Consider the birds. What a delicacy in their love-making, what old-world chivalry! For although the hormones produced in the body of the breeding hen predispose her to sexual emotion, their effect is neither so intense nor of so brief a duration as that of the ovarian secretions in the blood of the female mammal during oestrus. Hence the prevalence among male birds of bright plumage and of an instinct for courtship. And hence the conspicuous absence of these charming things among male mammals. For where, as among the mammals, the female's amorous desires and her attractiveness to the male are wholly determined by chemical means, what need is there of masculine beauty or the niceties of preliminary courtship?

Among humans every day of the year is potentially the mating season. Girls are not chemically predestined to accept, during a few days, the advances of the first male who presents himself. Their bodies manufacture hormones in doses sufficiently small to leave even the most temperamental of them a certain freedom of choice. That is why, unlike the dog and the bull, man has always been a wooer. But now the gamma rays have changed all that. Thanks to the supreme triumph of modern science, sex has become seasonal, romance has turned into rut, and the female's chemical compulsion to mate has abolished courtship, chivalry, tenderness, love itself.

(*The noise of the mating becomes louder.*)

DR. POOLE: (*lowering his glasses*): I wouldn't have thought it was possible.

ARCH-VICAR: With Belial all things are possible. (*He makes the sign of the horns.*) One tries to look at it objectively; but… Ugh! (*He makes a grimace of disgust.*) Nauseous! And this is nothing to what it'll be like later on. How thankful I am that I've been preserved from such ignominy! (*He turns to the* FIRST PRIEST, *who has approached and is also looking out through the window at was is happening in the arena.*) Don't you feel like that?

FIRST PRIEST: I certainly do, Your Eminence.

DR. POOLE (*after a moment of hesitation*): How old were you when you… when you entered the priesthood?

SECOND PRIEST: Just twelve.

DR. POOLE: Only twelve?

ARCH-VICAR: The surgical phase of the ordination is less dangerous at that age.

DR. POOLE: Quite, quite.

ARCH-VICAR: Any bright boy who shows signs of throwing back to the old-style mating patterns has his future assured. We save him from himself by making a priest of him.

DR. POOLE: I see.

ARCH-VICAR: For the Kingdom of Hell's sake. Not to mention the purely practical reasons. After all, the business of the community has to be carried on somehow; and obviously, at this season, the laity are in no position to do it. (*He raises his hand and points.*) Look over there. To the left of the High Altar. Do you see him?

DR. POOLE: See whom?

ARCH-VICAR: The Chief. There—running after that little vessel who was out at the cemetery.

DR. POOLE: Oh.

ARCH-VICAR: There, he's caught her. I ask you, what sort of a ruler is *he* going to be for the next three weeks?

DR. POOLE (*forcing a laugh*): Well, he certainly seems to be relaxing from the cares of State.

ARCH-VICAR: And until he and the other pigs stop being possessed, the Church has to take over.

(*He starts to close the shutter and, in so doing, bumps* DR. POOLE, *who is staring out so eagerly that he does not notice what the other is doing.*)

DR. POOLE: Oh, I beg your pardon. I didn't notice…

ARCH-VICAR: I'm glad you're enjoying it so much.

DR. POOLE: No, no. It's just… just scientific curiosity. (*He takes a last look. An expression of distress appears on his face.*) Oh, God.

ARCH-VICAR (*as he closes the shutter*): What's that?

DR. POOLE: Nothing, nothing. Let me bolt it for you.

ARCH-VICAR (*turning to the* FIRST PRIEST): I think it's time I went out to them, don't you?

FIRST PRIEST: I agree, Your Eminence.

(*He helps the* ARCH-VICAR *to put on his sacerdotal ornaments—a necklace of human vertebrae, a brooch set with a baby's skull—and hands him his pastoral staff, which is surmounted by gilded horns.*)

ARCH-VICAR (*to* DR. POOLE, *while he is being dressed*): I let the Patriarch conduct the Purification Ceremonies. But when it comes to the opening of the Hot Season, I always take over myself. I regard it as the most solemn moment of the religious year. (*To the* PRIEST) Is that straight?

FIRST PRIEST (*giving a final touch to the necklace*): Perfect, Your Eminence.

(*He holds up a mirror.*)

ARCH-VICAR: Good, good… Well, I think we're ready. You, Dr. Poole, will wait for me here.

DR. POOLE: Yes, Your Eminence.

FIRST PRIEST: Perhaps the doctor would prefer to come out and…

ARCH-VICAR: And join the ladies. Of course. I'd quite forgotten you weren't one of us. Come on.

(*He takes* DR. POOLE*'s arm.*)

DR. POOLE (*disengaging himself*): No thank you, Your Eminence.

ARCH-VICAR: Don't be bashful. You'll love it, once you've taken the plunge.

DR. POOLE: Really, Your Eminence.

ARCH-VICAR: You must learn to be docile to the Unholy Spirit.

DR. POOLE: I'd rather not, if you don't mind.

ARCH-VICAR: All right, all right. I won't insist.

FIRST PRIEST (*shocked*): But, Your Eminence, you *should* insist. On principle.

ARCH-VICAR: No, no. Why force things. Leave it all to Belial. He knows best. (*To* DR. POOLE) Well, I'll be back in about an hour.

(*He goes out through the door on the left, followed by the* FIRST PRIEST. DR. POOLE *goes to the window, opens and looks out. There is a flourish of trumpets and a screeching of thigh-bone flutes.*)

PRIESTLY VOICES: His Eminence, the Arch-Vicar of Belial. Make way for His Eminence. Out of the way there! Glory be to Belial. Silence. Silence, you swine. Silence.

NARRATOR: Slowly and majestically he crosses the arena, mounts the steps of the High Altar, bows before the gilded horns and dips his fingers in the blood of the sacrifices. Then turns towards the congregation and raises his staff.

(*There is a long silence. Then the chanting begins.*)

SEMICHORUS I:

This is the time,

SEMICHORUS II:
For Belial is merciless,
SEMICHORUS I:
The time for Time's ending
SEMICHORUS II:
In the blindness of desire.
SEMICHORUS I:
This is the time,
SEMICHORUS II:
For Belial is in your blood,
SEMICHORUS I:
Time for the birth in you
SEMICHORUS II:
Of the Others, the Aliens;
SEMICHORUS I:
Of Itch, of Tetter,
SEMICHORUS II:
Of tumid Worm.
SEMICHORUS I:
This is the time,
SEMICHORUS II:
For Belial hates you,
SEMICHORUS I:
Time for begetting
SEMICHORUS II:
Monsters, monsters;
SEMICHORUS I:
Time for the Soul's death,
SEMICHORUS II:
For the Person to perish;
SEMICHORUS I:
Time for the Human Being's
SEMICHORUS II:
Total defeat.
SEMICHORUS I:
Not your will, but His,
SEMICHORUS II:
That you may all be lost for ever.
CONGREGATION:
Amen, amen.

ARCH-VICAR'S VOICE: The curse of Belial be upon you, on your souls, on your bodies, on the souls and bodies of your children and your children's children to the end of time. Amen.

CONGREGATION:

Amen.

ARCH-VICAR'S VOICE: And now, that the curse may be fulfilled upon you, all things are made lawful.

(*A yell of delight goes up from the congregation.*)

NARRATOR: The women rush forward, surge up the altar steps, tear off their aprons and fling them in a mounting pile at the Arch-Vicar's feet. NO NO NO—and as each apron is discarded there rises a triumphant shout.

WOMEN'S VOICES: Yes, yes, yes.

MEN'S VOICES: Yes, yes…

NARRATOR: And now, one by one, the torches are extinguished. Let there be darkness; Let there be darkness. And there is darkness, and in darkness the frenzy of creatures that have ceased to be human without, however, achieving the innocence of beasts.

SEMICHORUS I:

Not your will, but His,

SEMICHORUS II:

That you may be lost for ever.

SEMICHORUS I:

Not your will but His:

SEMICHORUS II:

Lost for ever, lost for ever.

BOTH TOGETHER:

Lost for ever, lost for ever, lost for ever.

DR. POOLE: Christ!

(*He closes the window, and starts to walk up and down in a state of great agitation. The door on the left opens and the* FIRST PRIEST *enters, carrying several bloodstained garments.*)

FIRST PRIEST: Well, well, all dressed up and nowhere to go. There's still time. Why don't you go out and make a pig of yourself with the rest of them?

(*He walks over to the cupboard near the altar, lays the clothes he is carrying on a chair and starts to hang them up one by one.* DR. POOLE*'s attention is caught.*)

DR. POOLE: What's that coat? (*He gets up, goes over to the* PRIEST *and examines the coat.*) But that's Craigie's jacket.

(*He holds it up, exposing the dark bloodstain on the left side… He looks at the bloodstain, then at the* FIRST PRIEST.)

FIRST PRIEST: Don't ask any questions and you'll be told no lies.

(*He takes the coat and hangs it up.*)

DR. POOLE: Was he… was he killed?[22]

FIRST PRIEST: I'm under orders not to mention the matter. (*He holds up another jacket with an even larger bloodstain, looks at it and shakes his head.*) It's a shame. Such beautiful material! Do you think soap would take it out?

DR. POOLE: I don't know.

FIRST PRIEST: I think I'll try.

(*He goes out the door on the right.* DR. POOLE *sits down at the table and covers his face with his hands. The door on the left is opened and* FLOSSIE *bursts into the room.*)

FLOSSIE (*pausing to look about her*): Alfie! Where are you? (*She sees* DR. POOLE *and rushes towards him with outstretched arms.*) Honey boy!

(*She embraces* DR. POOLE.)

DR. POOLE (*struggling*): No, no.

FLOSSIE: Yes, yes!

(*She kisses* DR. POOLE *with violent enthusiasm.*)

DR. POOLE: Listen, Flossie. We can't…

FLOSSIE: Look—no apron.

DR. POOLE: I know, but… (*She makes a pass at him.*) Please…

FLOSSIE: But it's legal, honey; it's absolutely legal.

DR. POOLE: That's not the question. (*She makes another pass at him.*) Stop it. Stop it, I tell you. Get away.

(*He pushes her away and retreats towards the altar. She follows him and throws herself upon him, pinning him against the structure of bones.*)

FLOSSIE: Honey boy…

DR. POOLE (*trying to escape from her clutches*): Leave me alone.

FLOSSIE: You great big beautiful beast.

DR. POOLE: I don't want to have anything to do with you.

(*While they are struggling, the* CHIEF *enters through the door on the left. Without a word, he rushes across the stage, seizes* FLOSSIE *from behind and drags her away from* DR. POOLE.)

---

[22] ED: The following text on p. 56 is struck out in red pencil and replaced with sheets 56 (I), 56 (II) and 56 (III), connecting to "SEMICHORUS I: Not your will, but His" on p. 57 (see below, 66).

FLOSSIE: No. No. Let me go. I want Alfie. (*She struggles. The* CHIEF *clasps her more tightly and kisses her.*) I hate you. I hate you. No, don't. (*He continues to kiss her. Her resistance grows weaker, finally turns into enthusiastic consent.*) Honey boy. (*She kisses him passionately.*) You great big beautiful beast.

(*The* FIRST PRIEST *re-enters from the right, carrying the jacket.*)

FIRST PRIEST: Soap only seems to make it worse. (*He catches sight of* FLOSSIE *and the* CHIEF.) What are you doing here? Get out. Get out, I tell you. (*They pay no attention. Putting down the jacket on a chair, he picks up a whip that is lying in a corner.*) Get out, you pigs. Go and wallow somewhere else.

(*He strikes at the* CHIEF. *Still holding* FLOSSIE *by the hair with one hand, the* CHIEF *turns on him.*)

CHIEF: How dare you? Don't you know who I am?

FIRST PRIEST: Yes I do. You used to be the Chief. But for the next three weeks you're just a pig, like all the others. Get out. (*He strikes at* FLOSSIE.)

(FLOSSIE *squeals, breaks away from the* CHIEF *and runs towards the door on the left.*)

CHIEF: Where are you going?

(*He hurries after her.*)

FIRST PRIEST: Pigs, filthy pigs! (*He pursues them swinging his whip. They run out.*) I'll teach you!

(*He follows them, leaving the door standing open. The sound of chanting makes itself heard.*)[23]

SEMICHORUS I:

Not your will, but His,

SEMICHORUS II:

Not your will but His,

SEMICHORUS I:

That you may be lost for ever,

SEMICHORUS II:

Lost for ever, lost for ever and ever.

SEMICHORUS I:

Lost for ever, lost for ever and ever.

SEMICHORUS II:

For ever, for ever, for ever and ever.

---

[23] FC: The following passage up to "*and lays a hand on his shoulder*" (see below, 67) is not present in FC and is restored from ED.

SEMICHORUS I:
Ha ha ha ha.
SEMICHORUS II:
Ha ha ha ha.
ALL TOGETHER:
Lost for ever, lost for ever, lost for ever.

(LOOLA *enters softly through the door on the left. She stands on the threshold, looking around cautiously to see if the coast is clear, then tiptoes over to where* DR. POOLE *is sitting and lays a hand on his shoulder.*)

LOOLA: Alfie!

DR. POOLE (*starting and looking up*): Oh, it's you.

LOOLA: It was so wonderful what you did for Polly. I didn't know anybody *could* do a thing like that.

(*She takes his hand and kisses it. He withdraws it.*)

DR. POOLE: Leave me alone.

LOOLA: Alfie, what have I done wrong?

(*She tries to take his hand again. He pushes her away.*)

DR. POOLE (*violently*): Leave me alone, I tell you. Go away.

(LOOLA *stands uncertainly, not knowing what to do. Then her eye is caught by the jacket left by the* PRIEST *on the chair. She picks it up and examines the bloodstain. Then she sees the other jacket in the closet.*)

LOOLA: Oh, Alfie—it's your friends from the ship.

DR. POOLE: It's my friends, and it's my last hope of getting home. (*Turning on her with sudden fury*) Go away. Why don't you go away? Go back where you came from. Back to your precious Chief.

LOOLA: Oh, you saw what happened?

DR. POOLE: Of course I did. Quick! You can catch him if you run. He was here only a moment ago. Went out with Flossie.

LOOLA: Did Flossie come here?

DR. POOLE (*adjusting his tie, which is still crooked from* FLOSSIE*'s embrace*): For the same reason as you did. Luckily the Chief came after her. But you shouldn't find it hard to get him away from her.

LOOLA: Do you really think that I want to get him away from her?

DR. POOLE: Why not? The most important man in the country. Hurry up. Go and find him.

LOOLA: But, Alfie, he's horrible. He could never be my friend. None of them could be. They don't even know what it means. They just let themselves be possessed, that's all. And if you're not possessed in the same way… (*She shudders.*) It's horrible. It made me absolutely sick when he grabbed hold of me just now.

DR. POOLE (*after a pause*): Is that true?

LOOLA: I thought we were friends. Friends don't tell lies to one another, do they?

DR. POOLE: I'm sorry.

(*He takes her hand.*)

LOOLA: Oh, Alfie, I was afraid you didn't like me any more.

DR. POOLE: How did you get away from him?

LOOLA: Luckily Flossie was quite close. I called to her.

DR. POOLE: And she came and pounced on him?

LOOLA: Yes; that was when I gave him the slip. I don't know what happened then. I suppose she suddenly thought about you, and that made her come running here.

DR. POOLE: It's like some kind of obscene practical joke. I can almost hear that laughter the Arch-Vicar was talking about. (*He picks up the jacket from the chair.*) If it were just plain blood, it would be more bearable. But it has to be mixed with all this filth. (*He looks through the pockets of the coat and finds a wallet which he opens.*) Yes, I thought so. It's poor Tom Henderson's. That's his wife.

(*He shows* LOOLA *a photograph.*)

LOOLA: Oh, what lovely clothes! Alfie, do you have one of those?

DR. POOLE: What—a wedding dress?

LOOLA: No, no. I mean one of those… those wife-girls.

DR. POOLE: Oh, I see. No, I'm not married.

LOOLA: Then you don't have any pictures like this?

DR. POOLE: No. Just a snapshot of my mother, that's all.

(*He shows* LOOLA *a photograph, which he takes out of his own wallet.*)

LOOLA: She looks nice.

DR. POOLE: She is.

LOOLA: Do you like her?

DR. POOLE (*with a little laugh*): Quite a lot.

LOOLA: That isn't what Belial wants. It's in the Catechism. "What is your duty towards the source of your deformity? My duty is to hate it, despise it and turn from it with abhorrence."

(*The chanting of the* PRIESTS *outside in the arena becomes audible once more.*)

SEMICHORUS I:

Lost, lost for ever.

SEMICHORUS II:

For ever, for ever.

SEMICHORUS I:

Lost, lost, lost.

SEMICHORUS II:

Lost, lost, lost.

BOTH TOGETHER:

Ha ha ha ha ha…

CURTAIN

ACT THREE[24]

SCENE: *The same as in Act Two.*
TIME: *About three months later.* DR. POOLE *is seated at a table under the open window, looking through a microscope and making drawings of what he sees on the slides. The table is littered with notebooks, papers and various pieces of salvaged scientific equipment. There is a knock at the door on the left. He goes to the door and opens.* FLOSSIE *enters.*

DR. POOLE: Flossie! What a pleasant surprise!
FLOSSIE: Pleasant? What makes you think that? I want to have a talk with you, Alfie.
DR. POOLE: Come in. Make yourself at home. (*They go to the table; he pulls up a chair for her and himself sits down, talking as he does so.*) Do you remember the last time you were here?
FLOSSIE (*severely*): No, I do not.
DR. POOLE: Do you mean to say you've forgotten? I assure you I haven't.
FLOSSIE: Decent, Belial-fearing people don't remember those things.
DR. POOLE: But it only happened three months ago.
FLOSSIE: Three months or three days—it doesn't make any difference. When it's cold you don't recollect what happened when it was hot. It just isn't done. And anyhow, whatever anybody may remember, I didn't do it.
DR. POOLE: You didn't do it? But my dear Flossie…
FLOSSIE: Somebody else did it. Somebody who wasn't wearing this. (*She indicates her apron.*) I don't have anything to do with her. And I resent your vile insinuations. I'm not one of those filthy love-perverts. I'm normal, I'm law-abiding, I do what the Catechism says we ought to do. Ask anybody you like about my apron. It's unblemished. Which is more than can be said about some people I know of.
DR. POOLE: Are you referring to me?
FLOSSIE: You're a dirty foreigner; you don't know any better. But when I see one of our people doing those things—somebody that's been born and raised in the faith… I tell you, it makes me see red.
DR. POOLE: Will you kindly explain what you're talking about?
FLOSSIE: You know well enough.
DR. POOLE: I haven't the faintest idea.

---

[24] The first six pages of Act III appear to have been inserted instead of the earlier p. 61 of ED, as they are numbered 61(1) - 61 (6) and connect to "LOOLA: Yes—but where do those jokes end?" on the earlier p. 62 (see below, 72).

FLOSSIE: Who's been having reading lessons? Who's been sitting around in corners with a spelling book?

DR. POOLE: Oh, so *that's* the trouble!

FLOSSIE: I've seen her; I've heard her mumbling that stuff. "The cat is on the mat. The dog is in the fog."

DR. POOLE: Well, what about it?

FLOSSIE: What about it? Do you think I'm a fool? Do you think I don't know what happens when a foreign God-worshipper gets hold of a love-pervert and starts talking to her about cats on mats? Cats on mats indeed! *I* know what that means.

DR. POOLE: What does it mean?

FLOSSIE: I wouldn't sully my lips by saying it. (FLOSSIE *rises, goes to the altar and falls on her knees.*) Lord Belial, don't let them get away with it. Make an example of them. See that they're properly punished. (*She covers her face with her hands and goes on speaking in a low voice.*) Let them be whipped, let them have their ears cut off, let them be buried. Or just strike them dead. Lord, strike them dead. (*She rises, touches the horns on the altar, then touches her own forehead.*)

(*While* FLOSSIE *is at the altar,* LOOLA *appears at the open door.* DR. POOLE *sees her and wordlessly gesticulates, ordering her to go away. She looks for a moment at what is going on, then retires.*)

FLOSSIE (*turning to* DR. POOLE): Well, my prayer's been answered.

DR. POOLE: How do you know?

FLOSSIE: I can feel it.

DR. POOLE: How? By the pricking in your thumbs?

FLOSSIE: No, in the spine. It's like bugs running up and down.

DR. POOLE: Perhaps it *is* bugs. Would you like me to have a look?

FLOSSIE: Don't you dare touch me! (*She goes to the table, picks up her haversack, which she left on it when she came in, and slings it over her shoulder.*) Wouldn't you like to know what I'm going to do now?

DR. POOLE: I know exactly what you're going to do.

FLOSSIE: What?

DR. POOLE: Report me to His Eminence.

(FLOSSIE *stares at him in open-mouthed amazement.*)

FLOSSIE: How did you guess?

DR. POOLE: Surely it was pretty obvious.

FLOSSIE: Aren't you scared?

DR. POOLE: Why should I be? His Eminence knows all about it.

FLOSSIE: Knows all about it?

DR. POOLE: He dropped in here last week while we were having our reading lesson.

FLOSSIE: You mean, he caught you at it?

DR. POOLE: Red-handed. You should have heard how he laughed at some of our little friend's mistakes.

FLOSSIE: Laughed? His Eminence laughed?

DR. POOLE: Why not? Some of the mistakes were very funny.

FLOSSIE (*after a pause*): I don't know what we're coming to. (*She goes back to the altar and looks up at it with clasped hands.*) Belial, don't let them get away with it. Don't, don't!

(*She turns and walks towards the door.* DR. POOLE *follows her.*)

DR. POOLE (*solicitously*): Do you feel those bugs again? (*She ignores him.*) Well, goodbye, my dear. I did so enjoy your visit. Much more than last time, I may add. (*Still ignoring him,* FLOSSIE *walks out with an expression of haughty dignity.* DR. POOLE *stands in the doorway waving to her.*) Goodbye, goodbye.

(*When she is out of sight, he turns in the other direction and gives a low whistle of three notes. There is an answering whistle. A moment later* LOOLA *appears.*)

LOOLA: Alfie! (*They kiss.*) What did she want?

DR. POOLE: She was trying to find out about you and me.

LOOLA: I've been afraid of that ever since she first saw me practicing my reading.

DR. POOLE: She threatened to report us to His Eminence. So I just laughed and told her about what happened here last week.

LOOLA (*shuddering*): Oh, Alfie, wasn't that awful! I shall never forget it. Turning round and seeing him standing there with the sun shining on his horns. It scared me to death.

DR. POOLE: But why? The old boy took it so well. More as a joke than anything else.

LOOLA: Yes—but where do those jokes end? At the bottom of a hole in the cemetery. (*She shakes her head.*) I don't want to think about it any more. Look, I've got a present for you. (*She fumbles in her knapsack.*)

DR. POOLE: What is it?

LOOLA: Razor blades.

(*She hands him the packet of blades.*)

DR. POOLE: Just when the need was becoming really desperate. Thank you.

LOOLA: I found them in a bathroom on Eleventh Street. And I took this bottle too.

(*She hands a bottle to* DR POOLE.)

DR. POOLE (*reading the label*): "Milk of Magnesia. As an Antacid, one to two tablespoonfuls. As a Laxative, two to four tablespoonfuls. As a Purgative, six to eight…"

LOOLA: There were three of the cutest little baby skeletons I've ever seen. Just lying there in the bathroom. And a teeny-weeny dog, no bigger than that. (*She indicates the size.*) What do you suppose they died of?

DR. POOLE (*shrugging his shoulders*): They had a wide choice to select from. Radiation,[25] any number of toxic gases, bacterial action, or just plain thirst. I imagine[26] the aqueducts were cut within the first five minutes.

LOOLA: Aren't these the prettiest spoons?

(*She holds up a handful of spoons.*)

DR. POOLE: Very nice.

LOOLA: Oh, and I found this book. It's poetry.

(*She hands him a small volume.*)

DR. POOLE (*reading*): "*Selected Poems by Ella Wheeler Wilcox.*"[27] (*He puts the book down and picks up another from the table.*) I think perhaps we're better off with our Shelley. Would you like to have another shot at the reading?

LOOLA: Oh, yes, Alfie. I've been practicing secretly, whenever I could get a chance. (*He finds the page he has been looking for and hands her the book open.*) Where shall I begin?

DR. POOLE (*pointing*): There.

LOOLA (*reading slowly, with hesitations and mispronunciations*)[28]:

> "Warm fragrance seems to fall from her light dress
> And her loose hair; and where some heavy tress
> The air of her own speed has dis… dis…"

What's this word?

DR. POOLE (*who is playing with her hair*): "Disentwined."

LOOLA: What's "disentwined"?

DR. POOLE: This.

(*He separates lock from lock of her hair.*)

LOOLA: Oh, I see.

> "The sweetness seems to sat…"

DR. POOLE: "Satiate."

---

25 ED: Autograph insertion {Radiation,}; FC: [from, any number}.

26 FC: {thirst. Radiation; I imagine}.

27 Ella Wheeler Wilcox (1850–1919). Minor, but popular American poetess.

28 The following lines are from Shelley's poem *Epipsychidion* (1821), ll. 105ff.

LOOLA:

"Satiate the faint wind
And in the sowl..."

DR. POOLE: "Soul."

LOOLA: What's the soul?

Dr. POOLE: Well—let's see. It's something we all have; but most of us don't know it. We have to find it. Personally, I've done quite a lot of finding since I've been here.

LOOLA: What about me?

DR. POOLE: You too. Which is all the more remarkable, seeing that souls aren't permitted in Southern California.

LOOLA: You mean, like love?

Dr. POOLE (*nodding*): And for the same reason—they're against the Law of Belial. Now, go on.

LOOLA:

"And in the soul a wild odour is felt
Beyond the sense, like fiery dews that melt
Into the bow-some..."

DR. POOLE: "Bosom."

LOOLA: What's "bosom"?

DR. POOLE: Listen, we can't go into everything.

LOOLA: Sorry, Alfie.

"Into the bosom of a frozen bud."

DR. POOLE: Excellent! (*He takes the book from her and reads.*)

"See where she stands, a mortal shape indued
With love and life and light and deity,
And motion which may change, but never die,
An image of some bright Eternity,
A shadow of some golden dream, a splendour
Leaving the third sphere pilotless, a tender
Reflection of the eternal Moon of Love."

That's you. Do you like it?

LOOLA: I don't understand a word of it.

DR. POOLE: Neither did I, until these last few weeks.

LOOLA: Alfie, I thought you understood everything.

DR. POOLE: Here, yes; I understand it up here. (*He taps his forehead.*) But not here. (*He lays his hand on his heart.*) Not as a matter of experience. It's the difference between reading about a piece of music and actually hearing it.

LOOLA: You mean, I'm the music?

DR. POOLE: You're the music. A Mozart quartet in the seventh circle of hell. That's why it seems so supernaturally beautiful—because of all this. (*He points at the altar.*) Because of the Arch-Vicar and the Chief and the Purification Ceremonies. In a way I'm grateful to Belial.

LOOLA: What do you mean?

DR. POOLE: For helping me to understand everything that he isn't. You, for example, and Mozart and souls and the way all these things are related to… well, you know: the Other One. Back at home, I took everything for granted—from my mother to the "B Minor Mass" and *Don Giovanni.* Now I know what they really are. And I suppose I shall never see my mother again and never hear any more music.

LOOLA (*after a silence*): I wish I'd ever[29] heard any of those things you talk about.

DR. POOLE: How could they possibly allow any of that kind of music here? It's like what Shelley says about love—"An image of some bright Eternity."

LOOLA: That's another word I don't know.

DR. POOLE: And yet I'm pretty sure you know what it stands for.

LOOLA: What makes you say that?

DR. POOLE: Listen. I'll talk again about music; but if you think about love while I'm talking, I believe you'll understand.

LOOLA: All right, I'll think about love. As a matter of fact I never think about anything else nowadays.

DR. POOLE: Well, think about it a little more objectively, if you see what I mean.

LOOLA: I'll try to, Alfie. Now, tell me about music.

DR. POOLE: Well, how shall I put it? Good music is always more than itself. In itself it's just the notes. But it's also something else, something from outside, a kind of revelation.

LOOLA: Yes, yes. Go on.

DR. POOLE: Life can be terrible; but when you listen to music, you know there's something else.

LOOLA: And it makes you able to think of the terrible things in a different way.

DR. POOLE: Yes, that's it.

LOOLA: They could kill me; and yet in some way—I don't know how, I don't know why—in some way it would still be all right. In spite of having to leave you—just because I've loved you so much. I wouldn't

[29] ED: {~~n~~ever}; FC: {never}.

have felt like that before you came. (*She kisses his hand.*) What else does music tell you?

DR. POOLE: It tells you why Belial can never win more than a local and temporary victory.

LOOLA: Just imagine if they heard you say that! (*She laughs; then her face suddenly becomes apprehensive.*) Alfie, you don't suppose…? (*She gets up, goes to the window and looks out; then she turns back to* DR. POOLE.) I don't want to be killed, even if I do know it's somehow all right. (*After a little pause, as she approaches him*) Alfie, what about Polly and her baby? What about all the people who've never had a chance of finding out that there's something else? *They* don't feel it's all right.

DR. POOLE: And yet the sun's there, even if your eyes have been bandaged and you can't see it.

LOOLA: But if you can't see it, you're in the dark.

DR. POOLE: Yes, you're in the dark.

LOOLA: It isn't fair.

DR. POOLE: The only hope is that, some time, the bandage may be taken off and they'll see.

LOOLA: But it'll be too late.

DR. POOLE: No, it's never too late. What's going on here isn't the last word. The last word is what you begin to understand when you're listening to Mozart.

LOOLA: Or when you love somebody.

DR. POOLE: And it's always there—the image of some bright eternity. And not merely the image—the thing itself. Somehow it gets into time. A moment comes and suddenly it breaks through and transfigures time, delivers it from evil. I suppose that's the whole point and purpose of being a human being—to give the bright eternity its chance, to act and think and feel so that every instant of your life is an open window for the light to come in at.

LOOLA: Is that what people do where you come from?

DR. POOLE (*with a little laugh*): It's what we're supposed to do. But unfortunately we're apt to be a little forgetful. Especially when things are going well. Time seems so cozy and comfortable that we don't see any need for transfiguring it; we don't even notice the evil it has to be delivered from. "Go on improving the artificial light. Why bother about the sunshine outside?" I know that's how *I* felt about things. And then I came here and saw the consequences of precisely that policy. Home-made illumination, no windows, no bright eternity, but just time—time for its own sake, time unmitigated and unredeemed. Go on thinking and acting that way for a couple of centuries, and Belial inevitably takes over.

LOOLA: Do you think He'll ever be driven out?

DR. POOLE: As soon as people start opening the windows again and letting in a little light. (*He picks up the book, turns the pages, then reads.*)

> "That Light whose smile kindles the Universe,
> That Beauty in which all things work and move,
> That Benediction which the eclipsing Curse
> Of birth can quench not, that sustaining Love,
> Which through the web of being blindly wove
> By man and beast and earth and air and sea
> Burns bright or dim, as each are mirrors of
> The fire for which all thirst…"[30]

(*There is a silence. He strokes her hair. Suddenly he speaks again in another tone.*) But meanwhile there's Belial, there's the Chief and the Arch-Vicar.[31]

LOOLA: No, don't! Don't let's think about them.

DR. POOLE: We've got to—for the simple reason that they're thinking about us.

LOOLA: And I was so happy.

DR. POOLE: Did you find any more cans today?

LOOLA (*with a sign of resignation*): Yes, I forgot to tell you.

(*She extracts three or four cans from her knapsack.*)

DR. POOLE: No labels. (*He raises one to his ear and shakes it.*) Let's hope it's something nourishing. We shall need it.

LOOLA: Alfie, it's going to be so wonderful when we get up north. Nobody to spy on us, nobody to say we mustn't love each other.

DR. POOLE: I wish the getting there was going to be so wonderful. (*He goes to the smaller of the two closets near the altar, opens the door and puts away the cans on a shelf, on which numerous other cans are standing.*) Three hundred miles; no food on the way; precious little water; and all those troops and inquisitors scouring the country for fugitives.

LOOLA: Don't talk about it, Alfie. It brings bad luck.

DR. POOLE: Sometimes I wonder if it wouldn't be wiser to stay here and try to stick it out.

LOOLA: But, Alfie, we can't stay here, we can't.

DR. POOLE: And what if we can't get away?

LOOLA: Other people have done it.

---

30 Percy Bysshe Shelley, *Adonais* (1821), ll. 478–85.

31 Emendation: {and the Arch-Vicar}; ED and FC: {and Arch-Vicar}.

DR. POOLE: Precious few. And you saw what happened to the pair they caught two weeks ago.

LOOLA: Don't, don't!

(*She covers her face with her hands.*)

DR. POOLE: I'm sorry. But it's no good shutting one's eyes to the facts. (*A pause*) Do you know if they have bloodhounds?

LOOLA: I don't think so. I've never seen any.

DR. POOLE: Well, that's something. (*He closes the cupboard door and goes back to the table.*) Curious they shouldn't use bloodhounds.

LOOLA: Why?

DR. POOLE: For purely practical reasons, to start with. And then there's something really fiendish about the way they track a man down. He can run, he can hide; but it's no good. They always get him in the end. You'd think it would appeal to these people. On purely religious grounds.

(*He is interrupted by the sound of a trumpet being blown offstage. They turn and look at the window. The trumpet is blown again.*)

LOOLA: Alfie, it's the Chief.

DR. POOLE: Quick! (*He opens the door of the large closet and pushes her inside. Then he picks up her knapsack and hands it to her.*) Sit down on the floor. Don't stir.

(*He closes the door and bolts it; then goes to the other closet and closes that. The trumpet sounds again. He goes to the door on the left and opens it. The* FIRST PRIEST *and one of the men who were with the* CHIEF *in the cemetery enter and take their stand on the threshold.*)

FIRST PRIEST: His Eminence and the Chief.

GRAVEDIGGER: The Chief and His Eminence. (*He blows the trumpet.*)

(*The* ARCH-VICAR *and the* CHIEF *enter. Each bows to the other,* as *though requesting the other to go in first. Then both enter simultaneously.*)

NARRATOR:

Church and State,
Greed and hate
Two baboon-persons in one supreme Gorilla.

DR. POOLE: Welcome, welcome. This is a great honour, Your Eminence. A great honour, Generalissimo.

CHIEF (*delighted by the appellation*): Thanks, thanks. (*He points at the military tunic, covered with medals, which he is wearing.*) We were mining at Sawtelle, yesterday—that's the veterans' cemetery. Fits like a glove.

(*He turns around.*)

DR. POOLE: It might have been made to measure. (*To the* ARCH-VICAR) Won't you sit down, Your Eminence? And you, Generalissimo. (*He pushes up chairs.*)

(*The* ARCH-VICAR *sits down, holds out his hand to the* FIRST PRIEST *and snaps his fingers. The* FIRST PRIEST *produces a bottle and a drinking-horn, which he fills.*)

CHIEF: Just doing a little tour of inspection. Have you got anything to show us, Dr. Poole?

DR. POOLE: Well, I've been going on with my work on plant pathology. Incidentally, I'm delighted with this pre-Thing microscope. It's as good as new. (*He looks through the papers on the table.*) And I've just about finished my report on the present state of agriculture in Southern California. Ah, here we are. Would you like me to read it to you?

ARCH-VICAR: I should be delighted—though of course I can't speak for my distinguished colleague.

CHIEF: Four minutes—I can give you exactly four minutes. (*He takes out of his pocket a miniature hour-glass, such as is used for timing the boiling of eggs, and places it on the table.*) Then I'm due at the barracks. Fire away, man. Don't waste any time.

DR. POOLE (*reading*): "Preliminary Remarks. In true symbiosis there is a mutually beneficient relationship between two organisms. The distinguishing mark of parasitism, on the other hand, is that one organism lives at the expense of another. In the end this one-sided relationship proves fatal to both parties; for the death of the host entails the death of the parasite by which it has been killed. The relationship between modern man and the planet, of which, until so recently, he regarded himself as the master, has been that, not of symbiotic partners, but of tapeworm and infested dog, of fungus and blighted potato. Ignoring the obvious fact that his destruction of natural resources would result in the ruin of civilization and even in the extinction of the species, modern man continued, generation after generation, to exploit the earth with an almost complete disregard of the laws of Nature."

CHIEF (*yawning*): Couldn't you make it a bit snappier?

DR. POOLE: Certainly, Generalissimo. What about passing directly to the section on plant pathology?

CHIEF: I don't care, so long as you make it snappy.

ARCH-VICAR (*sententiously*): Impatience is one of Belial's favourite vices. Persevere in it, persevere.

(*He pats the* CHIEF*'s arm benignantly.*)

DR. POOLE (*turning several pages to find the relevant section, he starts to read again*): "Given the extent and seriousness of erosion in all its forms, yield per acre would be abnormally low, even if the principal food plants were reasonably healthy. But they are not healthy. After viewing crops in the field and after examining botanical specimens under an excellent pre-Thing microscope, I am convinced that there is only one explanation for the number and variety of the plant diseases now rampant in the area—namely deliberate infection of the crops by means of fungus-bombs, bacteria bearing aerosols, and the release of many varieties of virus-carrying insects. Otherwise how account for the prevalence and extreme virulence of *Giberella saubinetti* and *Puccinia graminis*? Of *Phytophthora infestans* and *Synchitrium endobioticum*? Of *Bacillus amylovorus*, *Bacillus carotovorus*, *Pseudomonas citri*, *Pseudomonas tumefaciens*, *Bacterium*…"

ARCH-VICAR: And you still maintain that these people weren't possessed by Belial? It's incredible how prejudice can blind even the most intelligent, the most highly educated…

CHIEF: Yes, yes, Your Eminence. We know all about that. Let's cut the cackle and get down to practical business. What can you do about all this?

DR. POOLE: It's going to be a long, hard job.

CHIEF: But I want more food now. I've got to have it this summer. In time for the campaign.

DR. POOLE: The campaign? You're not going to fight a war, are you?

CHIEF: To the finish. Unconditional surrender. We're going to stamp them out.

DR. POOLE: Who?

ARCH-VICAR: He's referring to our Good Neighbours of the North.

CHIEF: Filthy heretics. Mating all the year round. I'm told that some of them even worship God. You can't do business with people like that. Stamp them out, I say, stamp 'em out.

ARCH-VICAR: That's the right spirit. Persevere in it.

(*He touches his horns, then lays his hand on the* CHIEF*'s head.*)

CHIEF: Well, if I'm going to stamp 'em out, I've got to have food for my troops. This summer—do you get me?

DR. POOLE: But I can't perform miracles.

CHIEF: Well, you know what'll happen to you if you don't. Time's up.

(*He replaces his hour glass in his pocket and rises.*)

DR. POOLE: But, Generalissimo, you're asking for the impossible.

CHIEF:

"Bury him deep—
He won't keep."

DR. POOLE: Listen. You can't breed and test a new variety of disease-resisting plant in under ten or twelve years.

CHIEF:

"Bury him well—
He won't smell."

DR. POOLE: And then there's the erosion. Consider the labour of terracing, of building check dams, of re-foresting the watersheds. Consider the time it takes to lay down an inch of topsoil…

CHIEF: Listen, Doctor. I don't consider anything except the Will of Belial. Stamp 'em out—that's what He tells me. And if you can't help me stamp 'em out—well, it's just too bad for you. (*To the* ARCH-VICAR) Your Eminence!

(*He clicks his heels and salutes.*)

ARCH-VICAR (*making the sign of the horns in his direction*): You're a true Son of Belial. May you live and die in the shadow of His Horns. (*To the* FIRST PRIEST) Here! (*He hands him the drinking-horn.*) I shan't need you any more. You can take the evening off.

FIRST PRIEST: Thank you, Your Eminence.

(*The* CHIEF *marches to the door, which is held open by the* GRAVE-DIGGER, *who goes out after him, followed by the* FIRST PRIEST. *Outside we hear the sound of the trumpet playing a discordant version of "Onward, Christian Soldiers,"*[32] *diminuendo, into the distance.* DR. POOLE, *who has been looking after the retreating figures, turns back to the* ARCH-VICAR.)

DR. POOLE: How can he be so unreasonable?

ARCH-VICAR: How can a true Son of Belial be anything else? And, anyhow, what *is* reason? Man's instrument for achieving the ends which have been chosen for him by his passions. The God-given faculty, as it used to be called, has always been at the service of animals, lunatics or demons. They're the ones who decide what's to be done with the atomic bomb; reason merely designs it.

DR. POOLE: Quite, quite. But meanwhile I'm to be buried alive if I can't work miracles. Would he really do it?

ARCH-VICAR: Of course he would.

DR. POOLE: But it's monstrous!

---

32 "Onward Christian Soldiers." A nineteenth-century English hymn.

ARCH-VICAR: What do you expect? (*There is a pause.*) There's one very simple way out of your predicament.

DR. POOLE: What's that?

ARCH-VICAR: Put yourself under my protection.

DR. POOLE: I'd be only too delighted.

ARCH-VICAR: You understand, of course, that it would be necessary for you to become one of us?

DR. POOLE: One of you?

ARCH-VICAR: Yes, one of us.

(*He touches his horns.*)

DR. POOLE: Oh, I see…

ARCH-VICAR: Not only would you be entirely safe from our friend with the medals. You'd also enjoy a great many very valuable privileges and advantages. Better food, for example, more drink, superior accommodation, a higher social position. And, with your abilities and knowledge, you could look forward to very rapid promotion. Confidentially, I'm ready to guarantee you a bishopric within fifteen years. Only fifteen years—think of it.

DR. POOLE: That's very good of you, I'm sure.

ARCH-VICAR: I will not disguise from you that the surgery involved is not entirely painless, nor wholly without danger. But the advantages to be gained are so considerable as to outweigh any trifling risk or discomfort.

DR. POOLE: But, Your Eminence …

ARCH-VICAR (*holding up his hand*): One moment. Thank you. Nor must we forget that, if you were to undergo what I may call a physiological conversion, you would be delivered, and delivered for good, from all the temptations to which, as an unmutated male, you will most certainly be subject.

DR. POOLE: Quite, quite. But I can assure Your Eminence…

ARCH-VICAR: Where temptations are concerned, nobody can assure me of anything. And let me remind you of what happens to those who succumb to temptation. Fifty lashes, I am told, are the equivalent of a major operation. Without anesthetics, of course. And meanwhile the shocking events of last week are still fresh in my memory. I hope they are fresh in yours, Dr. Poole?

DR. POOLE: Yes, Your Eminence.

ARCH-VICAR: Just consider them for a moment from *my* point of view. With almost unheard-of condescension I come to visit you here, on foot, unannounced, without attendants. And what is my reward for such mistaken kindness? The disgusting spectacle of a man in the very act of teaching a young vessel how to read.

DR. POOLE: I should have thought that was a very innocent occupation.

ARCH-VICAR: Innocent? Are you trying to be funny?

DR. POOLE: No, I'm perfectly serious.

ARCH-VICAR: You're serious. You seriously expect me to believe that a man who takes the trouble to teach a vessel to read poetry is innocent of taking some special interest in that vessel? That he's innocent of feeling affection for it? Of harbouring designs upon it? You make me laugh. (*He laughs. Then he turns on* DR. POOLE *and addresses him with shrill emphasis.*) But don't imagine, because I laugh, that this is a laughing matter. Don't count on any repetition of last week's indulgence. From this time forth you are subject to the Law of Belial—to the strict letter of that Law. Do you understand?

DR. POOLE: Yes, Your Eminence.

ARCH-VICAR (*resuming his genial tone*): Then what about putting yourself out of jeopardy? What about becoming one of us? What about it, Alfred?

DR. POOLE (*after a pause*): I should like to be able to think it over, Your Eminence.

ARCH-VICAR: Of course, of course. Take your time. Take a week.

DR. POOLE: I don't think I could decide in a week.

ARCH-VICAR: All right, take two weeks. (DR. POOLE *still looks dubious.*) No? Take four. Take six, if you like. I'm in no hurry. I leave everything to Belial. (*He makes the sign of the horns.*) He sent you to us. I know it's His will that you should help us carry on His work. And I know, too, that sooner or later, by hook or by crook, His will is going to be done. So don't feel I'm trying to rush you into anything. I'm not. It isn't necessary. He'd get you, even if I didn't lift a finger. (*He rises and pats* DR. POOLE *on the shoulder.*) His Grace, the Bishop! You'll look stunning in horns.

(*He walks to the door, accompanied by* DR. POOLE. *They go out together. The stage is left empty for a moment. Then the door of the closet is noiselessly opened and* LOOLA *emerges. She goes to the door and looks out.*)

NARRATOR: In this city of two and a half million skeletons the presence of a few thousands of the living is hardly perceptible. Nothing stirs. The silence is total, and, in the midst of all these cozy little bourgeois ruins, seems conscious and in some way significant.

The sun is sinking. In the distance, above the roofs of the empty houses, one can see the mountains. Fold after fold the range recedes towards the east. The shadows are gulfs of indigo, and in the richly golden lights the far-off details stand out, distinct and small and perfect, like the images of things in a convex mirror. In the foreground, delicately chased and stippled by the almost horizontal light, even the baldest patches of parched earth reveal an unsuspected sumptuousness of texture.

There are times, and this is one of them, when the world seems purposefully beautiful, when it is as though some mind in things had suddenly chosen to make manifest, for all who choose to see it, the reality that underlies appearances.

"Didst thou ever descry a glorious eternity in a winged instant of time? Didst thou ever see a bright infinity in the narrow point of an object: Then thou knowest what spirit means—the spire-top whither all things ascend harmoniously, where they meet and sit contented in an unfathomed Depth of Life."[33]

(*There is a silence. Then we hear footsteps approaching.*)

LOOLA: Alfie. (DR. POOLE *enters. She takes his arm and they walk away from the door.*) I heard everything he said.

DR. POOLE: Well, there's one good thing about it. We don't have to hesitate any longer about what to do. I don't think he'll really give me six weeks. But a week, yes. I know we can be sure of that. That means we must be ready to start five or six days from now.

(*He opens the door of the smaller closet and starts to go through its contents.*)

LOOLA: How many more cans of food do we need?

DR. POOLE: At least a dozen. (*He holds up a metal water bottle, of the type used in the army.*) Try to find another of these, when you're out foraging next time.

LOOLA: I'll look out for one. What else?

DR. POOLE: A second machete, if you can get hold of it. Or a little hatchet would do and then some scissors—they always come in useful—and two spare pairs of moccasins, one for you and one for me.

---

[33] Quoted, with slight alterations, from Peter Sterry (1613–1672), *The Rise, Race, and Royalty of the Kingdom of God in the Soul of Man Opened in Several Sermons Upon Matthew 18.3: As Also the Loveliness & Love of Christ Set Forth in Several Other Sermons Upon Psal. 45. V. 1, 2* (London, 1683), 24 [see Early English Books Online—Proquest, 2010]: "Didst thou ever yet descry a glorious *Eternity* in each winged *Moment* of Time; a Bright *Infiniteness* in the narrow *points* of every dark Object? Then thou knowest what the *Spirit* means, that *Spire-top* of Things, whither all ascend harmoniously, where they meet, and sit together *recollected*, and *concentred* in an Unfathom'd Depth of Glorious Life."

LOOLA: I'll have to steal those from the quartermaster's office. It'll be pretty difficult.

DR. POOLE: Well, do your best. We shall need them before we've done. I've got two blankets here. That ought to be enough. And anyhow we've got to travel as light as we can.

LOOLA: What about a tinder-box?

DR. POOLE: Here, and this is a very nice magnifying glass. When the sun's shining, we can easily light a fire with it. Now, what else is there? I can't think of anything for the moment. Oh yes, iodine.

LOOLA: What's that?

DR. POOLE: It's something you'll find in the medicine cabinets in bathrooms. A little bottle with brown stuff in it. Or mercurochrome would be just as good.

LOOLA: What's that?

DR. POOLE: Mercurochrome. It's red.

LOOLA: Mercurochrome. Iodine or mercurochrome. OK.

DR. POOLE: And if you see any bandages lying about…

LOOLA: I'll take some.

DR. POOLE (*closing the door of the cupboard*): Collect all the bread you can lay your hands on during the next few days. And all the salt meat and salt fish. Anything that'll keep. (*He sits down at the table and from among the scattered papers produces a tattered road map of California, which he unfolds.*) One's got to be careful with this map. It is falling to pieces. (*They bend over the map and he traces their route with his forefinger.*) This would be the shortest way—across the San Fernando Valley. But it's much too risky. The only sensible thing to do is to make direct for the mountains. They mark a good road here. I imagine it's still more or less passable.[34] We'll take it as far as this, then drop down into the Mojave desert. We'll have to fill up our water bottles. I don't imagine we shall see another drop till we get into the foothills of the Tehachapis, here. That's about seventy miles. Three days. Maybe two and a half. The ground's level; it'll be easy walking. Then another two days at least in the mountains. (*He looks more closely at the map.*) I see they had the State Penitentiary for Women up here.

(*As he speaks these words, the door at the left is opened noiselessly and the* ARCH-VICAR *looks in. He stands on the threshold, while the others go on talking.*)

LOOLA: What's a penitentiary?

---

34 ED: Hereafter follows the autograph insertion {We'll take it as far as this, then drop down into the Mojave desert.}

DR. POOLE: It's another name for a prison.
LOOLA: Oh. What did they do to the women in that prison?
DR. POOLE: I don't know. Kept them locked up, I presume.
LOOLA: Did they get whipped?
DR. POOLE (*laughing*): They undoubtedly deserved it.
LOOLA: Seriously, Alfie.
DR. POOLE: No, of course, they weren't whipped.
ARCH-VICAR: Of course not. (*They turn with a start.* LOOLA *screams. The* ARCH-VICAR *advances, genially smiling, and sits down beside them at the table.*) They didn't enjoy the blessings of modern life, my pet. (*He pats* LOOLA*'s cheek. She shrinks in horror.*) Belial hadn't yet taken over completely. (*To* DR. POOLE) Curious, isn't it?—the inconsistency of those people. At the international level you had pure, unmitigated diabolism. But at home they went on behaving as though they were still more or less human—as though they believed in… in… what's that phrase they used to be so fond of? Ah, yes… "the fatherhood of God and the brotherhood of Man." (*He laughs and turns back to* LOOLA.) Just think of it, ducky. Putting a lot of little vessels in a penitentiary and then not whipping them. It's crazy, it's wasting your opportunities. (*He bends over the map.*) Now, let's see. From the Tehachapis[35] you make your way by easy stages down into the Central Valley. And here's Bakersfield. The ruins are picturesque, the moon is full; Cupid discharges his arrows, Hymen lights his torch. Etcetera, etcetera. After which you resume your journey to Fresno, where you live happily ever after. Isn't that the programme? (*He looks from one to the other. They do not speak. The* ARCH-VICAR *raises his voice to a scream of fury.*) Answer me, when I ask a question!
DR. POOLE: That *was* the programme.
ARCH-VICAR (*chuckling and rubbing his hands*): I guessed as much. That's why I came back to give you a little surprise. You shouldn't have left this book on the table. That gave you away. (*He picks up the volume of Shelley, which is lying open where* DR. POOLE *left it, and starts to read with excessive expressiveness.*[36])

"That Light whose smile kindles the Universe,
That Beauty in which all things work and move,
That Benediction which the eclipsing Curse
Of birth can quench not, that sustaining Love…"

Belial, what crap!

[35] Emendation: {From the Tehachapis}; ED and FC: {From Tehachapi}.
[36] See above, note 30.

"... that sustaining Love,
Which through the web of being blindly wove
By man and beast and earth and air and sea,
Burns bright or dim as each are mirrors of
The fire for which all thirst, now beams on me,
Consuming the last clouds of cold mortality."

Oh, I see, he thinks he's going to heaven after he's dead.

DR. POOLE: Perhaps it's true. Perhaps Belial's made a slight mistake and all these poor wretches will finally get away from him.

ARCH-VICAR: You think yourself clever, don't you? Now listen. Belial has always made good use of the materialists; but that doesn't mean that He himself is a materialist. Of course not. He knows perfectly well that death isn't the end. And that's precisely why He's given us this world where human nature has been degraded and a Law that compels its victims to behave like demons. Fear, hatred, anger, envy —that's all the Law of Belial permits them to feel. And if those are the feelings you have when you come to die, what happens? You're carried along by their momentum—like a stone rolling downhill. You go on feeling them indefinitely. Fear, hatred, anger, envy—for ever and ever. That's what they used to call hell in the old days. And that's what Belial is preparing his people for to-day. I tell you, He's got them coming and going, skewered on one horn in this life, skewered on the other in the next.

DR. POOLE: There's just one mistake in his calculations.

ARCH-VICAR: What's that?

DR. POOLE: The devil can never resist the temptation of going to the limit. But what happens when evil is carried to the limit? It destroys everything within range, including itself. After which the Order of Things comes to the surface again.

ARCH-VICAR: What do you mean?

DR. POOLE: Well, look what's happening here. Three or four more generations and you're finished.

ARCH-VICAR: Exactly as Belial willed.

DR. POOLE: Yes, and what then? The land goes back to nature and after a few hundred years it'll almost be fit for us to colonize. And I suspect something of the same kind goes on in the spiritual world. Fear and hatred and anger and envy—they're the most exhausting passions. They wear themselves out, they tend to their own annihilation. That's why hell can't be everlasting. It finally makes a clean sweep of itself and then the Other One rushes in to fill the vacuum.

ARCH-VICAR (*patting* DR. POOLE *on the shoulder*): For a cheap sophistry that's very pretty. When you enter the seminary, I'll get you to write a paper on it.

DR. POOLE: When I enter the seminary?

ARCH-VICAR: In about three or four weeks. That is, if we can arrange for the surgery tomorrow or the day after.

DR. POOLE: But… but I shan't be any good to you. I don't believe in what you believe.

ARCH-VICAR: Not now, perhaps. But you will, dear boy, you will. Perform the outward acts, and faith will come of its own accord. And that isn't all. Don't forget, I promised you rapid preferment, and I can assure you, on the basis of personal experience, that the higher you rise, the more intimate will be your sense of Belial's presence. Remember that question they used to debate in the Middle Ages: Can an arch-deacon be saved? Below a certain official position it was possible for a man to do the will of God. Above it, he could only do the will of the political and financial machine—in other words, the will of Belial, the will of the Great Blowfly in the heart of man. (*He makes the sign of the horns.*) That's how Belial managed to keep his end up. If the other religion had produced nothing but holiness, He'd have been done for. But fortunately it also produced churches, revenues, endowments, hierarchies; it produced ecclesiastical soldiers and politicians; it produced mitred financiers, stockbrokers in dog collars, Gestapo-men in cassocks. Everything that the Other One was able to achieve by means of holy individuals, Belial was able to undo by means of the religious organizations. That's why we here are so tremendously keen on organization. And that's why, as you go up through the hierarchy, you'll be able to say, ever more whole-heartedly, ever more sincerely: Not I, but Belial in me. (*There is a silence. Then the* ARCH-VICAR *rises.*) Well, the sun's down; we ought to be getting back to Headquarters. I'll send for the Surgeon-General first thing in the morning. (*He turns to* LOOLA.) As for you, my pretty little vessel, which would you prefer? (*He lifts her hair, exposing her ears.*) The ears? Or a hundred lashes?

LOOLA: Oh, Your Eminence…

ARCH-VICAR: Did I say a hundred? No, that's too little. Let's make it a hundred and twenty. Well, which is it to be? Make it a hundred and twenty—no, a hundred and twenty-five. Well, which is it to be? (LOOLA *stares at him in horror, unable to speak. He screams at her.*) Which is it to be? (*He shakes her violently.* DR. POOLE *seizes him and drags him away.*) What do you think you're doing? Let go. Let go, I say. (*He strikes at* DR. POOLE, *who returns the blow to the* ARCH-VICAR's *body.*) Ow. I'll have you buried for this.

(*He is choked by a fit of coughing.*)

DR. POOLE: Get back. Get in there. (*He indicates the closet in which* LOOLA *was hidden, the door of which stands open.*) Get a move on, quick!

(*He strikes the* ARCH-VICAR *again.*)

ARCH-VICAR: No, don't. Ow. Please. I'll make you a bishop tomorrow. Ow. No, no.

(*He is forced back through the open door.* DR. POOLE *administers a final punch, which sends the* ARCH-VICAR *staggering back to the end of the closet, then slams the door and bolts it. He turns to* LOOLA.)

DR. POOLE: Here, come and help me.

(*He goes to the other closet, takes out an army knapsack and some blankets and throws them onto the ground.*)

LOOLA: Alfie, they'll kill you when they find out.

DR. POOLE: Shut up! Pack these things.

(*He hands her cans, a loaf of bread, some bits of dried meat. From the closet comes a sound of shouting and hammering on the door.*)

ARCH-VICAR'S VOICE: Let me out. Let me out.

LOOLA (*apprehensively*): I'm so scared.

DR. POOLE: Do you want me to leave you behind? (*He hands her an army water bottle and two glass bottles with screw tops.*) Go and fill these. The bucket's in the next room.

(LOOLA *goes out through the archway on the right.*)

ARCHVICAR'S VOICE: Dr. Poole. (*No answer*) Dr. Poole. (*There is a hammering at the door.*) I insist on being heard. As Arch-Vicar of Belial I insist

DR. POOLE (*shouting, without raising his head from his packing*): Insist away, old boy.

ARCH-VICAR'S VOICE (*screaming*): Dr. Poole, Dr. Poole, Dr. Poole.

(*The hammering becomes louder than ever.* DR. POOLE *gets up and goes to the door of the closet.*)

DR. POOLE: If you don't stop that racket, I'll open the door and stop it for you. Do you understand? (*No answer*) I've got a club here, and if that isn't enough, I've got a machete. I killed a pig with it the other day. It's a messy business, but sometimes necessary.

ARCH-VICAR'S VOICE (*very mild and gentle*): Dr. Poole, be reasonable. (DR. POOLE *turns, quietly walks away and resumes his packing. The* VOICE *from inside the closet talks on.*) Consider the risks you're running.

The chances are a hundred to one that you'll be caught. And then, my dear sir, then… Well, I draw a veil. Whereas if you set me free, if you promise (and this is a very important point), if you swear by Belial to commit no further outrages upon my sacred person, you will find me ready to overlook what has passed. You will undergo your conversion and enter the seminary with honour, as though nothing had happened between us. Nay, more, I am even willing to show some leniency towards the young vessel by whom you have been led astray. She can choose between sixty lashes and only one of her ears. I ask you, could anything be more generous?

(*In the course of this speech* LOOLA *re-enters from the other room with the water bottles. The packs are strapped and hoisted onto their shoulders and they quietly go out through the door on the left.* DR. POOLE *puts the key in the lock before going out, and when he closes it, we hear the sound of it being turned. The final sentences of the preceding speech are addressed to an empty stage, which now begins to grow dark.*)

ARCH-VICAR'S VOICE: Could anything be more generous? (*Silence. He speaks more loudly.*) Could anything be more generous?

(*Silence. The* NARRATOR *starts to speak.*)

NARRATOR:

"…man, proud man,
Dressed in a little brief authority,—"

ARCH-VICAR'S VOICE (*now suddenly rising to a scream*): Answer me, damn you! Answer me!

NARRATOR:

"Most ignorant of what he is most assured,
His glassy essence—"

ARCH-VICAR'S VOICE: I'll teach you!

(*He hammers at the closet door.*)

NARRATOR:

"—like an angry ape"

ARCH-VICAR'S VOICE: If you don't let me out, I'll have you whipped to death.

NARRATOR:

"—like an angry ape
Plays such fantastic tricks before high heaven
As make the angels weep…"

ARCH-VICAR (*while the* NARRATOR *is speaking the last line*): Damn you, damn you!

SLOW CURTAIN

James Sexton
(University of British Columbia)

"A Particularly Painful Case of Overpopulation": Aldous Huxley's "Synopsis of a Film on Egypt"[1]

The untitled and unpublished film synopsis/scenario reprinted below is part of a series of linked writings by Aldous Huxley, perhaps beginning with *Science, Liberty, and Peace* (1947) but carrying over to 1948/49 with the *Ape and Essence* novel and play projects; "The Double Crisis" from *Themes and Variations* (1949); the chapter entitled "Overpopuation" in *Brave New World Revisited* (1958), extending into 1959 with *The Human Situation* lectures at Santa Barbara, as well as his preface to Alvah W. Sulloway's *Birth Control and Catholic Doctrine.* The common denominator in these works spanning the years 1947–59 was Huxley's belief that the planet was facing a catastrophe because of overpopulation and the abuse of science.

For example, in a letter dated 23 June 1956, Huxley tells his son Matthew of a recent meeting with Harrison Brown (1917–86), then a professor at Caltech, whose research during his years with the Manhattan Project, particularly at Oak Ridge, Tennessee, helped lead to the development of the atomic bomb, but who later became a social activist and environmentalist. Huxley had earlier featured Brown's ideas from *The Challenge of Man's Future* in his own article "Tomorrow and Tomorrow and Tomorrow," published in *Esquire* in March 1956, and it is clear that Huxley shared Brown's belief that humanity would regress to the kind of agrarian society depicted in *Ape and Essence* unless it "is able not only to make the technological transition to new energy sources and new raw materials, but also to abolish war and at the same time stabilize [the] population."[2] Huxley reported to Matthew that they had met at a party given by Robert Hutchins, then head of the Ford Foundation, and that he and Brown had been

> much impressed by the Academy of Science report on the genetic effects of radiation. How wonderfully close modern history is coming to the phantasies of the *Arabian Nights* [...]—the stories of the fisherman who let the djinn out of the bottle and couldn't put it back [...]. Atoms will give us all the power we want, but at the price of multiplying the number of monsters and, perhaps, bitching up the whole human species. (*Letters*, 798)

Although the prime mover in the film project appears to have been Huxley's friend Dr William Kiskadden, a key member of the group[3] would necessarily have been Dr Robert Hutchins, then head of the Ford Foundation, whose financial support would have been vital to the successful launching of a television movie on overpopulation and eventual international cinematic release.

Two months after writing to Matthew, on 30 August, Aldous informed his brother Julian of further developments, including his having completed a synopsis for the film. Moreover, Huxley was still optimistic about obtaining financial support from the Ford Foundation. Perhaps the main piece of news was that the group had persuaded the well-known Academy Award winning film director Fred Zinnemann to direct the film. Huxley elaborates:

> There seems to be a good chance of getting a big film on population done by the Ford people on their 'Omnibus' TV Programme. Zinnemann would do the directing, the necessary research into documentaries would be carried out probably by students in the Motion Picture school at the University of California; meanwhile I have written a very brief synopsis, suggesting ways in which the thing might be handled photographically. (This would be a general world population film, not a film for India alone; that will, I hope, come later. But meanwhile, if we can get Ford to do this, it will be a fine thing.) (*Letters*, 805–06)

In that letter, Huxley also mentioned a tentative meeting on 15 September 1956, involving Brown, Julian Huxley, Zinnemann, and Kiskadden, who, in an earlier letter to Brown, had stated his belief that "there was plenty of room and need for another agency in this field [conservation and population control]. One that perhaps might profit by short-circuiting the purely sociological approach.[4]

This agency soon became the Population Limited Foundation, and by 8 April 1957 Huxley informed Humphry Osmond of the slow progress that their foundation had made in their efforts to get the documentary film off the ground and of his plan, therefore, to "try to see some people in various Foundations, in the hope of getting someone to sponsor a documentary film for TV on population. (We have a little foundation of our own, called Population Limited, rich in talent [...]—but poor in money)" (*Letters*, 822). By then, the distinguished sociologist and demographer who coined the phrase "zero population growth," Kingsley Davis (1908–1997), had also joined their foundation. Huxley gives further details about the goals of Population Limited:

> I hope we may finally persuade someone to put up the necessary funds for doing a film to educate the American public—after which we shall try to see what can be done in such areas of dire need as India. I have written a synopsis of a film on Egypt—because it is better to attack the general through the particular, and because Egypt is a particularly painful case of overpopulation,

and is in a position to make the economic, sociological and political consequences of overpopulation extremely unpleasant to the rest of the world. Whether anyone will put up the money, I don't know. Everyone agrees that the population problem is the most important problem of the present century; but nobody wants to get in trouble with the Papists." (*Letters*, 822)[5]

Since no further reference to Population Limited appears in Huxley's letters, it is likely that neither the Ford Foundation nor any of the others Huxley had intended to solicit ever "put up the money," and the proposed documentary film was shelved.

---

[1] The editor wishes to thank the Margaret Herrick Library, Academy of Motion Picture Arts and Sciences, for permission to reprint this untitled film synopsis, located in "Fred Zinnemann Papers," Folder 1486. The folder is headed "Nectar and the Sieve [TV] correspondence." This heading might simply be Zinnemann's reference to the penultimate line of Samuel Taylor Coleridge's poem "Work Without Hope": "Work without hope draws nectar in a sieve, / And hope without an object cannot live." On the other hand, he may have decided to call the project "Nectar and the Sieve" as a deliberate allusion to the best-selling novel of 1954, *Nectar in the Sieve*, by the Anglo-Indian writer Kamala Markandaya (1924–2004), now considered to be an early classic of ecofeminist fiction. It is set in rural India and recounts the social and environmental damage caused by the introduction of a large tannery in the region. The title of this introduction refers to Huxley's use of these two phrases in his letter to Dr Humphry Osmond, dated 8 April 1957 (*Letters of Aldous Huxley*, ed. Grover Smith [London, 1969], 822; hereafter, *Letters*).

[2] Aldous Huxley, *Tomorrow and Tomorrow and Tomorrow* (New York, 1956), 109.

[3] The original members of the group involved in the attempt to have the documentary film produced were Dr William Kiskadden (1894–1969), Harrison Brown (1917–1986), Fred Zinnemann (1907–97), and Aldous Huxley. Huxley's brother, Julian Huxley (1887–1975), and Kingsley Davis (1908–97) joined the others as members of their foundation, Population Limited.

[4] Unpublished letter of 7 September 1956 from Kiskadden to Harrison Brown, Margaret Herrick Library, Academy of Motion Picture Arts and Sciences.

[5] In this context, Huxley must have welcomed the opportunity to add his arguments to Alvah W. Sulloway's "intelligent criticism" of the Roman Catholic birth control policy in his preface to Sulloway's book *Birth Control and Roman Catholic Doctrine* (Boston, 1959), xi. There Huxley labels the Catholic-supported rhythm method "sadly ineffective" (xv), adding, "[i]f you hope to be treated well by nature, and to live in accord with what theologians call the divine purpose, you must treat nature well and obey the Law of Equilibrium. [...] If we choose to upset the ecological balance by burning the forests, by overgrazing the mountains, by applying unsuitable agricultural methods to the prairie, we and our children will be punished by erosion, dust storms, and a sterile soil. And if we choose to upset the general ecological balance of the planet by practicing intensive death control without at the same time practicing intensive birth control, we and our children and our children's children [...]

will infallibly be punished by malnutrition, by world-wide famine, by promiscuous overcrowding in slums even worse than those of present-day Calcutta and Jakarta, by chronic political unrest, chronic war, and enslavement under totalitarian systems of government" (xvi).

Aldous Huxley

[Synopsis of a Film on Egypt][1]

(Edited by James Sexton)

Ours is a time of troubles. There are wars and preparations for wars; there are rebellions and revolutions. Freedom is everywhere menaced by Communist or Fascist tyranny. Peace is precarious and uneasy. Every month, almost every week, brings its new crisis.

On the screen we see a succession of headlines. HIROSHIMA. RIOTING IN INDIA. PALESTINE. ALGERIA. SUEZ. Sequences showing in brief glimpse the events recorded in the headlines. An A-Bomb exploding. Hindus and Moslems fighting. Battle scenes in Korea, etc.

These crises of our times exist on two levels. There is the surface level, the level of the headlines, the level of war and power politics, the level of revolutionary violence and mass hysteria. And there is also a lower level, where the crisis is less spectacular, but more fundamental and more continuous. This crisis of the depths is rarely discussed in international conferences or mentioned in the newspapers. And yet it is a crisis far more serious than any of the political crises which occupy the centre of the stage. This deeper, fundamental crisis of our age is the crisis of overpopulation, the chronic, deepening crisis of numbers pressing ever more heavily upon resources.

Sequences on the screen of a swarm of locusts. Of a plague of caterpillars. Of rabbits in Australia before the coming of myxomatosis.

For all his astonishing achievements, man is still a part of nature and is still subject to the laws of ecology. He cannot upset the balance with impunity.

Shot of an Asiatic slum in all its teeming squalor. Of the vast crowds assembled at the holy places of the Ganges.

---

[1] This is the later of two drafts kept among the "Fred Zinnemann papers," Folder 1486, at the Margaret Herrick Library, Academy of Motion Picture Arts and Sciences. It is dated 15 March 1957 and appears to have been considerably reworked by Huxley as compared with the earlier draft (see above, 12, note 20). I wish to thank the Aldous and Laura Huxley Literary Trust and the Margaret Herrick Library for permission to publish this draft in *Aldous Huxley Annual.* I also gratefully acknowledge the assistance of Matthias Kreimann for digitizing the text and of Dr Gerhard Wagner for formatting and proofreading it.

Let us illustrate our point by a concrete example. For some time now Egypt has been at the centre of an uninterrupted succession of international crises. That there are specifically political reasons for this state of things is obvious. What is less obvious is that, underlying these political reasons, there are deeper and more enduring reasons of another order. On the surface the Egyptian crisis is political. On a lower level it is biological. Egypt is an overpopulated country. Its numbers have outrun its resources. Hence all the troubles.

Sequences of Egyptian cotton fields, wheat fields, onion fields.

Egyptian agriculture is extremely efficient. An Egyptian acre yields almost as much wheat as an acre in Western Europe and about twice as much cotton as an average acre in the Southern states of America. On their irrigated lands Egyptian farmers raise three crops in every two-year period, and sometimes two or even three crops in a single year. And yet nowhere on earth is poverty more abject than in Egypt.

Shots of a village in middle or upper Egypt. The teeming squalor of an almost sub-human life, lived in mud huts, which are shared by the livestock. Close-up of blind adults, of children in the early stages of infectious ophthalmia.

The reasons for this poverty are simple. Every acre yields abundantly, but the number of fertile acres is too small to provide an adequate livelihood for the population.

Aerial shots from a plane flying high over the Egyptian desert. Vast expanses of sand and rock—then the Nile and the narrow strip of irrigated land along its banks. The plane follows the course of the river, and we see the cropland as a thread of green in the midst of the desolation. The air view turns into a map, in which the irrigated lands along the river and in the delta are shown as white, the desert as black.

Egypt has an area of two hundred and fifty-two million acres. Of these, only five and a half million acres can be irrigated. The remaining two hundred forty-six and a half millions consist of a waterless and completely barren desert.

The map gives place once more to an aerial view. The plane is now flying fairly low, and we see the villages of upper Egypt succeeding one another in an almost continuous rural slum.

On these five and a half million fertile acres live twenty-three millions of men, women and children. About fifteen hundred of them to every square mile of cultivated land.

More shots of Egyptian village life, then sequences showing first the slums of Cairo, then the quarters in which the rich have their houses and apartments.

To some extent the misery of the Egyptian peasantry is due to a social system under which most of the land has been owned by a few rich individuals and large corporations. The big estates are now being broken up and the land distributed among the peasants. As a result of these reforms, the gross product of Egyptian agriculture will, in the future, be more equitably distributed among the people. But, however just the distribution, the poverty of the Egyptian masses will still be abject—for the simple reason that the gross product of Egyptian agriculture is not sufficient to ensure a decent living for the present population of the country, to say nothing of the population ten or twenty years from now.

On the screen we see a diagrammatic cartoon, showing two squares representing one acre each, and one human being.

Two acres of well cultivated land are enough to supply the foods and fibres necessary to maintain a high standard of living. In Egypt every acre must support four human beings.

Diagram showing four persons on one square.

Five and a half million acres cannot be made to support twenty-three million people in any condition save that of abject poverty. Up till the end of the nineteenth century, Egypt was irrigated only in the autumn, when the Nile is in flood. There where lean years, as we know from the story of Joseph, and there where fat years—years of abundance after a high Nile, years of famine when the water was too low to cover the parched fields. In the nineteenth century all this was changed.

Shot of the Delta Barrage.

The Delta Barrage was completed in 1892. Ten years later the Asyut Barrage was built higher up the river.

Shot of the Asyut Barrage.

These barrages served to raise the water level of the river, and to make possible irrigation at every season of the year. The Great Dam at Aswan, completed in 1902, created a reservoir in which the surplus of a high Nile could be stored for future use. More land than ever before could now be irrigated, and it could be irrigated every year and at every season of the year. If the population had remained stationary, the standard of living for the masses of the people would have risen. But it did not remain stationary. It increased, during the first quarter of the present century, at almost exactly the same rate as the production of food.

An animated cartoon showing, on the left, a wheat plant, on the right the figure of a man. The wheat plant grows taller and for a time outstrips the man. Then the man puts on a spurt and comes up level with the wheat. The growth goes on, each one passing and being passed in turn, and finishing in a dead heat in the year 1925.

By 1925 most of the irrigation systems made possible by the building of the barrages and the Aswan Dam were in full operation. Thereafter agricultural production increased very slowly. But the rate of population increase remained constant.

The cartoon now shows the man outgrowing the wheat plant.

Slowly but surely the standard of living declined. The poverty of the Egyptian peasant became more extreme. And now, after the Second World War, a new factor made its appearance—systematic death control.

Shot of victims of malaria. Then a shot of stagnant pools being treated with DDT and kerosene.

The Anopheles mosquito was attacked in its breeding grounds, and in a very short time the incidence of malaria sharply declined. More important, under the health plan of 1944, thousands of Egyptian towns and villages were supplied with pure water. In the past the only drinking water had come from open ditches, polluted with sewage.

Shot of a ditch with women drawing the filthy water.

Dysentery was endemic, thousands died of typhoid. Then a great campaign of well drilling was launched.

Shot of one of the new Artesian wells in the delta.

For the first time in history the majority of Egyptians could enjoy the luxury of uncontaminated water. This was genuine progress; but unfortunately it was progress at a price.

Show the cartoon of the stationary wheat plant and the growing man. Suddenly the man begins to grow three times as fast as before.

For the past fifty years the population had been increasing at the rate of about one per cent per annum. Now, almost overnight, it began to increase at almost three per cent. As recently as ten years ago the experts were prophesying that Egypt would have a population of twenty-three millions in

1970. Clean water and DDT have falsified their forecasts. Egypt's population passed the twenty-three million mark in 1956, and it is still rising at the rate of three per cent per annum.

Shot of a baby in the arms of an Egyptian peasant woman.

By the time this little boy is thirty, Egypt may very well have twice its present population. How will those extra millions be fed?

Shot of the Aswan Dam.

The Aswan Dam was completed in 1902 and was made higher in 1912 and again in 1936. A new, much higher dam has been planned.

Animated drawing of a dam built up to several times the height of the present structure.

This high dam would store more water and would permit water piped from the lake behind it to irrigate large areas to which, under present conditions, no water can be brought.

Map of Egypt showing the areas now irrigated and then the areas which might be irrigated if the high dam were built.

A high dam at Aswan could make it possible for Egypt to add about two million acres to its croplands. Egypt is too poor to be able to finance the building of the high dam without foreign aid. Aid was offered by Britain and the United States; but in the summer of 1956 this offer was withdrawn. Colonel Nasser then seized the Suez Canal. When and if the high dam gets built, what will it do for the people of Egypt? Not so much as has been hoped. True, the high dam will increase the Egyptians' food supply by about one third. But it will take from ten to fifteen years to complete the dam and the irrigation systems which the dam will supply. By the time that everything is in working order, Egypt will have a population of thirty millions. The food produced by the two million acres of new cropland will not increase the peasant's daily ration by more than a few calories.

Illustrate this point by the animated cartoon of the wheat plant and the man. The man grows continuously for ten years; then the plant shoots up by a factor of one third. But at the conclusion of this sudden spurt of growth, it is still no taller than the man.

We talk hopefully of finding a speedy solution to the political and economic problems of the Middle East.

Newspaper headlines referring to Suez. Pictures of tanks and troops moving across the desert.

But these political and economic problems are, in large measure, merely the symptoms of an underlying biological problem, the increasingly intolerable pressure of numbers upon resources. The symptoms will persist until their cause is removed.

Show the cartoon of the wheat plant and the man. The wheat plant is now growing faster than the man.

If resources could be made to increase faster than numbers, all would be well—at least until the psychological effects of overcrowding became unendurable. But in Egypt, under existing circumstances, resources cannot possibly be made to increase more rapidly than numbers. The only hope lies in adjusting numbers to existing and foreseeable resources.

Shot of the wheat plant and the man. The wheat plant remains stationary. The man, who is considerably taller, gradually shrinks until he is somewhat shorter than the plant.

Systematic death control—the cause of the recent explosive growth of Egypt's population—must be balanced by systematic birth control. If it is not, we may expect the worst—more wars, more revolutions, more Fascist and Communist dictatorships and deepening poverty and wretchedness, wholesale famine and pestilence.

Shot of an Egyptian birth control clinic.

The rulers of Egypt have understood the country's biological predicament. With the sanction of the theologians of Islam, who can see no religious or moral objection to the practice of voluntary family limitation, they have set up a number of free clinics for the dissemination of knowledge about the methods of birth control. The case of Egypt is not unique. Throughout most parts of the world, numbers are pressing more and more heavily upon available resources.

Air view of an Indian crowd at the juncture of the Jumna and Ganges.

Here are a million human beings. Multiply this figure by forty.

Shots of Coney Island. Of Hong Kong from the air. Of a huge stadium in Japan. And go on flashing these images again and again.

This represents the annual increase of the human race. Every four years it adds to its numbers the equivalent of the population of the United States.

The camera travels over a map of the world. Each country's population is indicated and its annual increment—e. g. India 360 millions, increase 5 millions per year. China 600 millions, increase 9 millions per year.

Two thirds of the world's people are undernourished, and their present rate of increase is one and a half per cent per annum. To maintain the present entirely inadequate standard of living, the world's agricultural production would have to be increased at the rate of one and a half per cent per annum. To achieve any marked improvement, it would require an increase of two and a half or three per cent per annum. As things now stand, there is not the slightest prospect that such an increase can be made, much less maintained, year in year out, indefinitely. There is only one practical solution.

Show the wheat plant and the man. The wheat plant grows very slowly, the man shrinks until he is shorter than the plant.

Death control without birth control can lead only to deepening misery and ultimate destruction.

Above outline by Mr. Aldous Huxley
March 15, 1957

[Attachment III, "WSK:dw," in a letter to Harrison Brown signed William S. Kiskadden, dated 7 September 1956, giving an update and the reason for the proposed meeting on 21 September 1956]

Mr. Fred Zinnemann has suggested that the Ford *Omnibus* Television Program Committee might be interested in a script upon Problems of Population. Mr. Zinnemann stressed the fact that a brief synopsis showing the story possibilities, its probable development and the direction of its impact with conclusions was necessary. *Omnibus* has been an important TV program, and presented a number of outstanding programs of national interest. Its audience is the American public, but since often much of the program has been or is filmed, it could be international in its scope.

Such a film presentation could not begin to tell the entire story of Population. Hence its impact directed largely and primarily to the American public should be followed by an organized campaign of education and propaganda.

The following suggestions are offered for consideration:

1. This valuable opportunity should be fully explored by a group or agency other than those already in this field. The reasons for this are largely self-evident.

2. This group named, let us say, "Population Limited," would be organized on a foundation basis, and act as sponsor for the *Omnibus* film. Thus it could expend money on a tax-free basis, and, subsequently, solicit and receive funds.

3. The *Omnibus* film would present the problem of Population and Food to the public. It should be informative, thought-provoking, stimulating.

4. Because of religious and other prejudices the need for education should be the primary and basic point of attack of this group. It is only through knowledge of economics and of health that real progress will be made.

5. This film should be offered for international release.

6. The Foundation would hope to subsequently present films to the peoples of underprivileged areas framed to stress economic education, health of the individual resulting from smaller families. Correlation of this work with other agencies in this field should be made possible.

7. Methods of contraception—It would appear that these must vary as to the particular country and government. For example, India seems to have embraced the disappointing rhythm method while searching for other methods and 'perfect pills.' Japan, through clinics, education and abortion, is vigorously attacking the problem. This side of the problem should not be of immediate or first concern to the Foundation.

Elisa Fortunato
(University of Bari)

How to Escape a "Subhuman Lot": Aldous Huxley's *The Politics of Ecology—The Question of Survival*

Editing Huxley's 1963 pamphlet *The Politics of Ecology* first of all raises a terminological problem. It is no coincidence that the entry for the word 'ecology' in the *Oxford English Dictionary* has two sets of meanings. The first is: "The science of the economy of animals and plants; that branch of biology which deals with the relations of living organisms to their surroundings, their habits and modes of life, etc."; the second is: "Used *attrib.* (and *absol.*) with reference to ecological issues such as industrial pollution considered in a political context; *spec.* applied to various political movements (esp. in western Europe) which represent the environmental or 'green' interest."[1] With reference to the second entry, the *OED* mentions "1963 A. Huxley (title) *The Politics of Ecology*" as the earliest recorded evidence for the use of the word 'ecology' in this sense. In fact, it is in this paper, published just a few months before his death, that Huxley gives a detailed definition of *ecology*, shifting from the *OED*'s record to: "Ecology is the science of the mutual relations of organisms with their environment and with one another."[2] The definition is thus broadened with the addition of "with one another" and in that addition lies all its interest.

It was the German biologist Ernst Haeckel who coined the word *Oecologie* in 1866, "'to describe the complex web of relationships between living things and their environment.'"[3] While in this definition human beings were not assumed to be *things* and the *environment* was understood as everything that surrounded the "living things," in Huxley's these two assumptions are radically altered. On the one hand, Aldous Huxley was profoundly convinced that the "living things," including human beings, were not mere *things* but "parts of a vast living organism" and, for that reason, it is fundamental to treat nature and "our planet with intelligence and consideration," in order "to be well treated by nature" (*PE*, 6).[4] He believed in the importance of the intimacy between human beings and nature, which, in his opinion, had been undermined by Christian theology with its doctrine of human supremacy over other living creatures (called, indeed, *things*): "Animals have no souls; therefore, according to the most authoritative Christian theologians, they may be treated as though they were things" (*PE*, 6).[5] On the other hand, Huxley questions the definition of the term *environment*:

> In the nineteenth century, the environmentalist school spoke of environment as conditioning and creating cultures but left out of account altogether the fact that cultures condition the environment—that man has certainly done almost as much to change the environment as the environment has done to mould the course of history.[6]

The fact that in 1989 the *OED* defined *environment* still as "the conditions under which any person or thing lives or is developed; the sum-total of influences which modify and determine the development of life or character" shows that even then the relationship between human beings and the planet was still seen as a one-way relationship.

From 1937 to 1963 Aldous Huxley lived in California. It was there that he had the opportunity to get familiar with writings of two of the first American ecologists, William Vogt and Fairfield Osborn,[7] and also of Rachel Carson, the author of *Silent Spring*.[8] These and other relationships had made Huxley aware that the science of ecology was complex and systemic, the only science able to interconnect the single parts with the whole:

> The details of this binding up of ourselves with the world, and of all parts of the world, in a single quasi-organic whole are studied in the science of ecology, which is an extremely recent science [...] and has unveiled the basic facts that living organisms exist in exquisitely balanced communities and that this balance can be very easily upset. ("MNA," 34)

Huxley's goal is to overcome what later, in the 1980s, was called the "Anthropocene,"[9] in order to preserve and protect that highly fragile "balance." The essay *The Politics of Ecology: A Question of Survival* (1963) sums up his ideas about ecology, and suggests how twentieth-century man could respond to the ecological crisis he is facing.

The word *crisis* derives from the Greek word *krisis*, which means "decision." In the etymology of the word lies the answer Huxley was suggesting: in order to meet the crisis the planet (and humankind on the planet) is about to face, we have to realise that "the basic problem confronting twentieth-century man is an ecological problem" and, as a consequence, we have to make a choice by "shifting our attention from the now completely irrelevant and anachronistic politics of nationalism and military power to the problems of the human species and the still inchoate politics of human ecology" (*PE*, 6). This choice will naturally lead to the expansion of transnational institutions (UN, UNESCO, FAO, WHO) because, since the environmental and ecological problem is a global problem, the answer has to be found in global governance.[10]

The essay begins with a Shakespearean question: if "to possess power is *ipso facto* to be tempted to abuse it [...], what kind of institutions are effective" in order to "make it difficult for the powerful to be led into those temptations which, succumbed to, transform them into tyrants at home and imperialists abroad" (*PE*, 1)?

In Shakespeare's *Julius Caesar*, Brutus' ruinous answer was Julius Caesar's murder. In act II, scene i, Brutus has come to a decision; he has made his choice after experiencing a private and public crisis, and speaks out his famous twenty lines[11] because—as he continued to remind himself and playgoers during the funeral oration upon Caesar's corpse in act III—it was "not that I loved Caesar less, but that I loved Rome more."[12] For Brutus the answer was the *res publica*, Rome.

For Huxley, the answer is more complex, because it is linked with the ever accelerating progress of science and technology:

> [W]hen advancing science and acceleratingly progressive technology alter man's long-established relationship with the planet on which he lives, revolutionize his societies, and at the same time equip his rulers with new and immensely more powerful instruments of domination, what ought we to do? What *can* we do?" (*PE*, 1–2)

The first part of the essay, the *pars destruens*, rhetorically speaking, deals with these new and "powerful instruments of domination" and is divided into three subsections: one devoted to overpopulation; the second, to new technological weapons; the third, to nationalism and war.[13] These are three fundamental themes in Huxley's thought. From *Brave New World* (1932) to *Island* (1962), from *Ends and Means* (1937) and "The Double Crisis" (1948) to *Brave New World Revisited* (1958) and his lectures at Santa Barbara (1959), later published as *The Human Situation* (1977), he incessantly returns to these topics.

As regards overpopulation, due to an imbalance between death control (which is "easy, cheap, and can be carried out by a small force of technicians" [*PE*, 3]) and birth control (which, "on the other hand, is rather expensive, involves the whole adult population, and demands of those who practice it a good deal of forethought and directed will-power" [*PE*, 3]),[14] Huxley pinpoints how influential population increase is on the ecological equilibrium of the planet.[15] On the one hand, he highlights the depletability of the resources on our planet; on the other hand, he shows the difference between Western societies and "underdeveloped" ones:

> Within the next ten or twenty years, if war can be avoided, poverty will almost have disappeared from the highly industrialized and contraceptive-using societies of the West. Meanwhile, in the

> underdeveloped and uncontrolledly breeding societies of Asia, Africa, and Latin America the condition of the masses (twice as numerous a generation from now, as they are today) will have become no better and may even be decidedly worse than it is at present. (*PE*, 3)

And in this gap he sees the seeds of potential social unrest which will lead, inevitably, to dictatorship:

> Extreme poverty, when combined with ignorance, breeds that lack of desire for better things which has been called "wantlessness"—the resigned acceptance of a subhuman lot. But extreme poverty, when it is combined with the knowledge that some societies are affluent, breeds envious desires and the expectation that these desires must of necessity, and very soon, be satisfied. By means of the mass media (those easily exportable products of advancing science and technology) some knowledge of what life is like in affluent societies has been widely disseminated throughout the world's underdeveloped regions. But, alas, the science and technology which have given the industrial West its cars, refrigerators, and contraceptives have given the people of Asia, Africa, and Latin America only movies and radio broadcasts, which they are too simple-minded to be able to criticize, together with a population explosion, which they are still too poor and too tradition-bound to be able to control by deliberate family planning. [...]
>
> From disappointment, through resentful frustration, to widespread social unrest the road is short. Shorter still is the road from social unrest, through chaos, to dictatorship. (*PE*, 3)

The second subsection is devoted to new technological weapons. Huxley links the development of the A-bomb and H-bomb to the progress of science. He brings into question the common assumption "that political freedom was a necessary pre-condition of scientific research" (*PE*, 3-4) and shows how Russia and China have "demonstrated that poverty and primitive conditions of life for the overwhelming majority of the population are perfectly compatible with the wholesale production of the most advanced and sophisticated military hardware" (*PE*, 4). As a consequence, he says that the democratic institutions "are not at all necessary to the progress of science and technology, and that such progress does not of itself make for human betterment at home and peace abroad" (*PE*, 4). This conclusion brings us to another profound conviction which accompanies Huxley throughout his (literary) life and which is what we have called the third subsection: good ends are achievable only through good means, and good ends cannot justify bad means, as he explains for instance in *End and Means*: "For the means employed inevitably determine the nature of the result achieved; whereas, however good the end aimed at may be, its goodness is powerless to counteract the effects of the bad means we use to reach it."[16]

In fact, these technological weapons, seen as bad means, have led to modern war. And war is a by-product of culture, of a cultural prison built up by the "world's ruling minorities" which has "brought [men and women] up to regard nationalism as axiomatic and war between nations as something cosmically ordained by the Nature of Things" (*PE*, 4). The only way out of this prison, and here Huxley returns to the beginning of his essay, lies in "democratic institutions and libertarian traditions" (*PE*, 4); but this assertion comes with a warning:

> A rapid and accelerating population increase that will nullify the best efforts of underdeveloped societies to better their lot and will keep two-thirds of the human race in a condition of misery in anarchy or of misery under dictatorship, and the intensive preparations for a new kind of war that, if it breaks out, may bring irretrievable ruin to the one-third of the human race now living prosperously in highly industrialized societies—these are the two main threats to democracy now confronting us. (*PE*, 5)

In order to combat these threats we need what Huxley calls "ecological politics" (*PE*, 7). The description of such a policy constitutes the *pars construens* of the essay. Huxley suggests a completely new way of thinking. He advises us to shift "our collective attention from the merely political to the basic biological aspects of the human situation" (*PE*, 6). We have to ask ourselves a different set of questions,[17] we have to shift from a nationalistic, warmongering way of thinking ("Which is the best nation? The best religion? [...] The best form of government?") to an ecological one:

> How does the human race propose to survive and, if possible, improve the lot and the intrinsic quality of its individual members? Do we propose to live on this planet in symbiotic harmony with our environment? Or, preferring to be wantonly stupid, shall we choose to live like murderous and suicidal parasites that kill their host and so destroy themselves?" (*PE*, 6)

This set of questions mirrors a society's world-view and its culture that are "fundamental to the ways its members think and behave" (Sawyer, 224). We have adjusted technological progress to our anthropocentric, nationalistic world-view and, in so doing, we have lived, and we still live, "like a parasite living upon the host it infests."[18]

And in this idea of humans being just a part of the planet, not the rulers or owners of it, lies its prophetic originality. Man is not a host to the planet he lives on, man is equal just to plants, insects, animal, rocks, i.e., to the whole planet.

These questions are addressed to all humankind, not to the inhabitants of one or more particular nations, and they can be answered only through a collective effort. Ecology-oriented organizations, such as the UN, UNESCO, FAO and WHO, were, in the1960s, only just beginning their work,[19] and Huxley saw in them the only democratic possibilities to actualize human potentialities.

---

1 *Oxford English Dictionary*, V (Oxford, ²1989). Hereafter, *OED*.

2 Aldous Huxley, *The Politics of Ecology: The Question of Survival*, An Occasional Paper on the Free Society Published by the Center for the Study of Democratic Institutions (Santa Barbara, 1963), 6. Hereafter, *PE*.

3 Quoted in R. S. Deese, *We Are Amphibians: Julian and Aldous Huxley on the Future of Our Species* (Oakland, 2015), 159.

4 It is interesting to see how deeply this definition of *things* is linked with Huxley's religious view. Throughout his life, Huxley thought about the differences between Western faith and primitive and Eastern religions/beliefs, where man "has always regarded himself as a part of nature, as intimately and fundamentally concerned with and imbedded in it" ("More Nature in Art," *The Human Situation: Lectures at Santa Barbara, 1959*, ed. Piero Ferrucci (New York, 1977), 31; hereafter, "MNA" and *HS*). It is, in particular, in his last novel, *Island*, that Huxley fully developed his holistic view.

5 See also "MNA," 39, where Huxley states that in the Judaeo-Christian tradition "the fundamental notion is that man is the lord of creation and is in some way apart from nature and free to do what he wants with it."

6 Aldous Huxley, "Man and His Planet" [hereafter, "MHP"], *HS*, 13.

7 See *Letters of Aldous Huxley*, ed. Grover Smith (London, 1969), 587.

8 *Silent Spring* was published on 27 September 1962, documenting the environmental effects caused by the indiscriminate use of DDT in the United States. See also Deese, 18–19.

9 The "Anthropocene" is a proposed epoch dating from the commencement of significant human impact on Earth's geology and ecosystems, including, but not limited to, anthropogenic climate change. See Roy Scranton, "Learning How to Die in the Anthropocene," *The New York Times* (10 November 2013), <https://opinionator.blogs.nytimes.com/2013/11/10/learning-how-to-die-in-the-anthropocene/>, and Jonathan Safran Foer, *We Are the Weather: Saving the Planet Begins at Breakfast* (New York, 2019).

10 Aldous Huxley's older brother was Julian Huxley, the first Director-General of the United Nations Educational Scientific and Cultural Organization (UNESCO), and the founder of the World Wildlife Fund (WWF). See Deese, 9, 12.

11 "It must be by his death: and for my part / I know no personal cause to spurn at him / But for the general. He would be crowned: / How that might change his nature, there's the question. / It is the bright day that brings forth the adder, /And that craves wary walking. Crown him that, / And then I grant we put a sting in him / That at his will he may do danger with. / Th'abuse of

greatness is when it disjoins / Remorse from power; and to speak truth of Caesar / I have not known when his affections swayed / More than his reason. But 'tis a common proof / That lowliness is young ambition's ladder / Whereto the climber-upward turns his face; / But when he once attains the upmost round / He then unto the ladder turns his back, / Looks in the clouds, scorning the base degrees / By which he did ascend. So Caesar may. / Then, lest he may, prevent. And since the quarrel / Will bear no colour for the thing he is, / Fashion it thus: that what he is, augmented, / Would run to these and these extremities. / And therefore think him as a serpent's egg / Which, hatched, would as his kind grow mischievous, / And kill him in the shell" (William Shakespeare, *Julius Caesar* [hereafter, *JC*], II, i, 10–34).

12 "Romans, countrymen, and lovers! hear me for my cause, / And be silent, that you may hear: believe me for mine / Honour, and have respect to mine honour, that you may / Believe: censure me in your wisdom, and awake your / Senses, that you may the better judge. If there be any in / This assembly, any dear friend of Caesar's, to him I say, / That Brutus' love to Caesar was no less than his. If then / That friend demand why Brutus rose against Caesar, this / Is my answer: —Not that I loved Caesar less, but that I / Loved Rome more. Had you rather Caesar were living / And die all slaves, than that Caesar were dead, to live / All free men? As Caesar loved me, I weep for him; as / He was fortunate, I rejoice at it; as he was valiant, I / Honour him: but, as he was ambitious, I slew him. / There is tears for his love; joy for his fortune; honour / For his valour; and death for his ambition. Who is here / So base that would be a bondman? If any, speak; for / Him have I offended. Who is here so rude that would / Not be a Roman? If any, speak; for him have I offend/-ed. Who is here so vile that will not love his country? / If any, speak; for him have I offended. I pause for a / Reply" (*JC*, III, ii, 15–34).

13 See Peter Mortensen, "Tripping Back to Nature: Aldous Huxley, Psychedelics, and Pro-Technology Environmentalism," *AHA*, 15 (2015), 276: "From Huxley's perspective, the combination of population growth, dwindling resources and governments bent on economic growth increase the likelihood of war by pitting nations against each other in a deadly contest for 'wasting assets.'"

14 It is important to stress that Huxley wrote this essay when contraceptive devices and fertility-controlling drugs were first emerging (the first birth control pill, for example, was developed in the 1950s and became publicly available in the 1960s).

15 See, in particular, Aldous Huxley, "The Double Crisis," *World Review* (November/December 1948), 9–14, 33–38 (later included in *Themes and Variations* [London, 1950], 225–60), *Adonis and the Alphabet* (1956), *Brave New World Revisited* (1958), "MHP" (1959), "The Population Explosion" (1959), *HS*, 42–58. See also Dana Sawyer, "'Brave New World-View': Aldous Huxley, Environmental Prophet," *AHA*, 8 (2008), 221. As regards the relationship between overpopulation, natural resources, and birth control, it has been pointed out how crucial Huxley's forward-looking ideas were for the "Deep Ecology" movement (see Mortensen, 273–274; Rolf Lindemann, "Overpopulation and Sustainability—a Cultural Geographer's Reappraisal of Huxley's Pertinent Critical Essays," *Aldous Huxley, Man of Letters: Thinker, Critic and Artist*

—*Proceedings of the Third International Aldous Huxley Symposium Riga 2004*, ed. Bernfried Nugel, Uwe Rasch, Gerhard Wagner [Berlin, 2007], 113–21; Vita Fortunati, *Huxley: Una Società ecologica e pacifista* [Milano, 2017], 23–25).

16 *Ends and Means* (London, 1937), 52.

17 The set of questions to be posed is linked, inevitably, with each culture and its world-view. With regard to this topic, Dana Sawyer traces a path between Huxley's *weltanschauung* and what environmentalists today call 'belief paradigm'; see Sawyer, 223–25.

18 See Aldous Huxley, "MHP," *HS*, 15.

19 The United Nations, the United Nations Educational Scientific and Cultural Organization, and the Food and Agriculture Organization were founded in 1945, the World Health Organization in 1948.

Aldous Huxley

THE POLITICS OF ECOLOGY: THE QUESTION OF SURVIVAL[1]

In politics, the central and fundamental problem is the problem of power. Who is to exercise power? And by what means, by what authority, with what purpose in view, and under what controls? Yes, under what controls? For, as history has made it abundantly clear, to possess power is *ipso facto* to be tempted to abuse it. In mere self-preservation we must create and maintain institutions that make it difficult for the powerful to be led into those temptations which, succumbed to, transform them into tyrants at home and imperialists abroad.

For this purpose what kind of institutions are effective? And, having created them, how can we guarantee them against obsolescence? Circumstances change, and, as they change, the old, the once so admirably effective devices for controlling power cease to be adequate. What then? Specifically, when advancing science and acceleratingly progressive technology alter man's long-established relationship with the planet on which he lives, revolutionize his societies, and at the same time equip his rulers with new and immensely more powerful instruments of domination, what ought we to do? What *can* we do?

Very briefly let us review the situation in which we now find ourselves and, in the light of present facts, hazard a few guesses about the future.

On the biological level, advancing science and technology have set going a revolutionary process that seems to be destined for the next century at least, perhaps for much longer, to exercise a decisive influence upon the destinies of all human societies and their individual members. In the course of the last fifty years extremely effective methods for lowering the prevailing rates

---

[1] The editor wishes to thank the Aldous and Laura Huxley Literary Trust for permission to re-publish this essay. In this edition the 1963 pamphlet (P) is used as copy-text, checked against the typescript of an intermediate draft (ID) corrected in Huxley's hand. For the different states of the text, see Bernfried Nugel, "A Preliminary Catalogue of Aldous Huxley's Manuscripts, Typescripts and Proofs at Laura Huxley's Residence," *AHA*, 6 (2006), 184. For the original tape of Huxley's March 1962 lecture, see UCLA Special Collections, "Aldous and Laura Huxley Papers, 1925–2007," Box 94, Folder 4, Tape No. 141; for the original drafts and the published text, see *ib.*, Box 45, Folders 7–9. ID has a different title: {Democratic Institutions in the context of advancing Science and Technology}.

of infant and adult mortality were developed by Western scientists. These methods were very simple and could be applied with the expenditure of very little money by very small numbers of not very highly trained technicians. For these reasons, and because everyone regards life as intrinsically good and death as intrinsically bad, they were in fact applied on a worldwide scale. The results were spectacular. In the past, high birth rates were balanced by high death rates. Thanks to science, death rates have been halved but, except in the most highly industrialized, contraceptive-using countries, birth rates remain as high as ever. An enormous and accelerating increase in human numbers has been the inevitable consequence.

At the beginning of the Christian era, so demographers assure us, our planet supported a human population of about two hundred and fifty millions. When the Pilgrim Fathers stepped ashore, the figure had risen to about five hundred millions. We see, then, that in the relatively recent past it took sixteen hundred years for the human species to double its numbers. Today world population stands at three thousand millions. By the year 2000, unless something appallingly bad or miraculously good should happen in the interval, six thousand millions of us will be sitting down to breakfast every morning. In a word, twelve times as many people are destined to double their numbers in one-fortieth of the time.

This is not the whole story. In many areas of the world human numbers are increasing at a rate much higher than the average for the whole species. In India, for example, the rate of increase is now 2.3 per cent per annum. By 1990 its four hundred and fifty million inhabitants will have become nine hundred million inhabitants. A comparable rate of increase will raise the population of China to the billion mark by 1980. In Ceylon, in Egypt, in many of the countries of South and Central America, human numbers are increasing at an annual rate of 3 per cent. The result will be a doubling of their present populations in approximately twenty-three years.

On the social, political, and economic levels, what is likely to happen in an underdeveloped country whose people double themselves in a single generation, or even less? An underdeveloped society is a society without adequate capital resources (for capital is what is left over after primary needs have been satisfied, and in underdeveloped countries most people never satisfy the primary needs); a society without a sufficient force of trained teachers, administrators, and technicians; a society with few or no industries and few or no developed sources of industrial power; a society, finally, with enormous arrears in food production, education, road building, housing, and sanitation to be made good. A quarter of a century from now, when there will be twice as many of them as there are today, what is the likelihood that the members of such a society will be better fed, housed, clothed, and schooled than at present? And what are the chances in such a society for the maintenance, if they already exist, or the creation, if they do not exist, of democratic institutions?

Not long ago Mr. Eugene Black, the former president of the World Bank, expressed the opinion that it would be extremely difficult, perhaps even impossible, for an underdeveloped country with a very rapid rate of population increase to achieve full industrialization. All its resources, he pointed out, would be absorbed year by year in the task of supplying, or not quite supplying, the primary needs of its new members. Merely to stand still to maintain its current subhumanly inadequate standard of living, will require hard work and the expenditure of all the nation's available capital. Available capital may be increased by loans and gifts from abroad; but in a world where the industrialized nations are involved in power politics and an increasingly expensive armaments race, there will never be enough foreign aid to make much difference. And even if the loans and gifts to underdeveloped countries were to be substantially increased, any resulting gains would be largely nullified by the uncontrolled population explosion.

The situation of these nations with such rapidly increasing populations reminds one of Lewis Carroll's parable in *Through the Looking Glass*, where Alice and the Red Queen start running at full speed and run for a long time until Alice is completely out of breath. When they stop, Alice is amazed to see that they are still at their starting point. In the looking glass world, if you wish to retain your present position, you must run as fast as you can. If you wish to get ahead, you must run at least twice as fast as you can.[2]

If Mr. Black is correct (and there are plenty of economists and demographers who share his opinion), the outlook for most of the world's newly independent and economically non-viable nations is gloomy indeed. 'To

---

[2] The paragraph {The situation of these nations […] as fast as you can.} is not present in ID and has apparently been inserted before printing P. It resembles in part a passage in Huxley's Santa Barbara lecture "The Population Explosion," *The Human Situation: Lectures at Santa Barbara, 1959*, ed. Piero Ferrucci (New York, 1977), 49: "Another alternative is to increase industrial and agricultural production so that they can catch up with the increase in population. This solution, however, would be extremely like what happens to Alice in *Through the Looking Glass*. You remember that Alice and the Red Queen are running a tremendous race. To Alice's astonishment, when they have run until they are completely out of breath they are in exactly the same place, and Alice says, 'Well, in *our* country… you'd generally get to somewhere else —if you ran fast for a long time as we've been doing.' 'A slow sort of country!' says the Queen. 'Now, *here*, […] if you want to get somewhere else, you must run at least twice as fast as that!'"

those that have shall be given.'[3] Within the next ten or twenty years, if war can be avoided, poverty will almost have disappeared from the highly industrialized and contraceptive-using societies of the West. Meanwhile, in the underdeveloped and uncontrolledly breeding societies of Asia, Africa, and Latin America the condition of the masses (twice as numerous, a generation from now, as they are today) will have become no better and may even be decidedly worse than it is at present. Such a decline is foreshadowed by current statistics of the Food and Agriculture Organization of the United Nations. In some underdeveloped regions of the world, we are told, people are somewhat less adequately fed, clothed, and housed than were their parents and grandparents thirty and forty years ago. And what of elementary education? UNESCO recently provided an answer. Since the end of World War II heroic efforts have been made to teach the whole world how to read. The population explosion has largely stultified these efforts. The absolute number of illiterates is greater now than at any time in the past.

The contraceptive revolution which, thanks to advancing science and technology, has made it possible for the highly developed societies of the West to offset the consequences of death control by a planned control of births, has had as yet no effect upon the family life of people in underdeveloped countries. This is not surprising. Death control, as I have already remarked, is easy, cheap, and can be carried out by a small force of technicians. Birth control, on the other hand, is rather expensive, involves the whole adult population, and demands of those who practice it a good deal of forethought and directed will power. To persuade hundreds of millions of men and women to abandon their tradition-hallowed views of sexual morality, then to distribute and teach them to make use of contraceptive devices or fertility-controlling drugs—this is a huge and difficult task, so huge and so difficult that it seems very unlikely that it can be successfully carried out, within a sufficiently short space of time, in any of the countries where control of the birth rate is most urgently needed.

Extreme poverty, when combined with ignorance, breeds that lack of desire for better things which has been called "wantlessness"—the resigned acceptance of a subhuman lot. But extreme poverty, when it is combined with the knowledge that some societies are affluent, breeds envious desires and the expectation that these desires must of necessity, and very soon, be satisfied. By means of the mass media (those easily exportable products of advancing science and technology) some knowledge of what life is like in

---

[3] ID: {'To those that have shall be given.'}; P: {To those that have shall be given.}.

affluent societies has been widely disseminated throughout the world's underdeveloped regions. But, alas, the science and technology which have given the industrial West its cars, refrigerators, and contraceptives have given the people of Asia, Africa, and Latin America only movies and radio broadcasts, which they are too simple-minded to be able to criticize, together with a population explosion, which they are still too poor and too tradition-bound to be able to control by deliberate family planning.

In the context of a 3, or even of a mere 2 per cent annual increase in numbers, high expectations are foredoomed to disappointment. From disappointment, through resentful frustration, to widespread social unrest the road is short. Shorter still is the road from social unrest, through chaos, to dictatorship, possibly of the Communist Party, more probably of Generals and Colonels. It would seem, then, that for two-thirds of the human race now suffering from the consequences of uncontrolled breeding in a context of industrial backwardness, poverty, and illiteracy, the prospects for democracy, during the next ten or twenty years, are very poor.[4]

From underdeveloped societies and the probable political consequences of their explosive increase in numbers we now pass to the prospects for democracy in the fully industrialized, contraceptive-using societies of Europe and North America.

It used to be assumed that political freedom was a necessary precondition of scientific research. Ideological dogmatism and dictatorial institutions were supposed to be incompatible with the open-mindedness and the freedom of experimental action, in the absence of which discovery and invention are impossible. Recent history has proved these comforting assumptions to be completely unfounded. It was under Stalin that Russian scientists developed the A-bomb and, a few years later, the H-bomb. And it is under a more-than-Stalinist dictatorship that Chinese scientists are now in process of performing the same feat.

Another disquieting lesson of recent history is that, in a developing society, science and technology can be used exclusively for the enhancement of military power, not at all for the benefit of the masses. Russia has demonstrated, and China is now doing its best to demonstrate, that poverty and primitive conditions of life for the overwhelming majority of the population are perfectly compatible with the wholesale production of the most advanced and sophisticated military hardware. Indeed, it is by deliberately imposing poverty on the masses that the rulers of developing industrial nations are able to create the capital necessary for building an armament

[4] P: {very poor}; ID: {poor in the extreme}.

industry and maintaining a well-equipped army, with which to play their parts in the suicidal game of international power politics.

We see, then, that democratic institutions and libertarian traditions are not at all necessary to the progress of science and technology, and that such progress does not of itself make for human betterment at home and peace abroad. Only where democratic institutions already exist, only where the masses can vote their rulers out of office and so compel them to[5] pay attention to the popular will, are science and technology used for the benefit of the majority as well as for increasing the power of the State. Most human beings prefer peace to war, and practically all of them would rather be alive than dead. But in every part of the world men and women have been brought up to regard nationalism as axiomatic and war between nations as something cosmically ordained by the Nature of Things. Prisoners of their culture, the masses, even when they are free to vote, are inhibited by the fundamental postulates of the frame of reference within which they do their thinking and their feeling from decreeing an end to the collective paranoia that governs international relations. As for the world's ruling minorities, by

---

[5] In ID after this point (i.e., the end of p. 7) a page 7 A has been inserted, which provides a newly phrased passage instead of the deleted first half of page 8 (see below, note 6): {pay attention to the popular will, are science and technology used for the benefit of the majority as well as for increasing the power of the State. And even where democratic institutions exist, science, technology and preparation for war combine to pose a serious threat to civil and political liberty. A few days before he left the White House President Eisenhower delivered a farewell address, in which he urged his fellow countrymen to "guard against the acquisition of unwarranted influence, whether sought or unsought, by the military-industrial complex. The potential for the disastrous rise of misplaced power exists and will persist." And he added that "we must never let the weight of this (military-industrial) combination endanger our liberties or our democratic processes."

Most human beings prefer a measure of freedom to being constantly pushed around, prefer peace to war and would much rather be alive than dead. But in every part of the world, in democratically organized countries as well as in countries under dictatorships, men and women have been brought up to regard nationalism as axiomatic and war between nations as something cosmically ordained by God, or Faith, or the Nature of Things. Prisoners of their culture, the masses, even in those countries where they are free to vote, are prevented by the basic postulates, in terms of which they do their thinking and feeling, from summarily decreeing an end to the collective paranoia that governs international relations. As for the world's ruling minorities—by the very fact of their position and their power they are chained even}.

the very fact of their power they are chained even[6] more closely to the current system of ideas and the prevailing political customs; for this reason they are even less capable than their subjects of expressing the simple human preference for life and peace.

Some day, let us hope, rulers and ruled will break out of the cultural prison in which they are now confined. Some day… And may that day come soon! For, thanks to our rapidly advancing science and technology, we have very little time at our disposal. The river of change flows ever faster, and somewhere downstream, perhaps only a few years ahead, we shall come to the rapids, shall hear, louder and ever louder, the roaring of a cataract.

Modern war is a product of advancing science and technology. Conversely, advancing science and technology are products of modern war.[7] It was in order to wage war more effectively that first the United States, then Britain and the USSR, financed the crash programs that resulted so quickly in the harnessing of atomic forces.[8] Again, it was primarily for military purposes that the techniques of automation, which are now in process of revolutionizing industrial production and the whole system of administrative and bureaucratic control, were first developed. "During World War II," writes Mr. John Diebold, "the theory and use of feedback was studied in great detail by a number of scientists both in this country and in Britain. The introduction of rapidly moving aircraft very quickly made traditional gun-laying techniques of anti-aircraft warfare obsolete. As a result, a large part of scientific man-power in this country was directed towards the development of self-regulating devices and systems to control our military equipment. It is out of this work that the technology of automation as we understand it today has developed."[9]

---

6 In ID the passage before this point {pay attention […] chained even} (i.e., the first half of p. 8) was struck out but apparently later restored before printing P (p. 4).

7 In ID there is an extra sentence: {war. Nuclear fusion and nuclear fission have revolutionized war. But it}.

8 In ID there is an extra half-sentence: {forces, primarily for military purposes and secondarily (as a by-product of the A-bomb) as a source of industrial power. Again,}.

9 "Statement of John Diebold, President, John Diebold & Associates, Inc.," *Automation and Technological Change: Hearings Before the Subcommittee on Economic Stabilization of the Joint Committee on the Economic Report* (Congress of the United States, Eighty-Fourth Congress, First Session, October 1955) [Washington: United States Government Printing Office, 1955], 6–29; here, 9.

The headlong rapidity with which scientific and technological changes, with all their disturbing consequences in the fields of politics and social relations, are taking place is due in large measure to the fact that, both in the USA and the USSR, research in pure and applied science is lavishly financed by military planners whose first concern is in[10] the development of bigger and better weapons in the shortest possible time. In the frantic effort, on one side of the Iron Curtain, to keep up with the Joneses—on the other, to keep up with the Ivanovs—these military planners spend gigantic sums on research and development. The military revolution advances under forced draft, and as it goes forward it initiates an uninterrupted succession of industrial, social, and political revolutions. It is against this background of chronic upheaval that the members of a species, biologically and historically adapted to a slowly changing environment, must now live out their bewildered lives.

Old-fashioned war was incompatible, while it was being waged, with democracy. Nuclear war, if it is ever waged, will prove in all likelihood to be incompatible with civilization, perhaps with human survival. Meanwhile, what of the preparations for nuclear war? If certain physicists and military planners had their way, democracy, where it exists, would be replaced by a system of regimentation centred upon the bomb shelter. The entire population would have to be systematically drilled in the ticklish operation of going underground at a moment's notice, systematically exercised in the art of living troglodytically under conditions resembling those in the hold of an eighteenth-century slave ship. The notion fills most of us with horror. But if we fail to break out of the ideological prison of our nationalistic and militaristic[11] culture, we may find ourselves compelled by the military consequences of our science and technology to descend into the steel and concrete dungeons of total and totalitarian Civil Defence.

In the past, one of the most effective guarantees of liberty was governmental inefficiency. The spirit of tyranny was always willing; but its technical and organizational flesh was weak.[12] Today the flesh is as strong as the spirit. Governmental organization is a fine art, based upon scientific principles and disposing of marvelously efficient equipment. Fifty years ago an armed revolution still had some chance of success. In the context of modern weaponry a popular uprising is foredoomed. Crowds armed with rifles and home-made grenades are no match for tanks. And it is not only

---

[10] ID: {is}; P: {is in}.

[11] P: {militaristic}; ID: {bellicose}.

[12] P: {was weak}; ID: {was generally weak}.

to its ornament that a modern government owes its overwhelming power. It also possesses the strength of superior knowledge derived from its communication systems, its stores of accumulated data, its batteries of computers, its network of inspection and administration.

Where democratic institutions exist and the masses can vote their rulers out of office, the enormous powers with which science, technology, and the arts of organization have endowed the ruling minority are used with discretion and a decent regard for civil and political liberty. Where the masses can exercise no control over their rulers, these powers are used without compunction to enforce ideological orthodoxy and to strengthen the dictatorial state. The nature of science and technology is such that it is peculiarly easy for a dictatorial government to use them for its own antidemocratic purposes. Well financed, equipped and organized, an astonishingly small number of scientists and technologists can achieve prodigious results. The crash program that produced the A-bomb and ushered in a new historical era was planned and directed by some four thousand theoreticians, experimenters, and engineers. To parody the words of Winston Churchill, never have so many been so completely at the mercy of so few.

Throughout the nineteenth century the State was relatively feeble, and its interest in, and influence upon, scientific research were negligible. In our day the State is everywhere exceedingly powerful and a[13] lavish patron of basic and *ad hoc* research. In Western Europe and North America the relations between the State and its scientists on the one hand and individual citizens, professional organizations, and industrial, commercial, and educational institutions on the other are fairly satisfactory. Advancing science, the population explosion, the armament race, and the steady increase and centralization of political and economic power are still compatible, in countries that have a libertarian tradition, with democratic forms of government. To maintain this compatibility in a rapidly changing world, bearing less and less resemblance to the world in which these democratic institutions were developed— this, quite obviously, is going to be increasingly difficult.

A rapid and accelerating population increase that will nullify the best efforts of underdeveloped societies to better their lot and will keep two-thirds of the human race in a condition of misery in anarchy or of misery under dictatorship; and the intensive preparations for a new kind of war that, if it breaks out, may bring irretrievable ruin to the one-third of the human race now living prosperously in highly industrialized societies—these are the two

[13] P: {and a}; ID: [and everywhere a}.

main threats to democracy now confronting us. Can these threats be eliminated? Or, if not eliminated, at least reduced?

My own view is that only by shifting our collective attention from the merely political to the basic biological aspects of the human situation can we hope to mitigate and shorten the time of troubles into which, it would seem, we are now moving.[14] We cannot do without politics; but we can no longer afford to indulge in bad, unrealistic politics. To work for the survival of the species as a whole and for the actualization in the greatest possible number of individual men and women of their potentialities for good will, intelligence, and creativity—this, in the world of today, is good, realistic politics. To cultivate the religion of idolatrous nationalism, to subordinate the interests of the species and its individual members to the interests of a single national state and its ruling minority—in the context of the population explosion, missiles, and atomic warheads, this is bad and thoroughly unrealistic politics. Unfortunately, it is to bad and unrealistic politics that our rulers are now committed.

Ecology is the science of the mutual relations of organisms with their environment and with one another. Only when we get it into our collective head that the basic problem confronting twentieth-century man is an ecological problem will our politics improve and become realistic. How does the human race propose to survive and, if possible, improve the lot and the intrinsic quality of its individual members? Do we propose to live on this planet in symbiotic harmony with our environment? Or, preferring to be wantonly stupid, shall we choose to live like murderous and suicidal parasites that kill their host and so destroy themselves?[15]

---

14 In ID there is an extra sentence: {moving. We have to get it into our collective head that the basic problem now confronting us is ecological. How does}, whereas P has a new passage after {moving.} (see main text, above): {We cannot do [...] become realistic.}.

15 In ID there follows an extra passage: {It might be sensible to think less about the problem of landing a couple of astronauts on the moon and rather more about the problem of enabling three billion men, women, and children, who will soon be six billions, to lead a tolerably human existence without, in the process, ruining and befouling their planetary environment. Indeed, I believe that it is only by cultivating this kind of ecological thinking that we shall be able to reduce the threat of war. Rationalized and justified in terms of national ideals and dogmatic ideology, power politics raises problems that, except by war, are almost insoluble. The problems of ecology, on the other hand, admit of a rational solution and can be tackled without arousing the violent passions always associated with nationalism and ideology. There may be arguments}. Instead of this passage P has two new paragraphs and two new sentences in a third paragraph (see main text, above): {Committing that sin [...] nationalistic

Committing that sin of overweening bumptiousness, which the Greeks called *hubris*, we behave as though we were not members of earth's ecological community, as though we were privileged and, in some sort, supernatural beings and could throw our weight around like gods. But in fact we are, among other things, animals—emergent parts of the natural order. If our politicians were realists, they would think rather less about missiles and the problem of landing a couple of astronauts on the moon, rather more about hunger and moral squalor and the problem of enabling three billion men, women, and children, who will soon be six billions, to lead a tolerably human existence without, in the process, ruining and befouling their planetary environment.

Animals have no souls; therefore, according to the most authoritative Christian theologians, they may become treated as though they were things. The truth, as we are now beginning to realize, is that even things ought not to be treated as *mere* things. They should be treated as though they were parts of a vast living organism. "Do as you would be done by." The Golden Rule applies to our dealings with nature no less than to our dealings with our fellow-men. If we hope to be well treated by nature we must stop talking about "mere things" and start treating our planet with intelligence and consideration.

Power politics in the context of nationalism raises problems that, except by war, are practically insoluble. The problems of ecology, on the other hand, admit of a rational solution and can be tackled without the arousal of those violent passions always associated with dogmatic ideology and nationalistic idolatry. There may be arguments about the best way of raising wheat in a cold climate, or of re-afforesting a denuded mountain. But such arguments never lead to organized slaughter. Organized slaughter is the result of arguments about such questions as the following: Which is the best nation? The best religion? The best political theory? The best form of government? Why are other people so stupid and wicked? Why can't they see how good and intelligent *we* are? Why do they resist our beneficent efforts to bring them under our control and make them like ourselves?

To questions of this kind the final answer has always been war. "War," said Clausewitz, "is not merely a political act, but also a political instrument, a continuation of political relationships, a carrying out of the same by other means."[16] This was true enough in the eighteen-thirties, when Clausewitz published his famous treatise; and it continued to be true until 1945. Now,

idolatry.} These paragraphs draw on ideas already expressed by Huxley in his Santa Barbara lecture "More Nature in Art," *HS*, 31–32.

16 Carl von Clausewitz, *Vom Kriege* (Berlin, 1832) ['On War'], ch. 1, #24.

pretty obviously, nuclear weapons, long-range rockets, nerve gases, bacterial aerosols, and the "Laser" (that highly promising, latest addition to the world's military arsenals) have given the lie to Clausewitz. All-out war with modern weapons is no longer a continuation of previous policy; it is a complete and irreversible break with previous policy.

Power politics, nationalism, and dogmatic ideology are luxuries that the human race can no longer afford. Nor, as a species, can we afford the luxury of ignoring man's ecological situation. By shifting our attention from the now completely irrelevant and anachronistic politics of nationalism and military power to the problems of the human species and the still inchoate politics of human ecology we shall be killing two birds with one stone—reducing the threat of sudden destruction by scientific war and at the same time reducing the threat of more gradual biological disaster.[17]

The beginnings of ecological politics are to be found in the special services of the United Nations Organization. UNESCO, the Food and Agriculture Organization, the World Health Organization, the various Technical Aid Services—all these are, partially or completely, concerned with the ecological problems of the human species. In a world where political problems are thought of and worked upon within a frame of reference whose coordinates are nationalism and military power, these ecology-oriented organizations are regarded as peripheral. If the problems of humanity could be thought about and acted upon within a frame of reference that has survival for the species, the well-being of individuals, and the actualization of man's desirable potentialities as its coordinates, these peripheral organizations would become central. The subordinate politics of survival, happiness, and personal fulfillment would take the place now occupied by the politics of power, ideology, nationalistic idolatry, and unrelieved misery.

In the process of reaching this kind of politics we shall find, no doubt, that we have done something, in President Wilson's prematurely optimistic words, "to make the world safe for democracy."

February 1963

[*The Politics of Ecology: The Question of Survival* (Santa Barbara: Center for the Study of Democratic Institutions, 1963), 7 pp.]

---

17 In ID there follows the concluding sentence of the essay: {In the process of reducing these twin threats we shall find, no doubt, that we have done something, in President Wilson's prematurely optimistic words, 'to make the world safe for democracy.'} Instead, P has the new paragraph {The beginnings [...] misery.}, before concluding in a similar way as ID.

James Sexton
(University of British Columbia)

Aldous Huxley's "Matter, Mind, and the Question of Survival" and Two Connected Essays

In the late afternoon of 10 May 1960, as Aldous Huxley stood on the podium at the University of California, Berkeley, before a huge audience to begin the 22nd Foerster Lecture at Berkeley on his topic "Matter, Mind, and the Question of Survival," it is quite likely that he knew he would very soon have to confront the question of his own mortality, and before the month was over, he had taken action that he felt would prolong his increasingly lucrative public speaking career as a lecturer[1] and television pundit, but which would likely jeopardize his chances of *earthly* survival at least. We do not know whether Huxley was then aware that a malignant tumor had formed on the back of his tongue, but when, on 18 May 1960, he wrote to his son Matthew with news of his recent lecture tour, referring to his Berkeley lecture given the week before to "an overflow audience even more enthusiastic than at Lake Forest,"[2] he knew then that he had cancer but carefully kept the bad news from his son, because, as he told his friend, the physician William Kiskadden, in a letter dated 20 May 1960, "I don't want to worry anybody unnecessarily (including Matthew)" (*Letters*, 890). As his biographer Sybille Bedford puts it, "[r]adical surgery, which might have left him more or less speechless [...,] had been pressed on him as both urgent and inevitable" (Bedford, 262–263). Instead, on 31 May, he entered hospital under the assumed name of Matthew Leonard (see Bedford, 263) to undergo the less invasive treatment of radioactive needles recommended to him by the eminent surgeon and radiologist Dr. Max Cutler. The treatment temporarily kept the cancer at bay, but he had only a little more than three years left to live.

One tends to agree with Bedford, who says that his lectures are important because they "pull together so much of Aldous's thought" (272), and perhaps also because they provide a relatively clear point of entry into his more abstruse subjects such as "the immortality of the soul and other kindred topics," which were the terms of reference for the Foerster Lectures.[3] This lecture does, indeed, pull together ideas in which Huxley had long been interested. As early as 1931, in his play *The World of Light* (whose title he took from a poem by the seventeenth-century metaphysical poet Henry Vaughan), he explored topics which are usually considered ineffable and unscientific, such as spiritualism, and in an essay entitled "Science Turns to the Supernatural" (1934)[4] he continued to explore the boundaries between science and the supernatural. Here he first treated the ideas of James Esdaile, James Braid and other pioneers of hypnotic therapies, as well as those of J. B. Rhine and C. D. Broad, to whose ideas he returned in his 1954 essay "A Case for ESP, PK and PSI" (*CE*, V, 145–57) and in his 1960 lecture.[5] One might be dismissive, or one might be struck with the openness of mind with which he treats seriously subjects which many would label hocus-pocus, such as telepathy and clairvoyance, and which made him vulnerable to the charge of credulity levelled against him by some of his critics.

In his essay "Mind Reading," a Hearst essay published twenty-six years before his lecture at Berkeley, he wryly and characteristically tilts at the intolerant attitudes of "many excellent men of science," taking them to task for their treating "'supernormal' phenomena" in the same way "as Victorian spinsters reacted to Casanova's *Memoirs*."[6] Such phenomena are for them "the equivalent of indecent behavior; and they see in the literature of the subject a kind of scientific pornography" (*CE*, III, 165). In this lecture, given nearly thirty years later than the published essays quoted above, Huxley continues to criticize some of the "eminent men of science" such as Donald O. Hebb, who implicitly refuse to keep an open mind about such issues. Many readers, including this one, will be unable to share Huxley's position that "[t]he reality of telepathic communication was definitely established in the eighties of the last century," or his statement in reference to J. B. Rhine's research at Duke University, published in his book *Extra-Sensory Perception* (1934): "The result of the tests seems to leave no doubt as to the reality of telepathy on the one hand and clairvoyance on the other" (*CE*, III, 169). And perhaps he too easily accepts the accounts of mediums such as Mrs. Leonora Piper, who has been dismissed as a "'clever charlatan'" by science writer Martin Gardner.[7]

Perhaps more helpful are the ideas he here pulls together with a minimum of jargon about "undifferentiated consciousness," the nature of "personality," and his discussion of ideas contained in *The Tibetan Book of the Dead*, which he describes as "a kind of handbook for helping the dead person through the intermediate state between lives." Fifteen years earlier, he had described this intermediate state experienced by Uncle Eustace in a *tour de force* chapter in *Time Must Have a Stop*.

To document the continuity as well as consistent development of Huxley's pertinent thought, the two essays mentioned above have been included in this edition of "Matter, Mind, and the Question of Survival." In the case of the 1934 essay, the American version entitled "Science Views the Supernatural" (April and May 1935) has been chosen as copy-text, as it appears to be more complete and better edited than the British version. The 1954 essay has been collated with its original version published in *Life*, and the annotations for all three essays have been arranged and selected in such a way as to avoid repetitions.[8]

Unfortunately, the unedited transcript of the 1960 lecture, now held in UCLA Special Collections, is inaccurate in many places, but thanks to the availability of an MP3 tape of Huxley's talk in the public domain, it is now possible to publish the full text of this important lecture; see <http://www.language.berkeley.edu/SA_MP3files/SA0087/001_1.mp3>.

---

1 Huxley maintained a hectic pace as public lecturer and guest speaker on numerous television shows at the time. Shortly after he recovered from his radium-needle treatment, he was paid $ 9,000 for giving seven public lectures in the fall of 1960 as Carnegie Visiting Professor; see Sybille Bedford, *Aldous Huxley: A Biography* (2 vols., London, 1973–74), II, 264.

2 *Letters of Aldous Huxley*, ed. Grover Smith (London, 1969) [hereafter, *Letters*], 889.

3 See <https://gradlectures.berkeley.edu/series/foerster/>.

4 See *Complete Essays of Aldous Huxley*, ed. Robert Baker and James Sexton (6 vols., Chicago, 2000–02) [hereafter, *CE*], III, 167–79.

5 In this context it is of particular interest that Huxley also read Broad's own Foerster lecture on "Human Personality, and the Question of the Possibility of Its Survival of Bodily Death" (1954), see below, 173, note 24.

6 It is noteworthy that Huxley here uses the label 'supernormal' for such phenomena and not 'supernatural' as in the title of his 1934 essay—as a matter of fact, in the text of that essay he does not employ 'supernatural' either but speaks throughout of 'supernormal' phenomena. Even more significantly, in his 1954 essay on ESP he throughout substitutes 'paranormal' for 'supernormal.'

7 Harvey J. Irwin and Caroline A. Watt, *An Introduction to Parapsychology* (Jefferson, NC, 2007), 19.

8 I wish to especially thank Dr Gerhard Wagner for this new arrangement and for proofreading all three essays.

Aldous Huxley

SCIENCE VIEWS THE SUPERNATURAL (1934)[1] – I

Huxley is a famous name in English letters and science. Those who have borne it have been gifted with brilliant, inquiring minds, and Aldous Huxley is no exception. He is perhaps best known in this country as author of Antic Hay *and* Point Counterpoint.

What we now call supernormal phenomena show and have always shown a remarkable uniformity throughout the world. Thus, reports of fire walking come from Fiji, from India, from Japan, from Bulgaria. Every literature contains accounts of apparitions of the dying and the newly dead, stories of hauntings, of prevision, of second sight. Poltergeists always behave in the same way, as though obeying the laws of some mysterious code of ghostly bad manners. The adepts of almost all religions have been credited with extraordinary powers over matter; we are told that they can move objects at a distance, can raise themselves into the air, can produce extensive alterations in their own bodies. And so on.

The imagination is capable of such extravagant flights that the fact of a persistent uniformity is significant; it shows that there is some limiting factor that compels it to take the particular course it has taken and no other. Thus, the uniformity which we find in the myths of the world seems to be due to the similarity of human desires and human processes of thought. Myths are wish fulfillments and explanatory philosophies. But as wishes are everywhere much the same and as simple minds cannot help inventing similar explanations for what goes on in the world, it follows that all mythologies bear a strong family resemblance one to another.

With the phenomena we call supernormal the case is rather different. Here we are dealing not with tales about the gods but with what are reputed to be facts of human experience. That the gods (or the demons or the spirits of the dead) are somehow responsible is of course assumed by almost all of those who recorded these supernormal phenomena in the past and by many who record them at the present time. But this is merely an explanation after the event. The event itself, if any event it really is, remains purely human and mundane; therefore, unlike the events recorded in myths, susceptible of scientific investigation.

[1] The editor wishes to thank the Aldous and Laura Huxley Literary Trust for permission to re-publish this essay.

Of the earlier efforts at such investigation it is unnecessary to speak. Inquirers like Glanvill[2] in the seventeenth century did good work; but their notion of what constituted acceptable evidence was not, by modern standards, satisfactory. For our present purposes it may be said that the scientific investigation of the supernormal began in 1882, when the Society for Psychical Research [S.P.R.] was founded by F. W. H. Myers[3] and Henry Sidgwick.[4]

More than fifty years have passed since then, and the thick volumes of the Society's proceedings testify to the amount of work that has been done. Moreover, the work, as anyone who reads even a few of these many thousands of pages soon realizes, has always been careful, the evidence critically selected and of good quality.

Much fraud has been exposed, much irrelevant matter set aside. But these results, though excellent, are negative. What we are interested to know is whether this half century of patient research has had any positive result. In a word, what facts have been established? And, secondly, what is the significance of the facts, if facts they are? How can they be worked into the existing scientific world-picture?

The reality of at least one class of supernormal phenomena has been demonstrated, it seems to me, beyond all reasonable doubt. Cryptesthesia, as Richet[5] calls it, includes telepathy or thought transference, clairvoyance, psychometry, water divining, and all other forms of abnormal perception not passing through the ordinary channels of the senses.

II

Within the limits of this article I can do no more than briefly refer to the evidence for only one of them—telepathy. Telepathy is either spontaneous or deliberately induced, and the evidence for its existence is drawn from well-authenticated records of its random occurrence and from experiments carried out by investigators working with specially gifted subjects. In cases

---

2 Joseph Glanvill (1636–1680). Author of *The Vanity of Dogmatizing* (1661). Defended the reality of ghosts and witchcraft.

3 F(rederic) W(illiam) H(enry) Myers (1843–1901). Poet, critic, author. Huxley wrote the foreword to a 1961 reprint of his classic *Human Personality and Its Survival of Bodily Death* (1903).

4 Henry Sidgwick (1838–1900). Philosopher and first president of the S.P.R.

5 Charles Richet (1850–1935). French physiologist; winner of the 1913 Nobel Prize.

of spontaneous telepathy the percipient frequently receives his message in the form of an hallucinatory image of the transmitter.

It is to be noted in passing that the transmitter is often able, apparently, to transmit without being conscious of the fact that he is transmitting. Conversely, the transmitter may make violent conscious efforts to send his message to a given percipient, without the smallest result. In the combination of transmitter and percipient, the important person is the percipient. If his sensitivity is insufficient or if his state of mind is unfavorable to reception, nothing will be perceived.

The Society for Psychical Research has collected a great deal of evidence about hallucinations having reference to the dying. That apparitions of the dying may appear to their friends at a distance is an ancient and universal belief. As the chances of a given person dying on a given day are known (the odds against any particular date are about nineteen thousand to one), it is easy to calculate what proportion of deathbed hallucinations may legitimately be put down to mere coincidence.

An examination of three hundred fifty authenticated cases showed that thirty corresponded with the death of the person perceived, a figure hundreds of times higher than that which could be accounted for on the basis of simple probability.

Experiments in deliberate telepathy have been numerous. The most recent and successful are those recorded by an American psychologist, Dr. J. B. Rhine,[6] in his book *Extra-Sensory Perception*, published this year by the Boston Society for Psychical Research. Dr. Rhine made his tests with cards. In some cases these were first seen by the transmitter, and the percipient derived his extra-sensory knowledge of them from the transmitter's mind. In other cases the cards were not looked at, there was no thought transference, and the percipient was expected to 'see' them directly.

The result of the tests seems to leave no doubt as to the reality of telepathy on the one hand and clairvoyance on the other. Dr. Rhine found among students of Duke University a number of suitable subjects. None of them, however, seems to have been as highly gifted as those telepathists of genius who occasionally make their astonishing appearance among us. To work with one of these exceptionally gifted persons is an extraordinary and even rather disquieting experience. Of the nature of thought transference

---

[6] J(oseph) B(anks) Rhine (1895–1980). American botanist and parapsychologist; co-founder of Duke University's Parapsychology Laboratory. [*Forum* editor's note: See "Are We 'Psychic' Beings?" December Forum; "The Practical Side of Psychism," January Forum; "After Death—What?" *February Forum.*]

we are ignorant. All we can be sure of is that it is not a form of wireless. It seems to be a purely mental phenomenon.

The reality of cryptesthesia in its various forms may, I think, be regarded as established. (Water divining is regarded as so unquestionably a reality that landed proprietors, business firms, and even government departments will pay money to dowsers, in the confident belief that they are making sound investments.)

When we come to what are called the physical phenomena, we find ourselves on unsafer ground. The question that confronts us is this: How far are human beings able to affect matter directly, by means of their minds? For purposes of this investigation, matter must be divided up into three classes—matter included in the subject's own body, matter in the bodies of other human beings, and the matter of which the rest of the world, animate and inanimate, is made up.

In the past it was supposed that mind affected the matter of its body only in a few easily defined ways—as when, for example, mind willed that the hand should be lifted and the muscles duly performed the act. But recently the psychologists have made it clear that the influence of mind over its body is much greater than was supposed a couple of generations ago. There seems to be no doubt now that the symptoms of most diseases can be produced by the mind—that we are ill, in many cases, because, for some obscure and unrealized reason, we want to be ill. At one time it was thought that only functional diseases could be produced by the mind.

But inasmuch as derangement of function produces a corresponding derangement of the organs involved, it is now seen that the mind can actually produce organic disease. Moreover, it has been shown that, if you suggest to a man under deep hypnosis that (for example) the piece of stamp paper you are sticking to his hand is not stamp paper but a blister plaster, a blister will actually rise at the spot. The *Malade Imaginaire*[7] turns out to be really and physically ill. It will thus be seen that the 'supernormal' action of a mind on the matter of its body differs from its 'normal' action not in kind but only in degree.

That saints should receive the stigmata is a mysterious and astonishing fact but not much more mysterious, not more astonishing than that doctors should be able to raise blisters on their patients by means of suggestion and that the patients should be able by some process of subconscious autosuggestion to endow themselves with practically all the ills, outside a few

---

7 Compare Molière's comedy-ballet *Le malade imaginaire* (1673), translated into English as *The Imaginary Invalid.*

infectious diseases, that flesh is heir to. If the accounts of certain supernormal physical phenomena are true, then the mind's capacity to affect its body is even greater than the modern psychologist supposes it to be.

But are they true? To review all the evidence would be impossible. I will confine myself to a few brief comments on the curious phenomenon of fire walking.

III

Fire walking, as I have remarked before, is a rite practiced in almost every part of the world by peoples as widely different in race and culture as the Hindus, the Japanese, and the Maoris. These rites have frequently been witnessed by competent European observers, many of whom actually followed the native worshipers across the expanse of red-hot stones or burning charcoal prepared for the celebration of the ritual.

Andrew Lang[8] collected several reports of fire walking and published them in the fifteenth volume of the *Proceedings of the S.P.R.;* and this year, in *The Listener,* several more recent cases were described and illustrated with photographs. After reading these accounts, one is forced to believe that certain people are able by some unexplained mental process to immunize their bodies against the effects of intense heat. But this is not all. The rank and file of the native worshipers and the European observers are able to walk unscathed through the fire because they are in some way under the protection of the priestly organizers of the rite.

Yet more remarkable is the fact that, according to several of the accounts, the immunity to heat is extended not only to other human bodies but also to inanimate matter. Trailing garments belonging to the fire walkers are not scorched, though the heat of the stones or charcoal is sufficient to cause a dry branch to burst into flame. If the accounts of fire walking are reliable, we have evidence that certain minds can cause altogether abnormal modifications in all of the three classes of matter—the matter composing the bodies that belong to these minds, the matter of other human bodies, and the matter of which the rest of the world is formed.

I have selected fire walking as my main example of a supernormal physical phenomenon for the good reason that it is an event about which it is very difficult to make involuntary mistakes. A man who says he has walked over glowing charcoal so hot that a dry branch brought into contact with it bursts into flame is either speaking the truth or telling a lie. There is almost no psychological possibility of his merely thinking that he walked

[8] Andrew Lang (1844–1912). British man of letters; editor of Homer.

over something which he merely inferred to be hot. Fire walking has one great advantage over almost all other manifestations of supernormal physical phenomena: it is easy to observe and lends itself to unequivocal experimental test.

Most physical mediums refuse to work except in the dark or by a dim, red light, which, experiment shows, reveals practically nothing. I have attended a certain number of séances, and I can assert that, after sitting for half an hour in a dark and very stuffy room, listening to a gramophone playing the same tune over and over again, I am not prepared to accept even my own testimony of what occurs. I know that, in these circumstances, I shall almost certainly observe badly and remember inaccurately. The lamentable fallibility of human testimony has been demonstrated by many psychologists, and a few years ago experiments were carried out by the S.P.R. to test the reliability of trained and untrained observers in the séance room.

The results, published in the fortieth volume of the Society's proceedings, are really appalling. When the test was over, sitters were asked to answer in writing a series of simple questions about what had actually occurred during the half-hour of the séance. The examination papers were marked by the person who had arranged the details of the test. Out of a possible total of 100 the highest recorded marks were 61, the lowest 6, the average 34. The mistakes made were not merely mistakes of omission; several observers described remarkable phenomena which had never occurred at all. Thus, some of them declared that they had seen colored lights, others that they had heard raps. There were no raps, and except for some dabs of luminous paint, no lights.

These experiments show that it is really a complete waste of time to attend or read about any séance at which the supposed physical phenomena are not automatically recorded by fraud- and fool-proof instruments and at which the medium is not under complete control. Up to date very few properly controlled experiments with physical mediums have ever been made. One medium appears to have demonstrated his ability to interrupt a beam of infrared light passing between two points beyond his normal reach; and another medium has, in daylight and under laboratory conditions, caused pendulums enclosed in a glass case to vibrate. For the rest, we must be content to suspend judgment.

Hauntings are psychical phenomena that occur spontaneously and do not require the intervention of a medium. There is some tolerably good evidence for the ancient belief that in certain places noises and apparitions may be persistently heard and seen.

Poltergeists—those imps of mischief that delight in petty destruction—occupy an intermediate position between hauntings and the physical phenomena directly due to mediums. It is a fact of observation that the apparently supernormal smashing of crockery and furniture, characteristic of poltergeist activity, is almost invariably associated with a young person, generally a girl and often rather feeble-minded, of about the age of puberty.

IV

We now come to the problem of survival after death—or, to be more accurate, to the problem of communication between the dead and the living. For, of course, there is nothing illogical in the belief (it is that of all orthodox Christians) that souls survive bodily death but are not able to communicate with the living. Survival cannot be directly observed; it is a working hypothesis used to explain other phenomena. We regard a scientific hypothesis as 'true' if it explains the greatest possible number of facts in the simplest possible way.

Thus, many people believe that the observed facts of 'cross correspondence' between messages received by several automatic writers working independently is most simply explained on the hypothesis that a disembodied spirit is dictating to the various mediums disconnected fragments, which when put together reveal the existence of an intelligible literary whole. Others, on the contrary, think that such phenomena are most economically explained in terms of telepathy between living minds. Both hypotheses involve their supporters in considerable difficulties.

If there is survival, what is it that survives? The soul, comes the prompt reply. But what precisely is the soul? For the ancients the disembodied soul was a poor, miserable entity condemned, when deprived by death of its material instrument, to lead an ineffective existence in the dimmest of hereafters. This Homeric soul bears a close resemblance to what one of the acutest of contemporary philosophers, Professor Broad,[9] calls the "psychic factor"—a certain intangible something which, in conjunction with matter, constitutes the mind and which, when separated from matter, may preserve certain mental qualities but remains inferior to mind.

The Christians regarded the soul as immortal; but they insisted that, after the Second Coming, it would once more be associated with matter. "As the soul separated from the body is naturally imperfect, the consummation of its happiness, replete with every good, seems to demand the resurrection of

---

[9] C(harlie) D(unbar) Broad (1887–1971). British philosopher who wrote on the philosophical aspects of psychical research.

the body." So writes a modern Catholic theologian, Father Maas, S. J.[10] Like the Catholics, most Protestants profess to believe in this resurrection.

But it is worthy of note that the doctrine has now become extremely unfashionable and that many Christians who think themselves orthodox tend more and more to fall into the Manichaean and Albigensian heresy of regarding the future life as wholly immaterial. Many spiritualists, on the other hand, seem to think that, at death, the departed soul makes use of some form of attenuated matter. (See the description of the next world in Sir Oliver Lodge's *Raymond.*[11])

The view that survival is purely spiritual seems to find some support in the fact that the spirits (for I assume for the sake of argument that the entities that manifest themselves at séances are spirits) reveal themselves in most cases as being distinctly inferior in mental capacity to the living men and women they once inhabited. If the soul is what Homer, Professor Broad, and, with qualifications, even orthodox Christians imagine it to be—a thing which can attain perfection only in conjunction with a body—this decline of power after death is precisely what we should expect.

SCIENCE VIEWS THE SUPERNATURAL – II

Like all the sciences whose subject is man, psychical research can make practically no use of experiment. It is an observational and statistical science. Its aim is by careful and persistent 'field work' to provide a body of material sufficiently reliable to secure conviction that the phenomena investigated actually occur and sufficiently large to justify the psychist in making those generalizations which are called scientific 'laws.' How far has this aim been achieved?

We are justified in saying, I think, that psychical research has demonstrated the reality of at least some of the phenomena investigated. But as for generalizations, as for hypotheses satisfactory in themselves and compatible with the hypotheses of other sciences—for these we look in vain. Psychical researchers are still in the mental world of the egg collector and the naturalist, the world of irrational, brute fact, unorganized by the explaining intellect. No scientific philosopher has yet systematized the results of psychical research. Confronted by what are probably the facts, one can only

10 Anthony John Maas (1858–1927). American Professor of Scripture and noted Catholic exegete. The above quotation is ascribed to A. J. Maas (1911) in <http://www.newadvent.org/cathen/12792a.htm>.

11 Sir Oliver Lodge (1851–1940). British physicist.

throw out random reflections and speculations. Here are some of those which have occurred to me.

Orthodox men of science object to psychical research on the ground that its phenomena cannot be produced at will by anyone, at any time, and in any place. Indeed, they almost go so far as to assume that the phenomena cannot be credible because they are so rare. But this is an absurd attitude. The phenomena of musical genius cannot be investigated by anyone, anywhere, and at any time, for the good reason that Mozarts and Beethovens are not born every day of the week. And yet, in spite of its rarity, musical genius does exist and can, in favorable circumstances, be studied.

The capacity to produce supernormal phenomena appears to be a special gift like the gift for mathematics or music. But it is a gift that humanity has not yet learned systematically to exploit. Sir Isaac Newton was born in A.D. 1642; but there seems to be no biological reason why he should not have been born in 1642 B.C.

When Stonehenge was new, man was no less characteristically man than he is today. We have our deficients, our normals, our people of great ability, our men of genius. So, it is to be presumed, did the societies of antiquity. But now let us ask a question. Suppose Newton had been born in 1642 B.C. —what would he have achieved? The answer is: next to nothing.

In the England of 1642 B.C. there was no writing, no system of mathematical notation, no calculating instrument, such as the abacus of classical antiquity and the contemporary East. Born into such a world, the gifted mathematician would find himself unable to make use of his gifts. At times, no doubt, he would feel uncomfortably stirring within him the consciousness that there was something he could do—something wonderful and extraordinary; but what? In the forests and swamps of prehistoric England he would find no answer to his questions.

Mathematical geniuses, we may be sure, were born from time to time in that primitive England. But either they accomplished nothing, or else their natural gift exhausted itself in the discovery, enormous in the unpropitious circumstances, of some elementary piece of applied geometry or arithmetic. It was not till a long series of such mute, inglorious Newtons had gradually built up first an empirical system of mensuration, then the beginnings of a generalized theory of rational mathematics, that the geniuses ceased to be ineffectual and became the great mathematicians of recorded history.

Today a good telepathist or psychometrist is probably in much the same position as a good mathematician or musician would have been at the time Stonehenge was built. His gifts may be great, but they are untrained; he practices an art without any traditions and of whose fundamental rules he is ignorant. The remarkable thing is not that there should be so few psychically gifted individuals putting up such uncertain performances but rather that there should be as many as there are and that they should achieve as much as they do.

II

At this point a question inevitably suggests itself. If supernormal faculties are latent in the human mind, why is it that they have never been fully developed? Why are most of us still only potential telepathists and psychometrists? Why, if prevision is possible, has the power to look into the future remained in its present rudimentary state? We may suggest two possible explanations—a biological explanation and an explanation in purely psychological terms. We will assume for the sake of argument that mind can apprehend and influence external reality in two ways—directly, by what we now call supernormal means, and indirectly, by means of the sense organs, for perception, and of the nerves and muscles, for action. We will also assume that time is so constituted that the future has some kind of existence even 'before it happens' and that the mind can be so directed that this future is perceptible.

In all animals evolution has developed the second or indirect method of perception and action—presumably because it is the more efficient of the two. It has also orientated the mind in such a way that, in ordinary circumstances, there can be no consciousness of the future. This evolutionary process has gone very far among the higher animals, especially man. Our minds have become almost completely impervious to the future and at the same time extraordinarily efficient at perceiving things by means of the sense organs and at acting upon them by means of the nervous and muscular systems.

But capacity for extrasensory perception and direct action by the mind on matter must be regarded as still persisting, at any rate in a rudimentary state. It is a capacity that might, no doubt, be developed. That we have not developed it is due, perhaps, to the fact that it would not be biologically expedient for us to do so. Our organisms being what they are, it is quite possible that a well-developed power to pick up the thoughts of other minds would be not an advantage but a handicap. A society of highly trained telepathists would be a society in which no mental privacy was possible. But without mental privacy the individual as we know him could not exist. The development of direct perception would create entirely novel conditions, to which the species would certainly find it hard to adjust itself.

Foreknowledge of the future would be even more fatal; for it would probably induce an attitude of fatalistic resignation wholly incompatible with successful living. (It is significant in this connection that almost all the prophetic dreams recorded in Mr. Dunne's[12] remarkable book, *An Experiment with Time,* should concern events of the most trivial nature. It almost looks as though the mind were deliberately protecting itself against too much knowledge of coming events.)

Such, I suggest, are the biological reasons why the supernormal faculties have remained undeveloped. But there are also psychological reasons. Our civilization makes ever-increasing demands upon the conscious mind and its powers of logical analysis. But "it may be suspected," says Dr. T. W. Mitchell,[13] one of the most experienced of psychical research workers, "that mental dissociation is an indispensable prerequisite for the exhibition of supernormally acquired knowledge; and it may also be that some degree of mental dissociation is necessary for any knowledge to be so acquired."[14] Professor Rhine and other workers confirm this view.

Supernormal faculties seem to manifest themselves only when the conscious mind has to some extent been put out of action, when the powers of analysis are in abeyance. In other words, there is a certain incompatibility between the mental activity that makes for civilization as we know it and the mental activity that results in extrasensory perception, prevision, and the supernormal influence of mind on matter. There are psychic geniuses just as there are musical and mathematical geniuses. But whereas society rewards the composer and the geometer, it has, until quite recently, consistently persecuted the psychic, who was supposed to be in league with the powers of evil.

Psychic ability may be heritable and run in families. If this is so, the total amount of such ability in any European population must have been greatly reduced as a result of the persecutions of the witches. It has been suggested that the smiling skepticism of the eighteenth century towards the supernormal was due to the fact that it was a time when psychically gifted individuals were exceptionally rare. The people who would have been their

12 J(ohn) W(illiam) Dunne (1875–1949). Philosopher of time. His theories influenced Huxley and J. B. Priestley.

13 T(homas) W(alker) Mitchell (1869–1944). British physician who wrote on medical psychology and psychopathology. He studied cases of hypnosis and somnambulism.

14 A search for the precise source of the quotation showed no result, but in his article "Psychopathology and Psychic Research," *The Psychic Research Quarterly*, 1 (1920–21), 54–68, Mitchell discussed "supernormally acquired knowledge" at length.

ancestors had all been hanged or drowned or burned in the previous centuries. Voltaire and his contemporaries denied the very existence of the supernormal; and at that particular moment of history their denial was almost justified by the facts. Cessation of persecution has doubtless given the psychic strains an opportunity to reconstitute themselves.

III

It would seem then that there are adequate biological and psychological reasons why supernormal faculties have not been developed. The exponents of the Indian yoga psychology affirm that there are good ethical reasons why they *ought* not to be developed. The yogis have been working on their system of spiritual training for at least twenty centuries, and there can be no doubt that they have accumulated in this long span of time an immense mass of empirical knowledge about the workings of the mind, its potentialities, its relations with the body on the one hand and the *purusha* or spirit on the other.

The aim of yoga is to enable the individual to pass at will into the state of contemplation, and the way to this state lies through the acquisition of complete control, by means of long and arduous exercises, of all the mental processes. At a certain moment in his progress towards the ultimate state of blessedness the aspirant (so the yoga psychologists affirm) finds himself acquiring the power to produce all manner of supernormal phenomena. The exercise of this power is delightful; but the aspirant is solemnly warned against it. His goal is contemplation; the power of wonder working is only a halfway house. True, this halfway house offers all kinds of pleasant entertainment; but, if he succumbs to its charms and, instead of pushing on towards the final goal, remains a mere wonder worker, he is spiritually lost. In the eyes of the yogi psychologists, systematic cultivation of the supernormal powers is apparently a form of self-destroying self-indulgence. This Indian judgment, based as it is upon so long an experience, deserves the most respectful consideration.

Science is primarily concerned with facts and their explanation, not with ethical values. The systematic cultivation of supernormal faculties may be morally undesirable; but that does nothing to lessen the importance for science of supernormal phenomena. Hitherto psychical research has been carried out on a small scale and in the teeth of official scientific disapproval. It is greatly to be hoped that the scope of the investigations may now be extended.

For intensive research into the supernormal may be expected to throw light on some of the more obscure and the most important of our unsolved problems—on the nature of mind and its limitations; on the relations between individual minds and their bodies, the material world and other minds; on the nature of time and of our knowledge of it. These are matters of the highest scientific and philosophical importance; and the relevance of supernormal phenomena to all of them is manifest. A prima-facie case for the reality of at least some supernormal phenomena has now been firmly established; there is every possible reason why official science should make use of its resources to carry the investigation further.

In spite of which, it may be doubted whether official science will at present do anything of the kind. The subject is a disquieting one, and men, even men of science, do not like being disquieted. Moreover, the facts, if they came to be firmly established, could not be easily fitted into the existing world picture; long-cherished opinions would have to be dropped, current hypotheses stretched and altered. Men, even men of science, do not enjoy revolutionary changes.

IV

Let us consider, in this connection, the history of hypnotism in England. Mesmerism,[15] as it was always called before 1841, was violently denounced by the official representatives of English medical science. Their arguments were, first, that the phenomena did not take place and, second, that if they did take place they were quite unimportant. Thus, when Dr. Elliotson[16] (the man to whom Thackeray dedicated *Pendennis*) published an account of operations painlessly performed under the influence of hypnotism, his colleagues retorted by saying that he was a liar or, if not a liar, then a poor, credulous fool deceived by cunning patients who had merely pretended that they did not feel any pain while their legs were being cut off.

Finally, they admitted that he might be neither a liar nor a fool but insisted that it really didn't matter whether patients felt pain or not; nay, more, that pain was a very good thing and that patients ought to be made to feel as much of it as possible. Meanwhile, in 1841, Dr. Braid,[17] of Manchester, had invented the word "hypnotism" and propounded the

[15] Mesmerism. Therapeutic technique of Franz Mesmer (1734–1815).

[16] John Elliotson (1791–1868). British physician. According to Huxley in his essay "Morals in 1837" (1937), *Complete Essays of Aldous Huxley*, ed. Robert Baker and James Sexton (6 vols., Chicago, 2000–02) [hereafter, *CE*], VI, 365–71, the first English doctor to use the stethoscope and the first man in nineteenth-century England to wear a beard.

[17] James Braid (1795–1860). British surgeon.

psychological theory of its causation which is still accepted. And from 1845 to 1847 Esdaile,[18] in Calcutta, was developing a regular technique of hypnotic anesthesia for surgery. In two years Esdaile performed 260 operations on patients in the hypnotic trance, with a death rate of only 5 ½ per cent, a figure astonishingly low in the days before surgery was aseptic or even antiseptic. Then in the year 1848 there occurred two events which were fatal to hypnotism.

In Hydesville, New York, the Fox sisters[19] started to crack their toe joints; modern spiritualism was born. And chloroform, discovered some years before, began to be regularly used in surgical practice. Hypnotism fell into disrepute because it came to be associated with the new hocus-pocus; and at the same time its most obvious practical function—the production of anesthesia—was usurped by a drug. Chloroform was easier to use than hypnosis, and doctors naturally followed the line of least resistance.

It is interesting to speculate on what might have happened if the invention of chloroform had been delayed by another twenty years or so. There can be little doubt that Esdaile's example would have been widely followed. Doctors would have carried out intensive research into the possibilities of hypnosis; and a rapid and infallible technique of psychological anesthesia would probably have been developed. In the process of perfecting this technique much valuable information about the nature of the mind and its relation to the body would certainly have been made available—information which, for lack of a sufficient practical motive for research, either was not unearthed till much later or still remains to be discovered. But history decided against Esdaile and Braid. After 1848 hypnotism sank once more into disrepute, and it was not till 1892, just fifty-one years after Braid had done his classical work on the subject, that the British Medical Association at last officially admitted its existence and permitted its use. After 1892 doctors could practice hypnotism without running the risk of being hounded out of their profession.

Fifty-two years have now passed since Sidgwick and Myers founded the S.P.R., and the official representatives of English science still ignore the

---

18 James Esdaile (1808–1859). British surgeon and pioneer in the use of hypnosis for surgical anaesthesia. Huxley discusses his method of anaesthetic hypnotism in "A Case of Voluntary Ignorance" (1956), *CE*, VI, 59–68. He is the model for Dr. Andrew MacPhail in Huxley's utopian novel *Island* (1962).

19 Leah (1814–1890), Margaretta (1833–1893) and Catherine (1837–1892) Fox. They played a seminal role in the rise of spiritualism in the nineteenth century and were successful as mediums for a long time.

existence of psychical research. For how much longer will they persist in their present attitude?

If there is any value in historical analogies, we may expect a change to take place fairly soon. It took about thirty years for English doctors to accept the stethoscope; and it was, as we have seen, just over half a century before they admitted the respectability of hypnotism.

The supernormal phenomena with which psychical research deals are at least twice as odd as the noises heard through a stethoscope and perhaps twenty per cent odder than the results of hypnotism. If the length of time required for the official acceptance of a phenomenon is proportionate to its oddness, we may calculate that psychical research will be admitted to full citizenship in the kingdom of science some sixty years after its inception.

The first University Readership in Psychical Research should be founded, according to my computations, about the year 1942.

[*Forum and Century*, 93 (April 1935), 248–52; (May 1935), 308–11; in Britain this essay appeared under the title "Science Turns to the Supernatural," *Nash's Pall Mall Magazine* (December 1934), 12–13, 110–14. It was reprinted in *CE*, III, 167–79.]

Aldous Huxley

A Case for ESP, PK and Psi (1954)[1]

Mrs. A. woke up one morning during the war—the morning of Nov. 18—sobbing. "Jack is dead." Jack was her son, a soldier. Her husband, unable to calm her, called the family physician, who gave her a sedative. On the morning of Nov. 23, Mrs. A. again woke up crying. Again her husband was unable to calm her, and again the doctor prescribed a sedative. This time he also advised a psychiatrist. Before Mr. A. got to a psychiatrist, he and his wife received a letter Jack had written on Nov. 15, saying he was well. Mrs. A. still insisted that the boy was dead. That evening a telegram was delivered, reporting Jack's death on Nov. 17 in Hawaii. Mrs. A. said, "I knew it all the time, but you wouldn't believe me."

Here is another story, less tragic but, if anything, even odder. An English lady, Mrs. Atlay, the wife of the then Bishop of Hereford, dreamed one night that after reading the family morning prayers, she went into the dining room and saw an enormous pig between the table and the sideboard. The dream amused her and she told it, before prayers, to her children and their governess. After prayers she opened the dining room door and there was a pig exactly where she had dreamed it was. It had escaped from its sty while prayers were being read.

The first of these anecdotes is cited by Dr. Louisa Rhine[2] in *The Journal of Parapsychology*; the second one is told in the 11th volume of the *Proceedings of the Society for Psychical Research*.[3] Both have been vouched for by reliable witnesses, and there seems to be no good reason for doubting that the events actually occurred. How are they to be explained?

One answer, of course, is pure 'coincidence.' A mother dreamed that her son had died, and, as it happened, her son had died only a few hours before. A bishop's wife dreamed she saw a pig in her dining room, and a few hours later it happened that a pig came into her dining room and she saw it.

---

[1] The editor wishes to thank the Aldous and Laura Huxley Literary Trust for permission to publish this lecture.

[2] Louisa Ella Rhine (1891–1983). American botanist, but better known for her work in parapsychology, of which she was dubbed the first lady. She was the wife of J. B. Rhine.

[3] See Louisa E. Rhine, "Conviction and Associated Conditions in Spontaneous Cases," *Journal of Parapsychology*, 15.1 (1951), 164–191, here 171–72; see also *Proceedings of the Society for Psychical Research*, XI (London, 1895), 487.

Coincidences like these strike one as only moderately plausible. The alternative answer is more plausible but more disturbing: when the mother said that Jack was dead, she really *knew* Jack was dead. The bishop's wife actually could *see*, in her mind's eye, what was going to happen on the following morning.

If this hypothesis is correct, we must assume that human beings are endowed, at least potentially, with a paranormal—i.e., besides or beyond the normal—faculty. Modern research workers have given this faculty the blanket name of "psi" (the 23rd letter of the Greek alphabet) and have shown that it can manifest itself in a variety of ways—as telepathy, the direct awareness of events taking place in other people's minds; as clairvoyance, the direct awareness, with no help from sense impressions, of events taking place in the outside world; and as precognition, or foreknowledge, the direct awareness, apart from rational forecasting and logical inference, of future events. These are the three types of what is called extrasensory perception, or ESP.

But psi is not exclusively a form of knowing. There is some evidence that it is also a form of doing. There may be paranormal ways of action as well as paranormal ways of being aware.

Here, on the borderline between the normal and the paranormal, is a case reported by Dr. J. A. Hadfield,[4] an English psychiatrist who treated large numbers of shell-shock patients during and immediately after World War I. The doctor hypnotized a young sailor, Leading Seaman H. P., and then told him that his arm was being seared with a red-hot iron and that a blister would form at the point of contact. Actually Dr. Hadfield merely touched H. P. with his finger and bandaged the arm. When the bandage was removed six hours later, a small blister had formed. By the next day, Dr. Hadfield said, "there was a large quantity of fluid, giving the exact appearance of a blister produced by heat." The body had acted—with no physical reason for it to act.

From experimental medicine we pass to anthropology, specifically to a fire-walking rite in India observed by Mr. R. U. Sayce[5] in 1929. Some of the Indian participants had worn shoes all their lives and had feet as tender as the average Westerner's, but they walked over glowing ashes without being burned. They were followed by two Europeans. One got through with a

---

[4] J(ames) A(rthur) Hadfield (1882–1967). Pioneer of psychodynamic psychotherapy in Britain and believer in life after death and telepathy.

[5] See R. U. Sayce, "An Indian Firewalking Ceremony in Natal [South Africa]," *Man*, 33 (1933), 2–7.

few small blisters. The other European, whose attention was distracted by friends in the crowd, was badly burned.

It should be noted that fire walking in India is undertaken not for fun or as an experiment but for religious reasons. Perhaps the religious motive creates a kind of protective field within which the walker, if he remains confident and undistracted, finds himself safe.

Many persons who are prepared to accept the reality of ESP (extra-sensory perception) find it impossible to swallow PK, or psychokinesis, the direct action of mind on matter. Along with ESP, PK is the subject matter of modern parapsychology, which investigates these forms of doing and knowing with all the resources of contemporary science.

Perhaps the world's most distinguished parapsychologist is Dr. J. B. Rhine of Duke University, who for 25 years has been investigating psi in general and ESP and PK in particular. His latest book, published this winter, is called *New World of the Mind.* This new world, as he points out, is new only to modern science. To mankind at large it is as old as human experience. Prophets and oracles, ghosts and hauntings, poltergeists and apparitions, thought reading and second sight—we find them everywhere and at every period of history, in the Atomic Age and in the Bronze Age, in great cities and in the jungle and the tundra, among the most highly civilized as well as the most primitive of peoples. Up to about 1650 practically everyone in the Christian world accepted the reality of psi, and practically everyone attributed its manifestations to the intervention of supernatural agencies, in the main diabolic.

By the early 18th Century most educated people had begun to doubt the very existence of psi. Not all, however. Samuel Wesley[6] and his family, including the future founder of the Methodist Church, were besieged for more than a year by poltergeists, which are noisy ghosts. Swedenborg[7] based the whole of his elaborate theology on psi experiences and was believed by many of his contemporaries to have a genuine gift of clairvoyance.

Before the turn of the 19th Century, Mesmer and his followers discovered what we now call hypnosis and were investigating the properties, including psi, of what we now call the subconscious. Their work was fundamental to the development of modern psychology, but unfortunately Mesmerism, or animal magnetism as it was generally called, was appropriated by the cult

[6] Samuel Wesley (1662–1735). Clergyman of the Church of England, poet and writer. He was the father of John Wesley, the founder of Methodism.

[7] Emanuel Swedenborg (1688–1772). Swedish theologian, scientist, philosopher and mystic. His book on the afterlife, *De coelo et eius mirabilibus, et de inferno* (*Heaven and Hell*), appeared in 1758.

of Spiritualism, which burst upon the world in the 1840s. A scientific discipline was engulfed in a form of revivalism and came, in the popular mind, to be largely identified with it. As a result, for many years no British physician could use hypnotism without running the risk of being expelled from the British Medical Association. And not only hypnotism but psi phenomena in general were for decades the special reserve of a fringe commonly regarded as lunatic.

72 years of research

This situation came to an end in 1882 when a group of eminent men from the English academic world came together and, in the teeth of orthodox science and orthodox spiritualism, founded the Society for Psychical Research. Its journal, now in its 72nd year of publication, contains records of a prodigious quantity of careful work in the field of parapsychology. Hardly anybody bothers to read these records or the records of the similar societies in the U.S. and on the continent of Europe. This, I think, is a great misfortune. Nowadays, of course, for most people it goes without proving that mental events are caused by physical events, that they are indeed merely aspects of physical events. If this is the case, the incidents recorded in the proceedings of the S.P.R. cannot have taken place and it is only a waste of time to look at the evidence.

Another reason for the neglect, especially in academic quarters, of parapsychology is that much of the early evidence was biographical or anecdotal. It is not the sort of evidence by which one validates a scientific hypothesis. It relates, that is to say, to unique unrepeatable incidents in which psi was manifested in a particularly striking and dramatic manner. Now, unique, unrepeatable events are the very substance of human experience; but they are not, and they cannot be, the substance of a science, for science is (to borrow a phrase from Émile Meyerson[8]) the systematic "reduction of diversity to identity."[9] In human life unique and unrepeatable events are of cardinal importance. When we try to reduce men's diversities to identities, we run the risk of gross oversimplification in theory and the even worse risk of totalitarian dictatorship in practice.

We had better admit, then, that there will probably never be a completely adequate Science of Man. There are all sorts of useful partial sciences,

---

[8] Émile Meyerson (1859–1933). Polish-born French chemist, epistemologist and philosopher of science.

[9] Huxley refers at length to Meyerson in *Ends and Means* (London,1937), 11–12; he paraphrases him, for instance, as follows: "Science is [...] the effort to reduce diversity to identity" (12).

dealing with generalities and averages—such as economics and actuarial statistics, sociology and comparative religion, and various brands of psychology. But there is no genuine anthropology, no full Science of Man, in which the uniqueness of human beings takes its place along with their likeness, the irreducible diversities along with the unities. The art of living is still an art and is likely to remain one indefinitely.

The early investigators of psi collected a great mass of anecdotal material and published as much of it as could stand up to a searching examination. Juries are prepared, in good conscience, to send men to the gallows on less convincing evidence. And historians stoutly maintain the reality of past events for which the evidence is incomparably worse.

A second phase in the history of psi research began in 1930 with the foundation of the parapsychology laboratory at Duke University under Dr. Rhine. It was he and his coworkers who first developed fully controlled experimental conditions and subjected all results to statistical appraisal. The work has not been especially spectacular and its results do not make particularly interesting reading, but it has achieved what no collecting of anecdotal material could achieve. It has established the case for psi on a basis too solid to be explained away.

The new methods are beautifully simple. To test ESP the people at Duke invented a deck of 25 cards. There are five kinds in the deck, each with a simple symbol: circle, square, star, cross and waves. A subject is asked to guess the order of the cards—purely by extrasensory perception. He is separated from the experimenter by an opaque screen, or he sits in another room, perhaps even in a distant building. Sometimes the experimenter turns up the card before the subject makes his call, other times he does not look at the cards until afterward.

To test PK, Dr. Rhine and his aides use dice. The subject wills that a certain combination of faces turn up. The dice are then thrown, often by machine. With both dice and cards more and more elaborate precautions are constantly being taken against unconscious cues, improper shuffling, faulty observation and the like. It is doubtful whether any psychological experiments have been carried out under conditions so stringent.

The results of these simple tests are recorded and analyzed by standard statistical procedures. Statistical analysis cannot, of course, tell us anything about the laboratory conditions or about the causes of the observed results. It can and does state a degree of probability. It can say that some results were very likely due to pure chance. In other cases it can rule out pure chance as rather improbable, very improbable or overwhelmingly improbable.

What your chances are

If you try to guess the order of the cards in Dr. Rhine's deck, your chance of guessing correctly is one in five. In any one short run you may do better or worse and it will not signify much. But the more runs or throws, the more nearly will your score come to the expected average. (This is the reason why Las Vegas and Monte Carlo are still in business.)

If, over a long series of runs or throws, the score deviates markedly and consistently from the expected average, the deviation is called "significant," another way of saying that it was probably not due to chance alone but to some other factor. In most scientific experiments, odds of 100 to 1 or better are considered significant, odds of a few thousand to 1 are regarded as equivalent to a proof that some other factor than pure chance has been present.

In psi research, as in every other field of human or animal endeavor, some subjects are better and some circumstances more favorable than others. In one card experiment carried out in London by a mathematician, Dr. S. G. Soal,[10] the subject, Mr. Basil Shackleton,[11] was remarkably gifted. In more than 11,000 trials, carried out under elaborately controlled conditions, Mr. Shackleton scored so high that the odds against the results' being due to chance alone were of the order of 1 to 10^{35} (100,000,000,000,000,000, 000,000,000,000,000,000). But if chance were out of the question (as it obviously was) and if all other 'normal' explanations were ruled out by the stringency of the experimental conditions (as they were), how could Mr. Shackleton have managed it? Only by some form of ESP.

The first reports of the Duke experiments made their appearance in the early and middle '30s. (Dr. Rhine's book, *Extra-Sensory Perception*, appeared in 1934.) Orthodox psychologists immediately questioned the soundness of the statistical methods used. This matter was quickly cleared up in 1937 at the annual meeting of the American Institute of Mathematical Statisticians, which reached these conclusions:

> Dr. Rhine's investigations have two aspects, experimental and statistical. On the experimental side, mathematicians of course have nothing to say. On the statistical side, however, recent mathematical work has established the fact that, assuming the experiments have been properly performed, the statistical analysis

---

[10] S(amuel) G(eorge) Soal (1889–1975). Besides being a mathematician he was also a parapsychologist.

[11] Basil Shackleton was a professional photographer interested in telepathy. Dr. Soal and he carried out their experiments in 1936 and 1943, see <https://www.survivalafterdeath.info/articles/mccreery/shackleton.htm>.

> is essentially valid. If the Rhine investigation is to be fairly attacked, it must be on other than statistical grounds.

The critics took the hint and proceeded to attack on other grounds—the experimental setup. It did not take long to clear up this point either. Much of the early work at Duke had been of a somewhat free and easy nature—an exploratory foray into unknown territory, not intended to provide conclusive evidence. Later on, however, every conceivable precaution was taken to rule out in advance any 'normal' explanation of the results. In 1938, at the annual meeting of the American Psychological Association, the experimenters gave an account of how they conducted their experiments. Even the most hostile critics had to admit that their precautions were satisfactory. "There has been," says Dr. Rhine, "very little criticism of any kind since the ESP symposium in 1938."

Very little criticism—but also, we must add, very little interest. In 1952 Dr. Lucien Warner framed a questionnaire on ESP[12] and sent it to 515 Fellows of the American Psychological Association. About one sixth of the 360 Fellows who bothered to reply were of the opinion that ESP was either an established fact or a likely one; but only 14 had done any personal experimentation in the field. Two thirds of all the scientists answering the questionnaire had never, by their own admission, read an original scientific paper on the subject. Most of these are convinced, in the words of Psychologist D. O. Hebb,[13] that "we have no choice but to physiologize psychology." Psi phenomena do not lend themselves to being physiologized. Therefore they do not exist. "Personally," writes Dr. Hebb, "I do not accept ESP for a moment, because it does not make sense. Rhine may still turn out to be right, improbable as I think that is; and my own rejection of his views is—in a literal sense—prejudice."[14]

That a man of science should allow prejudice to outweigh evidence seems strange enough. It is even stranger to find a psychologist rejecting a psychological discovery simply because it cannot be explained. Psi is intrinsically no more inexplicable than, say, perception or memory; it is merely less common. We do not have the faintest idea how certain chemical and electrical events in the brain make us aware of a rose as being pink and perfumed. Nor are we any less ignorant of the way in which a mind recalls

---

12 See "A Second Survey of Psychological Opinion on ESP," *Journal of Parapsychology*, 16 (1952), 284–95.

13 D(onald) O(lding) Hebb (1904–1985). Canadian psychologist who was deeply influential in the field of neuropsychology.

14 Huxley used the same quotes again in "Matter, Mind, and the Question of Survival," see below, 167 and 163, respectively.

events in the past, of why some events in the nervous system should reappear in consciousness while others do not.

And how can events in a mind affect the fall of dice? We cannot say. But can we say how events in the mind can raise a blister on the arm of a hypnotized sailor? Can we say what hypnotism is? The mental state of a hypnotized person is very different from that of the same person unhypnotized. As far as the brain's activity can be measured by an encephalogram, the states are just about the same. Does this "make sense"? Not much more than anything else in the fascinating and bewildering field of our human nature. To refuse to accept psi because it does not conform to a hypothesis which is admittedly incapable of explaining the facts even of our everyday experience seems, to say the least of it, a little captious.

A hundred years ago, when Biblical fundamentalism was wrestling with geology, Philip Gosse,[15] the British naturalist, found himself in a position not unlike that now occupied by the anti-psi psychologists. The geologists could prove that life had existed upon the earth for millions of years and that every existing plant and animal species had undergone far-reaching changes in the course of its evolution. But to Gosse, as to millions of other intelligent people, Genesis was literally true, and the instantaneous creation of the world in 4004 B.C. was an unassailable fact. The evidence of geology had to be ignored or explained away. Gosse chose the latter course. The earth, he still maintained, had been created in a single instant, but it had been created in its present form, with all the appearances of having slowly evolved. In other words, "God hid the fossils in the rocks in order to tempt geologists into infidelity."[16] Today, it would seem, God is hiding Mind in the ESP cards to tempt psychologists into infidelity toward another brand of fundamentalism—the faith in Universal Matter.

In 20 years, more heretics

This temptation is of considerable potency, even for the professional physiologizers of the soul and for the academicians generally. At least one great European university has established a Chair of Parapsychology. Others have accepted endowments for parapsychological research and teaching and have allowed young men and women in pursuit of their Ph.D.s to write their theses on parapsychological subjects. Last summer an International Conference on Parapsychology was held at the University of Utrecht in

[15] Philip Henry Gosse (1810–1888). Father of poet, author and critic Edmund Gosse (1849–1928).

[16] Edmund Gosse, *Father and Son: A Study of Two Temperaments* (London, 1907), 120.

Holland, and some 60 psychologists, psychiatrists, physicists, engineers, mathematicians and philosophers from 14 countries attended, exchanged views, listened to papers and laid plans for future investigations. The heretics are more numerous and more articulate than they were 20 years ago.

For those who do not wish to ignore it on *a priori* grounds, the evidence would seem to point to the following conclusions:

▶ Some people can become directly aware of events taking place in other people's minds.

▶ Some people can become directly aware of events taking place remotely from them.

▶ Some people can become aware of events, either mental or physical, which have not yet taken place.

▶ Some people can influence the behavior of matter with which they are not in contact.

If psi is a reality, what is its significance? How does it fit into our scheme of things? What does it mean to us as thinkers and as doers, as individuals and as members of society, as political and moral beings, as believers and disbelievers?

Let us start with thinking. One of the most eminent of living philosophers, Dr. C. D. Broad of Cambridge, has remarked on "the extraordinary indifference of almost all professional philosophers to the subject of psychical research." Natural scientists, he says, "are not to be blamed if they confine themselves to their subjects of investigation, provided they do not dogmatize ignorantly about what they have never investigated." No such excuse is open to philosophers. Their business is to understand the world as a whole and they have no right to ignore any aspect of it. Philosophers may answer that, after all, psi is only an anomaly, a queer little exception to the majestic rule. But this will not do. "The odd, exceptional inexplicable facts, however trivial in themselves, are always the point from which the next great and fundamental advances in human knowledge may be made," writes Dr. Broad. "It is for this reason that I, as a philosopher, attach so much importance to psychical research and deplore the indifference of my colleagues to the subject."[17]

There is as yet no satisfactory philosophical theory about psi. Perhaps William James[18] was on the right track when he suggested that we live

[17] C. D. Broad "Philosophy and Psychical Research," *The Listener* (28 March 1934), 511.

[18] William James (1842–1910). American philosopher and psychologist, brother of Henry James.

immersed, so to speak, in "a continuum of cosmic consciousness,"[19] a World Mind, a little of which filters into every particular brain and is experienced by the owner of that brain as his private mind, or consciousness. Henri Bergson[20] went a little further. Mind in itself, he said, is aware of everything, everywhere, without regard to space or time, but the function of our brains is to shut out most of this (to us, irrelevant) knowledge, just in the interests of biological efficiency. On this hypothesis, psi would represent a leakage into personal consciousness of some of the mental material which the brain normally either excludes or directs into utilitarian channels.

The Jekylls and Hydes of psychology

From philosophy we return to psychology. The oddest thing about the orthodox physiologizers of psychology is their dual personality. As academic Dr. Jekylls they believe that all mental events depend on physical events and can be explained in physical terms. As common-sense Mr. Hydes they know that their will is, to some extent, free and that practically all their effective thinking about themselves and other people is done in mental terms. Dr. J. B. Watson, the founder of Behaviorism, once proclaimed that "no Behaviorist had ever observed anything that he can call consciousness, sensation, perception, imagery or will."[21] But I would suppose that even Dr. Watson must have had moments of aberration when he made the appalling discovery that he was thinking, that he was making a moral choice or that he was remembering, with a wealth of that nonexistent imagery, the scenes of his childhood.

Most of our experiences are mental. The physiologizers of psychology regard this fact as dangerously "mystical" (a favorite word with them) and try to explain it away. They say we may think we are thinking, but what is *really* happening is something electrical, something reassuringly chemical. The electrical, chemical and physiological facts should, of course, be investigated. But they should be investigated with an open mind (if the physiologizers will pardon the expression). It is surely significant that no educator or psychiatrist in his senses would ever dream of considering his problems exclusively, or even mainly, in terms of physics and chemistry. Indeed, many

---

19 *Memories and Studies* (London, 1911), 204.

20 Henri Bergson (1859–1941). French philosopher, awarded the Nobel Prize in Literature (1927).

21 J. B. Watson, "Behaviorism," *Encyclopædia Britannica* (14th ed., New York, 1932), III, 327. J(ohn) B(roadus) Watson (1878–1958). Famous American psychologist.

doctors believe that only by psychologizing physiology can they find cures for those innumerable psychosomatic diseases that plague the 20th Century.

Psychiatrists are apparently more ready to accept psi than are academic psychologists. Of some 700 psychiatrists who replied to a recent questionnaire, more than 200 stated that they were familiar with the current research in parapsychology, twice that number thought such research should be continued and extended, and about 160 reported that they had observed what appeared to be psi phenomena in the course of their practice.

What does psi mean to biology? A good deal of anecdotal evidence suggests that the lower animals may possess psi. This evidence has recently been supplemented by systematic experimentation with homing pigeons, carried out between 1949 and 1952 by Dr. G. V. T. Matthews[22] in England and Dr. G. Kramer[23] in Germany. In Matthews' experiments young birds were trained to 'home' from one direction only, the north. When all the birds had homed at least twice from distances of about 100 miles due north, they were taken in lightproof boxes to a point 80 miles west of the loft. With almost no hesitation the birds started to fly east. On their next test they were taken to a release point 90 miles south of the loft. Most of them at once headed north.

Kramer's birds, who had never homed from more than 10 miles, were taken 200 miles away in lightproof boxes and released. Within a very short space of time (in some cases 10 seconds) most were flying toward home. Of 27 birds, with no previous experience of long-distance flights, 14 were back in the loft on the day of the release. Ten more arrived the following day. Only three were lost.

Pigeons on turntables

How does a pigeon know which direction to take? A number of physical and physiological hypotheses have been put forward. There is, for example, the kinesthetic hypothesis: the bird always knows where it is, thanks to the semicircular canals of its inner ear. Thanks to the same remarkable canals, it is also supposed to be aware of what is called the Coriolis force, the force that results from the revolution of the earth on its axis. The hypothesis is ingenious, but it has failed to stand up under experiment. Birds were divided into two groups, one of which traveled to the release point in stationary cages, the other in cages placed on turntables that revolved at changing

22 G(eoffrey) V(ernon) T(ownsend) Matthews (1923–2013). British ornithologist and conservationist.

23 Gustav Kramer (1910–1959). German zoologist and ornithologist.

speeds through the whole outward journey. The most stupendous imaginable semicircular canals could not tell a revolving pigeon where it was in relation to its loft or to the equator. Consequently the revolving pigeons ought, when released, to have lost their way. But they got home just as well as the nonrevolving pigeons.

Then there is the magnetic theory. This assumes that pigeons are sensitive to terrestrial magnetism. The birds find their way home by combining the assumed awareness of the Coriolis force with the assumed awareness of the earth's magnetic field, which is different at different points of the planet's surface. This hypothesis can also be tested experimentally. Once again the birds are divided into two groups. Small magnets are attached to the wings of one, nonmagnetized objects of equal weight to the wings of the other. The birds with magnets fly in a homemade field so strong that terrestrial magnetism could not possibly be detected, but they do not lose their way any more often than the others do.

Finally there is the hypothesis that pigeons navigate by the sun. If they do, they must possess, built into their nervous system, the equivalents of a chronometer, a sextant, navigational tables and a calculating machine for correlating the solar data observed at the release point with those observed at the loft. In Dr. Kramer's experiments the birds were given 30 seconds, after a nocturnal journey in the canvas-covered cages, to adapt themselves to light. They were then released. Within 10 seconds most of them were flying homeward. If they were using the sun to guide them, they must have made all their observations and calculations in 40 seconds. All in all, solar navigation seems just as untenable as the canal theory or the magnetic theory. How, then, do the pigeons find their way home? We do not know. All we can say is that psi seems a likely possibility. That possibility is now being tested in this country by Dr. J. G. Pratt,[24] Dr. Rhine's associate at Duke. Several zoologists have recently begun to consider psi as a possible explanation for the equally extraordinary and hitherto inexplicable performances of migratory birds and fish, as well as the well-known ability of cats to find their way home from long distances. In Dr. Rhine's own North Carolina is one, Fluffy, which took two years to find its way back over a 350-mile journey. One biologist, Professor A. C. Hardy of Oxford,[25] is prepared to go a step further and to consider psi as one of the factors, along with individual variation and environment, in animal evolution.

---

24 J(oseph) G(aither) Pratt (1910–1979). American psychologist who specialized in the field of parapsychology.

25 A(lister) C(lavering) Hardy (1896–1985). English marine biologist with a lifelong interest in spiritual phenomena.

In *New World of the Mind* Dr. Rhine has some interesting chapters on the significance of psi for religion and ethics. Psi research, he points out, has led "by the application of strict scientific method" to the conclusion that "there is something operative in man that transcends the laws of matter [...]. The universe differs, therefore, from what the prevailing materialistic concept indicates. It is one about which it is possible to be religious."[26]

It is interesting to read what an eminent Catholic theologian, Father Victor White, O.P.,[27] has to say on the subject of psi. Scholastic philosophy recognizes the existence of "natural prophecy"—in our vocabulary, psi—which is sometimes used as the vehicle of divine revelation. "It is through the sub-rational [the deep Unconscious] that the super-rational is brought into human consciousness," writes Father White, or, in other words, psi is of interest to theology because its source in the Unconscious is very close to the door through which divine inspiration enters the human mind. But psi is not always spiritually and ethically desirable, or even neutral: the anecdotal evidence indicates that there are sometimes inspirations of pure unreason and radical evil. That was why Plato would have no truck with what he called "enthusiasts"—what we should call psychics, sensitives, automatists. "Though Plato could expel the inspired and the possessed from the Republic, they can never," Father White insists, "be expelled from the Church, which is built on the foundations of the prophets and the apostles."[28]

We are supposed to be waging a crusade against the godless materialism of the Communists. In actual fact our prevailing world differs from theirs only in degree and consistency, not in kind. On both sides of the Iron Curtain the effective religion of 20th-Century man, the only faith for which all are prepared to kill and die, is nationalism. The last few centuries have witnessed a general retreat from the beginnings of universalist monotheism to a new version of the parochial polytheism current in classical times, when every city had its own tutelary deities. Our gods are not the gods of cities but of nations. Associated with the worship of the 57 varieties of national gods is a philosophy compounded of physicalism and cultural determinism,

---

26 J. B. Rhine, *New World of the Mind* (New York, 1953), 226–27; Rhine originally writes: "The conclusion is inescapable that there is something operative in man that transcends the laws of matter [...]. The universe, therefore, does not conform to the prevailing materialistic concept. It is one about which it is possible to be religious" (227).

27 Victor Francis White (1902–1960). English Dominican priest. He corresponded and even collaborated with C. G. Jung.

28 Victor White, *God and the Unconscious* (Chicago, 1953), 140.

seasoned, this side of the Iron Curtain, with a dash of Freud. In Russia, to be sure, this philosophy has been worked out more systematically and applied with a stricter logic than in the West. We have been saved—insofar as we have been saved—by our inconsistency.

Our philosophy has no place for free will or for anything which might be described as the soul. And yet, with a blessed absence of logic, we go on behaving as though we believe in the uniqueness, the paramount value of human personality. Habit and the fact that our fundamental institutions were framed by men who were firmly convinced of the existence of all the things that "no Behaviorist has ever observed" make it quite easy for us to think one way while acting in another, incompatible way. How much longer can we continue to perform this curious feat? One fine day some dangerously logical demagogue may ask us why, if men and women are merely the by-products of physical and social processes, they should not be treated as such. After which we may expect to see the fiction of George Orwell's *1984* turn into appalling fact.

In the immediate future the most urgent task confronting the psi researcher is to discover, if possible, some way of bringing psi into consciousness, of using it consciously and controlling it. We already know a good deal about the conditions favoring the manifestation of psi. Certain mental attitudes militate against high scoring; certain personality traits tend to be associated with success in one kind of test, other traits with success in other kinds of tests. Boredom and monotony are as bad for psi as for every other kind of work. Scoring rates tend to fall off toward the end of each run of 25 calls and toward the end of every long series of runs. Similar declines appear in tests for learning and memory. The regularity with which they appear in the records of psi testing is another powerful proof that the results are due to psychological causes.

All this knowledge is valuable, but it is still woefully insufficient. Somehow or other we must learn to catch psi on the wing, to track it to its lair deep in the unconscious. But how? We may never find out, but that is no excuse for not trying.

Another problem for the psi researchers of the future will be that of human survival after death. If all mental events depend completely on physical events, survival is out of the question. But if there are some mental events that do not depend completely on physical events, survival certainly becomes a possibility.

The recipients of "spirit messages" are often convinced (and, it may be, quite rightly convinced) that they come from personalities known to them on earth, but this conviction is rarely shared by others. Perhaps no evidence of personal identity conveyed through a medium will ever be completely and universally accepted. Even in ordinary life our sense of the personal identity of other human beings is based on hearsay and intuition rather than on scientifically coercive evidence. Disquieting cases of mistaken identity turn up from time to time in the law courts. Mothers accept impostors as their long-lost sons, as in the famous Tichborne case[29]; wives, as in the more recent case of a returned Italian war prisoner, welcome smooth-talking strangers as their husbands. Passports, social security cards and even finger-prints can be faked. And somewhere in the world practically everybody has his or her double. (Stalin and Hitler are said to have employed half a dozen or more.) If it is so difficult, even here and now, to prove scientifically that I am I and you are you, how much harder must it be to demonstrate that the person speaking through the mouth of a medium is in fact the person he says he is, and not a projection of information acquired by means of ESP and dramatized, more or less convincingly, by a dissociated part of the medium's subconscious mind.

For this reason it seems unlikely that future research into the problem of survival will follow the lines laid down by the earlier workers in the field. How it will be conducted I do not pretend to know. We can only work at what lies immediately before us in the hope that new findings may suggest new ways of dealing with the old and still unsolved problems.

[*Life*, 36 (11 January 1954), 96–108 (used as copy-text); reprinted in *CE*, V, 145–57.]

---

29 Spectacular legal case which enthralled Victorian England in the 1860s and 70s. A man commonly referred to as "the Claimant" asserted to be the long-missing heir to the Tichborne baronetcy. Lady Tichborne immediately accepted him as her lost son though other family members considered him an impostor. He could not convince the courts, was convicted of perjury and had to spend fourteen years in prison.

Aldous Huxley

MATTER, MIND, AND THE QUESTION OF SURVIVAL (10 MAY 1960)[1]

I propose to begin this lecture with a rather long quotation from William James. It is extremely relevant to our purpose and it has a great deal of charm as all James's writing has. This is what he says:

> To no one type of mind is it given to discern the totality of Truth. Something escapes the best of us, not accidentally, but systematically, and because we have a twist. The scientific-academic mind and the feminine-mystical mind shy from each other's facts, just as they fly from each other's temper and spirit. Facts are there only for those who have a mental affinity with them. When once they are indisputably ascertained and admitted, the academic and critical minds are by far the best fitted ones to interpret and discuss them—for surely to pass from mystical to scientific speculations is like passing from lunacy to sanity; but on the other hand if there is anything which human history demonstrates, it is the extreme slowness with which the ordinary academic and critical mind acknowledges facts to exist which present themselves as wild facts with no stall or pigeon-hole, or as facts which threaten to break up the accepted system. In psychology, physiology, and medicine, whenever a debate between the Mystics and the Scientifics has been once for all decided, it is the Mystics who have usually proved to be right about the facts, while the Scientifics have had the better of it in respect to the theories.[2]

Now, the reluctance of the scientifics, the academic and critical minds, to accept wild facts, facts which don't fit into the current theories, has of course been recognized long before James drew attention to it. It was recognized, for example, by Lord Chesterfield when he said that if someone in our days were indubitably to rise from the dead the Archbishop of Canterbury would be the first to deny it. And it was recognized again by one of the early British historians of science, Playfair,[3] in the end of the eighteenth century, where he spoke about the difficulty with which people who had, so to say, an intellectual vested interest in an idea—the difficulty

---

[1] The editor wishes to thank the Aldous and Laura Huxley Literary Trust for permission to publish this lecture.

[2] William James, "The Hidden Self" (1890), *The Heart of William James*, ed. Robert Richardson (Cambridge, MA, 2010), 81. The text of the preceding quotation has been corrected against this edition.

[3] John Playfair (1748–1819). Scottish scientist.

that they had in changing their ideas. And similarly we find this trait of reluctance to accept wild facts going right on through the nineteenth century. A particularly flagrant example of this is the attitude of the official scientific mind towards what used to be called 'animal magnetism,' which came to be called after the days of James Braid 'hypnotism.' This is a really extraordinary story, when you find a man like Lord Kelvin[4] saying that hypnotism is half fraud and half bad observation; and when you find doctors, for example—eminent surgeons used to say in the early days before anaesthetics when amputations were performed under mesmeric trance, they used to say it was quite obvious that the man who was having his leg cut off was merely pretending not to feel pain just in order to spite the doctors. And other surgeons admitted that he probably wasn't feeling pain, but they said he ought to feel pain because pain was very good for people. The most extraordinary and monstrous example of this behaviour towards people who made experiments in this field is the case of James Esdaile, the young Scottish surgeon who went to India and performed several hundred major operations, many of which had never been performed before, under mesmeric trance. And the most startling fact was that not only did he perform these operations without pain to his patients, he also performed them with a then incredibly low mortality rate. The standard mortality rate after surgery in his day before anaesthetics and before antiseptics or asepsis was about 29 per cent, and Esdaile did his three or four hundred operations with a 5 per cent mortality. But all he got for his pains was to be violently attacked by his colleagues and hounded out of the medical profession.

This indicates very clearly how right James was to emphasize this fact that people with a vested interest in a certain kind of philosophy find it almost impossible to accept facts which go against that particular philosophy. And James himself went on to discuss the reaction in his own day to subjects like telepathy. The word was invented by F. W. H. Myers, and of course the thing was extensively studied in the early history, the early years of the Society for Psychical Research after 1882. And James has an interesting comment on this. He says:

> Why do so few "scientists" even look at the evidence for telepathy? Because they think, as a leading biologist, now dead, once said to me, that even if such a thing were true, scientists ought to band together to keep it suppressed and concealed. It would undo

[4] William Thomson, 1st Baron Kelvin (1824–1907). Irish-Scottish mathematical physicist and engineer.

the uniformity of Nature and all sorts of things without which scientists cannot carry on their pursuits.[5]

And this is not an exaggeration because about the time James was writing this, another eminent biologist, Ray Lankester,[6] denounced a group of his fellow scientists in Britain for taking part in an investigation of telepathy. He said it was a disgrace that any group of scientists should demean themselves by even inquiring whether such evidence as had been presented could possibly be true, because it could not be true. And as late as 1926 we get Professor Troland[7] of Harvard saying that the modern psychologist tends to regard alleged psychical phenomena as the modern physicist regards perpetual motion machines. And at about the same time we have Professor Joseph Jastrow[8] saying: "Obviously…"—this is curious, obviously—"Obviously, if the alleged facts of psychical research were genuine and real, the labours of scientists would be futile and blind." It is very difficult to see why they should be futile and blind. All that this seems to prove is that the theory of the world on which the scientists were basing their efforts required modification. I mean it doesn't mean to say in the least that their labours were futile. And yet we find at the present time certain extremely eminent psychologists such as Dr Hebb of McGill speaking in exactly the same way. Hebb has a very interesting comment on the work of Rhine, for example. He says: "Personally I do not accept ESP for a moment because it does not make sense. Rhine may still turn out to be right, improbable as I think that is, and my own rejection of his views is, in a literal sense, prejudice."[9]

This reminds me of an anecdote of my grandfather, Thomas Henry Huxley, where he said of Herbert Spencer that that philosopher's conception of a tragedy was a deduction foully murdered by a fact. And here again we have this strange phenomenon of the existence apparently of facts, which because they do not fit into a certain type of philosophical system are either denied or else blandly ignored, and we have to remember that this

5 William James, "The Will to Believe," *The Will to Believe and Other Essays in Popular Philosophy* (New York, 1897), 10. The text of the preceding quotation has been corrected against this edition.

6 E. Ray Lankester (1847–1929). British zoologist who held chairs at Oxford and the University of London.

7 Leonard Troland (1889–1932). American physicist and psychical researcher.

8 Joseph Jastrow (1863–1944). American psychologist.

9 Huxley used the same quote in "A Case for ESP, PK and PSI," see above, 151.

is a very deeply-rooted human tendency, and it is a deplorable tendency, but it seems to be very deeply-rooted and we must take it into account.

Now, we have to consider the problem of survival. If ESP is a fact, and I think it is a fact, then there would seem to be some *prima facie* reason to suppose that survival is a possibility. If, for example, it is possible to establish some kind of communication between people without the intervention of bodily signs and without the intervention of the sense organs, then, on the face of it, it is possible to imagine that some kind of survival after the death of the body may be possible. On the other hand, once we grant the existence of ESP or psi phenomena, the problem of validating what appear to be the evidences for survival becomes immeasurably greater, because practically every case—I don't think every case, but certainly a great majority of the cases which, on the face of them, appear to be veridical cases of spirit communication—can, on the hypothesis that ESP exists, be interpreted in terms of the medium's great ability in picking up information from the living. For example, a case becomes veridical, is regarded as verydical, if the alleged spirit communicator gives a piece of information which subsequently is found out to be true. But somebody then must know it is true, some living person must know it is true, and in this case obviously ESP becomes a possible explanation of the phenomena, so that we see that there is this curious paradox that with the establishment of ESP—and I personally believe it has been established—we have not only a certain intrinsic probability that there may be survival, but we also are confronted with an extraordinary difficulty in ever demonstrating that a given phenomenon is due to survival.

It is almost impossible, I think, to—well, anyhow it is very difficult, difficult to perhaps almost impossible—to devise an experiment which would definitely eliminate all possibility of explanation through ESP, and definitely demonstrate the spirit's survival. This of course is one of the problems which does confront parapsychologists at the present time who are interested in the problem of survival, the extraordinary difficulty of setting up an experiment which would definitely establish survival, as I say, without opening the way to an explanation through a kind of extended ESP. Practically all the mediumistic communications, the best of which can be studied in the proceedings and the journal of the Society for Psychical Research in London, and in the American society, practically all of these, with a few exceptions, do lend themselves to perfectly plausible explanation in terms of ESP.

Consequently, we have somehow to think of some alternative type of experiment in relation to survival. And something of the same, I think, is true in the cases of those veridical apparitions which have been studied ever since 1882, and have been studied recently with great thoroughness by Dr Louisa Rhine at Duke, and by Dr Hornell Hart,[10] who was at Duke—this, too, lends itself to the same kind of interpretation. Because we know now by experience that an apparition which appears to give veridical information may be not what it seems to be, something willed into existence by an incorporeal personality, but the creation of the percipient. It may simply be the percipient picking up out of the psychic medium some kind of veridical information and then by means of this extraordinary dramatizing and storytelling faculty which seems to lie at the back of so many minds, and especially at the back of the minds of sensitives, building up this figure, this apparitional figure. Dr Louisa Rhine in her enormous collection of cases sorts them out into degrees of probability of survival. The great majority, she thinks, are the actual creations of the percipient using ESP plus this dramatizing faculty, and she would regard as completely evidential only cases in which the percipient of the apparition had no active motive for seeing the apparition, whereas the hypothetical disembodied spirit would have a very strong motive for presenting himself to the percipient. And some of the cases that she has collected—she has collected many thousands of them and examined them very carefully—some of them come fairly near to this, but only one appears to fully come up to this standard of complete convincingness in this respect, and this particular one is not very well confirmed, unfortunately.

On the other hand, Dr Hornell Hart, who has also made a considerable study of the apparitional evidence, is of opinion that there are many apparitions apparently stemming from incorporeal personal agencies which cannot be distinguished from the apparitions of the living. One of the early classics of psychical research was Gurney's *Phantasms of the Living*,[11] where he brought together a very large number of very interesting cases of apparitional appearances of people actually alive—and this kind of census of phenomena has gone on since—and Hart points out that in many cases the apparitions of the dead appear to be of exactly the same nature as the apparitions of the living, and seeing that in many cases we know that apparitions of the living have been the vehicles of communication and action by personalities, we may, by analogy, perhaps imagine that some, anyhow, of the apparitions of the dead are also vehicles of personal thought and action. Well, be it as it may, there are, I think, a number of cases in

[10] Hornell Hart (1888–1967). American parapsychologist and professor of sociology.

[11] Edmund Gurney (1847–1888). English psychologist and parapsychologist.

which the weight of evidence seems on the whole to fall on the side of the survival hypothesis. There are cases in which it seems to be simpler and more plausible to adopt what is now called the IPA hypothesis, the incorporeal personal agency hypothesis, in favour of the ESP hypothesis.

There is another point, however, which I think has to be raised here, which is that as a matter of historical fact it is only fairly recently that it has been assumed that most of this kind of evidence did refer to spirits of the dead. It is interesting in this context to compare, for example, what Burton[12] in *The Anatomy of Melancholy* has to say on the subject with what one of the pioneers in psychical research, F. W. H. Myers had to say two hundred years later. Burton, in *The Anatomy of Melancholy*, dismisses as self-evidently absurd the idea that a departed spirit could possess what we should now call a medium and impart information through the medium. He says that information is given through mediums, but it does not come from departed spirits, but on the contrary, it comes from some non-human spiritual source, either divine or diabolical. F. W. H. Myers, on the other hand, completely dismisses this very ancient hypothesis in favour of the IPA hypothesis, the departed spirit hypothesis, and here—this again, I think, is a rather disturbing fact—[one can see] that essentially the same phenomena do lend themselves to interpretation either in terms of some kind of spirit possession, a non-human spirit possession, or to some kind of communication or possession by departed human spirits. Nevertheless, I think when we have taken all these things into account, it seems to me that there is enough evidence, for example, in the celebrated cross correspondence cases in the best work of Mrs Piper[13] and Mrs Leonard,[14] to make it reasonably plausible that something does survive bodily death.

Now, if we accept this evidence on its face value; if we assume that given the immense number of facts collected since 1882, since the foundation of the Society for Psychical Research, if we assume that these do point to some kind of survival of a personality or a part of a personality after the dissolution of the body, the next thing we have to inquire is: what sort of philosophy of the universe do we have to accept in order to be able to account for this? We have seen that an eminent psychologist of the present day such as Dr Hebb regards this whole thing as making no sense. Well, of course, it does not make any sense in terms of the particular hypothesis, the

---

12 Robert Burton (1577–1640). Oxford scholar and author of the encyclopaedic treatise on melancholy.

13 Leonora Piper (1857–1950). American medium and spiritualist.

14 Gladys Osborne Leonard (1882–1968). British medium and author of *My Life in Two Worlds* (1931).

theory of the world in terms of which he is carrying on his experiments and interpreting them. Obviously, if you believe that mind is an epiphenomenon of matter—the action of matter—or even if you believe that mind and matter are the manifestations of a single neutral substratum, unknown substratum; if you think, for example, that matter, so to say, is the outside of mind and mind is matter as experienced from the inside, then neither of these views seems to be compatible with the idea of survival. If you accept either of these views, then the evidence, I think, both for ESP and also for survival, which is much more difficult to accept than ESP, quite clearly doesn't make sense, but do we have to accept this view of the world? [Does] the fact that mental phenomena are so obviously a function of bodily phenomena drive us of necessity into postulating this kind of naturalistic, materialistic monism?

Well, this question was discussed many years ago by William James in his Ingersoll lecture on human immortality, and he said of course it does not necessarily mean that we have to accept this kind of view of the world. He says that mind may be a function of matter, but there are two kinds of functions: there is the productive function where we say that mind is actually produced by some kind of material activity, but there is also what he calls the transmissive function, that matter and especially the central nervous system is the organ, the reducing valve, through which a previously existing mind-stuff passes into the material world. This view, of course, was strongly supported by Bergson, and as I shall point out later on, it still has its adherents. And James points out that the theory of production is not a drop more simple and credible in itself than any other conceivable theory, it is only a little more popular.

Let us then distinguish between these two possible views of mind as a function of matter: is it the function of a productive nature or is it of a transmissive nature? Now, this debate has been going on ever since James's day, and let me quote here another remark of Dr Hebb's, where he says "we have no choice but to physiologize psychology."[15] Well now, the question is: who is 'we'? Because he does not speak for all biologists by any means. There are plenty of them who do not feel that they have no choice in the matter, that they have to physiologize psychology.

---

[15] Huxley used the same quote in "A Case for ESP, PK and PSI," see above, 151.

For example, take the case of an extremely eminent biologist, Professor Joseph Needham,[16] who doesn't feel anything of the kind. He does not feel at all that there is any necessity in the nature of the evidence to compel us to physiologize psychology. What he has to say on the matter is this—this is how he sums it up[17]: "Mind [...] and all mental [phenomena][18] cannot possibly receive explanation or description in physico-chemical terms, for that would amount to explaining something by an instrument [which is] itself the product of the thing [to be] explained"—because obviously all scientific theory such as the scientific theory of naturalistic, materialistic monism is a product of the mind, and as we know from the philosophers of science from Mach[19] onwards, all these scientific theories have an enormous subjective element in them, are themselves most characteristic products of the mind which they seek to explain, so that mind is being explained away in terms of something which is a product of mind, so that we see there is a profound logical fallacy here.

Now, Needham goes on to say that

> [t]he legitimacy of physico-chemical explanations in the realm of physical life [is] well grounded, but we have [...] found that as far as mental life is concerned biochemistry and biophysics have no authority. The opinion, therefore, which seems to me [...] most justifiable is that life in all its forms is the phenomenal disturbance created in the world of matter and energy when mind comes into it. Living matter is the outward and visible sign of the presence of mind, the splash made by the entry of mental existence into the sea of matter. (251)[20]

And he concludes this essay by saying: "The biochemist and the biophysicist can and must be thorough-going mechanists, but they need not on that account hesitate to say with Sir Thomas Browne,[21] 'There is something in

---

16 Joseph Needham (1900–1995). Prolific British scientist, who with Julian Huxley was a founder of the United Nations Educational, Scientific, and Cultural Organization (UNESCO).

17 Joseph Needham, "Mechanistic Biology and the Religious Consciousness," *Science, Religion and Reality*, ed. Joseph Needham (London, ²1926; ¹1925), 250 (the words in brackets are alterations introduced by Huxley).

18 Needham writes "processes."

19 Ernst Mach (1838–1916). Austrian physicist and philosopher of science.

20 Needham writes: "mental existences into the sea of inert matter."

21 Sir Thomas Browne (1605–1682). English physician and author. Huxley is quoting from *Religio Medici* (1643), Section IV, ch. 36: "Thus we are men, and we know not how: there is something in us that can be without us, and will be after us; though it is strange that it hath no history what it was before us, nor cannot tell how it entered in us."

us that can be without us and will be after us'" (257). Now, I quote this in order to show that the transmission theory is a perfectly live theory at the present time and that philosophically it seems to be better founded, perhaps, than the production theory. There is no compulsion for us to accept the production theory, and therefore no compulsion for us to accept a theory which means that ESP or even IPA are things which make no sense. They do make sense in terms of a transmission theory.

Now, the transmission theory obviously is related to the old Platonic and Cartesian theories, but is considerably more subtle, say, than the Cartesian theory. Descartes postulated the relationship of mind and matter in a much too limited way. He spoke of mind as being something whose essence is consciousness, being related to matter whose essence is extension, and each mind being completely watertight and separate from all other minds. But, of course, now we are able to see that his *cogito ergo sum*—'I think, therefore I am'—should be really modified as Von Baader,[22] the Romantic German philosopher of the early nineteenth century, modified it when he said that *cogito ergo sum* should be revised and that we should say *cogitor ergo sum*—'I am thought, therefore I am.' We are thought by an immensely much larger subliminal mind than this conscious ego of which we are aware, and in any kind of reasonable and realistic transmission theory we have to postulate, I think, that this subliminal mind in which our self-conscious ego floats, so to speak, like a kind of crystal within a solution, this subliminal mind is not cut off from all other minds, but it communicates somehow with all other minds in a kind of psychic medium: we are in a certain sense like crystals floating within this medium and communicating with other crystals through the medium.

Bergson accepted this view and maintained that intrinsically the mind was virtually omniscient, that it was not in fact omniscient here and now because for the benefit of the animal who has to survive on the surface of this planet we cannot be omniscient because we should be so full of irrelevant information that we should simply not be able to get out of the way of the cars in the street, and consequently the central nervous system and the brain exist in order to limit this virtually endless quantity of consciousness which we virtually have, to limit it and to funnel it through for the purposes of biological survival on the surface of this particular planet.

Well, my own feeling is, I would think that this idea of a completely omniscient mind seems to me a little fantastic, but I would think that there

22 Franz Xaver von Baader (1765–1841). German philosopher, theologian, physician and mining engineer.

is something to be said for a view which would say that this psychic medium, whatever it may be, is, let us say, virtually omniscient, that it could take on into itself every kind of specialized information, but what it is in itself is a kind of undifferentiated consciousness, and as I shall try to point out later on in this lecture, there is a lot of evidence on the part of the mystics both East and West to the effect that our particular specialized, individualized consciousness is underlain by an undifferentiated consciousness and that this undifferentiated consciousness possesses what the Catholic mystics call 'obscure knowledge.' This is a very curious and interesting phrase which we meet with very frequently in the literature of mysticism. Mystics constantly speak of this obscure knowledge of the world, which is not a particular knowledge of how to make sulphuric acid, or what is the distance of the nearest fixed star, and so on. It is a generalized knowledge in the individual, an awareness of this total underlying awareness which, as I say, underlies all particular awarenesses. This obscure knowledge of the universe is, I think, a direct awareness of the undifferentiated consciousness, mentoid state, which underlies all particular consciousnesses.

Now, we exist within this undifferentiated awareness as, so to speak, a succession of vortices in a liquid. Unfortunately our psychological vocabulary is so extremely poor that we are always driven back to use these material and spatial metaphors, but we must always remember that when we use material and spatial metaphors, that they are, necessarily, very misleading, inasmuch as this mental undifferentiated consciousness is not in space and time and it does not have the characteristics of a material medium. Nevertheless we have to—simply because we do not have the necessary vocabulary to speak in these sort of terms—we have to use analogies with vortices. Well, it is as though we were persistent vortices within a medium, and I think we have to postulate that by our experience in the embodied state we build up these particular awarenesses within the general undifferentiated awareness, and that we leave certain traces in the form of persistent vortices upon the undifferentiated medium—that these things go on.

Now the question then arises: what are these vortices within the undifferentiated awareness? Here I think we find some very interesting suggestions from the Oxford philosopher H. H. Price,[23] who speaks of these different types of, so to say, molecules of awareness which may be of any—the complexes of awareness—may be of any size, so to speak, from a single idea, from a haunting, for example, to go back to the question of survival—this purely non-personal thing which seems to remain attached to a certain

[23] H(enry) H(abberley) Price (1899–1984). Welsh philosopher noted for his work on the philosophy of perception and parapsychology.

place—up to large fragments of a personality and perhaps to a complete personality. Now, we pronounce this word 'personality,' and it is a word we use very glibly, but when we come to examine exactly what it means we are confronted by very great difficulties. What precisely is a personality? When we look closely at personalities—our own or other people['s]—what do we find?

Well, I think the first thing that we are struck by is that any given personality is certainly not a monolithic unity. The personality is a good deal more loosely bundled together than we ordinarily think, and it is a non-unitary thing. It is made of disparate elements, both in its temporal extension and in its cross section. In its temporal extension obviously we change very considerably as we grow older. But it is not merely a question of maturation that changes the personality. It is quite clear that if we look at the history of almost any life, that there may be profound changes of the personality brought about by particular circumstances.

Let us take a hypothetical case of a child whose mother dies, and who from having been a happy and completely healthy personality becomes a very wretched and neurotic personality; I mean, here is a startling change in the nature of the personality. And similarly, changes of surroundings, casual meetings, may make the most profound difference to people. I mean, one often hears of cases of people who seem to be almost moronic, who suddenly find what their talents are, what they can do: a chance meeting opens up a new world for them, and from having been practically idiotic they become alert and intelligent and efficient, and, well, one sees there is a profound change in the personality, and after all, it is one of the commonplaces of religious literature that certain types of religious experience will produce immense changes in personality, that the whole attitude towards life, towards other human beings, the whole way of behaving will change profoundly. And consequently, the whole stock of memories, which obviously become extremely important in the problem of survival, will be totally changed.

Similarly, in the cross section of a personality at any given time there are again obviously disparate elements brought together. After all, there is the conscious and unconscious, there is the rational and the childish in human beings, there is the respectable persona and the generally rather disreputable psycho-physiological reality which lies beneath it. All these things are there as very loosely connected bits of the personality. So this leads us to ask what exactly do we mean by a personality? Do we mean what I think I am or what I would wish to be or what the Freudian analyst interprets me as being, or what my friends think I am?

There are obviously a great many ways in which a personality can be thought about, and then on top of everything else we have to remember that there are, in every personality, immense numbers of—an indefinite number, I think—of potentialities which might have been developed in other circumstances, but which in the particular circumstances of the life have not been developed, so that over and above all the other enigmas of personality there is this immense enigma of the might-have-been, the fact that we carry about immense latent potentialities which have not, in fact, been actualized, but which might have been actualized.

Well, now, from this let us return to the question of survival. Let us assume that the evidence which points to something surviving is valid. Now, the question arises: what is it that is actually surviving? Now, I would agree with Professor C. D. Broad, who is one of the rather few philosophers who have really taken the trouble to study the literature of psychical research with great care and have devoted a lot of speculation to the problem, I would agree with Professor Broad in thinking that in most cases, certainly, what survives and what comes through in the communications with the medium or the percipient is perhaps not a complete personality—whatever exactly that may be—but is rather a fragment of a personality, that a piece comes through and establishes some kind of communication with the percipient in life. And in this case we would have to assume that these traces left in the psychic medium, the surviving vortices, have some sort of power of establishing communication with the percipient, and sometimes bringing through some kind of veridical information. But, as I say, in the majority of cases, it does look as though what is coming through is not a total personality, but only a piece of one. This may be because the communication is extraordinarily difficult between one mode of being and another. But, on the whole, I think we have to envisage this possibility that what in general is coming through is only a fragment of a personality.

Now, this means that it may be possible for the same human being to survive in several fragments simultaneously. For example, let us take the case of a boy X and a boy Y. These are close friends in their boyhood. The boy X dies. The boy Y goes on and lives to a ripe old age. Now, presumably if there is survival, the personality or some fragment of the personality of the boy X associates with the vortex left in the psychic medium by Y when he was a boy. He may be associating with something that Y has left behind him, even while Y is still alive. It seems to me perfectly on the cards that there may be this survival of bits of personalities which may communicate with disembodied personalities even while the first personality is still in life, and that the boy X and the boy who was Y will perhaps go on associating.

And here quite obviously, seeing that this is a purely mental and subjective life which is going on in the psychic medium, we must assume that the association is necessarily through similarity or through some other kind of psychological congruity. There is not an association through any spatial or chemical relationship, but solely through some psychic congruity between the two groups of surviving experiences.

Well, now we may pursue this still further and assume that Y, as he grows older, let us assume that he marries and that he loses his wife after a few years, marries again, and then in later life has an accident which, say, reduces him to imbecility. Well, here his personality is already broken up into a number of fragments each of which may leave its traces behind in the psychic medium and associate with those surviving fragments of the people with whom he associated during life, so that he will, as I say, perhaps survive in several forms at the same time. This, I think, is a genuine possibility.

We now have to come to a very curious and difficult point: suppose this kind of association of fragments of personality is possible within the psychic medium, what can happen? I mean, suppose that we assume that these vortices which remain can associate with similar vortices, what can we envisage in this posthumous life? Here let me quote a curious and interesting passage where C. D. Broad has discussed this. He says[24]:

> [When we consider analogies with persistent vortices, stationary waves, transmitting beams, etc.,] we can envisage a number of interesting and fantastic possibilities. [We can think of][25] the possibility of partial coalescence, partial mutual annulment or reinforcement, interference, etc., between the psi-components[26] of several deceased human beings, in conjunction perhaps with non-human flotsam and jetsam which may exist around us. There are reported [medium and mystic][27] phenomena, and pathological mental cases not ostensibly involving mediumship, which suggest[28] that some of these disturbing possibilities may sometimes be realized.

---

[24] “Human Personality, and the Question of the Possibility of Its Survival of Bodily Death,” *Lectures on Psychical Research: Incorporating the Perrott Lectures Given in Cambridge University in 1959 and 1960* (New York, 1962), 430 (the words in brackets are alterations introduced by Huxley). Broad originally delivered this lecture, as Huxley later did his, as a Foerster Lecture on the Immortality of the Soul on 20 May 1954, see <https://gradlectures.berkeley.edu/lecture/human-personality-and-survival/>.

[25] Broad writes: “Then we can conceive […].”

[26] Broad writes: “ψ-components […].”

[27] Broad writes: “mediumistic […].”

[28] Broad writes: “which would suggest […].”

And then he adds: "It is worth [while to remember][29] (though there is nothing[30] we can do about it) that the world as it really is may easily be a far nastier place than it would be if scientific materialism were the whole truth and nothing but the truth."

This is a rather characteristic summing up by Broad, who has said in a wry sort of way that he would be slightly more annoyed than surprised to find himself surviving, and it is characteristic of him to see only that the world might be a considerably nastier place. But he might have added, I think, that the world also may be a considerably nicer place, and for the evidence of this, let us turn for a moment to the whole mystical tradition. Here I cannot see why we should reject the evidential nature of much of this mystical tradition. This has gone on for an immense time, both in the East and West, the conception of this underlying, undifferentiated consciousness, this Divine Ground, this mother sea of cosmic consciousness, as William James called it, with which by suitable practices individuals can become unified, even during this life. And this operational process—for this is what essentially it is in all Oriental philosophies—[is] essentially a kind of transcendental operationalism which provides certain techniques for producing certain changes in consciousness, and which then goes out into speculation to give a metaphysical explanation for the nature of the change of consciousness. And the fundamental formula for describing, for interpreting, these changed states of consciousness is, of course, the ancient Indian formula *tat twam asi* ('thou art that'), or as the Buddhists say, mind with a small m from Mind with a large M is not divided, or again, as Eckhart[31] would say, that the ground of the soul is identical with the ground of the Godhead.

Now, in relation to survival, what does this mean? It means that immortality, in the sense in which the mystics use the word—they don't use the word 'survival' so much as 'immortality'—that immortality is the continuation into the post-mortem life of the kind of awareness of the Divine Ground which can be obtained in this life, and in this context I would like to make some quotations from perhaps one of the most remarkable of all pieces of religious literature, *The Tibetan Book of the Dead*, which is a kind of handbook for helping the dead person through the intermediate state between lives. This is a work of Tantric Buddhism, and the Buddhists, of course, assume that there is reincarnation. This has always been taken for

[29] Broad writes: "worth remembering […]."

[30] Broad writes: "nothing that […]."

[31] Meister Eckhart (1260–1328). German theologian and philosopher.

granted in the far East, and incidentally, in our own western tradition, David Hume[32] said that the only form of immortality which a philosophic mind could accept is that of reincarnation.

I don't think we have to discuss whether this is true or not, but the point is that *The Tibetan Book of the Dead* speaks of the possibility of communicating with the departed spirit immediately after death and helping it in this intermediate state between lives. If the person who dies can be made to be aware of the basic fact of the mind from mind being not divided, then he can escape from the wheel of birth and death, and enter into this timeless immortality. And *The Tibetan Book of the Dead* makes the following statement, that at the moment of death the dead person becomes aware of this undifferentiated consciousness, which in the language of Mahayana Buddhism is called the Clear Light. He becomes aware of this, and if, during his lifetime he has practised this awareness, he is able to associate himself with this. If he has practised during his lifetime the realization that 'thou art that,' that the foundation of his own—the ground of his own—existence is identical with the ground of the universe, then he can unite himself with the Clear Light and escape from the horrors of continuous birth and death.

But the chances are, of course, that he will not—I mean the overwhelming probability is that he will not have achieved this kind of enlightenment during life, and so will not be able to accept the pure light—the Clear Light—as it is presented to him. In fact it will seem intolerably brilliant and impossible to bear, and he will then have to go on to a series of less intense lights. In all these stages as he goes down he can get back to immortality, but the difficulty becomes greater and greater, and he will pass then through a stage of wild visionary illusions and finally will come down to the point where he has to re-enter a womb and be born again merely to escape from the intolerable purity and brilliance of the Clear Light. It is a very powerful conception which is not unlike St Catherine of Genoa's[33] conception of purgatory, where the pain of the suffering souls in purgatory is the pain of being impure in relation to this supremely pure light of God which is then experienced as fire. And in this conception in *The Tibetan Book of the Dead* we see something similar—that the Clear Light is of a degree of purity so great that the majority of people can't stand it, and have to go down finally into this comforting world of flesh once more.

---

32 David Hume (1711–1776). Scottish empiricist philosopher.

33 Saint Catherine of Genoa (1147–1510). Italian Roman Catholic saint and mystic.

Now, let me read the passage with which the priest speaks to the dying man and goes on speaking when the breath has ceased. [This is] what he says[34]:

> O nobly-born [you are now aware of the Clear Light seen at the moment of death.] Now thou art experiencing the Radiance of the Clear Light of Pure Reality. Recognize it. […] Thy present intellect, in [its] real nature void, [undifferentiated], naturally void, is the very Reality, the All-Good. Thine own intellect, which is now voidness, yet not to be regarded as of the voidness of nothingness, but as being [mind in] itself—unobstructed, shining, thrilling, and blissful—is the very consciousness, the All-Good Buddha. […] Thine own consciousness, shining, void, and inseparable from the Great Body of Radiance, has no birth, nor death, and is the Immutable Light. Knowing this is sufficient.

And this knowledge of the clear light of the undifferentiated consciousness underlying our ego-consciousness seems to be also among Western mystics the conception of the essence of immortality. For example, Meister Eckhart says that for an enlightened soul—and he was obviously speaking from personal experience—he says that for the soul which has purified itself, such a soul enjoys, even in this life, all that it will enjoy in the eternal life, that already there is eternity here and now in this knowledge of the undifferentiated ground of all particular awarenesses.

And I shall conclude with an anecdote which is told about Jacob Boehme,[35] the great Protestant mystic of the early seventeenth century. He was asked by a young friend: "Where does the soul go after death?" And he replied: "There is no need for it to go anywhere." The reason being that if the soul has been properly prepared, it is, so to say, "there" already. And this, over against the whole problem of survival, which *The Tibetan Book of the Dead* regards as ending necessarily in the reincarnation, is set over against this mystical idea of immortality, of participating in the Divine Ground of all being, and I think we should always make this distinction. I don't think we make it sufficiently strongly, that survival is not necessarily a divine state at all, it may be just exactly on a par with the sort of life that is being lived now by the average sensual man, but there is always a possibility for anybody who is prepared to fulfil the conditions, there is always a possibility of achieving this union with the clear light which is of the essence of immortality.

---

[34] *The Tibetan Book of the Dead*, ed. and trans. W. Y. Evans-Wentz (Oxford, 2000; [1]1927), 95–96 (the words in brackets are alterations introduced by Huxley).

[35] Jacob Boehme (1575–1624). German philosopher and mystic.

It may be, of course, a complete melting away into the totality of mind, or it may be, as the mystics have constantly assured us—what is possible during life—it may be a continuation of individualized awareness transfigured, so to say, by the light of this knowledge of the undifferentiated ground of all being so that there is a possibility both in this world and in the next of a kind of individual awareness in which the soul, so to say, makes the best of both worlds, where the absolute is not apart from the world, but is seen in the relative, where—as Blake[36] says—you "see infinity in a grain of sand, and eternity in a flower"[37]—that there is a possibility, as I say, if the ground of our own being has been realized as identical with the ground of all being, of a continuing personal existence which shall have the quality both of the absoluteness of the Divine Ground and of the individualized life. This is naturally, as all the fundamental truths of life are, this is a huge paradox which makes no sense, of course, except insofar as it is a fact of experience. Thank you.

[36] William Blake (1757–1827). English Romantic poet and painter.

[37] Compare Blake, "Auguries of Innocence" (1803/1863): "To see a World in a Grain of Sand / And a Heaven in a Wild Flower / Hold Infinity in the palm of your hand / And Eternity in an hour."

James Sexton
(University of British Columbia)

ALDOUS HUXLEY INTRODUCES EDNA ST. VINCENT MILLAY

In 1933, Eugene Saxton, Huxley's publisher at Harper's, sent Aldous Huxley some poetry by one of his other clients, Edna St. Vincent Millay, thereby eliciting a letter from Huxley, postmarked from the S. S. Statendam on his return voyage from Central America, thanking his publisher for the "very great pleasure" those poems had given him.[1] Five years later, Huxley had the opportunity to reciprocate by agreeing to give the introductory speech before Millay's poetry reading at the Los Angeles Philharmonic Auditorium on the evening of 5 December 1938.[2]

He clearly enjoyed the experience, because on 21 December 1938 Huxley sent a Christmas letter to Saxton, telling him, "Edna Millay was here recently, reading her poems (the most astonishingly accomplished performance!) and we have had some pleasant hours together. She is a very fascinating creature."[3]

A brief notice in a Los Angeles newspaper helps establish the date and venue for the reading at which Huxley introduced Millay:

> Edna St. Vincent Millay, known in some circles as America's greatest woman poet, will make one of her rare public platform appearances before the Los Angeles Modern Forum the night of Dec. 5 at the Philharmonic auditorium, Dr. Herman Lissauer, diorector, announced today.[4]

And Huxley is named as "Chairman" of the event in the previous day's notice in the *Los Angeles Times*:

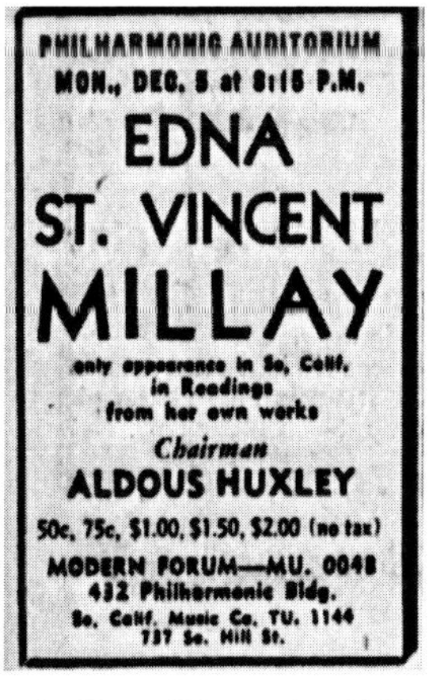

Los Angeles Times (4 December 1938), 6

Edna St. Vincent Millay, ca. 1933
(photo by Carl van Vechten, see Wikimedia Commons)

Millay's biographer Nancy Milford describes the demanding itinerary of Millay's 1938 poetry-reading tour: "She traveled by train, by car, and [...] very rarely by airplane. She crossed the country as far east as Boston, as far north as Buffalo, as far south as Fort Worth, and as far west as Los Angeles."[5] We know that on Sunday, 4 December 1938, the day before her Los Angeles reading, Millay gave a reading at San Francisco's Curran Theatre, described in detail by the reviewer who covered the event:

> Poetry lovers of the bay region, many from Mill Valley, gathered at the Curran Theatre Sunday [4 December] to see and hear Edna St. Vincent Millay. Swathed in a high-necked, long-sleeved clinging robe of old gold which exactly matched her hair, she tripped out on the stage as one dancing on air. Her beautiful voice immediately arrests the attention. Her personality changes like a chameleon—at times she seems a little girl, her gestures so natural, posture so similar to a child's. Then suddenly, she changes into a great dramatic actress, her acting quite as superb as her verse. Her repertoire consisted of several groups—old poems, familiar to most, proceeding to her latest verses which appeared in *Harper's* in October, yet unpublished in book form. In conclusion she recited her old poem, "The Train." Remarking that she must hurry now to catch a plane, she said: "But I still love to travel by trains."[6]

Presumably Millay flew that night to Los Angeles, and gave her reading the following evening, in front of Aldous Huxley and a fellow member of the packed house, a woman whose detailed description perhaps clarifies why Huxley described her performance as a "most astonishingly accomplished" one:

> "She was to give a reading at the Los Angeles Philharmonic—a big place, packed to the top gallery. Bare stage, except for a standing mike. She came out, alone, wearing the usual loose something, green, I think. Standing well away from the mike, she began. Almost at once came cries of 'Louder!' 'Can't hear!' and, insistently, 'Use the mike!' A crescendo that drowned her out. She stood there, waited while it sank to a grumbling, then gestured at the mike, and said something like—'I will not tell you my poems through this mechanical contraption. They come from me to you, direct. Please be entirely silent and I will make you hear me.' Oh no! It started up again, as she resumed. Twice. My seat was very near the front, and I never felt such tension. Growing, too. There was resentment in it, then anger, finally real antagonism. I suppose it took five minutes, while she stood still and fought them. Scary minutes, for there was a sort of peak when she almost lost them. But she didn't. Somehow they did settle and listen. She said every poem she'd chosen, just with her voice, an hour or so of speaking. Then she turned to go off—and then the house came down. Cheers. People stood up. Some cried. It was a show of guts and stubbornness and pride. And foolishness, I suppose." (Quoted in Milford, 122–23)

That Millay's reading took place in the venerable Los Angeles Philharmonic Auditorium is clear, but it is thanks to the presence that night of another audience member that we can be sure Huxley gave the introductory remarks that night. A minor poet named John G. Moore of Pasadena, California, also attended the Millay poetry reading that night in Los Angeles. In an unpublished memoir called "Huxley the Poet," begun in 1950 but not completed until 1965, Moore recalls, "the first time Aldous Huxley became for me an actual, tangible *fact* as a public man [...] was during the 30's." Recalling the Millay reading in Los Angeles, Moore says, "[Huxley] introduced the Poetess, Edna St. Vincent Millay, in Los Angeles, with some words about *words*, especially *poetry*, extolling the mission of the poets, as "more important than novelists" (7).[7]

The typescript containing Huxley's introductory remarks is housed in the Rauner Special Collections Library of Dartmouth College, which graciously granted me permission to reprint the text of Aldous Huxley's introduction of Edna St. Vincent Millay at her poetry reading (see below, 187–88),the time and venue of which was then unknown.[8]

[1] *Letters of Aldous Huxley*, ed. Grover Smith (London, 1969), 370.

[2] Celebrities as diverse as George Gershwin and Huxley's friend Igor Stravinsky gave concerts there; Pavlova and Nijinsky danced there; Jack Benny and Roscoe (Fatty) Arbuckle joked there. For a view of the building and more detailed information, see <https://losangelestheatres.blogspot.com/2018/10/philharmonic-auditorium.html>: "In short, almost everybody who was anybody in the performing arts of the 20th Century entertained there from the day its velvet curtains first rose in 1906 until its faded curtains dropped for the last time in 1964. And all during that time—and up until 1978—hundreds of thousands worshiped there."

[3] Aldous Huxley, *Selected Letters*, ed. James Sexton (Chicago, 2007), 360.

[4] *San Pedro* [CA] *News Pilot* (25 November 1938), 2. Besides Millay, other speakers recruited by Dr. Herman Lissauer for his Modern Forum were Stefan Zweig (13 February 1939; announced in *San Marino Tribune* [9 February 1939], 7) and Sinclair Lewis (5 January 1942; see <https://calisphere.org/item/d5464ee6a48425ab6d8013b0cf1b70a7/>. Interestingly, Aldous Huxley, too, gave a talk for Lissauer's Modern Forum at the L. A. Philharmonic Auditorium on 18 October 1937, according to an announcement in the *Los Angeles Times* (10 October 1937), 57.

[5] Nancy Milford, *Savage Beauty: The Life of Edna St. Vincent Millay* (New York, 2001), 419.

[6] *Mill Valley Record* (9 December1938), 1.

[7] The memoir, entitled "Huxley the Poet," is held in the Woodson Research Center, Fondren Library, Rice University. It was apparently begun in 1950 after Moore had interviewed Huxley in his Wrightwood, California, home. Moore states that the interview took place after Huxley had written *Ape and Essence* and mentions that in this period he was "writing 'special' articles for a certain periodical" (3).

[8] The editor is indebted to the Aldous and Laura Huxley Literary Estate and to the Rauner Special Collections Library, Dartmouth College, for permission to reprint the typescript, MS-286, Box 1.

(1)

Edna St Vincent Millay.

There is a story of which I have always been very fond --- a story which records a meeting between Degas, the painter, and the poet, Stephane Mallarmé. Like most people who do something supremely well, Degas was not content with ~~his~~ achievement. He wanted to ~~be a poet~~ make verses as well as ~~a painter~~ paint pictures. But, try as he would, he could not succeed. In despair he went ~~He came~~ to Mallarmé ~~txxxxxxxxx~~ for sympathy and advice. ~~"Why is it," he asked, "that I can't write anything decent? I have the most wonderful ideas."~~ "I have the most wonderful ideas," he said "And yet somehow I can't write anything that looks ~~like poetry~~ in the least like poetry." Mallarmé smiled indulgently. "You seem to forget," he said, "that poetry is not written with ~~the~~ ~~Mallarme shook his head. "But poetry is not written with~~ ideas, ~~he answered.~~ It is written with words."

"Poetry is not written with ideas. It is written with words." This is a saying which every would-be poet and every critic of poetry should remember and continually meditate. Poetry is written with words, and a poet is good or bad according to ~~the~~ his power of using words; his ideas will do nothing to help him out. The~~re~~ works of Whittier, for example, are full of what used to be called Great Thoughts. So is the hymn book. But felicitous combinations of words are conspicuously absent from these ~~There is no poetry in either~~ collections of verses. There is no poetry in them.

Poetry ~~isxxx~~, I repeat, is written with words. That is why, in introducing ~~Edna St Vincent Millayxxx~~ to you to-night a poet who needs no introduction, I shall speak only~~x~~ of Miss Millay's use of words. ~~xxxxxxxxxxxxxxxxxxxxxx~~ It would be easy to talk of ~~herx~~ the ideas which her poetry expresses --- ~~of~~ of that passionate love of life for its own sake, that capacity of intense and delicate feeling, that almost agonized perception of the world's beauty, a beauty the ~~more~~ poignantly lovely for being perpetually under the menace of death and the trampling brutality of insensitive men. It would be easy, I say; but quite unprofitable and beside the point. For the ~~statement~~ exposition of these ideas would not ~~explain why~~ account for the fact that Miss Millay is ~~the~~ a poet ~~that she is~~.

Page 1 of Aldous Huxley's corrected typescript

2/

I myself have just stated some of these ideas; but that statement was not poetry, because it was not couched in the right kind of words. This being so, let us confine ourselves to a consideration of the words of which Miss Millay's poetry consists. ~~which you are to hear to-night.~~

If I were asked to define Miss Millay's use of language in a single phrase, I should suggest some such formula as "orderly recklessness", or "elegant generosity" --- some phrase that should imply ~~simultaneously~~ the combination of wealth and refinement, of exuberance ~~extravagance~~ and control, of spontaneity and precision. The last twenty years have seen the emergence and the passing of several distinct poetical ~~fashions~~ conventions. There was a period, for example, when a kind of classicism was in fashion --- when young poets made use of the enormous treasures of the English language with a kind of stingy, cheese-paring parsimoniousness. ~~At other times and places the vogue has been for a socially conscious poetry … composed in a free verse so little organised and controlled … that it just poured out, like water.~~ In recent years there has been a reaction and we have witnessed, among others, the rise of the surrealist school, whose ideal it is to use language as the spiritualists use it in the paroxysms of automatic writing, or as it is used in dreams. Here, the linguistic vice is not stinginess and meanness but a wild extravagance. During the whole of her poetical career, Miss Millay has avoided both vices. And she has done so, as the Elizabethans long since contrived to do, by beautifully combining and balancing them --- by wedding economy of language with ~~careful … with reckless generosity~~ a kind of spendthrift eloquence, by joining the most delicate accuracy of statement with warmth and richness and splendour. Like the Elizabethans, she seems constantly on the verge of being swept off her feet by the impetuous current of her own eloquence; but just as it seems

Page 2 of Aldous Huxley's corrected typescript

3

inevitable that she should fall,the headlong movement is miraculously transformed before your eyes into a ~~beautiful~~ figure of the Dance, into some beautiful gesture,entirely unexpected and novel,and entirely satisfying. "Fools rush in where angels fear to tread." ~~Inxhanxx poetry~~ Miss Millay reverses the process. Her poetry is a repeated rushing of angels into situations where we common fools would ~~ignominiously tumble down~~ ~~cut ridiculous capers or ignominiously tumble down~~ ignominiously collapse.

And so,with this final evocation of bright wings and effortless movement, I shall ~~I'll now~~ give place to the poet ~~of~~ whose work I ~~have been trying to describe. Prosy words about poetical words soon become tedious. You have come here to listen to You will be eager to listen to the poetical~~

have been trying to describe. Words about words are apt to be tedious. You have come here to listen to poetry. Any further prosing on my part would be out of place. ~~Inxwillxspaxexmaxxanyxfurthernxn~~ Ladies and gentlemne,I have the pleasure and the honour to ~~introduce~~ introduce Edna St Vincent Millay.

Aldous Huxley

(183)
MR. HUXLEY INTRODUCES MISS MILLAY
*HUXLEY, Aldous. The ORIGINAL TYPESCRIPT, Signed, of his short speech introducing EDNA ST. VINCENT MILLAY for a poetry reading. $2\frac{1}{2}$ pp. with profuse autograph corrections. "She seems constantly on the verge of being swept off her feet by the impetuous current of her own eloquence...Her poetry is a repeated rushing of angels into situations where we common fools would ignominiously collapse." (From the Ms.)

Page 3 of Aldous Huxley's corrected typescript

[Mr. Huxley Introduces Miss Millay][1]

There is a story of which I have always been very fond—a story which records a meeting between Degas, the painter, and the poet, Stephane Mallarmé. Like most people who do something supremely well, Degas was not content with his achievement. He wanted to make good verses as well as paint good pictures. But, try as he would, he could not succeed. In despair he went to Mallarmé for sympathy and advice. "I have the most wonderful ideas," he said. "And yet somehow I can't write anything that looks in the least like poetry." Mallarmé smiled indulgently. "You seem to forget," he said, "that poetry is not written with ideas. It is written with words."

"Poetry is not written with ideas. It is written with words." This is a saying which every would-be poet and critic of poetry should remember and continually meditate. Poetry is written with words, and a poet is good or bad according to his power of using words; his ideas will do nothing to help him out. The works of Whittier,[2] for example, are full of what used to be called Great Thoughts. So is the *Hymn Book*. But felicitous combinations of words are conspicuously absent from these collections of verses. There is no poetry in them. Poetry, I repeat, is written with words. That is why, in introducing to you to-night a poet who needs no introduction, I shall speak only of Miss Millay's use of words. It would be easy to talk of the ideas which her poetry expresses—of that passionate love of life for its own sake, that capacity of intense and delicate feeling, that almost agonized perception of the world's beauty, a beauty the more poignantly lovely for being perpetually under the menace of death and the trampling brutality of insensitive men. It would be easy, I say; but quite unprofitable and beside the point. For the exposition of these ideas would not account for the fact that Miss Millay is a poet. I myself have just stated some of these ideas; but that statement was not poetry, because it was not couched in the right kind of words. This being so, let us confine ourselves to a consideration of the words of which Miss Millay's poetry consists.

---

1 Heading from the postscript typed on the manuscript probably by an antiquarian or librarian.

2 John Greenleaf Whittier (1807–1892). American Quaker poet and well-known abolitionist. His poetry, although popular, was sometimes considered overly sentimental. Huxley seems to have shared Nathaniel Hawthorne's estimation of Whittier: "'Whittier's book is poor stuff! I like the man, but have no high opinion either of his poetry or his prose'" (Roland Woodwell, *John Greenleaf Whittier: A Biography* [Haverhill, MA, 1985], 252).

If I were asked to define Miss Millay's use of language in a single phrase, I should suggest some such formula as "orderly recklessness," or "elegant generosity"—some phrase that should imply the combination of wealth and refinement, of exuberance and control, of spontaneity and precision. The last twenty years have seen the emergence and the passing of several distinct poetical conventions. There was a period, for example, when a kind of classicism was in fashion—when young poets made use of the enormous treasures of the English language with a kind of stingy, cheese-paring parsimoniousness. In recent years there has been a reaction and we have witnessed, among others, the rise of the surrealist school, whose ideal it is to use language as the spiritualists use it in the paroxysms of automatic writing, or as it is used in dreams. Here, the linguistic vice is not stinginess, but a wild extravagance. During the whole of her poetical career, Miss Millay has avoided both vices. And she has done so, as the Elizabethans long since contrived to do, by beautifully combining and balancing them—by wedding economy of language with a kind of spendthrift eloquence, by joining the most delicate accuracy of statement with warmth and richness and splendour. Like the Elizabethans, she seems constantly on the verge of being swept off her feet by the impetuous current of her own eloquence; but just as it seems inevitable that she should fall, the headlong movement is miraculously transformed before your eyes into a figure of the dance, into some beautiful gesture, entirely unexpected and novel, and entirely satisfying. "Fools rush in where angels fear to tread."[3] Miss Millay reverses the process. Her poetry is a repeated rushing of angels into situations where we common fools would ignominiously collapse.

And so, with this final evocation of bright wings and effortless movement, I shall give place to the poet whose work I have been trying to describe. Words about words are apt to be tedious. You have come here to listen to poetry. Any further prosing on my part would be out of place.

Ladies and gentlemen, I have the pleasure and the honour to introduce Edna St. Vincent Millay.

Aldous Huxley

[MS–286, Box 1, Rauner Special Collections Library, Dartmouth College, 3 pp.]

[3] Alexander Pope, *An Essay on Criticism* (1711), l. 625.

Bernfried Nugel
(University of Münster)

EXPERIMENTING WITH PEYOTE: AN UNKNOWN HUXLEY LETTER TO SEABURY EDWARDES

As we know from *Psychedelic Prophets*, the recently published correspondence between Aldous Huxley and Humphry Osmond, Huxley, in early spring 1954, must have passed on to Osmond an article that he had received from a hitherto unknown correspondent, for in a letter dated 30 April–1 May 1954 Osmond wrote:

> I liked the *Cactus and Succulent* writer's account of the peyote taking, most interesting. I shall keep it if I may and send for the articles mentioned.[1]

Who that writer was, becomes clear from the name of the periodical which Osmond mentioned: the article had appeared in the *National Cactus and Succulent Journal* in September 1953, and the writer was a certain Seabury Edwardes, who had described his experience with taking peyote.[2] If it had not been for the presence of the Centre for Aldous Huxley Studies on the Internet, the letter that Huxley sent to Edwardes in reply to the receipt of the latter's article would perhaps never have surfaced, for it was by a query from Edwardes' granddaughter Shani Davies that I first heard of its existence. In our subsequent correspondence I learnt more about Seabury Edwardes and his interests, and together with her brother Ian Edwardes we all finally agreed that the letter should be published in *Aldous Huxley Annual.*

Before presenting the letter, I would think it apposite to summarize the few biographical details conveyed either by Edwardes' grandchildren or retrieved from sources on the Internet[3] and from Edwardes' own article.

Born in London in 1884, Seabury Cyril Donaldson Edwardes travelled to Burma (nowadays Myanmar) in 1902 and entered British Government Service in 1906, eventually working as Superintendent in the Burma Excise Department at Moulmein (nowadays Mawlamyine) until his retirement "from a career devoted to the control of Drugs and drink" in 1939 (Edwardes, 59). During his thirty-three years' service he was stationed in thirteen different districts spread from one end of Burma to the other and in this capacity gained an intimate knowledge of the country. In his spare time he worked as a dedicated photographer—many of his Burmese photos can still be found on the Internet—and after his retirement "built a house near Rangoon with a fine Ophidiarium to start a snake-farm" (59), with the purpose to collect snake venom and send it in vacuum-sealed glass vials to Europe and local medical facilities for making anti-venom serum and anti-blood-clotting medicines. When the Japanese invaded Burma in 1942, Edwardes and his family packed whatever they could into two cars, set out on a hazardous trek to the north of Burma and eventually reached the relative safety of India.[4] After World War II, Edwardes returned to London. He continued pursuing his interest in drugs and cultivating, among other plants, the peyote cactus. He died at Muswill Hill, London, in 1968.

Reading Edwardes' article, Huxley must have been highly pleased to realize that Edwardes and he had independently experimented with peyote and mescaline at almost the same time, Edwardes in September and October 1952, and Huxley in May 1953. As Edwardes noted in his article, he had prepared himself for his self-experiment by reading "Mr. Proctor's superb articles on the subject of Peyote which probably contain all that is known on the subject with one exception, that of personal experience about which I am going to tell you now" (59). According to various Internet sources, this "Mr. Proctor" was R. C. Proctor, a cactus expert and cactus flower photographer,[5] who was also mentioned in a 1966 publication of the National Cactus and Succulent Society as one of three writers on the effects of mescaline, the other two being Huxley and Edwardes.[6] Relying on Proctor's knowledge of peyote, Edwardes undertook his experiment in three steps: on 22 September 1952 he started with a mild dose, viz. with eating one head of a peyote plant, and for about an hour experienced "a wonderful series of visions in colour" (59). Eleven days later, he ate two heads and for two hours enjoyed a different kind of "entertainment":

> This time there was more of radial geometric design, like huge spider webs and fine lace, designs like some of the circular Diatoms. In one vision they seemed to cover the dome of an enormous hall. Then there were long vistas of rows of flowers reaching to the end of sight and always things were moving and in the most brilliant colours changing into each other. No flower show could ever equal this. (59)

The last step of his self-experiment took place on 20 October 1952. Edwardes emphasized that he made "many notes at the time about mental and physical effects, and these are the only evidence which has any scientific value" (59). Apparently this session was the most intense of all three, but he described in detail only a few of the "most striking" visions:

> I was in a huge building like a museum, rather in the style of the Alhambra. Chamber after chamber was filled with marvellous objects in the most brilliant colour. The first show was a sort of

> laboratory with much slender glass apparatus on the benches, all shimmering with Neon colours. Then there was a chamber full of ceramics in all sorts of modernistic as well as ancient designs. Only one image appeared to have any erotic significance, there was a room filled with ancient musical instruments and as I looked at them one fixed my attention.
>
> It was a rather large viola, it did not have a face and yet it seemed to have a personality and was certainly alive. It or she was pregnant and was making coy gestures at me. It was then I made the discovery that to an abnormal mind everything has a personality. Every chair, table, vase or other thing in a room is alive and moving and watching you, but the moment you fix your attention on anything it freezes. I remember saying to myself, "If you let things start making faces at you there will be no end to it, you must not let them get out of control." (60)

Another vision presented "a long procession of heads [...], just heads and shoulders":

> They moved from left to right. They were not trying to frighten me but were intent on something over my right shoulder. A note made at the time by the light of a single candle at the end of the room which was all the light I cared to have, reads, "All queer, some horrid, look mentally deformed, a few pleasant and innocent." I recalled de Quincey's words "Now I knew the tyranny of the human face." He must have had some sort of vision like this, he alludes to "Endless processions."[7] [...] While this drug is acting, the supreme "I" at the centre, what the sailors call "the little cherub that sits up aloft and looks after poor Jack," is not deceived by the show and yet enjoys it all the same. (60)

Finally, Edwardes drew the following balance:

> On the Debit side there was an amount of discomfort comparable to, say, one day's Malaria. Nothing to talk of in the case of one who is used to Malaria.
>
> On the Credit side—Firstly an increased appreciation of colour which seems to persist to this day as well as some lovely memories and an increased ability to call up images in colour. Secondly, I think, a better comprehension of Art. I begin to understand how some of the Artists get their images and figures which may seem bizarre but have a real significance to them. The Surrealists, of course, definitely claim to be portraying some of the contents of the subconscious. After this experience I can feel more kindly towards abstracts even though I may not like them. [...] I feel that to have had the subconscious partly accessible even for an hour or two was a very thrilling experience, one that is confined as a rule to Artists, Poets and Madmen. (60)

Now how did Huxley respond to Edwardes' account? He replied in a four-page letter dated 10 April 1954, which follows in facsimile and transcription.

Cunard Line

R.M.S "Queen Elizabeth"

10. IV. 54

Dear Mr Edwardes,

Thank you for your letter & the interesting paper. When I am next in the neighbourhood of a library, I will look up Proctor's paper. Much work has been, & is being, done in America on peyote among the Indians — I have read some of it — but by no means all.

Pure mescalin produced in me a mild ~~[illegible]~~ queasy

1

feeling, like the feeling of
being on a boat on a
moderate sea. It passed off
in about half an hour. There
was no hangover. It is advisable
to eat a lot of sugar as
the effects wear off. This
counteracts the lingering hypo-
glycaemia which may follow
the ingestion of mescalin.

The drug is synthesized by
the Swiss firm of Hoffmann
Laroche. I took it under
the auspices of a doctor, &
I presume that only a medical
man can obtain it in
England — even tho' it isn't
on the dangerous list. I am
trying to help my young psych-
iatrist friend, Dr Osmond, to get
a grant from one of the

2/

Cunard Line
R.M.S "Queen Elizabeth"

big Foundation for a systematic ~~psychological~~ study of the remoter regions of the mind by means of mescalin & lysergic acid. So far without success. But I still hope we may get the thing started sooner or later. Even after 70 years of experimenting nobody knows what happens when mescalin is taken e.g. by a congenitally blind person, by a colour blind person, by a first-rate

natural musician, by
a highly developed analytical
~~the~~ thinker, such as a ~~of~~ mathematician,
by an alcoholic (there is
some reason to suppose that
mescalin & alcohol are
incompatible & that the former
may help in curing alcoholism)
by a devout follower of
Christianity, Buddhism,
Islam etc, by a mentally
deficient person, by a
monkey (but we know that
rabbits are unaffected, while
dogs under mescalin bark
at what observers regard as
empty space). So there is
plenty of work to be done.

Sincerely yours

Aldous Huxley

Transcription:[8]

Cunard Line
R.M.S. "Queen Elizabeth"

10.iv.54

Dear Mr Edwardes,

Thank you for your letter & the interesting paper. When I am next in the neighbourhood of a library, I will look up Proctor's paper. Much work has been, and is being, done in America on peyote among the Indians: I have read some of it—but by no means all. Pure mescalin produced in me a mild queasy feeling, like the feeling of being on a boat on a moderate sea. It passed off in about half an hour. There was no hangover. It is advisable to eat a lot of sugar as the effects wear off. This counteracts the lingering hypoglycaemia which may follow the ingestion of mescalin.
The drug is synthesized by the Swiss firm Hoffmann-La Roche. I took it under the auspices of a doctor, & I presume that only a medical man can obtain it in England—even tho' it isn't on the dangerous list. I am trying to help my young psychiatrist friend, Dr Osmond, to get a grant from one of the big Foundations for a systematic psychological study of the remoter regions of the mind by means of mescalin & lysergic acid. So far without success. But I still hope we may get the thing started sooner or later. Even after 70 years of experimenting nobody knows what happens when mescalin is taken e.g. by a congenitally blind person, by a colour blind person, by a first-rate natural musician, by a highly developed analytical thinker, such as a mathematician, by an alcoholic (there is some reason to suppose that mescalin & alcohol are incompatible & and that the former may help in curing alcoholism), by a devout follower of Christianity, Buddhism, Islam etc., by a mentally deficient person, by a monkey (but we know that rabbits are unaffected, while dogs under mescalin bark at what observers regard as empty space). So there is plenty of work to be done.

Sincerely yours
Aldous Huxley

Written shortly after the publication of *The Doors of Perception*,[9] during Huxley's passage to Cherbourg on the Queen Elizabeth,[10] this letter shows that Huxley found Edwardes' paper more than "interesting" in several respects. He admits that he has not come across Proctor's articles mentioned by Edwardes but readily announces that he will look them up in a library. At the same time he excuses his pertinent lack of knowledge stating that he could not possibly have read all studies on peyote. Then he compares his own mescaline experience with Edwardes' and points out that he ingested pure mescaline, which had no side effects ("no hangover"), whereas Edwardes had eaten the raw tops of a peyote plant and suffered slight discomfort. Thus Huxley implies that, by taking pure mescaline, he already started from improved test standards, and he also presents himself in the advanced position of giving specific advice about how to avoid hypoglycaemia or "cerebral sugar shortage" as he calls it in *The Doors of Perception* (*DP*, 20). He even enlarges his advice by telling Edwardes how best to procure pure mescaline from the Swiss firm Hoffmann-La Roche.

While so far he has only moderately intimated his superior knowledgeability, he concludes his letter with a directer display of his expertise, stressing the importance of taking mescaline "under the auspices of a doctor" and explicitly naming Dr Osmond, who appears only implicitly as "investigator" in *The Doors of Perception* (*DP*, 13). What is more, he also draws up a long list of specific future research topics, most of which go beyond those mentioned in his just published book. For instance, neither the cases of a mathematician or a musician, nor those of an alcoholic or of religious persons or of animals[11] are discussed in *The Doors of Perception*. Therefore it can be said that this list more distinctly reflects Huxley's key concern at the time, viz. "a systematic [...] study of the remoter regions of the mind by means of mescalin & lysergic acid." Similarly, it is true, throughout *The Doors of Perception*, he emphasizes the scientific nature of his self-experiment, pointing out that he is familiar not only with the history of pertinent scientific research but also with current studies in the field[12] and that he carried out the test under medical supervision, but it is certainly striking that Edwardes' letter should have induced Huxley to reveal in detail his and Osmond's plans of raising funds for an overall research project on the effects of mescaline and LSD.

---

1 *Psychedelic Prophets: The Letters of Aldous Huxley and Humphry Osmond*, ed. Cynthia Carson Bisbee, Paul Bisbee, Erika Dyck, Patrick Farrell, James Sexton, and James W. Spisak (Montreal & Kingston, 2018), 103.

2 See Seabury Edwardes, "An Experiment with Peyote (Lophophora Williamsii)," *The National Cactus and Succulent Journal*, 8.3 (September 1953), 59–60.

3 See, e.g., <http://www.shwepla.net/Replire.mv?622>; <http://www.nationaltrustcollections.org.uk/results?Maker=Seabury+Edwardes+(photographer)>; <https://www.thegazette.co.uk>, *The London Gazette* (22 February 1968), issue: 44530, 2241.

4 Their story of this trek has been recorded by the BBC World Service Omnibus programme under the title "The Flight of Tiny Feet" (14 February 2003), see <https://www.bbc.co.uk/sounds/play/p0376mlk>.

[5] See, e.g., W. Taylor Marshall, "Cactus and Succulents," *The National Horticultural Magazine* (January 1948), 42; see <https://docplayer.net/ 120155638-Horticultural-magazine.html>.

[6] See Philip E. Downs, "The Uses of Succulent Plants," *The National Cactus and Succulent Journal*, 21.3 (September 1966), 73: "Alkaloids extracted from the cactus *Lophophora williamsii* [i.e., peyote] have achieved much religious significance. The main active principle of the plant, the dried, cooked or raw tops of which are utilised, is Mescaline [...] and articles on its effect have been written by Aldous Huxley, also by R. C. Proctor and Seabury Edwardes in earlier N.C.S.S. [i.e., National Cactus and Succulent Society] magazines."

[7] Compare Thomas De Quincey, *Confessions of an English Opium-Eater* (1821), ed. pdfbooks.co.za: "[A]t night, when I lay awake in bed, vast processions passed along in mournful pomp" (52); "now that which I have called the tyranny of the human face began to unfold itself" (56).

[8] Minor inconsistencies of spelling and punctuation have been silently adjusted to current standards.

[9] *The Doors of Perception* (London, 1954) [hereafter, *DP*] came out in February 1954, see "Chronology," *Letters of Aldous Huxley*, ed. Grover Smith (London, 1969) [hereafter, *Letters*], 17.

[10] See Sybille Bedford, *Aldous Huxley: A Biography* (2 vols., London, 1973–74), II, 165.

[11] The case of "a congenitally blind person," listed in the letter, does not appear in *The Doors of Perception* either, but is significantly mentioned in a Huxley letter to Osmond, dated 2 March 1954: "Have you ever tried the effects of mescalin on a congenitally blind man or woman? This would surely be of interest" (*Letters*, 699).

[12] See, for instance, the beginning of the essay (*DP*, 5–7, and note 1).

Hisashi Ozawa
(Meiji University)

Aldous Huxley and D. T. Suzuki: A Biographical Consideration of Their Relationship

Introduction

In his later career, particularly from the latter 1930s, Aldous Huxley came to explore human consciousness more seriously from various angles. The development of his research has been known as being concurrent with his encounters with those who were especially concerned with the field, such as mystic philosophers Gerald Heard and Jiddu Krishnamurti, educator F. M. Alexander, psychiatrist Humphry Osmond and psychologist Timothy Leary. However, there has been little consideration of another of his friends, Daisetsu Teitaro Suzuki (1870–1966), whom Huxley called "the great Japanese scholar to whom the West owes most of its knowledge of Zen Buddhism."[1] As Jake Poller indicates, "

> [i]n the final phase of his career, Huxley's experiments with psychedelics enabled him to perceive nirvana in samsara, the divine in the mundane, and this breakthrough led him to turn away from the life-denying asceticism of Vedanta in favour of the life-affirming creeds of Tantra, and Mahayana and Zen Buddhism."[2]

In order to understand Huxley's concern with human consciousness and other facets of his later work and life, it is thus important to pay attention to Suzuki and his writings. In this article, I discuss biographically Huxley's relationship with Suzuki, not only by analysing their published work but also by considering Huxley's little-known letters to Suzuki and the contents of Suzuki's personal library, both of which aspects were the interest of my investigation at the Matsugaoka Bunko Foundation.

Overview of the relationship between Huxley and Suzuki

In 1870 Teitaro Suzuki was born into a family of doctors in Kanazawa, Japan. His father was a first-rate intellectual who was familiar with Western medicine and Confucianism. His family was from the Rinzai school (one of three sects of Zen in Japanese Buddhism), but because of his mother, Suzuki was also influenced by Shin Buddhism (a school of Japanese Pure Land Buddhism), which was more popular in Kanazawa. The loss of his father in 1876, his brother in the following year and particularly his mother in 1890 led Suzuki to believe in something that could not be elucidated by science. In his teens, Suzuki was so full of intellectual curiosity that he devoted himself to reading numerous ancient and modern classics from Eastern to Western, from philosophy to science, such as the works of Confucius, Laozi, Jean-Jacques Rousseau, Ralph Waldo Emerson, Charles Darwin, Herbert Spencer, T. H. Huxley and Yukichi Fukuzawa. However, due to his poverty and his deepening interest in religion, Suzuki did not graduate from any schools where he studied, including the University of Tokyo. In 1891 he took up Zen practice at Engaku-ji in Kamakura, and was trained over the next several years by Soyen Shaku, a pioneering international master who had learned modern science at university before studying Buddhism in Ceylon, India and China, and under whom Suzuki began to call himself Daisetsu (or Daisetz). In 1893 Shaku attended the World Parliament of Religions in Chicago, organised by clergyman John Henry Barrows and theologian Paul Carus. For this, Suzuki translated his master's manuscript into English. Though Suzuki did not attend the conference, Shaku became acquainted with Carus, and upon his request, Shaku sent his student to America to help him translate Laozi's *Tao Te Ching*.

Between 1897 and 1908, Suzuki worked in America for the publisher Open Court, studying Eastern philosophies, translating the Mahayana text *Dàshéng Qǐxìn Lùn* into English as *Awakening of Faith* (1900) and writing his own book, *Outlines of Mahayana Buddhism* (1907). As Judith Snodgrass points out, "[b]y the end of his apprenticeship with Carus [the advocator of a 'religion of science'], Suzuki had acquired an appropriate philosophical vocabulary and intellectual framework for presenting Japanese Buddhism to Western audiences."[3] In his time in America Suzuki became familiar with the Christian mysticism of Meister Eckhart and Emanuel Swedenborg, and in Japan, between 1910 and 1915, he published the Japanese translations of the latter's work and wrote a biography of him. In 1911 Suzuki married Beatrice Erskine Lane, an American Theosophist who also influenced his ideas. In 1921 he was appointed to a professorship at Otani University in Kyoto, and founded *The Eastern Buddhist*, the first journal on Buddhism in English. In 1927 he published *Essays in Zen Buddhism, First Series*, thereafter energetically writing and lecturing in English and Japanese about Eastern philosophies, particularly Zen Buddhism. Between 1950 and 1958, he lived in America, made the rounds of many universities and formed friendships with celebrities in the fields of religion, literature and other areas, including Aldous Huxley. After returning to Japan, he continued his activities until his death at the age of ninety-five in 1966.[4] Suzuki's idea of Zen developed in a hybrid manner, reflecting his deep learning about Western culture, his actual life in the West and his mother country, which was then being radically Westernised. In other words, it was such a background that led Suzuki to not only interpret but also reconstruct Buddhism or construct his own 'Buddhism.'

His activities were not limited to religion. For the public in Japan, Suzuki wrote a large amount of criticism on politics and culture. Rather than conservative or progressive, his political stance was on the whole liberal and pacifist.[5] As early as the beginning of the twentieth century, Suzuki expressed his sympathy with advocation of democratic socialism, not based on economics but religion, and believed that social progress, both in the East and the West, would largely depend on the advance of socialism.[6] After the Second World War, Suzuki repeatedly argued for the need of combining the wisdoms of the East and the West in order to create a new culture and a better world, in which human beings could harmoniously live together and with nature.[7] As a Buddhist, he also made an appeal for peace by expanding the renunciation of war, which was stipulated in the newly enacted constitution of Japan, into establishing the World State.[8] Furthermore, Suzuki inspired the leaders of the counter-culture by his view of nature based on Zen Buddhism; to take only two examples, the philosopher Alan Watts (Suzuki's and Huxley's common friend) and the poet Gary Snyder came to reject Western anthropocentrism and reconsider humanity without separating it from the natural environment.[9]

According to his diaries, Suzuki actually met Huxley at least five times in the 1950s:[10]

(1) 20 February 1950:
In the afternoon Suzuki called on Huxley in Los Angeles. At Huxley's, he met Jay Barrie and Gerald Heard, both interested in Zen. (On the previous day, Suzuki had telephoned Huxley.)[11]

(2) 12 December 1951:
Suzuki went to the Huxleys in Los Angeles to have lunch with them.[12]

(3) 24 January 1952:
In the afternoon Suzuki visited Huxley and Heard at Huxley's home in Los Angeles.[13]

(4) 2 September 1954:
Suzuki went out in the evening to the Warwick Hotel in Manhattan to dine with the Huxleys, who were staying there at the time.[14]

(5) 18 May 1957:
Huxley and Robert Richman called Suzuki in New York in the morning as arranged.[15]

What did Huxley and Suzuki talk about in their meetings? Why were they so much drawn to each other?[16] To answer these questions, let us consider their reviews of, and possible influence upon, each other.

Huxley's comments on Suzuki: the influence of Suzuki on Huxley

According to his letters and essays, it can be confirmed that from the 1940s Huxley became increasingly interested in Suzuki's writing for several reasons. Huxley first referred to Suzuki in a letter to George Sewell, dated 12 January 1940: "From what I have read about the doctrine of the Void, in Suzuki and [Louis de] La Vallée Poussin [a Belgian scholar of Buddhism], I should say it corresponded very closely with the Taulerian [a German mystic, Johannes Tauler's] conception" (*Letters*, 449). In *The Perennial Philosophy* (1945), Huxley sought for the common basis of various religious traditions, and named in the reference list Suzuki's *Studies in Zen Buddhism* (London, 1927), *Studies in the Lankavatara Sutra* (Kyoto and London, 1935 [¹1930]) and *Manual of Zen Buddhism* (Kyoto, 1935).[17] In the sixth chapter, "God in the World," Huxley presented "salvation" as "a reconciliation of time and eternity," by citing passages from Taoist and Zen Buddhist texts, which he was familiar with, particularly Suzuki's *Manual of Zen Buddhism*, which "contains translations of the most interesting writings of these Chinese and Japanese mystics—mystics who made use of world-denying self-discipline for the purpose of being able and worthy to become world-accepting on that higher level where a man can say, with Augustine, *Ama et fac quod vis*" (*Letters*, 534). In a letter to psychotherapist Hubert Benoit (the author of *The Supreme Doctrine* [1955], to which Huxley wrote a foreword), dated 10 December 1949, Huxley showed his interest in the *koan* technique, which "aims at the exhaustion of the ego by prolonged effort," and admitted he owed his understanding of *koan* to Suzuki's writing (*Letters*, 613). In another letter to Benoit, dated 3 February 1950, Huxley recommended Suzuki's latest volume, *Zen Doctrine of No-Mind* (1949), which he said was "a commentary on the Sutra of the Sixth Patriarch and contains a great deal of interesting material from Chinese sources hitherto inaccessible to European readers" (*Letters*, 618).

After his first meeting with Suzuki in 1950, Huxley wrote: "[I] had a very pleasant and instructive talk with him. I find the whole Zen approach, together with Chinese and Japanese Zen literature, peculiarly satisfying" (*Letters*, 639). In a letter to his and Suzuki's common friend, Humphry Osmond, dated 1 June 1957, Huxley mentioned his fifth meeting with Suzuki, and appreciated his latest book, *Mysticism: Christian and Buddhist*

(1957), as "very good," and a short pamphlet, *The Essence of Buddhism* (1947), as "even better":

> This last is really admirable. It makes one realize how much subtler these Far Eastern Buddhists were, in matters of psychology, than anyone in the West. They know all about 'existential experiences' and the horrors of the human situation as described by Sartre, Camus and the rest—and they know how to come through to the other side, where every relative manifests absolute Suchness, and where Suchness is identical with mahakaruna, the Great Compassion. (*Letters*, 825)[18]

In a letter to Julian Huxley, dated 10 September 1957, Huxley insisted that a "sensible and realistic religion" should help individuals to "become conscious of the Unconscious (this is Suzuki's definition of enlightenment) and [...] of other human beings ('mutual forgiveness of each vice,' in Blake's words)" (*Letters*, 827). In "The Education of an Amphibian" in *Adonis and the Alphabet*, published in the previous year, Huxley applied Suzuki's notion of the Unconscious to his discussion of the ideal education, and while comparing Suzuki with a Roman Catholic theologian, Fr. Victor White, argued for "the art of spiritual insight" as the "most important branch of non-verbal education" (*CE*, V, 205–07). His admiration of Suzuki continued until his late years, and in a letter to Lucille Kahn, dated 8 August 1961, Huxley still recommended Suzuki's *Essays in Zen Buddhism* and *Zen Doctrine of No Mind* as "books on oriental philosophy and religion which I valued" (*Letters*, 918).

Following up on Huxley's references to Suzuki in his non-fiction allows us to realise that Huxley was influenced by Suzuki in thinking about not only religion but also other general subjects such as human psychology and education. Through reading Suzuki, Huxley viewed Buddhism not as just an object of his research but as a perspective for considering his society and time. For Huxley, Buddhism could be compared with and supplement Western culture; East could be associated with West, ancient with modern. Indeed, the leitmotif of his last novel, *Island* (1962), i.e., making the best of the Western and Eastern worlds,[19] can be grasped as an extension of that vision. Although a detailed analysis of this point is for another paper, we will find the novel has some similarities with Suzuki's thought, particularly with his argument that Buddhism is supported by two pillars, namely the Great Wisdom (an insight into the significances of life and the world beyond dualism) and the Great Compassion (a love of all things, including evil) (see *Essence*, 46), and with his view of Zen Buddhism as a practice of daily life rather than speculation.[20]

Huxley was drawn to Suzuki not only for his religious charisma but also as a human being. Their direct relationship started at the beginning of May, or possibly the end of April, 1949. In a letter to Harold Raymond at Chatto & Windus, dated 8 May 1949, Huxley wrote:

> I have just had a letter from Dr. D. T. Suzuki, the well-known Japanese scholar who is the leading authority in the field of Mahayana Buddhism. He writes that he has a friend [Shosaku Fukazawa] who w[oul]d like to translate *The Perennial Philosophy* and who is competent to do so adequately. [...] If none [arrangements by Raymond] have been made, I think Suzuki's friend might have the preference, if his competence is vouched for by such an authority. (*Letters*, 597)

In later 1949, Huxley received another letter from Suzuki, and because of his deepening interest in Zen he came to "hope very much to see him" (*Letters*, 608).[21] After the first meeting, Huxley confessed his impression of Suzuki: "He is a little Old Japanese of more than eighty, with the tiniest hands I have ever seen on any human being, and with an extraordinary charm and gentleness. I [...] was greatly taken by him, would like very much to talk with him again" (*Letters*, 638).[22] His praise of Suzuki never changed, and after their final meeting in 1957 he remarked on Suzuki: "What a really wonderful old man!" (*Letters*, 825)

Although not included in the published collections edited by Grover Smith or James Sexton, Huxley's letters to Suzuki are preserved in the Matsugaoka Bunko Foundation in Kamakura, Kanagawa. The institution was established in 1946 to store Suzuki's collection of books, and Suzuki spent his last years there; since his death, it has maintained Suzuki's house and library and worked for the promotion of research on Suzuki and Zen Buddhism. On 8 March 2017, through the courtesy of Ms Katsuyo Ban, Administrative Chief of the Foundation, I examined Huxley's two letters, dated 14 and 24 October 1951, and an envelope with no letter, postmarked 13 November 1951.

The first letter reads:

> 740 North Kings Road,
> Los Angeles 46, California
> October 14th 1951
>
> Dear Dr Suzuki,
> We shall be very happy to see your friend & yourself whenever it suits you.
> Just let us have a card or a phone call in advance.
> Gerald Heard is out of town until Christmas.
> Very sincerely yours,
> Aldous Huxley

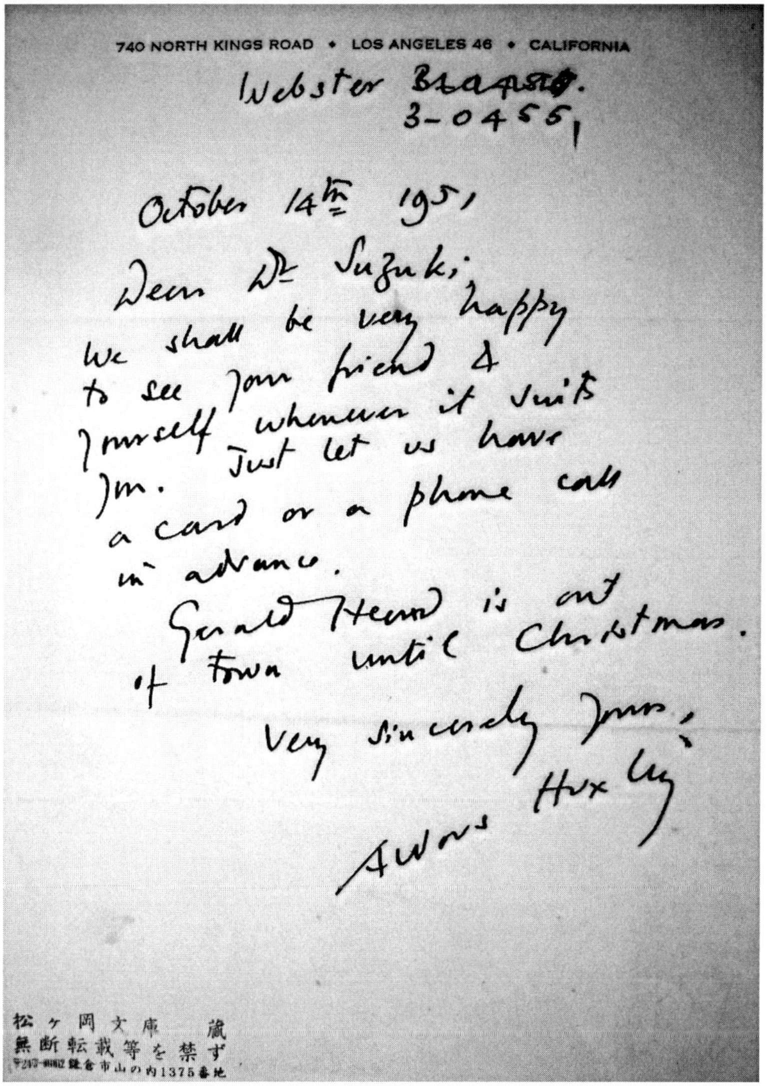

740 NORTH KINGS ROAD • LOS ANGELES 46 • CALIFORNIA

Webster [illegible].
3-0455,

October 14th 1951

Dear Dr Suzuki,
We shall be very happy to see your friend & yourself whenever it suits you. Just let us have a card or a phone call in advance.

Gerald Heard is out of town until Christmas.

Very sincerely yours,
Aldous Huxley

Eleven days after this, Huxley wrote the second letter:

740 North Kings Road,
Los Angeles 46, California
October 25th 1951

Dear Dr Suzuki,
Someone told me that you were once again in California.

I hope very much that, if ever you come to Los Angeles, you will do us the pleasure of visiting us here.

The phone is Webster 3-0455, & we are almost always at home until about 2.0 p.m.

So please let us know if you can come one day to lunch or tea or dinner—whichever suits you best.

Very sincerely,
Aldous Huxley

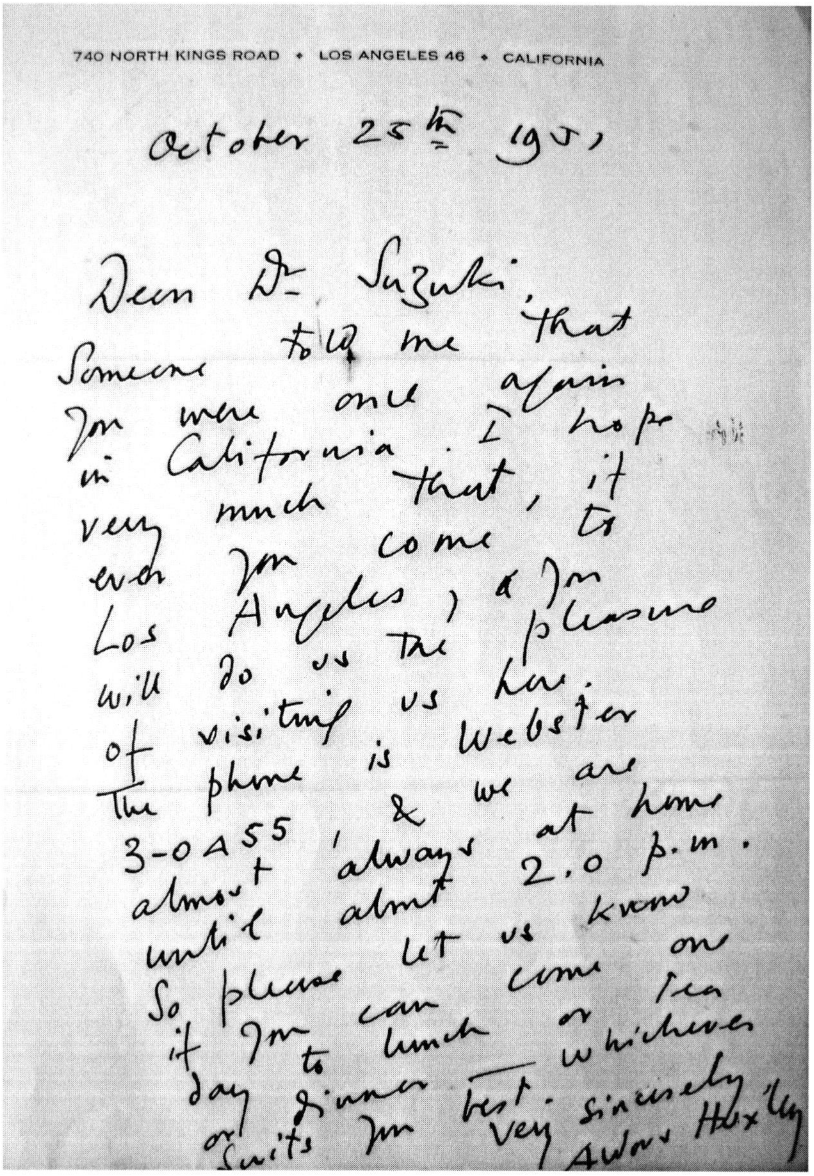

740 NORTH KINGS ROAD • LOS ANGELES 46 • CALIFORNIA

October 25th 195[illegible]

Dear Dr. Suzuki,
Someone told me that you were once again in California. I hope very much that, if ever you come to Los Angeles, you will do us the pleasure of visiting us here. The phone is Webster 3-0455, & we are almost always at home until about 2.0 p.m. So please let us know if you can come one day to lunch or tea or dinner—whichever suits you best.

Very sincerely,
Aldous Huxley

The meeting which Huxley proposed in these letters was realised on 12 December 1951 (see above, 201). From what Huxley said in his letters, it may be gathered that he was sincerely fascinated by Suzuki.

Suzuki's comments on Huxley: the influence of Huxley on Suzuki

On the other hand, how familiar was Suzuki with Huxley's work? Was it possible that he was also influenced by Huxley in a similar way? My investigation of Suzuki's library,[23] as well as *A Catalogue of Foreign Books in the Matsugaoka Bunko* (2008), shows that his library contains seventeen books written by Huxley. Among them, seven books were donated by his disciple, R. H. Blyth (the author of *Zen in English Literature and Oriental Classics* [1942], which Huxley read[24]) after his death in 1964, and it is highly probable that Suzuki did not read them.[25] Excepting these, the library has the following ten books by Huxley:

> (1) *The Olive Tree* (Harper & Brothers, 1937 [^{1}1936]): probably Suzuki's underlines and a third person's signature
> (2) *Ends and Means* (Chatto & Windus, 1938 [^{1}1937])
> (3) *The Perennial Philosophy* (Harper & Brothers, 1945): Suzuki's signature
> (4) *The Devils of Loudun* (Chatto & Windus, 1952): Suzuki's numerous notes in margins and insertions (news clippings, name cards, letters, etc.)
> (5) *The Devils of Loudun* (Harper & Brothers, 1953 [^{1}1952])
> (6) *The Doors of Perception* (Harper & Brothers, 1954): Suzuki's underlines
> (7) *The Genius and the Goddess* (Chatto & Windus, 1955)
> (8) *Heaven and Hell* (Harper & Brothers, 1956): Suzuki's underlines
> (9) *Tomorrow and Tomorrow and Tomorrow* (Harper & Brothers, 1956)
> (10) *Brave New World Revisited* (Harper & Brothers, 1958)[26]

Because of various indications such as his notes, the volumes listed 1, 3, 4, 6 and 8 can be judged to be the ones that Suzuki read closely.

As a matter of fact, Huxley's name often appeared in Suzuki's later writings in English and Japanese. The first mention is seen in his essay, "Tōyō wa sekai bunka ni nani o kōken shiuru ka" ['How can the East contribute to world culture?'] (1948; lectured in 1947), in which Suzuki takes up *The Perennial Philosophy* by 'a famous British writer,' Aldous Huxley: 'Even if not being systematised by philosophers, we, human beings, naturally have perennial philosophy in ourselves. Huxley explains this in the book, introducing many pieces of Eastern thought. He seems to pay considerable attention to Buddhism and Zen.'[27] A few years later, Suzuki came to contact Huxley through their common acquaintance(s) because of the aforementioned translation. In a letter in March 1949 (unknown date and recipient), Suzuki wrote:

> A friend of mine translated A. Huxley's [*The*] *Perennial Philosophy* into Japanese and asked me to communicate with the author. But as I don't know him personally, I wish you would write the letter on behalf of myself and my friend about the translation that my friend [did] to get from Mr. Huxley the right of translation and publication into Japanese.[28]

Probably this unknown recipient came to send the letter which Huxley mentioned in his letter to Raymond. Fukazawa's Japanese version of *The Perennial Philosophy*, entitled *Kuon no shinri*, was published in 1951, with a preface by Suzuki.[29] Although Suzuki wrote this before meeting Huxley, the preface was helpful in understanding what impression he had about Huxley (see the "Appendix" to the present article). Here, Suzuki stated that he had 'somehow entertained friendly sentiments' towards Aldous Huxley since he was a grandchild of T. H. Huxley, whose work Suzuki had read to learn English, and because he was also deeply affected by Eastern thought. Then Suzuki recommended to the Japanese, especially the young, *Kuon no shinri*, with which he sincerely empathised and from which they could learn about Eastern thought.[30] In fact, probably partly inspired by Huxley's *The Perennial Philosophy*, Suzuki later published a book with a similar theme, *Mysticism: Christian and Buddhist*, in which he also sought after the "underlying chain of relationship" between Western mysticism (Eckhart) and Eastern mysticism (Zen and Shin Buddhism).[31]

Huxley's later motif of making the best of the West and the East was also shared by Suzuki. In "Tōyō gakusha no shimei" ['The mission of Eastern scholars'] (1961), included in *Tōyō-teki na mikata* ['The Eastern outlook'] (1963), Suzuki found the 'deadlock of the Western way of thinking' in the contemporary state of human beings being mechanised and deprived of their liberty, and expressed his deep concern: 'Societies imagined by Orwell and Huxley may come earlier than expected.'[32] In his belief, the Eastern way of thinking was becoming more important in order to live peacefully with other people and nature, and to produce a new world culture in collaboration with the Western way of thinking. Suzuki often repeated such an opinion in his writings and lectures after the Second World War.[33]

In his grasp of human psychology, Suzuki also echoed Huxley's pessimistic or realistic vision. Immediately after the Second World War, Suzuki expected world peace, but as the situation grew worse due to, above all, 'politicians and diplomats' obsessed by 'power,' he became a sort of 'cynic,' frankly confessing in an essay, "Amerika no sakkon" ['America today'] (1955):

> A reading of Aldous Huxley's *The Devils of Loudun* made me sense the actuality of devils. Though science appears to be omnipotent nowadays, I want to believe that "devils" nevertheless lurk in the depths of a human's heart. What cannot be modified or removed by science hides in the bottom of the human "unconscious." It is no easy matter to repress this once it comes to the fore. It seems the only way for humans themselves to fall into ruin.[34]

This pessimistic view may also remind us of the dystopian image of human mentality in Huxley's *Ape and Essence* (1948).

However, Suzuki did not agree with all aspects of Huxley's work. Apart from religious meditation, Huxley was also drawn to the effects of psychedelics upon the human mind, conducted his own experiments with them, and published *The Doors of Perception* and *Heaven and Hell.* According to *The Doors of Perception*, while looking at flowers after taking mescaline, Huxley remembered a passage of Suzuki's essay in which, to a novice's question "What is the Dharma-Body of Buddha?," the Master answers, "The hedge at the bottom of the garden." Then, Huxley, for the first time, understood the meaning of this seemingly nonsensical answer (*CE*, V, 161–62).[35] Although Osmond wrote in a letter to the Huxleys, dated 16 April 1954, that "[a]pparently Suzuki was greatly interested in *The Doors of Perception* and had insisted that his students read it" (*Prophets*, 94),[36] Suzuki was actually critical of the book and a series of social phenomena in which the liberation achieved through Zen meditation came to be compared with that obtained from psychedelics. According to Suzuki's "Religion and Drugs" (1966),

> [i]n his book *The Doors of Perception*, Aldous Huxley described his own experience with the drug (mescaline). He saw a hitherto unknown world upon opening this 'door.' He then tried to relate this experience with that of Zen. Though Mr. Huxley had taken an interest in Zen, he did not have the guidance of a Zen teacher. He thus sets forth to writing a detailed description of the world of illusory vision brought on by mescaline.[37]

Although it is not clear that in *The Doors of Perception* Huxley tried to relate psychedelics with Zen, Suzuki might have received such an impression through his meetings with Huxley or his friends. More probably, when he made the above comment, more than ten years after the publication of *The Doors of Perception*, Suzuki had in mind not so much Huxley's work but the subsequent fashion for psychedelics in the counter-culture movement, which of course could not be fully attributed to Huxley.

In *Island*, Huxley fictionalises such a debate. Murugan attacks the Palanese practice of taking psychedelics for the reason that it does not bring "real" liberation like religious meditation, but Vijaya and Dr Robert, whose position is closer to the author's, argue back: "'He's outraged by the fact that, with four hundred milligrammes of *moksha*-medicine in their bloodstreams, even beginners—yes, and even boys and girls who make love together—can catch a glimpse of the world as it looks to someone who has been liberated from his bondage to the ego'" (*Island*, 137); "'[s]o maybe the whole thing does happen inside one's skull. Maybe it *is* private and there's no unitive knowledge of anything but one's own physiology. Who cares? The fact remains that the experience can open one's eyes and make one blessed and transform one's whole life'" (139). Indeed, by taking the *moksha* -medicine, Will, the main character, ultimately reaches a momentary liberation, in which he can first look into the truth of everything (see 279–83). To enlarge upon this, it may be argued that in his view of Zen Buddhism (or the liberation obtained by religious training), Huxley differed from Suzuki, for whom "Zen is not to be conceptualized" but to be "experientially grasped."[38] However, Suzuki did not completely negate Huxley's research and at least displayed sympathy for him.[39] Following the cited passage from "Religion and Drugs," Suzuki continued: "Zen experience is quite often confused, even by some so-called Zen people, with the hallucinatory state (makyō) experienced by Hindu saints as is described in the *Śūraṅgama Sutra*. It is of little wonder, therefore, that an outsider is prone to making similar mistakes" (*SW*, III, 234). In a letter to Lunsford P. Yandell, dated 30 September 1950, Suzuki also remarked: "The main trouble with the Zen writers of the West is that they are not acquainted with the original texts, and another serious defect they all have is that they have never actually trained themselves in Zen."[40] Later, in an interview in 1965, he commented that psychedelics would be 'fine as a clue to starting Zen but are still not Zen.'[41]

Even so, Suzuki certainly felt friendship with Huxley, and prided himself on Huxley's interest in his work. For example, in a letter to Kofu Edson, dated 4 July 1955, Suzuki showed his concern for Huxley, who had lost Maria in February that year: "Too bad that Mrs. Huxley passed away. He was so dependent on her. It is especially sad in his case. I like to see him again while he is still in this neighborhood [New York]."[42] Suzuki was also conscious of Huxley's evaluation, as he wrote in a letter to Buddhist author Christmas Humphreys, dated 3 September 1954: "I understand *Manual of Zen Buddhism* is now out of print. In that case would it not be better to have it reprinted? When I saw Aldous Huxley a few days ago in New York, he was referring to it as an eye-opener to him. I know some other people who think it valuable" (*CW*, XXXVIII, 86). In a letter to Alan Watts, he somewhat proudly states: "The *Manual of Zen Buddhism* is liked very much by Aldous Huxley as you may know" (*CW*, XXXVIII, 208). In his above-mentioned interview in 1965, Suzuki talked about 'Zen boom' with regard to psychedelia on the East Coast of America and the Beat Generation on the West Coast (he met Jack Kerouac and his friends, who called Suzuki's writing 'the Bible'), and revealed his wish to develop such a 'worldwide boom of Zen,' which contained misunderstandings, into authentic 'thought' ('Zen Boom,' 300–02). He also recollected that the late Huxley was 'fascinated by Zen and said that he would have definitely taken Suzuki's book if he had been exiled to a desert island' (302). In this way, Huxley was a good stimulus for Suzuki's research into, and propagation of, Zen Buddhism.

Conclusion

The biographical consideration of Aldous Huxley's relationship with D. T. Suzuki suggests that they influenced each other in their views on religion, mysticism, psychology, education and other subjects of their common interest. For Huxley, who was then sincerely exploring human consciousness, Suzuki's writings on Eastern thought, particularly Zen Buddhism, contained perspectives that were different from Freudian psychoanalysis and could supplement Western mysticism. Suzuki echoed Huxley's work on the perennial philosophy and his pessimism towards human beings, and was stimulated by Huxley's quest for the ultimate truth about human consciousness. Their different attitudes towards psychedelics never hurt or shook their bonds and respect for each other. Their common friends, such as Gerald Heard and Alan Watts, also probably contributed to deepening their relationship.

In the background of their friendship lay points of commonality or similarities between Huxley and Suzuki. Both of them were born to intellectual families of scientists or doctors, and acquired encyclopaedic intelligence by pursuing learning, mainly through self-study, whether the sciences or humanities, Eastern or Western. Having experienced the deaths of members of their families, they became concerned, early in their lives, with the realm beyond the material, and came to develop their own notions of religion by absorbing Christianity, Buddhism, Theosophy and various sorts of mysticism. Politically, they both resolutely opposed any form of totalitarianism, showed ethical or religious sympathy with support of socialism, and advocated a peaceful and ecological vision based on the wisdom of the

West and the East.[43] In their five meetings, Huxley and Suzuki may have talked about these general topics beyond rigidly religious themes.

Comparison of Huxley's and Suzuki's writings and life will provide us with crucial insights not only for our research into their later careers but also, possibly, for our discussion of contemporary issues, from religious conflicts to environmental devastation. In accordance with their principle of non-attachment, Huxley and Suzuki, on the whole, were not deeply committed to political campaigns or controversies and have thus been at times criticised for not being more engaged with the actual problems of their day.[44] Yet their non-attachment never meant that they were uninterested in reality. Rather, these independent intellectuals struggled with reality by keeping a moderate distance, and partly because of this, their works are still fully worthy of our reading and investigation.

---

1 Aldous Huxley, "The Education of an Amphibian," *Complete Essays*, ed. Robert S. Baker and James Sexton, V: *1939–1956* (Chicago, 2002), 205; hereafter, *CE*, V.

2 Jacob Robert Poller, "'Dangerously Far Advanced into the Darkness': The Place of Mysticism in the Life and Work of Aldous Huxley" (Diss., Queen Mary, University of London, 2011), 396.

3 Judith Snodgrass, *Presenting Japanese Buddhism to the West: Orientalism, Occidentalism, and the Columbian Exposition* (Chapel Hill, 2003), 262. In his writings, including *The Religion of Science* (1893) and *The Gospel of Buddha* (1894; translated by Suzuki into Japanese in 1895), Carus anticipated some aspects of Suzuki's lifework, particularly the dissemination of Buddhism in the West and the exploration of the relation between science and religion.

4 For the above outline of Suzuki's life, see Ryōmin Akizuki, *Suzuki Daisetsu* (Tokyo, 2004 [[1]1967]), 13–43.

5 In particular, Tomoe Moriya's recent anthology of Suzuki's essays and letters, *Zen ni ikiru: Suzuki Daisetsu korekushon* ['Living in Zen'] (Tokyo, 2012), has shed light on his liberal and pacifist nature.

6 See Suzuki, "Shakaiminshutō no kettō kinshi ni tsukite (Shakaishugi no shūkyō-teki kiso)" ['On the Prohibition of the Formation of the Social Democratic Party: The Religious Foundations of Socialism'] (1901), *Suzuki Daisetsu zenshū* ['Collected Works of D. T. Suzuki'; hereafter, *CW*], ed. Shin'ichi Hisamatsu, Susumu Yamaguchi and Shōkin Furuta, XXX (Tokyo, 2002), 266.

7 See Suzuki's series of essays included in *Tōyō-teki na mikata* ['The Eastern Outlook'] (Tokyo, 1997 [[1]1963]).

8 See Suzuki, "Nihon no reisei-ka" ['Spiritualising Japan'] (1947), *CW*, VIII (Tokyo, 1968), 227–28, 418–19; see also *The Essence of Buddhism*, trans. Christmas Humphreys (London, 1983 [[1]1946]) [hereafter, *Essence*], 81; Suzuki was also nominated for the Nobel Peace Prize in 1963, see "Nomination Database, Daisetz T Suzuki," <https://www.nobelprize.org/nomination/

redirector/?redir=archive/show_people.php&id=12957>, accessed 27 May 2019. For the closest analysis of Suzuki's pacifism, see Kemmyō Taira Satō, "D. T. Suzuki and the Question of War," trans. Thomas Kirchner, *The Eastern Buddhist*, 39.1 (2008), 61–120.

9 See Makio Takemura, *Buddisuto ekorojī: Kyōsei, kankyō, inochi no shisō* ['Buddhist Ecology'] (Tokyo, 2016), 54–59.

10 See also Kiyohide Kirita, ed., *Suzuki Daisetsu kenkyū kiso shiryō* ['Basic Information Concerning Research on D. T. Suzuki'] (Kamakura, 2005), 157, 172, 192, 207.

11 See Suzuki, "English Diaries IV: 1950 to 1951," ed. Kiyohide Kirita, *The Annual Report of Researches of the Public Interest Matsugaoka Bunko Foundation* [hereafter, *ARR*], 22 (2008), 6–7. On 29 March 1950, Suzuki wrote a letter to Huxley (see the same volume, 10), and on 11 November 1950, he went to Fulton to watch Huxley's dramatized *The Gioconda Smile* (see 36).

12 See Suzuki, the same volume, 78.

13 See Suzuki, "English Diaries IX: 1952 to 1953," ed. Kiyohide Kirita, *ARR*, 27 (2013), 3.

14 See Suzuki, "English Diaries X: 1954 to 1955," ed. Kiyohide Kirita, *ARR*, 28 (2014), 31.

15 See Suzuki, "English Diaries XI: 1965 to 1959, 1962," ed. Kiyohide Kirita, *ARR*, 29 (2015), 33. See also Huxley's letter to Humphry Osmond, dated 1 June 1957, *Letters of Aldous Huxley*, ed. Grover Smith (London, 1969), 825; hereafter, *Letters*.

16 In an interview in the mid-1990s, Mihoko Okamura, Suzuki's secretary in his late years, remembered Aldous Huxley as one of the 'most impressive' people who met Suzuki (Mihoko Okamura and Shizuteru Ueda, *Omoide no kobako kara: Suzuki Daisetsu no koto* ['The Memoirs of D. T. Suzuki'] [Kyoto, 1997], 85).

17 Here, I cite reference information as described by Huxley, see *The Perennial Philosophy* (London, 1945), 306. However, instead of *Studies in Zen Buddhism*, he possibly meant Suzuki's famous and important work *Essays in Zen Buddhism, First Series*, which was published in London in 1927. In his reference list, Huxley also cited Suzuki's wife, Beatrice Lane Suzuki's *Mahayana Buddhism* (1938).

18 In a reply to Huxley, dated 8 June 1957, Osmond writes: "I must see Suzuki again. Yes we are primitives psycho-spiritually and usually unwilling to admit our primitiveness. […] I shall get the essence of Buddhism" (*Psychedelic Prophets: The Letters of Aldous Huxley and Humphry Osmond*, ed. Cynthia Carson Bisbee, Paul Bisbee, Erika Dyck, Patrick Farrell, James Sexton and James W. Spisak [Montreal, 2018], 339); hereafter, *Prophets*.

19 See Huxley, *Island* (London, 2005), 129; hereafter, *Island*.

20 See Suzuki, *Essays in Zen Buddhism (First Series)* (New York, 1949 [[1]1927]), 302.

21 The letter to Hubert Benoit is dated 5 November 1949.

22 The letter to Elise Murrell is dated 4 November 1951.

23 Again, I am grateful to Ms Ban for allowing me to enter Suzuki's library and examine his books.

24 See Huxley's letter to Elise Murrell, dated 4 November 1951, *Letters*, 638; letter to Roger Godel, dated 23 December 1951, *Letters*, 639. Blyth, an English literature scholar who spent the latter part of his life in Japan, discusses Huxley in *Zen in English Literature and Oriental Classics* (Tokyo, 1942) (see 334, 403–05) and *A Survey of English Literature* (Tokyo, 1957) (see 362–63).

25 The donated books are, in chronological order, *Two or Three Graces*, *Jesting Pilate*, *Point Counter Point*, *Texts and Pretexts* (two copies), *After Many a Summer* and *The Perennial Philosophy*. Suzuki's library also contains, excepting Blyth's books, T. H. Huxley's *Science and Education* (1901 [[1]1893]) and Julian Huxley's *Religion Without Revelation* (1957 [[1]1927]), *Science, Religion, and Human Nature* (1930), *Man in the Modern World* (1948 [[1]1947]) and *Evolution in Action* (1953). See *A Catalogue of Foreign Books in the Matsugaoka Bunko* (Kamakura, 2008), ed. The Matsugaoka Bunko, 127; hereafter, *Catalogue*.

26 For the above information (1) to (10), see also *Catalogue*, 126.

27 *CW*, XXXIII [Tokyo, 2002], 234.

28 *CW*, XXXVII [Tokyo, 2002], 210–11.

29 In 1988 another Japanese translation of *The Perennial Philosophy* was published by Yasuo Nakamura. Incidentally, all of Huxley's novels, excepting *Those Barren Leavers* (1925), have been translated into Japanese.

30 On 7 December 1955, Suzuki wrote a letter to Fukazawa to thank him for having sent a copy of his translation. See *CW*, XXXVIII (Tokyo, 2003), 284.

31 D. T. Suzuki, *Mysticism: Christian and Buddhist* (London, 2002 [[1]1957]), vii.

32 *CW*, XX (Tokyo, 1970), 222.

33 Suzuki's (and more or less Huxley's) use of the terms East and West was not necessarily geographically or biologically determined, but from a contemporary perspective, their discourse appears to be essentialist, even though they hoped for a harmony between East and West.

34 *CW*, XXXIV (Tokyo, 2002), 97. On 12 March 1953, Suzuki also wrote: "Huxley's *Devils of Loudun* is a terrible book in more than one sense. The 'possession' at the Convent, exorcists; Public show, devils, superstitions, Sexualities, &c. are almost beyond the reach of modern man's imagination. But all these things I believe are going on though differently masked and patterned. Fundamentally, we are not changed" ("English Diaries IV: 1950 to 1951," 48).

35 I cannot identify the source here, but one of Suzuki's best-known titles, *Zen Buddhism and Its Influence on Japanese Culture* (1938), cites a similar passage from *Blue Cliff Record* (see the enlarged 1959 version, *Zen and Japanese Culture* [Princeton, 2019], 348).

36 In the same letter, Osmond also wrote: "Suzuki looks like a small yellow monkey. He talks like the sage that he is and he emanates a serene wisdom that warms the heart. How little and moth-eaten the old body is, so like a Chinese print. What a pity he wears our ugly Western clothes. [...] He had a Chinese (or Japanese) book in front of him. He is remarkably acute and asked whether many of our subjects had experiences 'like Huxley's.' We went over the whole matter of mescaline and he said that he thought that it would be valuable and useful 'with metaphysics' but not so valuable without. I agreed with him. He took the same view that you do that there are many ways to this strange vision.

The Zen masters he said had often discussed this, though not so much in recent years as in the past" (*Prophets*, 95).

37 Suzuki, "Religion and Drugs" (1966; trans. 1971), *Selected Works of D. T. Suzuki*, ed. Jeff Wilson, Tomoe Moriya and Richard M. Jaffe [hereafter, *SW*], III: *Comparative Religion* (Oakland, 2016), 234.

38 See Suzuki, *Zen Buddhism: Selected Writings of D. T. Suzuki*, ed. William Barrett (New York, 1996, [1]1956), 260. Of course, he also admits that "we are all human in the sense that we cannot remain dumb, but have to express ourselves in one way or another" and that, to a certain extent, the "conceptualization of Zen is inevitable" (260).

39 In his lecture "Thought Currents of Today and Buddhism" (1954), Suzuki criticised Western materialism, and sympathetically cited Huxley's comments on "systematic reasoning" in *The Doors of Perception*: "Systematic reasoning is something we could not, as a species or as individuals, possibly do without. But neither, if we are to remain sane, can we possibly do without direct perception, the more unsystematic the better, of the inner and outer worlds into which we have been born" (*ARR*, 28 [2014], 101; Huxley, *CE*, V, 190).

40 *CW*, XXXIX (Tokyo, 2003), 171.

41 "Zen būmu sekai ni hirogaru: 'Shisō' to shite teichaku sasetai" ['Zen Boom Worldwide'], *CW*, XXXV (Tokyo, 2002), 302–03; hereafter, 'Zen Boom.'

42 *CW*, XXXVIII (Tokyo, 2003), 199. Suzuki continued: "Do you know where Mr. Heard is at present? I also like to see him" (199). On the whole, in his work in English, Suzuki did not directly criticise Huxley's discussion of psychedelics. Here, we may see Suzuki's consideration of, or concern for, his friend. It is not clear that Huxley was aware of Suzuki's disagreement.

43 For Huxley's pacifism, see e.g., David King Dunaway, *Huxley in Hollywood* (New York, 1989), Chapter 1. For his environmentalist perspective, see Dana Sawyer, "Brave New World-View: Aldous Huxley, Environmental Prophet," *AHA*, 8 (2010), 221–38. For his support of socialism not so much from the angle of economics as from that of pacifism and ethics, see David Bradshaw, "Introduction," *The Hidden Huxley* [London, 1995, [1]1994], viii-ix and xxiv, note 6; Stephen Ingle, *Narratives of British Socialism* (Basingstoke, 2002), 103–05.

44 For instance, Charles M. Holmes severely attacks Huxley's "deep distaste for the political" and criticises him for "never want[ing] to join any kind of organization himself" ("The Sinister Outer World: Aldous Huxley and International Politics," *Now More Than Ever: Proceedings of the Aldous Huxley Centenary Symposium Münster 1994*, ed. Bernfried Nugel [Frankfurt, 1995], 204). For a debate on Suzuki's attitudes towards imperialism and militarism, see Richard M. Jaffe, "Introduction," *SW*, I: *Zen* (Oakland, 2015), xvii-xix.

Appendix

D. T. Suzuki

Preface to *Kuon no shinri* (1951), the Japanese Translation of *The Perennial Philosophy*[1]
(Translated into English by Hisashi Ozawa)

Although I am sure the author of this book needs no introduction to Japanese readers, I will reveal a few aspects of my personal relationship with him.

When I was still young, probably over sixty years ago, Japanese learners of English often read the following works—if I remember correctly—historical writings, such as [Thomas] Macaulay's accounts of [Robert] Clive, [Warren] Hastings and [John] Milton (these are not exactly biographies but criticism), philosophy books such as [Herbert] Spencer's, studies of economics by [John Stuart] Mill, physics by [John] Tyndall, and biology by [Charles] Darwin and [T. H.] Huxley. I was still twenty or less, with not enough English skills, and I doubt very much that I could really understand these books written in English. But because it was an age when no Japanese translation was available, those who had even a little appetite for knowledge would read whatever they could lay their hands on.

Ever since I heard that the author of *The Perennial Philosophy* was a grandchild of the aforementioned biologist, I have somehow entertained friendly sentiments towards him. Especially because he was attracted to Eastern thought and spread it in his writings, I felt as if he had not been a perfect stranger to me. Because I knew that he paid attention to my writings, I even thought that we might meet each other somewhere, at some time.

When I first read *The Perennial Philosophy*, I could not help shouting, "That's very true!"

When I went to Honolulu in summer last year, I heard that Mr Huxley was in the city of Los Angeles, and thought that I would be able to see him in the near future. In February this year, I came over to the American Continent to lecture about Japanese culture at Claremont Graduate University in California.

---

[1] The original text is Daisetsu Suzuki, "Jo" ['Preface'], Aldous Huxley, *Kuon no shinri* ['The Perennial Philosophy'], trans. Shosaku Fukazawa (Tokyo: Mikasa Shobō, 1951), 1–3. This preface is also reprinted in *Suzuki Daisetsu zenshū* ['Collected Works of D. T. Suzuki'; hereafter, *CW*], ed. Shin'ichi Hisamatsu, Susumu Yamaguchi and Shōkin Furuta, XXXV (Tokyo, 2002), 47–50. Additional information is included in square brackets.

In March or April, I was invited to his home in Los Angeles, where I was treated to tea.[2] Then I was introduced to Gerald Heard, a famous believer in Vedanta philosophy. As a badly informed person, I had known nothing about Mr Heard, but his appearance immediately made me guess that he had a personality very different from a Westerner's.

Although I have now forgotten most of the conversation, I remember it probably centred on *koan*[3] in Zen Buddhism. Both Mr Huxley and Mr Heard were immensely interested in it. After talking for a good while, we parted with a promise to meet again.

Each of us has been busy, and life in America, especially in Los Angeles, is extremely inconvenient for those who do not own or drive a car. Thus we have missed a chance to meet again.

Now (October) Mr Huxley may have returned to New York City from Europe. I can probably confirm this if I ask someone from the Vedanta school, but I have had no time to do so and left it. I have recently read in the newspaper that one of his stories, which was cinematized before, has been staged this time. The article reports his impressions of it. The story is called "The Gioconda Smile." This is the subject-matter of a famous picture by Leonardo da Vinci, and the smile on Mona Lisa's lips is often referred to by people as a kind of mystery. I heard that the last smile of Mr Huxley's heroine equals this mysteriousness.

I want to watch the play when I am free, but I still have not had the opportunity.[4] This 'Gioconda smile' might give a glimpse of something mysterious that is said to reside in the psychology of Easterners.

It is possibly just because I have been greatly attracted to the field these days that I have the impression that a stream of books on Eastern mystic thought have been published in Europe and America. There are, however, good reasons for this trend.

I remember that recently [in 1949], when the establishment of the Ford Fund (over twenty million dollars) was officially announced, a passage from its prospectus mentioned the decline of human creativity with through

---

2 The accurate date is 20 February 1950. See Suzuki, "English Diaries IV: 1950 to 1951," ed. Kiyohide Kirita, *The Annual Report of Researches of the Public Interest Matsugaoka Bunko Foundation*, 22 [2008], 6–7.

3 *Koan* is a paradoxical anecdote or riddle, used in Zen Buddhism to show the inadequacy of logical reasoning and provoke enlightenment (see *The Concise Oxford English Dictionary, Eleventh Edition, Revised*, ed. Catherine Soanes and Angus Stevenson [Oxford 2004], 790).

4 On 11 November 1950, Suzuki watched *The Gioconda Smile* in Fulton. See *The Annual Report of Researches of the Public Interest Matsugaoka Bunko Foundation*, 22 [2008], 36.

modern mechanization. This is also what I have realized more deeply since coming to this country, and I sense that, if things continue like this, American strength of mind, too, will necessarily lack creative profundity and liberty.

At any rate, I fear that young people in the East, especially in Japan, being Westernized one way or another, might lose their Eastern depth and liberty. There is a danger that an ideology like communism, developing a marked totalitarian tendency, could also mechanize and enslave humans. The same danger can be sensed in the West's, particularly America's, attempts to do everything by machinery. Individualism, democracy and communism seem to have something in common. They are probably the direct outcome of the fashion for modern thought or scientific thought.

I hope that young people perceive the deep Kegon[5] wishes for unity with nature itself at the bottom of Eastern psychology. Kegon thought has something different from the current Western ways of thinking and living. They must recognize this.

Mr Huxley's grandfather was a scientist and his eldest brother is also one of the most outstanding scientists of this age. Given that a person like Mr Aldous Huxley was born into the same lineage, I believe beyond all doubt that at the bottom of the hearts of scientists, too, there is something that ultimately impels them towards the Eastern.

It may also be a trend of the times that Easterners are given an opportunity to reflect on themselves through the writings of Westerners.

October 1950
At a residence of the Union Theological Seminary in the City of New York —To the right looking at Grant's tomb, to the left looking up at the tall tower of Riverside church,

Daisetsu Suzuki

[5] Kegon (Chinese: Hua-yen) is one of the major schools of Chinese Buddhism and one of the oldest schools of Japanese Buddhism. This school teaches the equality of all things and the dependence of all things on one another. Its teaching is known as the teaching of totality, since according to the Kegon view all things participate in a unity and this unity divides itself into the many, so that the manifold is unified in this one (see *A Concise Dictionary of Buddhism and Zen*, ed. Ingrid Fischer-Schreiber, Franz-Karl Ehrhard and Michael S. Diener, trans. Michael H. Kohn [Boston, 2010, [1]1991], 93).

Gilles Iltis
(Sanary-sur-Mer, France)

THE HUXLEYS IN SANARY (1930–1937): THE STORY OF FOSCA GORI

Since the fall of the Berlin Wall, German historians and scholars have conducted studies on the German-speaking intellectuals who had stayed in Sanary, this little Provençal fishing village called by Ludwig Marcuse, somewhat ironically, the "Capital of German Literature."[1] From Hitler's rise to power in 1933 until the declaration of war in 1939 dozens of writers, painters and poets settled in this quiet part of the French Riviera.[2]

As a consequence of these studies, the city of Sanary-sur-Mer published in 2004 a booklet in three languages showcasing the most famous names and their respective fates in relation to the events which took place during the war, along with a map indicating the location of the villas in which they had lived. Also, a plaque with a picture and a short notice was set up on each of the selected sites. Although Aldous Huxley's nationality logically excluded him from the group, he is nevertheless mentioned, with the privylege of having one plaque in his name on the site near the beach of La Gorguette where once stood the 'Villa Huxley,' called today 'Les Flots.' This plaque reads that the famous writer came to Sanary in 1929, where he wrote *Brave New World* in 1932, and that his home became an essential meeting point for the German intellectuals of Sanary.

None of the three pieces of information mentioned above was quite correct. During the icy end of January 1929, en route from Paris to Florence, Aldous Huxley, with his wife Maria behind the steering-wheel of their roaring automobile, made a stop in Bandol, a coastal village two miles west of Sanary, in order to visit D. H. Lawrence and his wife Frieda, who had been living there for a couple of months already. They stayed for ten days at the Hôtel Beau Rivage, where the Lawrences had first resided—just like Katherine Mansfield way back in 1915. At this time Lawrence was in the last phase of the illness which took his life in Vence thirteen months later.

Lawrence's recommendation to settle there and the sight of the lovely Bandol bay certainly caught the Huxleys' attention. After their stay in Italy they had purchased a house in Suresnes, but Aldous was already looking for a new place to live, for the Paris climate and environment did not suit him at all, so it was the Hôtel Beau Rivage that the couple drove back to soon after D. H. Lawrence's death on the second day of March 1930. They looked for a house to buy and within a week the owner of the hotel had found the right one: "We are just moving into a little house here on the sea, not far from Toulon. A l[ovely] place. If you ever condescend to revisit [the] Old World, remember our address," Aldous wrote to Dorothy Brett in June 1930.[3]

It was in this house at La Gorguette that from May to August 1931 Aldous Huxley wrote his most remarkable and most famous novel, *Brave New World*, published in London in February 1932. Between 1930 and 1937 he wrote a steady flow of articles for various English, American and even French publications, several essays, a play called *Now More Than Ever* (unpublished till 2000) and *Beyond the Mexique Bay*, a travel book. Another major novel, his most autobiographical one, *Eyeless in Gaza*, was written between 1934 and 1936 with much pain and effort, quite unusual for the fast writer Huxley had proved to be.

If it is not incorrect to say that a number of selected friends were invited to the house, Julius Meier-Graefe, Edith Wharton or the Noailles among them, 'Villa Huxley' was no open house, for, the creator he was, Aldous needed to work regular hours in a quiet environment, Sundays included. It was a place to meditate, read, study, paint and write, certainly not a place to entertain the international community, as some of his most famous neighbours, William Seabrook or Lion Feuchtwanger, did. Everything indicates that beside Sybille Bedford, the only German-born person in their entourage, and Eva Herrmann, who was half American, the Huxleys had little genuine contact with the German community. Klaus Mann later would be another exception with Huxley's participation in Mann's *Die Sammlung*.[4] Although his famous father, Thomas Mann, laureate of the Nobel Prize for Literature, crossed Huxley's path in Sanary first and later in Los Angeles, the two acclaimed men never developed an intellectual relationship as Huxley did with other prestigious minds of their times. Partly culture, but also language most certainly were responsible for that.

My encounter with Aldous Huxley

Having being raised in Toulon, like many teenagers I once laid my hands on a copy of *Brave New World* that I read with the same interest and passion which led me to devour Orwell's *1984*. Later, in adult life, I developed a passion for travelling. For many years I lived the life of an expatriate in the UK and the US (NYC and Southern California), and visited other countries like Italy, Spain, Tunisia, Mexico, Guatemala, Barbados, Malaysia, Singapore, Japan—in a way inadvertently following Huxley's footsteps. In 2000, after a full year in Australia (this time in Lawrence's footsteps), I then chose to settle in Sanary-sur-Mer, the favourite summer playground of my youth, precisely where Aldous Huxley had resided in the 1930s. But up until the 1990s nobody in the vicinity was aware of that fascinating detail.

In December 2004 I had just enrolled in a two-year course in English Literature and Civilization when Henri Ribot (a local scholar, historian and a friend), who had heard that I was planning to start some research on Aldous Huxley, informed me that an acquaintance of his knew quite well a lady of eighty-four years of age, Fosca Gori, who happened to have spent her teenage years at the 'Villa Huxley' during the writer's stay. He told me that the lady still had vivid memories of this period and had kept interesting documents and memorabilia that I should look at.

Within days I managed to see copies of these documents; I felt that they were just waiting for me! What I had in hand was superior to anything I had found so far on the subject; several dozen original photographs as well as postcards and letters, written in Italian and French by Maria Huxley and her sisters, sent or given to Giulia Gori, Fosca's mother, who at that time was in charge of the Huxley household.

Soon after this first discovery I contacted Fosca, a sweet grandmother living in Angoulême, and I had with her a long and most inspiring conversation. She told me that between her ninth and sixteenth birthdays she had visited the Huxleys' villa almost every day and sometimes even slept there overnight. She had had the chance to play with English children of her age, and to witness the simple—yet, by local standards, somewhat eccentric—daily life of these famous foreigners. She recalled very well the sophisticated man of letters Huxley was, the simplicity of his manners, and his constant devotion to his wife, whom he seemed to adore. Moreover, Fosca remembered the exquisite personality of Maria Huxley, her profound humanity, her genuine interest in people and true love for everyone involved in her life.

Fosca explained the special bond which attached her family to the Huxleys even long after the Sanary period. At the height of the war, during the harshest time, Maria had managed to send packages with clothes, food and some money to her own family as well as to her dearest Giulia, whom she never forgot. Parcels were still sent long after the war with, as always, these touching letters to enquire about the well-being of the Gori family and especially young Fosca, her favourite.

Fosca had always cherished these photographs and these letters which personified Maria, who had left an indelible mark upon her. Needless to say that Fosca was more than happy to hear that someone living in Sanary had the desire to make her story exist outside the family circle. By the fact that

I rapidly laid my hands on this first-choice material and that I had now a rare opportunity to record Fosca's original testimony, I was convinced that writing a paper on that very period of time would make full sense.

As much as Huxley in his novels had extensively described the Tuscany region and the life of rich British expatriates living there, he did not write a single paragraph on Sanary until *Eyeless in Gaza*, where one can find a description of the Morocco-type terrace of the villa and a flavour of the surrounding wilderness:

> From the flat roof of the house the eye was drawn first towards the west, where the pines slanted down to the sea-a blue Mediterranean bay fringed with pale bone-like rocks and cupped between high hills, green on their lower slopes with vines, grey with olive trees, then pine dark, earth red, rock-white or rosy-brown with parched hearth. Through a gap between the nearer hills, the long straight ridge of the Sainte-Baume stood out metallically clear, but blue with the distance. To north and south, the garden was hemmed in by pines; but eastwards, the vineyards and the olive orchards mounted in terraces of red earth to a crest; and the last trees stood, sometimes dark and brooding, sometimes alive with tremulous silver, against the sky.[5]

It is true that in his essay "Music at Night" there are a few poetic lines which appear to refer to the nocturnal atmosphere of the villa's garden:

> Moonless, this June night is all the more alive with stars. Its darkness is perfumed with faint gusts from the blossoming lime trees, with the smell of wetted earth and the invisible greenness of the vines. There is silence; but a silence that breathes with the soft breathing of the sea and, in the thin shrill noise of a cricket, insistently, incessantly harps on the fact of its own deep perfection. Far away, the passage of a train is like a long caress, moving gently, with an inexorable gentleness, across the warm living body of the night.[6]

In terms of Huxley's writing on Sanary, however, that is all that there is. The only descriptions of the 'Villa Huxley' along with some day-to-day anecdotes were to be found in two of Sybille Bedford's novels, *Jigsaw* and *Quicksands*, and in her famous authorized biography of Aldous Huxley in two volumes.[7]

By themselves Fosca's photographs were a valuable base to work on; I knew that Maria had taken most of them, but who were the more or less known persons posing in them? At what time approximately had these shots been taken? Concerning the letters and the postcards, it was much easier to decipher them because despite the fact that the majority were written in Italian (luckily they were typed) most of them were dated and described in accurate details Maria Huxley's impressions when discovering the new country which was to become her and Aldous' home until the end of their respective lives.

Maria's correspondence

Obviously Maria's letters could not compete with Aldous' in terms of style and content, but they were lively, peppered with eccentric spelling mistakes, and full of trivial details and heart-breaking observations on the state of the world and the practical difficulty to communicate with loved ones. In any case, they well reflected the expatriate couple's state of mind at that time. We learn that from the Huxleys' departure from Sanary in February 1937 until the end of 1939 Giulia Gori was in charge of the villa and was paid for her trustful work and presence, except for the summer months when members of the family and other guests resided there. Billux (Sybille Bedford) lived there, Suzanne Nys Nicolas, together with her husband, Dutch artist Joep, and their two little girls, Claire and Sylvia, spent the whole summer of 1938 at the Sanary villa.

After they had left Sanary Maria rented out the villa to "Little monsieur," or "Il Signorino"—Eddy Sackville West. A new life had begun:

> Dearest Giulia. We are really lost in the distance of mountains and deserts. We chose to spend the summer in a small mud and earthen house at 3000 meters in altitude, 6km from the main road by a steep and very bad road. [...] I am obliged to do everything on my own and I often think of you and I regret having been so lazy when I was at ease in the house and every time he writes me the "little monsieur" tells me so many beautiful and good things about you that I feel really melancholy. [...] I'm sending you a cheque for the month of April. We agree that I do not pay you for the summer months. I hope you are as satisfied with "Signorino" as he is delighted with you. I imagine that you all take care of him so well because you know how much I love him. (Letter from San Cristobal, New Mexico, May, 1937)[8]

During the year of 1937 staying in America did not seem to be a certitude:

> As we approach Christmas, I send you this check for you to have a party and remember us. Keep half for the salary of this month of November and celebrate with the other half. We do not know yet what we will do in February. For the time being we have to stay here for Monsieur. I cannot say if we will return home. (Letter from Rhinebeck, N. Y., 14 December 1937)

In April 1938 Maria announced that she would stay longer than planned:

> In my last letter I said it would not be long before we returned to Europe. I did not want to talk about it so as not to risk making false joys or disappointments and I was right. For now we are far

> away and once again in Hollywood. We will not even come back for the summer. (Letter from 1340 N. Laurel Avenue, Hollywood, CA, 13 April 1938)

In mid-1938 Maria was still uncertain:

> Dear Giulia, as we expect to return in the autumn to spend the winter in our house I think it would be better not to lend anything to my friends since I might need all that the house contains. Your Maria Huxley (Letter from 1340 N. Laurel Avenue, Hollywood, CA, 5 June 1938)

After the summer of 1938 Maria was making plans again:

> For the moment we do not return to France. Monsieur is not completely cured and the doctors say that we have to stay in this climate for a few more months. We will go to the mountain when my rental will end in 15 days [...]. I embrace you very much and I hope that you will be refreshed when you receive my letter. My thoughts are with you and your whole family. I wish you all the best for this winter. We are so anxious because of this war. God preserve us. I think so much of you all. (Letter from 1340 N. Laurel Avenue, Hollywood, CA, 12 September 1938)

With the declaration of war, 1939 turned out to be a year of 'no return.' To her sister Jeanne, Maria wrote on 15 November that she received Sanary's "accounts" and that she would not transfer anything more to Giulia, but that for Christmas she would send her a cheque.[9] Which, of course, she did.

In many letters Maria reported to Jeanne the difficulties in getting supplies for her family in Europe. She did not, however, forget to add: "And I hope that if necessary and if possible you will help Giulia a little. This woman has always been extremely good to me and devoted to us all. She must feel part of your family. Accept her a little."[10] And indeed, when Jeanne Nys married French writer and theatre director Georges Neveux at the Sanary Town Hall in August 1940, Giulia and her husband Guigo were the two witnesses.

The documents mentioned above seemed to be the most valuable testimonies. What I needed was to find the stories related to the photographs and find witnesses who could help me sort it all out in spite of the time elapsed. At first I thought I could wholly rely on Fosca Gori, but most of the pictures were in the then fashionable small format, and following a recent ocular degeneration her sight was now deficient. I had no choice but to count on Fosca only for what she remembered well; fortunately what she had always affirmed in several interviews had never changed or drifted into imprecision or fantasy.

The main witness

I first decided to turn to Matthew Huxley. In 2005, thanks to the Internet, I rapidly managed to contact Dorris Halsey, his Los Angeles literary agent, who sent him my request. Two days later I received the following answer:

> My agent Dorris Halsey forwarded your email to me. As Aldous' son, I have memories of the time we lived in Sanary and the house, La Gorguette. I was a boy when Aldous was writing *Brave New World* so how informative I can be is questionable. I am intrigued with your observations about Sanary with relation to *BWN*. Further, I am curious about your project. A bit more detail would provide me with a clearer idea of what you are looking for; and if and how I might be able to help you [...]. I look forward to hearing from you.

My first idea was to show him photographs of him as a nine-year-old boy playing on the beach with his father in Forte dei Marmi or, a little older, with friends of his age in the Sanary garden. There was a chance that Matthew would recall some of the photographs of his boyhood and that they would bring back a faraway past I knew he still cherished. He himself had had several opportunities to travel back to Sanary, once for his honeymoon with his wife Ellen, and years later when he had the luck to locate the paintings which had been left to Rina Rontini, the other faithful Italian servant from Tuscany. There were two full-length paintings of Aldous and Maria done around the 1920s by Sir John Collier, a member of the family,[11] two portraits of Maria by Aldous, plus some photographs and correspondence. Matthew proposed to buy them from Marcel Eustration, Rina's second husband and then widower, but the old man knew the sentimental value these pieces had had for his wife during her lifetime and he graciously gave them all to Matthew, who brought everything back to his home in Pennsylvania where I expected it to be at the time when I thought of visiting him.

I had heard the story directly from Rina and Marcel Eustration's niece who happened to have met the Huxleys once when a child in Dieulefit. I was ready to mention the photographs to Matthew Huxley when I learned the sad news:

> Author, NIMH Epidemiologist Matthew Huxley Dies at 84. Thursday, February 17, 2005. Mr. Huxley was born in London and came to the United States in 1937. He attended high school in Colorado before graduating from the University of California at Berkeley, and receiving a master's degree in public health from Harvard. His first marriage, to documentary filmmaker Ellen Hovde, ended in divorce. His second wife died in 1983. Survivors include his third wife, Franziska Reed Huxley of Washington and

> Morgantown, Pa., two children from his first marriage, Trevenen and Tessa Huxley, both of New York City; and two grandchildren. (*Washington Post*, 17 February 2005)

Unhappy stroke of fate, may Maria and Aldous' son rest in peace.

The young witnesses: Guy and Jean Kisling

There were two brothers, Jean and Guy—sons of the famous neighbour Moïse Kisling—who I hoped would remember a few things. In her account of one of the last picnics with the Huxleys, Sybille Bedford writes:

> It was a mid-day one and the site chosen by Renée Kisling an almost inaccessible cove beyond Le Brusc. A vanguard consisting of Maria, Renée, the two Kisling boys, tough little devils blackened by the sun, Matthew and myself, went early to bathe and reconnoitre. We left the cars on a promontory, Maria and the Kislings danced down a precipitous goat track, Matthew did creditably; I shut my eyes. [...] At noon Edith Wharton, Lalla Vandervelde, Paul Valéry and Mme Valéry, frail septuagenarians, shepherded by Aldous, were seen approaching the edge of the cliff. (Bedford, I, 327)

Sybille Bedford in her biography talks extensively of the relationship between Renée Kisling and Maria Huxley. Aldous did not particularly enjoy the company of his all too famous neighbour from La Plage Dorée, Modigliani's friend of the last moments, the rich and celebrated Montparnasse painter that was Moïse Kisling. Although a generous heart and a decent man, Kisling was too much of a show-off and a womanizer for the rather shy Huxley. On a few occasions they had dined in each other's homes, but Aldous was not particularly attracted by the artist's life-style. It was Kisling's vigorous and charismatic wife Renée who kept the relationship alive as Maria and Renée had meanwhile discovered that they shared a passion for plants, cats, and the outdoor life. The two were part of a group of women who socialized, meeting frequently at the 'Villa Huxley,' but only when Aldous was not present. When the Huxleys left for California in 1937, Maria as a token of friendship gave her famous red Bugatti to Renée.

It wasn't difficult to contact Guy and Jean Kisling, who had lived through the second half of the twentieth century in the shadow of their celebrated father. When I introduced myself to Guy Kisling, the older of the two brothers, it was to ask him if he had any recollection of the Huxleys, if he knew about the fate of the red Bugatti. He did in fact remember well the episode and after two meetings he invited me to lunch at his place. Guy Kisling still lived in the original family house 'La Baie,' on a large property nestled between the narrow coastal road and the Marseille-Toulon railway, yet offering the most beautiful view over the Bay of Bandol and the rocky promontory of La Gorguette, in the past named by some 'Huxley Point.' The one-level house built in 1939 and the nearby annex, which was once the studio in which Kisling had painted numerous portraits of the local beauties, still echoed the painter's presence.

If Guy Kisling was able to confirm that Maria Huxley offered the Bugatti to his mother, he was also able to tell me that the automobile ended in the snares of the German occupiers in 1942. He could well remember the car for he had driven it to Saint-Tropez without permission, only to be arrested for driving underage and sent home guarded by two gendarmes.

That was the only event Guy Kisling was able to recall; otherwise there were countless anecdotes of a spoiled brat, most of them post-war, but alas not many memories of Aldous and Maria, which is understandable for they were strangers belonging to the world of adults, of which he himself was not yet part. Guy Kisling had a slightly clearer recollection of Matthew because of their similar age, but most of it consisted of fishing and beach picnics, which is confirmed by biographers.

When in Paris I later visited his brother Jean Kisling, who had made a career as pilot for Air France, he couldn't tell me much either, but he was able to show me amazing photographs of the various celebrities with whom 'Kiki' (i.e., Moïse Kisling) had been acquainted during his life as a famed painter, and later sent me an original picture of Billux with a friend on the beach of our respective teenage years.[12]

Mrs Sybille Bedford

As I had already noticed, the name of Sybille Bedford seemed to be a sesame in the Huxleys' circle. The day I called Mrs Bedford in Chelsea, London, we engaged in a passionate conversation lasting more than forty minutes, in English at first, but rapidly switching to French, which she still spoke fluently. When I called she was just days away from the publication of *Quicksands*, the last opus of her memories, at ninety-five! The conversation with Sybille Bedford was touching for we conversed on the Sanary of today, which still bears numerous resemblances to that of the thirties. But when it came to the Huxleys she did not really show a willingness to talk. She told me that everything she had to say on that account was to be found in her books, particularly the new one, to be out soon. Mrs Bedford was getting weary with the conversation, nevertheless she expressed her support for my initiative, and I wished her well. A few weeks later I called her again after sending her some pictures on which I needed her advice, but she wasn't feeling well, so I did not insist. Before we said goodbye she had the time to give me a contact in the person of Noële Neveux, Aldous and Maria's niece for whom they had had a particular affection.

The story of Fosca Gori

On the whole, a good part of the material I had found had already—but sometimes only partially—been referred to in the books I knew of. If there had been omissions and errors here and there, a reading of Huxley's letters sometimes helped me to sort out the true from the inexact. Yet there was no need to repeat what others had said. The logical approach was to publicize what Fosca Gori had revealed, in parallel to the letters sent by Maria to her own family and to Fosca's own mother.

If Mrs Sybille Bedford had been called by a journalist "The Sphinx of Sanary,"[13] Mrs Fosca Gori for her part was more than willing to share her memories of the sweet days of her youth, as according to her it was "le meilleur des mondes," the best of worlds in the French sense of the expression. For me it became obvious that along with the material I had assembled, I should put Fosca's precious testimony in the centre of a monograph detailing at best the life and work of Aldous Huxley in relation to the world but also the domestic events which often reveal little-known details of the life of a famous public man and obviously those of his spouse, who was somewhat part of his legend.

All his life Huxley had been criticized by those who knew how brilliant he was and always expected a lot from him. But Huxley was all too human with his physical limitations and psychological flaws, as much as anyone else considering the illness and sorrow endured when he was young. Some of those critics had been hard on him—the British, particularly, never totally forgave him for not staying in England for the duration of the war—but he had never really lived long in England anyway, simply because warmth and light suited him better. In the course of their lives Maria and Aldous Huxley spent a great deal of time, energy and money helping relatives, friends and people who had worked for them. Fosca Gori's story is worth being told so that Huxley's readers, old ones just like new ones, will know for sure that the Huxleys applied early on, and on an everyday basis, what Aldous would declare as the sum of his thinking towards the end of his life: "'[T]he best advice I can give to people is to be a little kinder to each other.'"[14] Below there are condensed excerpts of Fosca's recollections as recorded on tape by herself and later on by myself, the two narratives having been conflated. The translations are mine.

"For me it was 'the best of worlds'"

"I was born in Florence in 1921. When I was eighteen months old my parents left Italy to work in Belgium. We did not stay there long because my mother Giulia did not like the climate. So we went back to Italy and my father left again for France to find work. He arrived in Sanary where he had cousins. We joined him soon after.

Then came the time when my mother met Mrs Huxley at the Hôtel Chardon (also called Hôtel de la Gorguette), as they had bought their villa, which was nearby, and they were having their renovating modifications done and were sleeping there. There was not yet the Aricot [a famous fish restaurant facing Bandol], even the little harbour that there is now was very small as compared to nowadays.

The Huxleys had bought this house because it was the only decent one that existed there at the time, above a rocky promontory only surrounded by vineyards and olive groves. It was not right at the beach so the area was very quiet, there was no one, it was a 'desert,' just a small dirt road from where you could hear the mighty red Bugatti coming. Down the hill was the sandy beach of La Gorguette with the big house of the eccentric American writer [William Seabrook], his house was the only one on the beach! There were only tamarisk shrubs, everywhere! There was a little path through this kind of jungle, we passed under the railway and we arrived at our place.

At the Hôtel Chardon nearby there were very few guests at that time who came here on vacation. Mémé [Fosca's mother Giulia] worked there as a chambermaid when Mrs Huxley met her. She asked what nationality she was, and when she said she was Italian that was a great joy because Aldous and Maria themselves had lived in Italy in the 1920s, where, before that, Maria had already spent part of the 1914–18 war years with her family, and after which she had cherished a love for Italy because the Italians had always been nice to her: so she was delighted to meet an Italian—and from Montecatini, so much the better! She still loved Italy, but she and Aldous had decided to leave it because of the Fascists there! She would always write to us in Italian, she spoke with no accent, she loved Italian.

When Maria started to talk to her she was so pleased my mother was Italian, and she said, 'I'm so sorry I have hired all the staff already, but come to see me anyway.' After several visits, when it was clear that they got along well, Maria said to Giulia: 'I absolutely want you to come to work for us, you will clean the car.' That's how she took on my mother.

At that time we usually came over with my young brother Erasmo. When Maria first saw us she was so nice! She complimented us and she asked what

I would like as a gift. She was told that I liked sewing and that I dreamed of having a doll, so she had one sent directly from Paris, and later she bought a real little *Singer* machine, adorable!

After a while she gave my mother lots of clothes that Matthew did not wear anymore, little pants, shirts all for Erasmo, who must have been three or four years younger than her son, and so my brother was wearing the clothes that did no longer fit Matthew, and even if he wore somewhat oversized clothes it did not matter. My brother did not realize it but he was suddenly dressed like a prince. Madame Huxley, she was a woman as you cannot imagine, extraordinary, a heart… a heart of gold!

Soon Madame Huxley met all sorts of problems with the young locals she had hired, and she often cried over the situation. Being between eighteen and twenty of age, their main concerns naturally were love affairs, things were going wrong because of that and so on. If Mrs Huxley was worried about the torments of youth, she was also annoyed to see that the young locals abused her kindness and good heart. There was Marcelle, who went off to get married, Camilla, who often had her child to look after. Rina, who had come with them from Tuscany and who was in charge of the household, had been a squanderer it seemed.

Point Counter Point had brought in a lot of money, but it was disappearing too fast! At one point Rina fell in love and she left with her Emile, the American writer's driver, so Madame Huxley confided to my mother, feeling sorry: 'Rina I had raised, having promised her mother that I would take care of her, and she leaves with a man…' She told my mother all of this, and she was crying because she was really in pain. So my mother said to her: 'Do not worry, you'll see, with me—I'll save you money!'

The other girls finally gone, my mother took care of everything: the cooking, the cleaning, picking the fruit, making preserves and so on… Then my father started to come over, and as he was good with the garden, he finally took care of it. 'How beautiful the flowers are, Guigo, I never had such beautiful roses!' Madame Huxley was never short of compliments!

My mother Giulia was an illiterate peasant from Tuscany, but she worked well and fast. She had a lot of common sense and wisdom that made Maria admire her. She stopped unnecessary expenses and excessive tariffs for foreigners, such as the exorbitant cost of fitting out the villa at the beginning. Giulia became the confidante and the support Maria needed in this foreign country.

When accompanying Maria to Sanary to do the errands Giulia would invariably sit in the passenger seat of the red Bugatti, and whichever member of the family or friend was coming along, everyone was summoned to help carry the baskets home. There was no master-domestic relationship because Madame did not want it so. When Giulia answered the telephone hanging on the wall of the entrance, one of the very first in Sanary, my mother was supposed to name herself 'the intendant,' not the maid. 'You are my intendant, there is no servant in my house,' insisted Madame Huxley.

They were extremely nice people. Every day I would eagerly wait for the moment to go to their home. I was young, but I did appreciate this sophisticated atmosphere; you should have seen them together, caring for each other, holding hands, delicate, nice and polite with everyone.

Over the years I would spend a lot of time in the house, where I stayed overnight so many times. Madame Huxley would prepare me a bath, make breakfast for me, she would share all kinds of stories as if I were another child of the house. I even had dinner with famous guests and Madame Huxley would ask me gently: 'What do you want to do, Fosca? Do you want to say goodbye to everyone or slope off like a Brit?' When they left for Italy or elsewhere they would always come back with heaps of presents for everybody. Madame would send us postcards from their trips, Mexico, Barbados… She had such a good heart, immense! She loved everybody, and him [Aldous] as well!

Monsieur Huxley, at the end of writing *Brave New World* [it was actually *Eyeless in Gaza*]—I can tell you that he was depressed and sick because he was unable to find the ending, he could not finish the book, and it was my mother who took care of him: 'Don't give him grape juice! You will harm his intestines even more.' Mémé knew how to take care of him and she gave him a decoction of herbs, so Aldous felt alive again and found the ending he was looking for! She healed him and that must not be forgotten!

From age nine until sixteen at the time they left for America, it was for me the best of all worlds!

Love from my family, affection from a family of the heart! I will eternally thank God for having me cross their path, and they will remain, especially Madame Huxley, an inspiration for the rest of my existence!"

From a walk on the site of the 'Villa Huxley'

After having phoned Fosca on several occasions, we finally met in the middle of summer at the house she still owns, not far from La Gorguette. It is not common to try to imagine someone's face after having seen it in photographs taken almost seventy years ago. In the later photographs Fosca was a beautiful girl in her twenties, and even now she still showed a certain striking elegance, even when dressed in simple clear-coloured sports wear. I found her to be much taller and thinner than I had imagined, unlike her mother in the photos. She was still wearing on her finger the ring Madame Huxley had given to her mother ages ago and that she had inherited.

The conversation naturally centred on the Huxleys, but also on her own life, which seemed serene at the evening of her existence. After a brief moment I sensed very well that she had been expecting this instant for a long time, the moment she would discuss her youth spent in the presence of those famous people whom the world had talked about for so long. Without boasting or exaggerating she was simply proud of the chance she had had to have been blessed by the presence of people like Maria and Aldous Huxley, adding that even when very young she had always sensed the privilege of it. In her heart and mind Maria Huxley was still alive, Fosca loved her the same way she had confessed to her mother seventy years ago.

One warm evening in August we walked down to the seashore to visit the site of this once deserted stretch of land between La Gorguette and La Pointe de la Cride. We stopped at 'Les Flots' in the Allée Thérèse where once had stood the 'Villa Huxley,' now a vacation centre for 'PEP13,' a Public Education Wards Network. We asked the young director permission to visit the garden. To him and the young women of the staff Fosca narrated her story while showing me around. She was moved because now the place bore little resemblance to what it had been in the past, but she managed to describe what it had looked like at that time, and she talked about the persons who had once lived there as if they had left only a few years ago, certainly not as far back as 1937! The young staff had always been intrigued by the plaque at the entrance, so after Fosca's moving story they could value this unexpected visit even more because now they knew the importance the writer and his wife had in the hearts of many people.

And Fosca went on and on: the description of the garden, the coloured fields of sweet peas, the ever perfumed house, the famous picnics in the garden and the beach parties with the inflatable rubber boat; Maria's mirrored room where she danced to keep a gracious line (she had once been a student of Vaslav Nijinsky's), the Siamese cats, Charlotte Wolff, the palm reader and psychologist, who came to read everyone's hand palms, the quiet atmosphere where no one was authorized to raise their voices when Mr Huxley was working, but, Fosca said, "besides that he spoke to us all the time! When Madame Huxley was away he would eat with us in the kitchen and tell us stories and stories… He and Madame Huxley even came to our place for Erasmo's 'Première Communion,' and on the day of my 'Certificat d'Etude' Madame Huxley came with my mother to pick me up with the Bugatti at the school without telling me beforehand. When I said I had succeeded my mother and Maria herself were so proud of me! Oh, mon Dieu!

The house was very pretty, it was not at all a Provençal house, it was like a house in Morocco. There were green shutters, she liked green. There was nothing upstairs, there was no roof, just a terrace where Madame Huxley used to sunbathe.

A palm tree was there, there was a magnificent *tilleul* ('lime tree') at the corner that has long since disappeared. It was beautiful, this *tilleuil*, beautiful and it smelled so good! What remains is the garage where she parked the Bugatti, with the painting workshop above. Monsieur Huxley only painted there. Once he took an interest in gardening, he was literally burrowing through the garden, but it did not last long.

At one point he painted every afternoon, relaxing from his writing, but when he worked in his office you were never expected to speak, there were no voices, we heard nothing, not a sound; but at noon it was all over, when we heard the gong we sat down at the table. Then later they had tea together, they sat side by side, he caressed her hands the moment they had tea… it was beautiful, it was so beautiful.

The entrance has always been there, at the reception a big phone hanging on the wall. Further inside there was the dining room and there the veranda, but they have demolished everything, what a horror! In the big living room there were huge pearly gray curtains, shiny, heavy, and often drawn, she did not want white curtains: 'Oh, nature is much more beautiful than white curtains,' she said! She did not like furniture; later she had her piano here, and her typewriter, next to the piano. And then there was the large glassy veranda, and over there his library—he was surrounded by books—here on the same floor, and he had a small terrace for himself in the front. It was she who typed everything or retyped it, I guess, but I know he did a lot of work here.

The kitchen was downstairs, in the veranda where they took their meals, and where they had tea every day at exactly 5 pm. They both dined downstairs and when there were guests it was upstairs in the beautiful dining room, but not all the time.

They were not always at home together. He often left alone, but sometimes it was she who left and then Monsieur Huxley stayed writing his books and we took care of him. He ate with us in the kitchen and he was so nice to us! A love, he told us stories without end, how funny he was!

Later, at the beginning of the war, my parents were the two witnesses at the Neveux' wedding in Sanary, Jeanne and the Parisian gentleman who was also a writer. I knew them all, the most beautiful of the four [sisters] was

Suzanne; Rose, she was very cute, very kind, she had married a nobleman, de Hauteville or something like that.[15] There was also Madame Huxley's brother-in-law, the painter [Joep] Nicolas, who came from Holland. He immediately painted me, he made me sit on an armchair—and there was one who painted me, and another one who drew me. The one who made the biggest picture was Nicolas. I wonder what became of this painting, oh! how I would like to see the paintings again… But what I remember is when Monsieur Huxley painted Sophie,[16] and he often painted her, but, between us, he did not paint well, oh no, one should not exaggerate, what he was doing was awful!"

Over a telephone call to America, where they live, I asked Sylvia and Claire Nicolas, Suzanne and Joep's daughters, about their father's painting of Fosca. They told me a few anecdotes in French, which they still spoke fluently. They remembered very well their dear childhood friend Fosca and her brother Erasmo, but they had no memories of the fate of the painting.

Fosca continued: "When he was at home, Monsieur Huxley did not want to receive anyone who was not invited, nobody. One day a member of the Royal Family[17] even came ringing unexpectedly, and he was not received![18] When Monsieur Huxley went to England, Maria in return socialized a lot. Often Sybille and Eva were at the villa, together with other friends who came when the gentleman was not there. They ate, they laughed. Madame Huxley was friends with the Kislings—with her, I specify, not him. Renée, when she spoke… she was warm, but vulgar. I do not understand how Madame Huxley could get along with a woman like that. She was educated, but she swore like a fishmonger, she so often took to the sea with her fisherman on his *pointu* [a local wooden boat], and she seemed happy." On his side Kisling was known to have made portraits of, and gone to bed with, many local beauties.

"They bathed at the Gorguette or at the small beach of l'Aricot. At that time there was no one else there, no vacationers, you tell me! It was much prettier then! The tall pines that leaned over the beach… It was not the port that it is today. Madame Huxley had bought a small square of land just above the beach, maybe she wanted to keep a boat there? We went to the beach a lot for swimming, but we did not stay long. Madame and Monsieur bathed together, sometimes naked; they went off a little and they discussed, she with her big straw hat… And then, in the late afternoon, they regularly went for a walk in the quiet little lanes all around the villa and along the sea shore.

They were always dressed simply but with great originality considering the region. Madame Huxley was often dressed in navy clothes which she regularly bought at the military port of Toulon. She wore beautiful white shorts, shorts which, however, made the coast guard at the time remark to her, 'Madame Huxley, shorts are good for little girls, but a lady like you…' She laughed.

They left at the beginning of 1937, when I was not a little girl anymore. But meeting them had enriched me enormously, and I still maintain a boundless admiration for these exceptional people. I grew up in all that, and following their example I accepted everything in life.

They sensed the war was coming. After its declaration Madame Huxley sent us a picture that showed her with sad eyes [this picture seems to have been lost]. They were philosophers who wanted people to be happy on earth. There was a great love between them, but I had the impression that he loved her more than she loved him, indeed she saw a lot of women, her lifestyle was more unconventional. When Madame Huxley left she said, 'Take whatever you want,' but my mother replied, 'I do not want to take anything, it's theft! The house will stay like that!' After Mrs Neveux at the beginning of the war had sold 'Villa Huxley' and bought the other house,[19] she hired some of the old staff again and it is said that quite a lot were taken on. Madame Huxley gave us a clock that I still have at home and her own engagement ring, which I hold so dear."

Further investigations

It is said that Huxley had always been ahead of his time, expressing visionary views on important issues facing our societies. As I have already mentioned, when I learned that Huxley had completed *Brave New World* in Sanary as early as 1931, my intention was to comprehend his creative process of working on the uncommon theme of this negative utopia which, indeed, became a gloomy picture of the future. What puzzled me most was that he had written it in less than four months in the familiar environment I knew so well: sun-drenched beaches, pine groves and cicadas, so far away from the technocracy depicted in his book. What kind of background did he possess to have mastered so well such a scientific subject? How did he manage to find the sources he needed?

Sanary was a picturesque fishing village, but at the time there were no fast trains and it was a long day journey to London. After having settled in his new environment he had in mind to write a satire on the utopian visions of H. G. Wells, whom he knew well. He got carried away by the subject and ended up writing his best-known novel. With *Brave New World* Huxley took a step forward, drifting away from what he had done before to write almost exclusively on human potentials and the capacity, or incapacity, of man to be one with the world surrounding him.

One has to remember that in *Brave New World* Huxley described a modern but authoritarian world—perhaps like the one he had discovered in Italy in the mid-1920s? So could this be the answer? Not really, according to what we learn from his correspondence. At the beginning of the Huxleys' stay there, Italy was a model of socialism on the surface, but in reality a rather disorganized feudal society, nothing compared to the iron fist of Stalin's Communism, which at this period went largely unpublicized, or the kind of society not yet established by the Nazis.

Aldous Huxley had already travelled the world: from India, where he had seen the dismay of the inferior castes, and America, which he had crossed, briefly stopping in the Indian reservations, but generally witnessing the cruel poverty bred by the Great Depression, to Northern England, where he had been shocked to see the miserable life of the coal miners. He then gathered basic sources from the London libraries and the rest he found within the realm of his own fertile imagination, and in hard work.

My investigations show that reports of excesses in his social life were exaggerated and that the accusations of snobbism and racism by British or even French reviewers were quite unjustified. This is why, among other testimonies, the memories of a family of simple servants are more valuable decades after the facts. They confirm just how much the couple cared for others.

Having been her employer for seven years, the Huxleys had a profound affection for Giulia and her family, to the point where they managed to provide them with legal papers, even offering them a piece of land on their own property to have a house built for them there. Some days before they left for America they proposed to take the entire family with them. Fosca's mother declined the offer, but although they were far away, the Huxleys did not forget Giulia and her family. Maria's letters are here to prove it:

> Dearest Giulia, I heard from Count Noailles, who wrote to me after visiting you. But since then there is the immense danger of war that we follow every moment while listening to the radio and this causes us great anxiety [...], perhaps we will never see each other again. It would be nice to kiss you again and look at your face because Madame Jeanne sent me a big, beautiful picture of you with her and I hung it on the wall of my room. So I see you at least once a day. (24 November 1938) [My translation]

The Villa 'Huxley,' La Gorguette at Sanary-sur-Mer

With its seething cultural life and its venerable libraries London remained Huxley's main place of research, but how agonizing the atmosphere must have been for someone deprived of the breeze and light of the Mediterranean, the latter being the indispensable fuel for the writer's inspiration. Sanary had no library at all nor any cultural life beside the one Huxley's presence automatically triggered wherever he lived. Yet, this small and all traditional fishing village met the necessary conditions for him to practise his profession as a writer according to his own standards, midway between living a hermit's life and that of a socialite, depending on his inspiration and the publication of his books. While in Sanary Aldous Huxley altogether published ten of them, plus hundreds of articles.

Years passed, almost seven, during which every summer was spent sunning and basking on the nearby beach, working endless hours, painting, gardening, reading out aloud while making jam, listening to Beethoven and Bach on the old gramophone, travelling a lot and socializing with faithful friends.

There were ups and downs, years better than others. 1933 saw the arrival of the German refugees in Sanary, nothing would ever be the same. 1935 was called the "terrible year" by Maria because Aldous could not finish a difficult, yet pivotal work for his future orientation, *Eyeless in Gaza* (1936). The Bloomsbury years gone, Italy fallen into the hands of the Fascists, and the European skies becoming darker and darker, Huxley could not stay idle; he had to defend what he had always praised. In 1935, on the advice of his friend Gerald Heard, he got himself involved in the pacifist movement of the Peace Pledge Union (PPU), in which numerous people suddenly found hope. Huxley wrote many PPU speeches and attended congresses in London and Paris. But the terrible events of 1936 in Spain, which prefigured the upcoming war, were to put a definitive halt to the philosophical discourse.

In April 1937 Aldous Huxley, together with Maria and Matthew and his friend and mentor Gerald Heard, left Europe for America. The main reason was to find a new school for Matthew. They had planned to stay for a year; they would not come back for another ten years, for the Old World had lost its head.

Two years before his death in California in 1963, a brush fire in the Hollywood Hills completely consumed the house Aldous Huxley and his second wife, Laura, inhabited, destroying most of their personal belongings, his library of 4000 books, and a life's worth of precious archiving. This is the main reason why so many documents from Aldous's and Maria's time in Sanary were irretrievably lost.

The Fosca Gori documents

The appearance of these documents, along with the lively testimony of Fosca Gori, a first-rate witness of these somewhat blessed years, sheds a touching light on the Huxleys' family life.

During their seven-year stay Maria Huxley regularly sent postcards from their travels and gave numerous photographs to Giulia Gori. Once in America she sent her letters in Italian. Giulia barely spoke French, she did not write it, but she knew how to count and she had an interesting point of view of life and people. Sybille Bedford said that Giulia was able to get the measure of people, apparently well enough for Maria to put her trust in her. Maria was also very fond of Giulia's daughter Fosca, the bright little girl she could never have. She took care of her, bathed her, watched her progress and her first little children's joys with a porcelain doll as well as her first sewing machine directly procured from London.

The Gori collection counts over seventy rather small pictures, most of which had to be restored, and a dozen letters plus some postcards, all in Italian. These letters, although not numerous, bear witness to the intensity and depth Maria felt for personal relations. They very well show her attachment to this faithful Italian family, as well as her state of mind from her arrival in New Mexico, where she experienced a totally different lifestyle, until the announcement that the war was over, a touching moment in history. Throughout the Sanary years—and also in America—Maria relied on faithful assistants such as Giulia Gori to lighten her workload and make life easier for her visually handicapped husband, who was always in need of practical support.

Maria's sense of responsibility towards her whole family grew in importance with the outbreak of the war, and then became an inevitable misfortune that broke her heart. A heart of gold she had, but also a frail constitution and a weak immune system which, over the years, got the better of her, probably precipitating her too early death.

Out of seventy pictures I have selected about thirty worth being shown in a future publication. I can put a name to most of the people in the photos, but there are a few mysterious faces left, and I will challenge specialists to recognize them. In this selection of pictures you will see Aldous Huxley in the most relaxed atmospheres: during the famous picnics, resting in the garden, bathing with Maria while discussing the world. A snapshot taken from behind exists of Huxley swimming naked, but we will keep that as a 'hidden Huxley'… Beside his family, the most famous personalities one can recognize are Thomas Mann and his wife, Gerald Heard, Moïse Kisling, Eddy Sackville-West. Maria also gave Giulia three versions of the famous picture of Lawrence and Huxley sitting in the grass in Tuscany.

The first photograph that I wish to present here from my Gori collection was probably taken by Maria in the garden of the 'Villa Huxley' in June 1932. One can recognize Aldous Huxley with longtime friends Raymond Mortimer and Eddy Sackville-West, who were known to be visiting at that time. But who are the two ladies standing next to Raymond and Eddy? An answer from the Huxley community will be welcome.

Five friends in the Sanary garden

The next photo, ending this article, is in memory of Fosca Gori and Noële Neveux. In this picture taken in the Neveux's garden on a spring day in 1941 we can see Fosca holding Noële and looking after her—Fosca, daughter of the proud Giulia Gori, without whom my research would never have started, and Noële, daughter of Jeanne Nys and Georges Neveux, to whom I promised to write the full account of the Sanary years. I owe them both their precious testimonies, they passed on to me their admiration for Maria Nys Huxley, who lived in the shadow of the great man, without ever being fully overcast by it.

Fosca Gori and Noële Neveux

[1] Jean-Michel Palmier, *Weimar in Exile: The Antifascist Emigration in Europe and America*, trans. David Fernbach (London, 2006), 196.

[2] A large number of German and Austrian intellectuals chose to flee their countries after the Nazi book-burning nights. Between spring 1933 and the outbreak of World War II hundreds of them, mostly Jewish, settled in Le Lavandou, Bandol and Sanary, which by itself lists 78 names on the marble plaque put up on the front of the Tourist Office. If some, like Thomas Mann, Arnold Zweig or Bertolt Brecht, decided early on to find refuge in other parts of the free world, most of the refugees had no choice but to stay longer in Sanary, where living conditions were favourable even with little or no means.

[3] *Letters of Aldous Huxley*, ed. Grover Smith (London, 1969), 339.

[4] A monthly anti-Nazi literary magazine published between September 1933 and August 1935 by Klaus Mann. Along with Aldous Huxley Bertolt Brecht, Jean Cocteau, Albert Einstein, Lion Feuchtwanger, Bruno Frank, André Gide, Ernest Hemingway, André Maurois, and Klaus Mann's brother Golo and uncle Heinrich Mann were the most famed contributors.

[5] Aldous Huxley, *Eyeless in Gaza* (London, 1936), 19.

[6] Aldous Huxley, *Music at Night* (London, 1931), 43.

[7] Sybille Bedford, *Jigsaw: An Unsentimental Education* (London, 1989); *Quicksands: A Memoir* (London, 2005); *Aldous Huxley: A Biography* (2 vols., London, 1973–74) [hereafter, Bedford].

[8] My translation, as in the following letters to Giulia written in Italian.

[9] Letter of Maria to Jeanne Nys, 15 November 1941, Nys Fund, Royal Library Bruxelles, Belgium.

[10] Letter of Maria to Jeanne Nys, 31 July 1941, Nys Fund, Royal Library Bruxelles, Belgium.

[11] See Bedford, I, 275. These large-size pieces were given to Rina for her own wedding with Emilio, William Seabrook's driver, in 1933.

[12] I myself spent numerous summers at Plage Dorée, Plage de Beaucours or Plage de la Gorguette near-by the 'Villa Huxley.'

[13] Martin Mauthner, *The Spectator* (17 March 2001), 42.

[14] Quoted in Laura Archera Huxley, *This Timeless Moment: A Personal View of Aldous Huxley* (London, 1969), 117.

[15] Baron Eric De Haulleville, surrealist poet, who died in Vence in 1941.

[16] Sophie Moulaert, Jeanne Nys' daughter from a first marriage with René Moulaert, a Belgian theatrical decorator, whom she divorced in 1929. Sophie was three years younger than Matthew, whom she was very close to; the Huxleys almost considered them brother and sister. Sophie left France in November 1939 to live with them in California. Maria thought of adopting her if the situation in France was to deteriorate. Her sister Jeanne, however, who had founded a new family with Georges Neveux, dismissed the idea. After five years in America Sophie finally went back to France in1944 to take part in the Liberation with the Free French Forces.

[17] That was Edward VIII, Prince of Wales, who regularly visited Hyères and the region. With Wallis Sympson he once stayed at the Count and Countess de Noailles' home, the famous modern masterpiece designed by Robert Mallet-Stevens and called till today 'Villa Noailles.' The local newspaper *Le Petit Var* published (date unknown) the following anecdote concerning Edward VIII and Aldous Huxley: "Here is an example of the charming modesty of Edward VIII at the time when he was free, or nearly so, to live his life as he pleased. As he was having lunch this summer at Sanary where he had come on a tour from Cannes, the restaurant's owner asked the most illustrious Englishman to leave his signature in his book of honour. With a smile the Prince showed him the great writer Aldous Huxley, who makes long stays each year in the charming little Provençal port and who was precisely eating at a neighbouring table: 'No, my friend,' replied the Prince of Wales. 'Sanary's most famous Englishman is not me, it is this gentleman.'" (My translation.)

[18] Perhaps it was because of the Prince of Wales' pro-Nazi feelings that Huxley refused to open his door? (Author's note.)

[19] With the German invasion arriving the Huxleys feared that with such a famous British owner their villa would be more easily requisitioned. Upon Maria's request (letters dated 11 and 16 March 1941, Nys Fund, Royal Library Bruxelles, Belgium) 'Villa Huxley' was sold by her sister Jeanne in mid-1941. Jeanne then purchased a villa under her own name, 'Villa La Rustique,' where she, her husband Georges and the young Noële spent many summers. It was at the 'Villa La Rustique' near the centre of Sanary that the Huxley couple stayed (from 30 August to 18 September 1948) when they came back for the first time since 1937. Matthew and his first wife Ellen spent their honeymoon there, and in August 1950 the Huxleys came again for a full month. That was their last visit to Sanary.

Jerome Meckier
(University of Kentucky)

Aldous Huxley and the Cure Scene in Modern Literary Utopias[1]

In the prototypical cure scene from Samuel Butler's *Erewhon* (1872), confusion develops as to what constitutes sickness and what health. Shortly after Higgs stumbles upon Erewhon, he is nearly "imprisoned" for catching cold.[2] On the other hand, Mr. Nosnibor, "'lately recovered from embezzling a large sum of money'" (*E*, 68), continues to be greatly respected because in Erewhon, sickness is a crime; crime is considered a sickness. Victorians punished criminals severely but coddled the sick. Butler laughed at both countries but especially at Britishers like Higgs, who "cannot bear having much to do with people who think differently" (71). The real danger, Butler surmised, was that in the future the state might manipulate concepts of sickness and health to enforce its policies: conformity would be regarded as health; anyone disagreeing would have to be cured.

From *Erewhon* to *Island*, a cycle of roughly a hundred years, one society after another reveals that it is not the utopia it pretends to be by proposing to rehabilitate a protagonist who seems healthier and saner than it is. Novelists outdo each other trying to invent a more insidious cure scene. There is a constant redoing, each utopist striving to be more diabolical. It appears that no one can resist the almighty state's penchant for perverse corrections. Finally, Huxley intervenes with a cure for the cure scene itself; he offers a genuine rehabilitation as proof of his final utopia's perfection.

Yevgeny Zamiatin's *We* (1924) was the first major utopia to replace Butler's playful ambivalence with painful ironies.[3] The government is clearly the sick party, not D-503, whom it presumes to cure. The totalitarian One State coerces a deviant back into the fold by persuading him that he has fallen ill. Its cure makes it impossible for D-503 not to embrace the government's perverse doctrines ever after. In the novel's thoroughly absurd happy ending, a lobotomized D-503 and the One State seem pleased with each other.

The One State's totally regimented citizens have numbers in place of names. All wear the same "pale blue unifs" (uniforms) (Z, 5) and do everything with mathematical precision, even chewing each mouthful of food a prescribed number of times. They obey the Benefactor unreservedly. D-503, the One State's leading scientist, is building "the *Integral*," a rocket ship designed to "subjugate" planets "still living in the primitive condition of freedom" (Z, 1).[4] I-330, a *femme fatale*, awakens the heretofore rational D-503's second self, which proves to be poetic and sensual. Confused, he consults a doctor: "'You're in a bad way!'" he is told; "'You have developed a soul'" (Z, 89). "'Is it very dangerous?'" D-503 inquires. "'Incurable'" is the unfortunate reply.

Actually, the One State, fearing an "epidemic" of "soul sickness" (Z, 91, 195), has devised an invidious cure: "excision of the imagination" (Z, 81), whereby the last traces of one's creativity and rebelliousness are removed. Being "ill," D-503 becomes convinced, means acquiring "individual consciousness" (Z, 128) in lieu of universal depersonalization. Such awareness is "merely a sickness," he decides, just "a miserable little nodule in the brain" that one can be "cured of" by its extraction (Z, 180). Tied to a table, D-503 is "subjected to the Great Operation" (Z, 232). "I am well," he subsequently writes in his diary without a trace of regret: "a kind of splinter was pulled out of my head," which now "feels light and empty" (Z, 231), hardly the ideal mental state. D-503 tells the Benefactor "everything" he knows about I-330 and her confederates, the Mephi,[5] who are promptly condemned as "enemies of happiness" (Z, 232). In *We*'s cure scene, which is both scary and funny, sickness and health trade places more disconcertingly than they do for Butler's Higgs. By its method of curing D-503, the One State indelibly stamps itself a negative utopia.[6]

In the first of three climactic cure scenes in *Brave New World* (1932), John the Savage disrupts the distribution of the daily "*soma* ration" (*BNW*, 171) to the menial staff of the Park Lane Hospital for the Dying, an unpromising setting for a cure. "'Lend me your ears,'" John begins; "'Don't take that horrible stuff. It's poison.'" He insists he has "'come to bring [them] freedom'" (*BNW*, 173) by ending the drug dependency that keeps them happily servile.

Unfortunately, the "khaki mob" of maggoty twins prefers euphoria to independence. "Exasperated" by such "brutal stupidity" (*BNW*, 174), the Savage begins throwing pill-boxes of *soma* out the window. When the infuriated Deltas charge, John is soon discarding *soma* with one hand and punching "the indistinguishable faces of his assailants" with the other (*BNW*, 175). The disturbance quickly escalates into a riot as a well-meaning visitor fails to cure a group of dystopia's unheeding citizens of their *soma* addiction.

"A full head" taller than his attackers, John swings away at a swarm of "less than human monsters" mad enough to "kill him" (*BNW*, 171, 174, 175). At once ludicrous and frightening, Huxley's cure scene parodies the funeral oration Mark Antony delivers after Caesar's murder: "'Friends, Romans, Countrymen, lend me your ears!'" He subtly convinces the Plebeians that Brutus and his allegedly "honorable" accomplices are actually "traitors."[7] Like John, Antony achieves a different result from his ostensible purpose but does so intentionally. Huxley's Shakespeare-quoting Savage, an outsider who fails to impress the society in which he finds himself trapped, winds up fighting the workers he intended to save.[8]

No one gets cured in the two cure scenes with which *Brave New World* ends. In Chapter XVI, Mustapha Mond banishes Helmholtz Watson to the Falklands for fighting alongside John at the Park Lane Hospital. Watson is clearly not about to be reformed. The World State seems more anxious to purge itself than to discourage Watson's new-found penchant for solitude and independent thought. As in Zamiatin, the unhealthy party here is the government. Exile to an island, Watson's punishment, is less draconian than D-503's lobotomy, but it reveals an unsound society's determination to maintain a meretricious status quo by deporting its healthiest citizens. The World State is more demented than the One State. This "insane" utopia (*BNW*, viii), as Huxley calls it, dispenses with the one person who might do it some good. A nascent poet-mystic, Watson has begun pursuing loftier ideals than the brave new world's limited concept of "happiness" as "well-being," i.e., bodily health.

Island exile may be more prize than punishment, an ironic misfortune.[9] Although Watson selects the "thoroughly bad climate" of the Falklands over the Marquesas or Samoa—allegedly it will prove more conducive to composing—Mond calls it "really a reward" (*BNW*, 186, 187). Along with Bernard Marx, Watson is

> "being sent to a place where he'll meet the most interesting set of men and women to be found anywhere in the world. All the people who, for one reason or another, have got too self-consciously individual to fit into community-life. All the people who aren't satisfied with orthodoxy, who've got independent ideas of their own. Every one, in a word, who's anyone." (BNW, 186)

"'I almost envy you,'" Mond concludes. The "almost" is worrisome, but Watson seems destined to associate with talented misfits like himself, a blessing in disguise. If he continues to poeticize, he will make himself sicker by brave new world standards. Ironically, island exile can only aggravate the so-called illness it purports to cure.

In the novel's best-known cure scene (Ch. XVII), the World Controller, speaking for the brave new world, tries unsuccessfully to convert an outsider to its spurious views. Parallel lines, Mond and John the Savage argue to a stalemate, neither convincing the other, which leaves readers with a counterpoint instead of resolution. Freedom, which John champions, and happiness, the World State's *summum bonum*, turn out to be as contrapuntal in Huxley's opinion as Fulke Greville found "passion and reason, self-division's cause."[10] Apparently, one cannot have both of the former simultaneously yet neither satisfies without the other.

Mond advocates a prelapsarian happiness. Blissfully ignorant, thoroughly conditioned to glorify their lot as the best possible, brave new worlders enjoy the "perfect health" that Adam and Eve knew before the Fall; an unquestioning happiness predicated on the absence of "inconveniences" (*BNW*, 196, 197) such as sin, introspection and, above all, suffering. "'People are happy'" in the brave new world, Mond boasts; "'they're never ill'" (*BNW*, 180). Happiness means never getting sick, never having to worry. John objects that life on such terms is "'too easy'" (*BNW*, 196), mindless and meaningless. "'I want freedom,'" he declares, such as our first parents acquired by eating forbidden fruit from the Tree of Knowledge. Mond accuses John of "'claiming the right to be unhappy,'" i.e., the right to grow old as did Adam and Eve, to contract typhoid, syphilis, and cancer, to suffer "'unspeakable pains of every kind'" (*BNW*, 197). "'I claim them all,' said the Savage at last." At the end of a debate supposed to win John over to the World State, he embraces every known sickness and disease rather than become a healthy brave new worlder.

Huxley outdoes Zamiatin with three cure scenes as variations on a theme: not a single genuine cure is effected. John the Savage fails to liberate the Deltas; given "a fresh supply of pill-boxes," they are soon "kissing and hugging one another" (*BNW*, 176). Watson may signal the next evolutionary advance for humankind, an expansion of consciousness. Yet even if he becomes poet laureate of the Falklands, maturing into a full-fledged poet and mystic by actualizing the "extra latent power (*BNW*, 149), he senses within,[11] his breakthrough can have little impact on the brave new worlders left behind. The debate between Mond and the Savage improves upon *We*, wherein the Benefactor invites D-503 to "argue" with him (Z, 213), then brushes aside his objections.[12] Huxley's World State is irrevocably certified as a dystopia when the incurably disillusioned Savage hangs himself rather than continue to live there.

D. H. Lawrence believed that, by 1928, an industrial dystopia already existed for dehumanized coal miners in and around Nottingham as well as for the deformed steel-workers from Sheffield.[13] The former appear as permanently "blackened" as the countryside, whereas the latter are "weird, distorted, smallish beings" who frighten Connie (*LCL*, 142, 143). In *Lady*

Chatterley's Lover (1928), industrialists such as her husband have sucked the vitality—the instinctive, passionate side of human nature—out of Tevershall's work-force. Thanks to their underground existence, Sir Clifford's miners have been reduced to "less than humanness" (*LCL*, 143); this "new race" of dwarfish "creatures" seems worse off than Wells's subterranean Morlocs, whom they resemble, or Huxley's subhuman Deltas.

Unlike the time traveler, Connie need not journey into the distant future to learn "what has man done to man" (*LCL*, 143). A simple car ride through "the long squalid streets of Tevershall" gives her a sense of the future as "utter negation" (*LCL*, 142). Under conditions that continually imperil "the life of the body," destroying its "living intuitive faculty" (*LCL*, 219, 142), Mellors and Connie, Sir Clifford's wife and his gamekeeper, struggle to resurrect each other: each strives to bring the other back to the fullness of physical life. Despite their adulterous affair, they are the only ones who remain faithful to the feelings and instincts industrial society has betrayed. Inspired by Mellors, Connie goes so far as to predict victory, complete recovery for life-worshippers like herself and Mellors: the body "'is really rising from the tomb,'" she cries (*LCL*, 220).

By novel's end, Connie and Mellors develop into full-blown life-worshippers, ardent proponents of unrestricted physical awareness here and now, in which "the body is really wakened to life" (*LCL*, 219). They accomplish this by violating taboos, not just the one prohibiting adultery but also England's supreme sexual taboo forbidding sodomy—anal copulation with a member of the opposite sex. Through a starting transgression comparable to Adam and Eve's, Lawrence sought to liberate society-in-general along with Connie from all self-imposed constraints due to guilt or fear. Living with Clifford and his ilk is literally killing Connie. Her health, her state of mind as well as her physical condition, deteriorates rapidly until Mellors begins giving lessons in love. He is still bitter from his failed marriage to Bertha, so Connie in effect forces him to wake up and make a new start. Their mutual restoration culminates in an intense cure scene on their "last night" in Mellors' hut before Connie and Hilda leave for Venice.

The irony in Lady Chatterley's cure scene is that through perversity, that is, by means of what society considers sick behavior, lies a path to physical, bodily health, not to mention a peace of mind akin for Lawrence to spiritual contentment. Two malcontents in an industrial dystopia cure each other by violating society's ultimate taboo. Indirectly, almost in Connie's own words, Lawrence recounts her "night of sensual passion":

> [S]he was a little startled and almost unwilling: yet pierced again with piercing thrills of sensuality, different, sharper, more terrible

> than the thrills of tenderness, but, at the moment, more desirable. [...] [S]he let him have his way, and the reckless, shameless sensuality shook her to her foundations, stripped her to the very last, and made a different woman of her. [...] Burning out the shames, the deepest, oldest shames, in the most secret places [...] to burn out the false shames and smelt out the heaviest ore of the body into purity. [...] the shame died [...] the deep organic shame, the old, old physical fear which [...] can only be chased away by the sensual fire [...] by the phallic hunt [...]. She felt, now, she had come to the real bed-rock of her nature, and was essentially shameless (*LCL*, 231–32).

Almost painfully, Connie savors a sexual emancipation that Lawrence believed all persons must experience, in one form or another, if they are to recapture the shamelessness that Adam and Eve knew prior to original sin. Thanks to Mellors, Connie regains a certain paradoxical "purity," complete freedom from "the old, old physical fear," namely, fear of the physical; in short, she recovers a utopian state of bodily wellness not unlike bliss. Without this state, says Lawrence, there can be no ideal place. Shaken "to her foundations," having reached down to "the real bed-rock of her nature," Connie sheds the last of her inhibitions; decisively uninhibited, she turns into "a different woman," someone completely cured, entirely healthy, indeed, virtually reborn. Ironically, her transformation, a form of enlightenment, takes place amidst the "nightmare" of a dystopia that threatens to engulf her as modern life becomes increasingly "mechanical" (*LCL*, 143, 146), more and more hostile to all things physical. Mustapha Mond, one recalls, censors a heretical paper that dared to posit the "refining of consciousness" as life's purpose (*BNW*, 145). Lawrence's heroine finds the "refinements of passion," unimpeded delight in the body from moment to moment, quintessential for living well even in dystopia.

Regrettably, Connie's redemptive feat remains a secret from everyone except Mellors. Not rebels so much as social outcasts thanks to Connie's infidelity, their really serious offense goes undetected[14] by a society whose mores seem impervious to change. The only chance Mellors and Connie have of not being the last full-bodied man and woman is to transmit their outlook, Lawrence's so-called 'blood philosophy,' to the next generation.[15] Hence the importance of Connie's pregnancy. Occurring out of wedlock, it violates a third taboo. Separated at novel's end, Connie and Mellors plan to reunite "next year" after she secures a divorce (*LCL*, 282). They must keep Connie's child out of Sir Clifford's clutches. Whether these things will happen Lawrence seems uncertain. An additional irony remains possible: the novel's cure scene could prove to be transitory, its traducing of society's moral code a breakthrough best seen as an anomaly, if not a last gasp. I-

330's frank sexuality discombobulates D-503 and a "pneumatic" Lenina Crowne (*BNW*, 40) unsettles John the Savage. Lawrence longs to invest the physical attraction between Mellors and Connie with utopic possibilities yet cannot be confident of having done so. Albeit the cure Mellors applies to Connie works, the need for it condemns the ethos of an anti-human industrialized system whose victims may still include Mellors and Connie.

In the lengthy cure scene from Huxley's *Ape and Essence* (1949), the Arch-Vicar of Belial fails to persuade an outsider, Dr. Alfred Poole, to enter the devilish priesthood that rules a post-nuclear society in Southern California. It is 2108, more than a century after atomic bombs pounded most of the world back into the Stone Age.[16] A simian community in and around Los Angeles is convinced that only diabolical possession—indeed, the devil himself—could have driven the twentieth century, especially "between 1945 and the beginning of the Third World War" (*AE*, 97), to the brink of universal self-destruction. Consequently, survivors worship Belial[17] and take orders from the Arch-Vicar, a shabbier version of "his fordship" (*BNW*, 37), Mustapha Mond in Huxley's previous dystopia.[18]

Alfred Poole is chief botanist for the New Zealand Re-Discovery Expedition. An isolated New Zealand was spared the "radioactive conditions" prevalent everywhere else (*AE*, 28); its reconnaissance boat, a make-shift time machine, has reached Southern California in search of signs of life. A thirty eight year-old virgin, whom his colleagues have nicknamed "Stagnant," Poole is captured by "villainous-looking" workers and taken to the Arch-Vicar (*AE*, 44). Once it becomes clear that Poole can help everyone get "more to eat," the Arch-Vicar invites him to "become one of us" (*AE*, 55, 138). Joining the devil's priesthood, however, involves castration. All priests, Poole suddenly realizes, are beardless contraltos. The Arch-Vicar urges Poole to undergo "physiological conversion," a cure which will free him from all temptations besetting "an unmutated male" (*AE*, 139).

Poole is subjected to a long history lesson reminiscent of Our Ford's lecture in Chapter III of *Brave New World*—except that it is too much a straight forward sermon to be nearly as effective. The Arch-Vicar reviews disasters that culminated in a third world war: overcrowding (i.e., the population explosion), hubristic misuse of technology, depletion of natural resources, heavy industrialization resulting in widespread pollution, etc. (see *AE,* 92–94). All the economic and political mistakes that Huxley's essays warned against throughout the 1940's have had predictably calamitous consequences. The lecture stands as Huxley's redoing of Mond's debate with the Savage in Chapter XVII of *Brave New World*, but Poole's infrequent and feeble objections are easily dismissed by the devil's advocate.

During Belial Day ceremonies in the Los Angeles Coliseum, deformed babies born during the past year are systematically slaughtered. Rounding up these victims of radioactivity is not difficult: all babies are conceived during the "five weeks" following Belial Day (*AE*, 102). When the Arch-Vicar's lecture and the slaughter of the innocents conclude simultaneously, Poole participates in the orgy that opens this dystopia's annual mating season. For the other forty-seven weeks, girls wear a patch saying "No" over each breast (*AE*, 46) and on the seat of their trousers. Poole's shedding of inhibitions seems almost farcical compared with Connie Chatterley's. No longer restrained by "the conventions in which he was brought up" (*AE*, 109), he copulates repeatedly with Loola, a sexually precocious eighteen-year-old, whose "extra pair of nipples" (*AE*, 63), did not merit extermination.

In Zamiatin's *We,* the One State removed D-503's soul; the dystopian society of twenty-second century California wants to do likewise with Alfred's testicles. Instead, Poole and Loola escape to a "little community up north, near Fresno" that is supposed to be "[e]ighty-five per cent Hot" (*AE*, 103), a sexually robust Lawrencian enclave in northern California instead of in New Mexico.[19] Ironically, Poole effects his own cure by avoiding the one Huxley's dystopia has in mind for him. Having discovered the joys of year-round sex, he and Loola become "normal" human beings with "normal human feelings" (*AE*, 145), a recovery akin to that of Connie and Mellors. But Huxley's couple will not settle for a Lawrencian fullness of bodily life. Once fully humanized, they are allegedly poised to take the next step towards spiritual enlightenment. As Huxley puts it, they are prepared to move from Shelley's *Epipsychidion*, which Poole quotes at novel's end, to the same poet's *Adonais* and then "beyond" to what the narrator calls "the wordless doctrine of the Pure in Heart" (*AE*, 149). Presumably, this is a state of mystical awareness vastly superior to the "purity" a sodomized Connie regains courtesy of Mellors (*LCL*, 232).

Poole and Loola pale in comparison with Mellors and Connie, but both couples find maintaining a healthy sexual relationship in a dystopian social environment risky business, as will Orwell's Winston and Julia, the even more depleted version of Connie and Mellors in *Nineteen-Eighty-Four*. Indeed, a love affair's chances for success provide a reliable means of gauging a society's lack of utopic potential. Connie's blasphemous vision of her revivified physicality emerging Christ-like from "the tomb" has a certain gravity (*LCL*, 220). Its comical equivalent in *Ape and Essence* finds the pseudo-Lawrencian Poole, in search of Loola, "advancing from behind the tomb of Rudolph Valentino" (*AE*, 123).[20] Poole's is the weakest of Huxley's several cure scenes, but when Alfred is offered a choice between year-round sex and castration, he easily decides which cure to embrace.

Seated at his "speakwrite" machine in the Records Department of the Ministry of Truth,[21] Winston Smith is George Orwell's time traveler. He sends Winston back in time to rewrite historical events in light of the Party's current policies. "The past was brought up to date," says Orwell (O, 36); Winston, in effect, recreates it to suit the present. But his "defective memory," as O'Brien calls it, his ability to remember things that the Party has decided never happened or should have happened differently, is one of several criminal acts (i.e., thought crimes) that lead to his and Julia's arrest for heresy by the Thought Police. Then commences the longest and one of the most painfully ironic cure scenes in modern utopian fiction: the "drama" involving O'Brien and Winston is "played out" in the misnamed Ministry of Love for "seven years" (O, 221), incredibly longer than Poole's lecture from the Arch-Vicar. "'Fortunately,'" claims O'Brien, Winston's "'heresies,'" more so than D-503's, are "'curable'" (O, 203, 221). "'I shall save you, I shall make you perfect'" (O, 201), Oceania's Inquisitor promises.

Combining brainwashing and physical torture, Oceania attempts to set to right one of the few remaining relatively healthy intellects in its midst, thereby unmistakably revealing its fundamental wrongness. In a society which subscribes to the "mutability of the past" (O, 25) and thus continually revises it to please itself, only Winston clings to what T. S. Eliot calls "the historical sense": this involves a perception of the continuing presence of an unchanging past.[22] The more abuse Winston suffers and the more debilitated he becomes, the sicker the social system professing to help him appears. Winston must be convinced that truth at any given moment is whatever the Party claims, even if it stipulates that "TWO AND TWO MAKE FIVE" (O, 228). If the Party can "control the mind," it can determine what is real because, O'Brien argues, "Reality" is mental, only existing "inside the skull" (O, 218). After being attached to a "heavy piece of apparatus," Winston feels "as though a piece had been taken out of his brain" (O, 211-12). Similarly, D-503 underwent "The Great Operation," whereby a "splinter," allegedly his imagination, was removed from his head (Z, 232). But Orwell is more emphatic: the goal, O'Brien repeatedly informs Winston, is "'[t]o cure you! To make you sane!'" (O, 209). Sanity and insanity change places here, more disturbingly than crime and sickness do in *Erewhon*.

Regarding sex, Oceania is more restrictive than the simian society in *Ape and Essence*. The Party has determined "to kill the sex instinct" altogether (O, 57). Julie wears a "narrow scarlet sash, emblem of the Junior Anti-Sex League [. . .], around the waist of her overalls," the equivalent of the patches saying "No" on women's breasts and trousers in Huxley's novel. Nevertheless, the rebel in her worships the sex instinct "because it created a world of its own which was outside the Party's control" (O, 110). Finding something the Party cannot control becomes the goal. Unfortunately, Winston and Julia are soon under surveillance even during their lovemaking. Nor does sex between them prove as liberating as intercourse outside the mating season is for Poole and Loola; nor does their behavior, perverse in the eyes of the state, rejuvenate Orwell's lovers as sodomy did Connie and Mellors.

Winston's "heart lept" when Julia claims to have had illicit sexual encounters "scores of times" (O, 104). "Anything that hinted at corruption filled him with a wild hope," Orwell writes (O, 105). He has Winston ask, "'You like doing this?'" and Julia reply, "'I adore it'" (O, 105). Thanks to this virtual but surely unintentional parody of a Lawrencian exchange, sexual intercourse, although "successfully performed," remains no more than "a political act" in *Nineteen-Eighty-Four* (O, 105), never physically curative or a step towards enlightenment. Orwell either did not share, or perhaps could not mimic, Lawrence's confidence in a bodily path to redemption. Consequently, Charrington's shop, where Winston and Julia carry on, cannot rival the sacred wood where Connie and Mellors romp and she becomes pregnant. "Out of their bodies," Winston sadly realizes with respect to Julia and himself, "no child would ever come" (O, 181), no procreative consequences as in Lawrence to sanctify rebellion.

On the subject of freedom versus happiness, O'Brien disagrees vehemently with Huxley. Winston asks why the Party cherishes power. He expects to hear that "the choice for mankind lay between freedom and happiness" but that "for the great bulk of mankind, happiness was better" (O, 216), just as Mustapha Mond maintains. O'Brien rejects the suggestion that the Party rules "for the good of the majority" who are "not fit to govern themselves" (O, 216). "'The Party seeks power entirely for its own sake,'" O'Brien declares, because power is "'an end'" not a "'means'" (O, 217). What makes O'Brien more diabolical than Huxley's Mond and Zamiatin's Benefactor put together is the sadistic pleasure he takes in perverted cure scenes such as Winston's. Oceania in effect creates rebels and heretics, encouraging and nurturing the misfit's disobedience. Then it enjoys seizing and executing them, but only after they have been reformed, that is, once they have been made to renounce dissent and love Big Brother.

Zamiatin believed "heretics" keep the world alive; their recurrence allegedly frustrates totalitarianism by preventing ideals from hardening into "official dogma."[23] Orwell found such confidence naïve. The truly authoritarian state of the future, he informed the Russian, will play devilish games; it will lure dissidents into the open with rumors of "vast underground conspiracies" against itself (O, 18). Winston is led to believe in a secret "Brotherhood" intent on overthrowing Big Brother. But its leader, Emmanuel Goldstein, is probably a myth. His book of heresies, *The Theory and Practice of Oligarchial Collectivism*, exposes how unscrupulously Oceania and its sister superstates operate. Most likely it is a fabrication by the Party to arouse false hopes in malcontents like Winston. O'Brien actually procures a copy for him. Mistaking O'Brien for a member of the Brotherhood, Winston and Julia are easily caught; they step forward, eager to "incriminate" themselves as "enemies of the Party" (O, 140).

In other words, Oceania is the only modern utopia in which the sole outlets for rebels and dissidents are traps set up by the state. To justify itself, to prove itself to itself, a self-perpetuating Oceania is "not content with negative obedience, nor even with the most abject submission" (O, 210); again and again, O'Brien explains, it must completely disabuse the heretic of disloyalty. If every "erroneous thought" can be eradicated, the Party's ideas will become as infallible as "laws of nature" (O 210, 218). O'Brien tells Winston how cures in Oceania work:

> "When finally you surrender to us, it must be of your own free will. *We* do not destroy the heretic because he resists us; so long as he resists us *we* never destroy him. *We* convert him, *we* capture his inner mind, *we* reshape him. *We* burn all evil and all illusion out of him; *we* bring him over to our side, not in appearance, but genuinely, heart and soul. *We* make him one of ourselves before we kill him." (O, 210; italics added)[24]

O'Brien, Winston decides, "is not a hypocrite; he believes every word he says" (O, 211). Yet he sounds like an agent of the Gestapo when he denigrates Zamiatin's confidence in the persistence of heresy and heretics. O'Brien concedes that both "will live forever" but only because Oceania wants them to:

> "Every day, at every moment, they will be defeated, discredited, ridiculed, spat upon—and yet they will always survive. This drama that I have played out with you during seven years will be played out over and over again, generation after generation, always in subtler forms. Always we shall have the heretic here at our mercy, screaming with pain, broken up, contemptible—and in the end utterly penitent, saved from himself, crawling to our feet of his own accord." (O, 221)

In short, says Orwell, in the dystopia of the future, heretics will be cured over and over again to satisfy the state's hunger for power and gratify its need to demonstrate to itself its absolute authority. Thanks to Hitler and Stalin, Orwell could imagine horrific cure scenes beyond Zamiatin's ken and totally contrary to the pleasure-oriented brave new world.

The prolonged contest between Winston and O'Brien seems meant to trivialize Mond's debate with the Savage, in which no one wins. Orwell's is not an ironic cure scene just because the sick person is in charge; in addition, each side thinks it has triumphed when, possibly, neither has. Winston resolves to die "hating" the Party with one last "heretical thought" in his head, undetected and unpunished (O, 231). "'They can't get inside you,'" Julia counsels; the Party allegedly "had never mastered the secret of finding out what another human being was thinking" (O, 137, 138). But O'Brien denies that the heretic is ever able to "carry rebellion locked up in his skull" until the last minute when he is "waiting for the bullet" (O, 210). At first, O'Brien appears to be correct. The "final, indispensable, healing change" takes place after Winston's release from the Ministry of Love when he gazes up at "the enormous face" of Big Brother: "Forty years it had taken him to learn what kind of smile was hidden beneath the dark mustache. O cruel, needless misunderstanding! O stubborn self-willed exile from the loving breast! [...] He loved Big Brother" (O, 245).[25]

Emblazoned with exclamation marks, the cure, a "healing change," involves a return to "the loving breast." This sounds maternal rather than fraternal.[26] Winston, one remembers, has always been ashamed of grabbing his sister's chocolate ration years ago and fleeing from his mother's admonitions. "He never saw his mother again," Orwell notes (O, 135). Behind Big Brother's "dark mustache," Winston discovers a mother surrogate with whom to reconcile, putting an end to his life-long guilt feelings. If so, he professes love for Big Brother due to reasons beyond the Party's grasp. Arguably, it has not gained control of his "inner heart" (O, 138). On the other hand, the Party remains unaware of its failure, as does everyone else except Winston, who is too befuddled on Victory Gin to capitalize on his breakthrough and is probably about to be shot. His victory, if it is one, goes unproclaimed. O'Brien observes that "posterity" will not "vindicate" Winston; it "'will never hear of you,'" he predicts (O, 210), just as Helmholtz Watson's influence seems likely to be confined to the Falklands. Orwell delivers an ironic cure scene in which no cure may have transpired although the Party believes its perverse idea of one has. Even if Winston has found a cure for his guilty conscience, it is more solipsistic than

Connie's sexual liberation; nor does it include Julia the way Poole's does Loola.

Little Alex's crimes in Part One of Anthony Burgess's *A Clockwork Orange* (1962) are revolting. But one begins reluctantly to sympathize with the fifteen-year-old hooligan in Part Two because the state, when it cures Alex of anti-social tendencies, turns out to be worse. In the first of two ironic cure scenes, Alex is conditioned literally to throw up at the thought of committing violent acts. One sees him "heaving away" (*CO*, 104) when forced to watch film clips in which individuals are raped, viciously beaten, or burned alive. The state cures Alex by making him get sick whenever he witnesses violence or is tempted to behave badly. The Erewhonians viewed crime as a sickness. Alex's captors cure him by turning into a sickness his urge to commit crimes.

In the second cure scene (Part Three), public outcry compels the government to undo Alex's reclamation; he becomes well again once he recovers his appetite for criminal behavior. Sickness and wellness change places in Burgess's modern satirical novel until it is uncertain which is which. So, too, with good and bad, right and wrong, sanity and insanity. Ironically, Alex seems better, healthier, saner as a victimizer in Part One, where his inclinations are detestable, than as a victim in Part Two, after he is rendered incapable of wrongdoing. The novel's tripartite structure takes Alex from bad to worse, then back again to where something more terrible may yet await him. There can be no utopia for Burgess because whatever comes next always seems likely to be worse.[27]

"Badness is of the self," Alex theorizes; it is an inseparable part of the individual, indisposable if not essential. States "cannot allow the bad because they cannot allow the self," Alex decides (*CO*, 43). They want only docile individuals who have been "deprived of the ability to make an ethical choice" (*CO*, 95) and behave properly automatically. The real danger, Burgess contends, as he muddies conventional moral distinctions, stems not from sociopaths like Alex and his "droogs" (gang), but from the desire of the state, always inherently totalitarian, for model citizens, even if their obedience is involuntary. It may be "horrible to be good," that is, to have to be good, the prison chaplain "Charlie" warns after little 6655321 (aka Alex) agrees to undergo the "Reclamation Treatment" (*CO*, 96, 95).[28] If it is bad to have to be good, it may be good to be bad, right to be wrong, healthier to be sick.

Individuals are kept human, Burgess claims, by their ability to choose, even to choose wrongly, thereby refusing to become automatically perfect. Retaining the individual's capacity to do wrong, the freedom to make bad choices, is more important to Burgess than attaining perfection, which he considers contrary to human nature. To achieve flawlessness, one would have to become what Alex indignantly protests against being made into: "a clockwork orange," someone who is conditioned to "ooze juicily," surrendering his or her "sweetness" (i.e., goodness) unnaturally like clockwork, without having to be squeezed by the state (*CO*, 27). "'Am I just to be like a clockwork orange?'" Alex shouts in Part Two after allegedly being cured (*CO*, 126). Without fully understanding it, he quotes the title of F. Alexander's book deploring the state's eagerness to turn everyone into a "mechanical creation." Alex and his gang tore up this manuscript when they invaded the liberal author's home in Part One.

Burgess's constant theme is "the perpetual conflict between authority and the individual"; he foresees "the State […] taking on more and more control […] of the individual life."[29] In his opinion, only imperfection, one's determination to remain incurably less than prefect can preserve humankind's fundamental humanness. Consequently, an unlikely protagonist emerges: the despicable hero, a person like Alex who relishes making bad choices, becomes the last person likely to be reformed; he stands the best chance of thwarting the totalitarian state's plans to impose a uniform goodness. Ironically, Alex is good for humanity when bad, bad for it when good, saner and healthier as a criminal than as a citizen programmed for perfection. O'Brien calls a broken-down Winston Smith, who is literally "falling to pieces," "the last man," a kind of human being soon to be "extinct" (O, 222).[30] For Burgess, the final holdout is more likely to be Alex than Oliver Mellors or Helmholtz Watson. As the saint of reprehensibility, Alex is "a kind of martyr," says Burgess, "for man's power to choose" no matter how wrongly (Bunting, 523). Zamiatin and Huxley find certain types of utopia, Wells's scientific utopias in particular, highly objectionable; Burgess considers utopia *per se*, state-engineered perfection in any shape or form, undesirable.

As a general election nears, the anti-liberal incumbents need all the prison cells for political prisoners. In order safely to release the currently incarcerated, the Governor decides the state must "[k]ill the criminal reflex" (*CO*, 193) in malefactors like Alex. This reflex, not the sex instinct as in *Nineteen Eighty-Four*, is allegedly the state's real enemy. Imprisoned for bludgeoning an old lady to death, Alex can have his sentence commuted if he signs up for "Reclamation Treatment" (*CO*, 95). "'You are to be made into a good boy, 6655321,'" the chaplain explains. "'Never again will you have the desire to commit acts of violence or to offend in any way whatsoever against the State's peace'" (*CO*, 95-96). Foolishly confident in his incurable criminality, Alex laughs "at everybody's like innocence" (*CO*, 99) when only he is unaware of what can be done to him. Upon release, he expects to resume his old ways. Ironically, the gleeful rapist and willful murderer comes to seem more innocuous than the devious state that presumes to reform him. Burgess shakes the readers' confidence that one can readily tell guilt from innocence, just as he unsettles one's ability to distinguish sickness from health.

Doctors Brodsky and Branum sound like O'Brien when they assure Alex that, thanks to Ludovico's Technique, he is "being made sane [...,] being made healthy" (*CO*, 109). Strapped to a table, prevented from closing his eyes, Alex receives injections that leave him trying to throw up as he watches film after film of people being savagely beaten. Formerly, he savored doing or watching vicious acts; now he finds himself "not feeling all that well" (*CO*, 103). His nausea, Dr. Branum insists, is a sure sign that he is behaving like "any normal healthy human organism" witnessing evil deeds (*CO*, 109).

More so than D-503's lobotomy or Winston Smith's, Alex's cure scene is extremely funny, the idea of illness as a cure, of vomiting as a healthy reaction, being as absurd as it is disgusting. "'What you've been doing,'" Alex objects, "'is to make me feel very very ill'" (*CO*, 109). The cure is not complete, Brodsky warns, until Alex, "without medication," vomits at the mere suggestion of violence (*CO*, 116). Ludovico's Technique is crudely Pavlovian: at first, chemically induced sickness whenever Alex is exposed to violent behavior; eventually simple exposure makes him ill. Pavlov's dog salivated at the sound of a bell whether or not it signaled dinnertime. Alex sickens even without injections whenever he sees blood.

Alex, one realizes, is Burgess's portrait of an artist; his medium is violence. When he beats up an "old veck" (old man) or robs and assaults a female shopkeeper, he describes his actions and their physical consequences with a poet's zest; becoming a conductor, he orchestrates blows "that brought the red out like an old friend" (*CO*, 14, 17). Unfortunately, Ludovico's Technique robs Alex of this creativity, perverse though it is; it destroys his love of music, especially Beethoven's Ninth Symphony, which now makes him sick because all the violent films he watched contained musical scores. Ceasing "'to be a wrongdoer,'" laments the chaplain, Alex "'ceases also to be a creature capable of moral choice'" (*CO*, 126), i.e., a human being.

For Burgess, one must reiterate, good and bad in the individual are hopelessly intertwined; one cannot cure, that is, eliminate, the latter without hampering the former, hence no utopia. Dr. Brodsky boasts of creating in

Alex "your true Christian [...] ready to turn the other cheek" (*CO*, 128), no matter how severely abused. In Burgess's opinion, only a patsy can be truly Christ-like, genuinely faultless, so Church and State want the same modified harmless person; they are equally enemies of one's real self. Burgess's ironic metaphor for both a genuine Christian and the model citizen is a mechanical orange, voluntarily yielding its juicy goodness without having to be squeezed. In future, says Burgess, there will be no need to lobotomize dissidents as in Zamiatin, or to dose them regularly with *soma* as in *Brave New World*, or for the "boot stamping on a human face—forever" that O'Brien predicts (O, 220).

In Burgess's second ironic cure scene, Alex is cured of the cure Dr. Brodsky administered. In Part Three, having been released by the incumbents, Alex is victimized by nearly everyone towards who he behaved badly in Part One; his insurmountable goodness renders him defenseless. The "old veck" Alex mugged in the first chapter incites a pack of "dirty old men" to beat him up until the police come (*CO*, 114). Led by Billyboy, Alex's "old enemy" (140), the "millicents" (i.e., police) give him a second beating. Without realizing his whereabouts or being recognized, Alex finds refuge in the home of F. Alexander, the expert on clockwork oranges. Alexander and his fellow liberals decide to exploit the harm that was done to Alex in order to "dislodge" the incumbent Government (*CO*, 154). But when Alexander begins to recognize Alex as his wife's assailant, the latter escapes by jumping out a window. He lands back in the arms of the state. It cracks down on the liberals, imprisons F. Alexander for Alex's protection, then proceeds to undo Ludovico's Technique. Alex regains his love of "ultra-violence" and "the old in-out in-out" (rape); again he takes pleasure in "the glorious Ninth of Ludwig van" (172, 174). Without sensing a trace of the irony Burgess intends, one of the Government's "doctor vecks" observes: "'You seem to be cured.'" He credits "[d]eep hypnopaedia," apparently an improvement upon sleep-teaching techniques invented by the brave new world (*CO*, 172; see *BNW*, 21).

"I was cured all right," these are Alex's last words and Burgess's, a scary declaration that makes *A Clockwork Orange* the only modern utopian novel with a second ironic cure scene to reverse the first. Alex has been cured wrongly—twice. He signs another mysterious document, "not knowing what [he] was signing and not [...] caring either" (*CO*, 175), just as earlier he signed up for reclamation. Part Three in the American edition has six chapters compared to seven apiece for One and Two.[31] The novel seems on the verge of a new cycle, ready for another swing of the pendulum. Unless readers are familiar with the British edition, in which, surprisingly,

Alex settles down in the cancelled seventh chapter, they are left wondering what atrocities a twice-cured delinquent is capable of and doubtful whether the Government has really given up on mechanical oranges.

Conditions remain endlessly dystopian for Burgess because one's "capacity to choose"—he calls it "the only thing we have"—is unreliable, yet tampering with it only makes matters worse (Bunting, 523, 521). One is "always taking the wrong side," Burgess laments, because "by definition" the "right side" is "the other side" (Bunting, 520). That is, once one chooses, the choice not taken begins to look better.[32] Thus one sides against Alex in Part One, only to discover in Part Two that one has taken the wrong side. By the end of Part Three, the reader wonders if there is a right side. In Zamiatin and Orwell, sickness and health trade places, but in *A Clockwork Orange* one can no longer tell one from the other,[33] nor can one still believe in the individual's capacity to make good choices. For this loss of confidence in choosing, the ability Burgess considers one's only asset, *A Clockwork Orange* offers no cure.

The cure scene reaches its apotheosis in *Island* (1962), Huxley's last completed novel. A cynical Westerner is washed ashore on Pala after a freakish boating accident. Although Will Farnaby's physical injuries are minor, his outlook on life is sickeningly negative: a low opinion of humanity in general combined with a strong sense of personal guilt and consequent self-loathing. He cannot forgive himself for mistreating his wife, Molly, who died in a car crash shortly after their breakup. Nor can he forget the degrading death from breast cancer of his beloved Aunt Mary. As a journalist, Will has traveled "from hell to hell," always covering the "current horrors," which he feels make existence an "enormous joke" (*I*, 27, 15, 13). *Island* extols the virtues of utopian Pala by telling the story of Will Farnaby's rehabilitation, the only eminently successful cure in modern utopian literature.

Butler's Erewhonians threaten Higgs for getting sick. The Palanese, enlightened Mahayanist Buddhists who practice Vedanta's perennial philosophy, immediately put their unexpected visitor to bed and begin his therapy. Led by Dr. Robert MacPhail and Susila, his widowed daughter-in-law, a host of benign islanders recount Pala's history and praise its present workings. Nurse Appu, Ranga, Vijaya, Mrs. Rao, Shanta, Mr. Menon, and Mrs. Narayan extend the recovery process by lecturing Will at length even after he is up and around. Collectively, they persuade him that Pala is as utopic as life gets. "'The more I see of you people the better I like you,'" Will admits; "'I want to find out more about you'" (*I*, 11). Thus the process of Will's recovery and the unfolding of Huxley's positive utopia become one and the same. The more Will learns about Pala, the higher his revised estimate of human potentialities and the better he understands and accepts the good and bad in himself. Will's conversations with Pala's detractors—the Rani, Murugan, Mr. Bahu—are not so much setbacks in his recovery as counterpoints to be overcome in Huxley's final discussion novel of ideas.

Unlike the Savage who grows increasingly disillusioned the more he sees of the brave new world, Will is delighted to learn about Mutual Adoption Clubs, the yoga of love, innovative methodologies for agriculture and education, "DF and AI," etc. (*I*, 192). He studies the Old Raja's *Notes on What's What*, Pala's guide book to spiritual health. Having made sufficient progress, a rejuvenated Farnaby is given a pill to accelerate his cure. Susila asks Will if he is ready to take "the *moksha*-medicine" (*I*, 270). The novel's climax and the cure scene overlap in Chapter XV: Will swallows "the reality revealer, the truth-and-beauty pill," that accomplishes the erstwhile cynic's "mental transformation" and makes him "fully human" (*I*, 138). While listening to Bach's Fourth Brandenburg Concerto more rewardingly than Alex savors Beethoven's Ninth, Will transcends his egotistic "selfhood," briefly becoming "blissfully one with Oneness" (*I*, 270). Huxley outdoes all previous cure scenes by granting a recuperating Will a glimpse of the Beatific Vision. Presumably, like most Palanese from the time of their initiation into adulthood, Farnaby will take a pill periodically as part of his spiritual regimen while also striving towards further enlightenment by means less pharmaceutical.

Island is unique among modern utopias in that it contains a cure scene within a cure scene. As part of Will's therapy, Dr. Robert relates how Pala came into being. A cure scene proved instrumental. In the 1850s, Dr. Andrew MacPhail, Dr. Robert's great-grandfather, was recruited to treat the island's Raja; a tumor "had filled the nose, [...] pushed up into the socket of the right eye, [...] [and] had half-blocked the throat" (*I*, 123). Using Professor Elliotson's technique for "painless operations [...] on patients in the mesmeric trance" (*I*, 123), Dr. Andrew removed the tumor and saved the Raja's life. Dr. Robert's history lesson, a positive counter to Mustapha Mond's in Chapter III of *Brave New World*, goes on to tell how, together, the Scottish doctor, a "Calvinist-turned-atheist," and the Palanese King, a "pious Mahayana Buddhist" (*I*, 129), made Pala into "the best of both worlds, the Oriental and the European, the ancient and the modern" (*I*, 130): Eastern spirituality married to Western know-how.

Pala began when an outsider cured its ruler. Ironically, it ends when its cure of an outsider, who behaves like a tumor or cancerous cell, has disastrous side effects for the body politic. It is as if the island's demise is the price it must pay for helping Farnaby. Modern utopists fear that oncoming oppressive societies will devise perverse cures to stifle non-conformists and muzzle dissent. Huxley fears that any utopia diligent enough to effect genuine rehabilitation will be exposed to fatal contamination, which is what happens to Pala thanks to Will.

Pala is called "the forbidden island, the place no journalist had ever visited" (*I*, 8). The island trusts to its isolationist policies to protect it from European imperialists and outside corporations anxious to gain access to its oil. "No oil concessions to anyone" is the rule; but a "pro-oil minority" (*I*, 21) consisting of Mailendra Murugan (Pala's future ruler), the Rani (his mother), and Mr. Bahu, the ambassador from neighboring war-like Rendang, hope to strike a deal with Joe Aldehyde's Southeast Asia Petroleum. Coincidentally, Farnaby is a journalist who works for Aldehyde and thus penetrates Pala as Joe's "secret agent" (*I*, 111). Assurances he can offer of Aldehyde's support encourage the pro-oilers to invite Rendang's Colonel Dipa to overrun Pala. Murugan, his new ally, proclaims "the United Kingdom of Rendang and Pala" (*I,* 293), which undoubtedly will grant oil leases to Southeast Asia Petroleum on its way to becoming a westernized industrial state.

Dipa's invasion interrupts Will's cure, his *moksha*-medicine experience; the commotion outside turns inward bliss into chaos and nightmare. Asked earlier how he survived the boating accident and climbed a steep cliff from the shore, Will says: "'Remember the beginning of *Erewhon* [...]. As luck would have it, Providence was on my side'" (*I*, 17). But providence is no longer on Pala's. As Huxley fashions the modern utopia's supremely ironic cure scene, Will acknowledges the novel in which the cure scene began.

Pala has managed to stay healthy (i.e., independent) by keeping aloof from a sick world, in effect quarantining itself. Rendang's "magnificent harbor" invited invasion by Arabs, Portuguese, Dutch and English; less accessible, Pala, as Ranga explains to Will, "escaped" all of these "infestations" (*I*, 81). "'So long as it remains out of touch with the rest of the world,'" Mr. Bahu lectures Will, "'an ideal society can be a viable society'" (*I*, 55). But he sees "'the outside world closing in on this little island of freedom and happiness. Closing in steadily and inexorably, coming nearer and nearer'" (*I*, 56).[34] Farnaby's arrival constitutes a loss of immunity, the next-to-last step in this unfortunate process. After it comes colonialization, commercial exploitation of its natural resources that Pala has resisted for a century.

As befits a novel that is practically one long cure scene, disease imagery abounds. Besides the Raja's "tumor" and Randang's "infestations," there is oil itself. "'Pala's full of oil,'" Joe Aldehyde tells Will (*I*, 21), as if the island was infected by it. Murugan says "the island is fairly oozing with the stuff" (*I*, 41); he could be describing open sores. When the Rani insists that "'Pala's smooth bright skin concealed the most horrible rottenness'" (*I*, 51), her disapproval of its liberal attitudes makes it seem terminally ill, as indeed it is, for the healthier Will becomes thanks to the Palanese, the closer Pala is to expiring due to his promise to the pro-oil conspirators. The patient gets better as the caregiver declines. Will operates as a cancerous cell, sickening Pala and hastening its demise. Pala dies figuratively from cancer the way Will's Aunt Mary literally did: "a little piece of her body" started to work against the good of the whole (*I*, 242), just as the pro-oilers plot Pala's downfall.[35] The utopic island's symbol is Lakshmi, who perishes from incurable cancer. Throughout the novel, Dr. Robert's wife is "slowly wasting to extinction" (*I*, 25). The closer to death she comes, the less time Pala has left: her death is followed a chapter later by Will's *moksha*-medicine experience, which is interrupted by Colonel Dipa's invasion. Appropriately, Will attends Lakshmi's deathbed, underlining the ironic interconnections Huxley establishes between her death, Will's cure, oil, and a doomed utopia.[36]

Utopias from *Erewhon* to *Island* regularly feature ironic cure scenes. Remedies imposed rarely display genuinely utopic qualities but reveal, instead, a society's fundamental malignancy. Supposedly utopian communities implement self-serving cures designed to neutralize deviants while safeguarding their own socio-political perversities. Thus the sick party administers what it regards as a cure; a rebel or heretic is allegedly straightened out by a benighted society. The cure is doubly ironic inasmuch as the so-called sickness being eradicated is usually a strength that society should profit from. A cure may transpire in spite of society, that is, without its assistance but contrary to its wishes. Ironically, such cures are too personal to change anything. A cure scene can have unwelcome consequences when a benign community actually rehabilitates an unwanted visitor only to succumb to forces from the insane outside world he represents. Cure scenes are often the funniest episodes in modern utopias, but always among the scariest.

In sum, as much as any other feature, a society's treatment of problem cases determines whether it merits consideration as the good place. An allegedly utopian community gives itself away by the manner in which it handles uninvited guests or responds to indigenous dissidents, be they rebels, heretics, or malcontents. Hence the preponderance of climactic cure scenes in modern British utopias. Beginning as a humble episode in *Erewhon*, the cure scene takes over increasingly larger portions of the narrative. Inability to imagine a non-ironic cure scene is one of the primary reasons few positive utopias appeared in the approximately hundred-year cycle from *Erewhon* to *Island*, heyday of the modern British literary utopia.[37] Nicholas Berdiaeff warned that utopias were not only realizable but rapidly approaching; he doubted the twentieth century would be able to avoid them.[38] The profusion of ironic cure scenes reveals an even more deep-seated anxiety, namely, that a negative utopia, once it materializes, will learn to prevent or defuse alternatives so that a genuine cure becomes impossible or unsustainable. No one manipulated cure scenes better or more often than Aldous Huxley, whose three utopias contain six of them: three in *Brave New World*, one in *Ape and Essence*, and two again in *Island*. The final cure, Will's, revalues the negative cure scenes in Zamiatin and Orwell. With Nurse Appu, Will discusses Pala's aptitude for finding the right "cure" for life's problems (*I*, 65). She contends "there is no single cure"; one must "attack on all the fronts at once"—diet, autosuggestion, meditation—the goal being a fully "integrated man" (*I*, 66). As the end of the cycle from *Erewhon* to *Island*, Higgs to Farnaby, only Huxley was able to produce one.

---

1 Revised version of a lecture held at the international conference "Excellence in Arts and Sciences: The Huxley Family" at Eötvös Loránd University in Budapest on 9 November 2019.

2 Samuel Butler, *Erewhon* (New York, 1961), 67 [hereafter, *E*]; other utopias and dystopias mentioned in the following include: Anthony Burgess, *A Clockwork Orange* (New York, 1963 [[1]1962]) [hereafter, *CO*]; Anthony Burgess, *The Long Day Wanes: A Malayan Trilogy* (New York, 1964 [[1]1956-59]); Aldous Huxley, *Ape and Essence* (London, 1949) [hereafter, *AE*]; Aldous Huxley, *Brave New World* (London, 1950 [[1]1932]) [hereafter, *BNW*]; Aldous Huxley, *Island* (New York, 1963 [[1]1962]) [hereafter, *I*]; D. H. Lawrence, *Lady Chatterley's Lover* (New York, 1959 [[1]1928]) [hereafter, *LCL*]; William Morris, *News from Nowhere* (London, 1993 [[1]1890]) [hereafter, *NN*]; George Orwell, *Nineteen Eighty-Four* (New York, 1951 [[1]1949]) [hereafter, *O*]; H. G. Wells, *A Modern Utopia* (Lincoln, NE, 1967 [[1]1905]); H. G. Wells, *The First Men in the Moon* (New York, 1965 [[1]1901]); H. G. Wells, *Men Like Gods* (New York, 1923); H. G. Wells, *The Time Machine* (New York, 1964 [[1]1895]) [hereafter, *TM*]; Yevgeny Zamiatin, *We* (New York, 1972 [[1]1924]) [hereafter, Z].

3 Although translated from the Russian, *We* must be considered a vital part of the modern British utopian tradition: Zamiatin warned readers of the totalitarian tendencies in H. G. Wells's scientific utopias; *We* strongly influenced *Brave New World* and *Nineteen Eighty-Four*.

4 The *Integral* is Wells's time machine retooled for nefarious purposes, a perfect example of misuse of science.

5 Mephi is short for Mephistopheles, the devil who tempts Goethe's Faust.

6 Huxley, one is reminded, used 'negative utopia' instead of 'dystopia,' although its opposite, positive utopia, sounds redundant (see "Utopias, Positive and

Negative (1963)," edited and with an afterword by James Sexton, *AHA*, 1 (2001), 1–5).

7 See *Julius Caesar*, III, ii, 78.

8 Huxley also parodies the cure scene in *The Time Machine*, although it was already ironic. H. G. Wells's time-traveller journeys to the year Eight Hundred and Two Thousand Seven Hundred and One expecting to behold the triumph of evolution. Instead he discovers an Overworld of effete, cattle-like Eloi and an Underworld of cannibalistic Morlocs who prey on them. Desperate to escape these "human rats," the traveller sets forest and hillside ablaze, incinerating hundreds (*TM*, 107, 105). Instead of basking in the "perfect world," Wells's traveller lights up tomorrow like a pyromaniac Prometheus. As Huxley's time-traveller, John journeys to Fordian London by Blue Pacific Rocket. This time machine carries him forwards from Malpais, a primitive Indian reservation where time stands still, to A.F. 632.

9 See Jerome Meckier, "'My Hypothetical Islanders': The Role of Islands in *Brave New World* and *Island*," *AHA*, 12/13 (2012/2013), 319-40.

10 See Huxley's epigraph to *Point Counter Point.*

11 This power could be unexpended evolutionary energy. Upon seeing listless Eloi and degenerate Morlocs, Wells's time-traveller feared none was left.

12 Peter Firchow attributes resemblances between *We* and *Brave New World* to the "debt" both owed to H. G. Wells. See *The End of Utopia* (Lewisbury, 1984), 40, n. 5.

13 See Jerome Meckier, "Dickens and the Dystopian Novel: from *Hard Times* to *Lady Chatterley*," *The Novel and Its Changing Form*, ed. R. G. Collins (Manitoba, 1972), 51–58.

14 In his closing speech for the prosecution at the novel's obscenity trial in 1960, Griffith-Jones singled out this passage, saying it was "not very easy [...] to know what in fact [Lawrence] is driving at." See *The Trial of Lady Chatterley*, ed. C. H. Rolph (Baltimore, 1961), 221. This was disingenuous innuendo designed to shock jurors without specifying sodomy. Brenda Maddox points out that "penetration per anum" was "a felony in English law" in 1960, but states wrongly that the "act of anal intercourse went unrecognized" during the trial (Brenda Maddox, *D. H. Lawrence: The Story of a Marriage* [New York, 1994], 426, 425). Had the prosecution been more explicit, Lady Chatterley might have been convicted.

15 To Ernest Collins, in January 1913, Lawrence wrote: "'We can go wrong in our minds. But what our blood feels and believes and says, is always true.'" In short, "'the blood, the flesh [is] wiser than the intellect'" (quoted in John Worthen, *D. H. Lawrence: The Life of an Outsider* [London, 2005], 129).

16 Huxley saw *Ape and Essence* as an opportunity to correct a "vast and obvious failure of foresight" in *Brave New World*: in his 1946 "Foreword," he regrets the omission of any "reference to nuclear fission" (*BNW*, x).

17 According to A. C. Grayling, "evidence of the world is in fact more consistent with the existence of an evil deity than a good deity." See A. C. Grayling, *The God Argument: The Case Against Religion and for Humanism* (New York, 2013), 26.

18 Dominic Baker-Smith, in "The World to Come: Aldous Huxley and the Utopian Parable," miscalls the Arch-Vicar, who wants to emasculate Poole, a "more engaging version of Mond." See *Aldous Huxley Between East and West*, ed. C. C. Barfoot (Amsterdam, 2001), 107.

19 In the 1946 "Foreword" to *Brave New World*, Huxley wishes he had afforded the Savage an escape to "a community of exiles and refugees from the Brave New World, living within the borders of the Reservation" (*BNW*, ix).

20 In *Aldous Huxley: Satire and Structure* (London, 1969), Jerome Meckier notes Poole's "failure to move convincingly from comic butt to mystic hero" (195).

21 Misnomers abound in Oceania, not just a Ministry of Truth where falsehoods prevail by a "speakwrite" apparatus that speaks wrong.

22 T. S. Eliot, *The Sacred Wood* (New York, 1960), 49.

23 See "Afraid of Tomorrow," quoted in Mirra Ginsburg's introduction to Zamiatin's *We*, ix.

24 "We" appears eight times in this passage, a not-so-subtle allusion to Zamiatin, who allegedly underestimated the totalitarian state's coercive powers. "Burn" is a faint allusion to Lawrence's cure scene in which Connie's deepest shames are burnt out of her.

25 If Winston is "thirty-nine" at the outset (O, 5) and forty when he embraces Big Brother, the length of his struggles with O'Brien becomes problematic. The latter's declaration that he has "watched over" the former for "seven years" (O, 201) could simply mean that Winston has been suspected since he was thirty-two, not that the cure scene *per se* runs nearly a decade. Yet O'Brien's subsequent statement that it has "played out [...] during seven years" (O, 221) surely suggests that it does. Perhaps "forty" refers to Winston's life prior to arrest and the commencement of his cure, in which case he is forty-six when earmarked for extermination.

26 Zamiatin's D-503 dreads the thought of being torn "away from the maternal breast of the One State" (Z, 197). He speculates that he might not have gone wrong "[i]f [he] had a mother, [...] mine—yes, precisely—my mother" (Z, 216). To Lenina, Bernard remarks: "'I often think one may have missed something in not having had a mother'" (*BNW*, 91). See Marcus Smith, "The Wall of Blackness: A Psychological Approach to *1984*," *Modern Fiction Studies*, 14 (Winter, 1968-69), 422-3.

27 In *The Long Day Wanes: A Malayan Trology* (1956–59), Burgess has little sympathy with British rule in Malaya, which is coming to an end, but implications are that conditions in the new, independent country will be even less satisfactory.

28 An egregious play on words: "Charlie," the prison chaplain, the actor Charlie Chaplin.

29 See Charles T. Bunting, "An Interview in New York With Anthony Burgess," *Studies in the Novel*, 5 (Winter, 1973), 151.

30 In *Lady Chatterley's Lover*, Mellors is the last man, the only male who remains fully alive physically. When Watson joins the Savage in the fight to liberate the Deltas from *soma*, the latter exclaims, "'Men at last!'" (*BNW*, 175). More

directly than Huxley, Orwell may be alluding to Mary Shelley's *The Last Man* (1826), in which the narrator is the only person on earth to survive the plague.

[31] For Burgess's explanation of how his novel lost its final chapter in the American edition, see Bunting, 525. Omitting the last chapter, Michael Schmidt argues, "sacrificed [...] the symbolism of twenty-one chapters," which he equates with "coming of age." See Michael Schmidt, *The Novel: A Biography* (Cambridge, 2014), 628. However, Alex is still only fifteen or sixteen at the end of a parodic *bildungsroman* in which a relapse substitutes for maturation.

[32] In Burgess's *The Wanting Seed* (1962), society alternates between a Pelagian phase of belief in human perfectibility and an Augustinian phase, in which man is seen as inherently sinful. Different policies are put in place to accompany each phase. Gradually, the other phase, be it Pelagian or Augustinian, begins to look superior and a change is made.

[33] One can endorse Robert K. Morris's positive view of the novel's "tribunal division" as "Alex damned, Alex purged, Alex resurrected," but he does not rebound as successfully as Mellors or Connie. See Morris's *The Consolations of Ambiguity* (Columbia, 1971), 57.

[34] Brave new worlders, one remembers, could not have freedom and happiness both; in 1932, these are one of life's counterpoints which it took Huxley thirty years to resolve.

[35] See Jerome Meckier, "Cancer in Utopia: Positive and Negative Elements in Huxley's *Island*," Dalhousie Review, 54 (Winter, 1974-75), 619-33.

[36] "Failure to convert [i.e., cure] Murugan to Palanese values," Peter Firchow objects, has "far greater and more immediate social consequences than Will's very private conversion." Success in curing Will is more than offset by Pala's apparent indifference to its failure with Murugan. See Peter Firshow, "Brave at Last: Huxley's Western and Eastern Utopias," *AHA*, 1 (2001), 161.

[37] William Morris's *News from Nowhere* (1890) and Edward Bellamy's *Looking Backward* (1888), though optimistic, contradict each other. Both contain dreams about the future, not forecasts. Guest awakens in his own bed, doubtful if he can turn his "dream" of a return to pre-industrialized England into a "vision" (*NN*, 228). Julian West, having slept for a hundred years, has a nightmare in which he returns to the nineteenth century, then is relieved to awaken from it still in the twentieth, where, implausibly, he remains (see *Looking Backward*, ch. XXVIII). West's ideal society functions like a gigantic corporation, a machine-driven monopoly that disgusted Morris. In positive utopias such as *A Modern Utopia* (1905) and *Men Like Gods* (1923), H. G. Wells tried to ameliorate the pessimism in the *Time Machine* (1895) and *The First Men in the Moon* (1901); instead, he triggered negative responses from Zamiatin and Huxley.

[38] See Huxley's epigraph to *Brave New World*.

Bernfried Nugel
(University of Münster)

THE ANTI-UTOPIAN DRIFT IN ALDOUS HUXLEY'S LITERARY UTOPIAS[1]

Aldous Huxley's world-famous negative utopia *Brave New World* (1932) is still widely praised for its amazing topicality even in our twenty-first century. But to disregard his other three literary utopias —*Ape and Essence* (1948), *Brave New World: A Musical Comedy* (1956) and *Island* (1962)—is an unfair reduction of Huxley's overall achievement as a utopian writer spanning thirty years of his career. Seen together, his utopias are not only characterized by an impressive scope and variety of subject-matter but also by intriguing experiments in different literary forms within the larger utopian genre. Above all, instead of pleading for optimistic blueprints of a perfect society in the vein of H. G. Wells, Huxley from the start rather aimed at a fundamental critique of utopian thought. Perhaps his concept of a literary utopia can best be understood from a classification that he proposed in retrospect in a lecture given in 1962 on "Utopias, Positive and Negative."[2]

Speaking of "Utopia in general, Utopia in its historical manifestations down the centuries," he postulates:

> Positive or negative, all Utopias belong to one or other of two main classes. There are the near-in Utopias, where people like ourselves have solved their social and psychological problems in ways which to us are unfamiliar. And there are the far-out Utopias, inhabited by creatures unlike ourselves—creatures whose problems are either non-existent or so different from ours as to seem irrelevant. ("UPN," 2)

From Huxley's further differentiation of types it becomes clear that "the far-out Utopia can never be regarded as a blueprint, a plan of possible and desirable action" (2) and that even the more realistic near-in utopias "have never been realistic as a whole, practical in [their] totality" (3). Thus he pleads for an overall conception of utopia as a literary genre that allows for a great variety of types, whether one calls them positive and negative utopias or, as many literary critics prefer to have it, 'eutopias or good utopias'[3] over against 'dystopias' or 'anti-utopias'[4]; even the term 'meta-utopia' has been coined to denote a conceptual framework for all conceivable utopias[5] or a kind of self-reflexive utopia à la Wells's *A Modern Utopia.*[6] At the same time Huxley's extreme scepticism about the realisation of utopias in general is evident, which is understandably more pronounced in the case of far-out than near-in utopias. This scepticism constitutes a basically anti-utopian current in his thinking that tends to deny the very principle of devising utopias.[7] Combining Huxley's suggestions and the insights of more recent literary criticism, one may venture to propose a working definition of a literary utopia as follows:

> A literary utopia, whether of the far-out or the near-in type, is the fictional representation of a comprehensive image or counter-image of a perfect society naively or critically set off against the contemporary reader's conditions of life.

According to this working definition, *Brave New World* certainly is a satirical far-out utopia, or more specifically, a negative utopia or dystopia. Dystopia as well as anti-utopia, *Brave New World* satirizes seemingly positive concepts, such as genetic and social engineering, community, identity and stability, technological and cultural progress, the pleasure principle including free love and happiness induced by drugs as well as pleasant substitutes for religion. Since the novel has been profusely studied as a literary work of art in terms of themes, structure, characters and style, it seems apposite here to focus on its critical potential with regard to its social and cultural dimensions and above all on its anti-utopian tendencies.

The structure of *Brave New World* emphatically establishes a socio-cultural contrast between the World State and the Indian reservation in Malpais (which in Spanish means 'bad land'). The five-caste system of the brave new world ensures a hierarchy that leaves little room for individuals and achieves stability by manipulating its citizens with the help of genetic standardization and social conditioning, whereas the Indian reservation is organized by traditional tribal structures and primitivistic religious rituals. In the penultimate chapter of the novel Huxley presents the unavoidable clash of the two civilizations in a confrontation between their respective representatives, the World Controller Mustapha Mond and the so-called Savage John, who has been brought up according to Indian tradition and, amusingly, by reading the works of Shakespeare. Eventually he finds himself compelled to defend traditional concepts of Western civilization over against the pleasure principle of the Utopian State. But he has no real chance because he sticks to obsolete values, whether Indian or Shakespearean. To the World Controller's remark, "'We prefer to do things comfortably,'" he can only reply: "'But I don't want comfort. I want God, I want poetry, I want real danger, I want freedom, I want goodness, I want sin.'"[8]

By resorting to keywords of the Western mindset, such as God, poetry, bravery, freedom, goodness and sin, the Savage has to admit that he is on the horns of an insoluble dilemma between two sets of values, viz. the code of happiness in the brave new world and the mixed morality of his tribal and humanistic education. With pointed sarcasm the World Controller hints at the unacceptable consequences of that world-view:

> "In fact," said Mustapha Mond, "you're claiming the right to be unhappy."
> "All right, then," said the Savage defiantly, "I'm claiming the right to be unhappy."
> "Not to mention the right to grow old and ugly and impotent; the right to have syphilis and cancer; the right to have too little to eat; the right to be lousy; the right to live in constant apprehension of what may happen tomorrow; the right to catch typhoid; the right to be tortured by unspeakable pains of every kind."
> There was a long silence.
> "I claim them all," said the Savage at last.
> Mustapha Mond shrugged his shoulders. "You're welcome," he said. (*BNW*, 197)

Quite consistently, the novel ends with the Savage's suicide and, by implication, with the complete defeat of all that he had argued for.

On a larger scale, this ending, like so many other utopian features in the course of the novel, inescapably demonstrates the absurdity of utopian thinking in general, which appears to offer the Savage as well as the contemporary reader no more than an impossible choice, as Huxley put it himself in his 1946 foreword to the novel, between the "insanity" of the brave new world and the "lunacy" of a primitive society in an Indian reservation (see *BNW*, viii).

This distinctly anti-utopian drift of *Brave New World* as a whole has often been neglected by critics even though it is overtly announced by Huxley in his epigraph to the novel, where he warns the reader against too absolute a belief in the realisation of utopias. Ironically, in a kind of transnational approach, Huxley uses a French quotation from the Russian philosopher Nicholas Berdyaev[9] and thus alerts those educated English readers who are able understand French:

> Les utopies apparaissent comme bien plus réalisables qu'on ne le croyait pas autrefois. Et nous nous trouvons actuellement devant une question bien autrement angoissante: Comment éviter leur réalisation définitive? …
> Les utopies sont réalisables. La vie marche vers les utopies. Et peut-être un siècle nouveau commence-t-il, un siècle où les intellectuels et la classe cultivée rêveront aux moyens d'éviter les utopies et de retourner à une société non utopique, moins "parfaite" et plus libre.

[Here is my English translation:

> 'The present utopias appear much more realisable than one should have thought in earlier times. And currently we find ourselves confronted with an otherwise disquieting question: how can one prevent their definitive realisation? …
> The utopias are realisable. Life marches in the direction of the utopias. And perhaps this is the beginning of a new century, a century in which the intellectuals and the cultured class will dream of means of avoiding utopias and returning to a non-utopian society, less "perfect," but freer.']

In spite of this serious critique of utopian thought, however, *Brave New World* still has a somewhat playful note inasmuch as it is presented as an experiment in utopian planning gone wrong some 600 years in the future. Huxley later, i.e., after World War II, admitted that, as a satirist writing in 1931, he found the impossible choice between insanity and lunacy amusing and that he himself would never have thought "the nightmare of total organization" so imminent as it appeared in the 1940s and 1950s.[10]

In comparison, his second negative utopia, *Ape and Essence*, published in 1948, reflects a much more embittered attitude: part I is set in a contemporary Hollywood film studio and describes how an odd film script is saved from being burnt in the incinerator and how a search is carried out to find its deceased author William Tallis, a Swift-like satirist. Here Huxley sarcastically satirizes the Hollywood film industry, particularly its practice of fabricating trivial illusions and easy utopian worlds. This distinctly anti-utopian tendency is further enhanced in part II, which presents the full contents of the film script: it depicts a totalitarian state at the beginning of the twenty-second century ruled by a hierarchy of Satanic priests after an atomic war that in fact amounts to another Fall of Man, only much more fatal, if conceivable, than the first Fall related in the Bible. By resorting to atomic warfare, mankind has abused its free will in order to choose extreme evil, and consequently church and state observe an inverted Christianity, with Belial, i.e., the Devil, as the highest deity and with all the Christian rites turned inside out. In the title and in several passages of his negative utopia Huxley uses a quotation from Shakespeare's *Measure for Measure* that contrasts man's good and evil qualities, i.e., his essence and his apishness (see *AE*, 25).[11] Evidently Huxley's trust in human potentialities has greatly suffered, because he seems bent on driving home an insight that he formulated in *The Perennial Philosophy* (1945), an anthology of texts chosen from the tradition of Western and Eastern mysticism:

> But it must be remembered, of course, that the capacity for supreme good is achieved only at the price of becoming also capable of extreme evil. Animals do not suffer in so many ways,

> nor, we may feel pretty certain, to the same extent as do men and women. Further, they are quite innocent of that literally diabolic wickedness which, together with sanctity, is one of the distinguishing marks of the human species.[12]

And only two years before the publication of *Ape and Essence*, in his belated foreword to *Brave New World*, Huxley scathingly criticizes the dire consequences of a humanistic education that was not capable of preventing the atrocities of World War II. Significantly, he points to the demolition of European and Japanese cities, when he sarcastically proposes to build a Pantheon for the "benefactors of humanity":

> It should be located among the ruins of one of those gutted cities of Europe or Japan, and over the entrance to the ossuary I would inscribe, in letters six or seven feet high, the simple words: SACRED TO THE MEMORY OF THE WORLD'S EDUCATORS. (*BNW*, viii)

This remark shows that he was fully aware of the amount of destruction inflicted on Japan by nuclear warfare, and the fact that, in his negative utopia, he represents Los Angeles and California as victims of an atomic war may well be understood as a sign of poetic justice aimed at American society. Moreover, the brutal regime of Satanic Church and State is shown to lead to excesses of dehumanization never heard of in *Brave New World*: because of the general denunciation of the body and, with it, all individual sexuality, women, for instance, are denigrated as "'vessel[s] of the Unholy Spirit'"[13] radiating "'Malicious Animal Magnetism'" (*AE*, 69) and are cruelly whipped by the priests in obedience to Belial. Another excess and certainly one of the most horrifying scenes is the public sacrifice of mutated babies in so-called "Purification Ceremonies" (*AE*, 58) on Belial's Day, ceremonies highly reminiscent of a Christian service misused for diabolical purposes. All this is traced back to solely human defects in the Arch-Vicar's historical account of the triumph of Belial:

> "By purely natural means, using human beings and their science as His instruments, He created an entirely new race of men, with deformity in their blood, with squalor all around them, and ahead, in the future, no prospects but of more squalor, worse deformity and, finally, complete extinction. Yes, it's a terrible thing to fall into the hands of the Living Evil." (*AE*, 99)

Against the backdrop of this sinister world and the accompanying sombre mood there is little room for hope, except in the flight of a pair of lovers trying to escape to a group of people beyond the Mojave Desert, who have survived the war without deformities. In this context Dr. Poole, the male protagonist, voices his—and, to some extent, also Huxley's—trust in what he calls "the Order of Things":

> "[R]emember, He [Belial] can never win for good. [...] Because He can never resist the temptation of carrying evil to the limit. And whenever evil is carried to the limit, it always destroys itself. After which the Order of Things comes to the surface again." (148)

But the "Order of Things" is certainly not the utopian dream of a man-made perfect order, for, according to a remark at the beginning of the novel, "the dream of Order begets tyranny, the dream of Beauty, monsters and violence" (*AE*, 7),[14] and inevitably results in apish behaviour (see the novel's title) and frightening consequences like an atomic war. Such behaviour clearly proves that man is inherently incapable of devising truly perfect societies, and it is this implication that unmistakably points to the anti-utopian drift of Huxley's thinking: whatever kind of order man strives to perfect is doomed to failure. Thus, the above-mentioned "Order of Things" rather corresponds to mystical notions, such as "ultimate reality" or the "Divine Ground," which Huxley began to cherish from the late 1930s onwards and which are correlated in the human sphere with man's essence (see the novel's title) and Huxley's concept of "sanity," as promoted in his 1946 foreword to *Brave New World*. Working with the Order of Things, as Dr. Poole attempts to do, would mean to actualize one's desirable human potentialities, as Huxley later came to call man's inborn capacity for supreme good[15]; in *Ape and Essence*, however, this is indeed the only little ray of light in an overall ludicrous and depressing anti-utopian nightmare.

It seems hardly conceivable that Huxley could have surpassed the anti-utopian intensity of *Ape and Essence*, but, as a matter of fact, he wrote another negative utopia which, in my view, even goes beyond its precursor in several respects. In 1956 he embarked on reworking *Brave New World* in the form of a musical comedy, but unfortunately the script was never produced in his lifetime although Huxley tried to win over Leonard Bernstein and Igor Stravinsky to set it to music. However, it was at last rediscovered and published almost fifty years later in *Aldous Huxley Annual*, 3 (2003).

Deceivingly harmless, the first scene of the first act introduces work and life at the Central London Hatchery in a fashion similar to the novel, but more light-hearted and even funny in places, as one might expect of a musical comedy. This mood is carried on into the second scene, which is set in the Predestination Hall. Here is, for instance, the song of the Epsilons, the lowest caste of brave new worlders:

No more Mammy, no more Pappy:
Ain't we lucky, ain't we happy?
Everybody's oh so happy,
Everybody's happy now!

Sex galore, but no more marriages;
No more pushing baby carriages;
No one has to change a nappy—
Ain't we lucky, ain't we happy:
Everybody's happy now.

Dope for tea and dope for dinner,
Fun all night, and love and laughter;
No remorse, no morning after,
Where's the sin, and who's the sinner?
Everybody's happy now.

Girls pneumatic, girls exotic,
Girls ecstatic, girls erotic—
Hug me, Baby; make it snappy.
Everybody's oh so happy,
Everybody's happy now.

Lots to eat and hours for drinking
Soma cocktails—no more thinking.
NO MORE THINKING, NO MORE THINKING!
Everybody's happy now.[16]

But this funny note abates as soon as Bernard appears and asks the Director of Hatcheries and Conditioning to countersign a permit for him to visit the Indian reservation: the Director openly criticizes Bernard's "extra-curricular activities" (*BNWMC*, 56) and announces a severe screening after his return. Thus a sense of conflict and serious import arises, which is needed for satirical effects in the later course of action.

The first scene in the second act presents Bernard and Lenina in the Indian reservation at Malpais, New Mexico, and just by directly mentioning an American place name Huxley alerts the audience to the fact that the story is much closer to contemporary American society than it seemed in the first act. This drift is reinforced in the second scene, in which Bernard's return together with the Savage John surprises the Director with the embarrassing discovery that he is John's father: the Director's secretary is called Gromyka Franco in allusion to two representatives of totalitarian regimes of the 1950s, one being a leading government official and later foreign secretary of the Soviet Union, Andrej Gromyko, and the other the then dictator of Spain, Generalissimo Franco. In addition, the Director's office is described as similar to "*the office of any twentieth-century Big Shot—only considerably more so*"

(*BNWMC*, 71) so that the spectators—in contrast to the far-away oddities of the first act—are not only reminded of the familiar US State of New Mexico but also of the decade in which they themselves live. In act three, finally, the story closes in fully on contemporary American society by alluding to elements of the current lifestyle: the first scene presents a TV advertising spot and a broadcast of the celebration of GLOBAL LOVE WEEK, culminating in the choice of a Queen of Global Love, which clearly resembles popular competitions like the Miss World contest. Thus American society is implicitly equated with the brave new world and silently accused of the loss of values, such as freedom, individuality, and morality. Even more drastically, the second scene turns the shallow comedy into downright farce: in the Hospital for the Dying, where John's mother Linda is dozing off toward death under the influence of soma, a nurse practises death conditioning with small children and sings them a truly macabre song:

Death is like that scrumptious coma,
Into which you fall
After seven grammes of soma—
Nothing to worry about at all.

How satisfactory to feel quite certain
That this queer farce will have no sequel,
That death rings down the final curtain,
And that all men are chemically equal!

Alpha and Epsilon—in the sanitarium
Each is merely calcium, carbon and a pinch of barium.
Beta Plus and Delta—out of the crematorium
Comes only chlorine and phosphorus and the tiniest trace of thorium.

Nitrogen turns into lettuce in the spring,
Phosphorus puts apples on the autumn tree.
Oh grave, where is your victory?
Oh death, where is your sting? (*BNWMC*, 92)

Here the clue "farce" is explicitly mentioned in connection with death, and the statement "all men are chemically equal" sarcastically alludes to the article of equality in the American constitution. But the very height of black humour is reached in the ending of the musical comedy. When Helmholtz Watson, John and Lenina have just decided to go into exile to Tahiti, the brave new world's place for outsiders, a female TV newscaster interrupts the conversation, preposterously combining a kind of modern reality TV with advertising:

> Newscaster: "…and our candid camera transports you to beautiful Tahiti."
> (*Momentary blackout. The* Newscaster *is removed and when the lights come on again we see a brilliantly coloured set which reproduces, on a large scale, the background of one of Gauguin's South Sea paintings.*
> *Two men rush in from either side of the set, one in a blue, the other in a black uniform.*)
> Blue Islander: "Long live Humanity!"
> Black Islander: "Long live God!"
> (*They fight with butcher's knives. Two more men rush in from either side of the set.*)
> Second Black Islander: "Death to the Infidels!" (*He fires a revolver and the* First Blue Islander *falls.*)
> Second Blue Islander: "Down with the Reactionaries!" (*He fires his revolver. The* First Black Islander *falls.*)
> Second Blue Islander: "Justice!"
> Second Black Islander: "Truth!"
> (*Both fire simultaneously. Blackout. The light comes on again and we see the female* Newscaster.)
> Newscaster: "And now, ladies, I'd like to tell you something about Voluptua hand cream. Voluptua is the only hand cream enriched with ethyl acetic aldehyde. Laboratory tests by famous scientists have proved that the effect of ethyl acetic aldehyde on anthropoid apes is little short of miraculous."
> (*Music as in the previous commercial*)
> "So buy Voluptua in the Jumbo Economy Jar today."
> (*BNWMC*, 102–03)

That the outcasts, who are supposedly superior to the brave new worlders, should still be ready to kill each other in the name of ideas that form the backbone of the Western mindset, such as humanity, God, justice and truth, is certainly anti-utopian enough in itself, but that all this happens against the backdrop of Tahiti—an island that conjures up utopian dreams of a South Sea paradise—makes it doubly anti-utopian; that, however, a TV commercial for Voluptua hand cream—presumably an erotic name—should in its triviality follow the atrocious scenes from reality TV, clearly reflects the mindless pleasure principle at work also in American society. All in all, in his satiric musical comedy, which forestalls any sympathy, pity or even tragical effects by employing a mixture of songs, ridicule and farce together with a most macabre ending, Huxley raises his anti-utopian thrust to a maximum of intensity seldom reached before.

After three negative utopias and his concomitant critique of utopian thought, Huxley at last thought it was time that he got down to writing a positive utopia of the sort that he had envisaged in his 1946 foreword to *Brave New World*:

> If I were now to rewrite the book, I would offer the Savage a third alternative. Between the utopian and the primitive horns of his dilemma would lie the possibility of sanity [in a community where] economics would be decentralist [...] and politics [...] co-operative. [...] Religion would be the conscious and intelligent pursuit of man's Final End, the unitive knowledge of the immanent Tao or Logos, the transcendent Godhead or Brahman. (*BNW*, viii–ix)

One can see here that Huxley's profound knowledge of the mystical tradition in West and East paved the way for his novel *Island*, which he began to compose in 1956, the very year in which he wrote his anti-utopian musical comedy.

After the publication of *Island* in 1962 he stated in retrospect how difficult it was "to be interesting and convincing about happiness and rationality, about the common decencies and the uncommon ecstasies and illuminations" ("UPN," 1). Indeed, he had to avoid the defects of utopian thinking that he had criticized so hard and at the same time had to give life on his utopian island an ideal orientation that human beings could realistically hope to approximate to. This aim is reflected in the novel's epigraph, taken from Aristotle's *Politics*: "*In framing an ideal we may assume what we wish, but should avoid impossibilities.*"[17] Therefore, *Island* could not be a far-out utopia but had to be a near-in one, to use Huxley's own classification cited above: in such a utopia, he argued, "people like ourselves have solved their social and psychological problems in ways which to us are unfamiliar" ("UPN," 2). Consequently, the novel depicts a sane contemporary society on a fictitious island in the Indian Ocean, "completely surrounded," as Huxley said, "by a sinister world."[18] The inhabitants of Pala are eager to actualize their desirable human potentialities and aspire to become "fully human beings" (*Island*, 210) on the physical, intellectual and spiritual levels. This means that they are involved in a permanent process of self-education and adopt only the most suitable things from the Western and Eastern civilizations to "make the best of both worlds" (*Island*, 129). In particular, they avoid the three great dangers for modern societies that Huxley had pointed out in his collection of essays entitled *Brave New World Revisited* (1958): over-population, over-organization and over-simplification. Basically, Huxley tries to apply the philosophical insights of his late career to suggest ways of living that are geared to forestall the pitfalls of modern life, though not in any final sense but always according to the standards of contemporary scientific knowledge. The underlying assumption is neatly formulated in the Old Raja's little book called *Notes on What's What*:

> One third, more or less, of all the sorrow that the person I think I am must endure is unavoidable. It is the sorrow inherent in the

> human condition, the price we must pay for being sentient and self-conscious organisms, aspirants to liberation, but subject to the laws of nature and under orders to keep on marching, through irreversible time, through a world wholly indifferent to our well-being, towards decrepitude and the certainty of death. The remaining two thirds of all sorrow is home-made and, so far as the universe is concerned, unnecessary. (*Island*, 86)

Therefore, the Palanese are resolved to fight on all fronts:

> *Patriotism is not enough.* But neither is anything else. Science is not enough, religion is not enough, art is not enough, politics and economics are not enough, nor is love, nor is duty, nor is action however disinterested, nor, however sublime, is contemplation. Nothing short of everything will really do. (*Island*, 132)

Thus many of the problems raised in *Brave New World*, from genetic and social engineering to the question of "man's Final End" (*BNW*, ix) are tackled, if not solved, in *Island* in different ways with the help of reason, mutual understanding and techniques of Buddhism, such as awareness, meditation and self-transcendence. In contrast to Huxley's rather static negative utopias, in which a seemingly perfect stability has been achieved, *Island* depicts a society in progress and can therefore be called a dynamic utopia.[19] Surely Huxley's severe critique of definitive utopian blueprints of the static sort has not in the least abated—he now rather presents realistic, if tentative, attempts to develop desirable human potentialities with a view to creating a social community of fulfilled individuals. Nevertheless the novel ends on an extremely pessimistic note, with the island being invaded by its militarist neighbours, who serve the interests of global materialism and consumerism. To quote from the late David Bradshaw's introduction to the novel:

> *Island* is [Huxley's] poignant acknowledgement that in a world of increasing greed, mass communication, oil-guzzling transport, burgeoning population and inveterate hostility, a pacific and co-operative community like Pala's 'oasis of freedom and happiness' has little hope of survival.[20]

Even if considered not equally hopeless as *Ape and Essence*, the tragical implication of this ending seems at least to suggest that it will take a long time for the world to move in the direction of Pala and will require a good deal of intelligence, good will and charity from all parties involved.

In conclusion, one may return to Huxley's lecture on "Utopias, Positive and Negative" (1962) and hear his reasons for radical anti-utopian thinking, which, as has been shown, is essentially directed against static utopias:

> [T]hough some Utopias have been shrewdly realistic and practical in patches, not one, I venture to say, has ever been realistic as a whole, practical in its totality. [...]
>
> There are two cogent reasons for this state of things. In the first place, all writers [...] are victims of that Original Sin of the Intellect, the urge to oversimplification. [...]
>
> From Plato's time to the present the majority even of near-in Utopists have failed to do justice to individual psychology. They tend to assume that natural religion, moralistic education and a judicious reform of our social, political and economic arrangements will lead, inevitably and automatically, to universal happiness, permanent peace and generalized virtue. [And there is] that other most common manifestation of Original Sin—the lust for tidiness [, i.e.,] the immoral excess, perversion and misdirection of that beneficent urge to order, which is at the root of all art, all philosophy, all science, all civilization. ("UPN," 3)

In Huxley's view these two "manifestation[s] of Original Sin" obviously are inveterately ingrained in the make-up of all human beings and inevitably induce utopian writers to devise static utopias. Quite consistently, he appears to return, in the concluding paragraph of his 1962 lecture, to Berdyaev's *caveat* that he had chosen as epigraph to *Brave New World*:

> By their creators all these Utopias were intended to be positive. But in every case an oversimplified view of human nature, combined with the lust for tidiness [for perfect order], has reversed the sign and transformed these ideal states into negative Utopias which, in spite of their authors' underlying good will and sporadic good sense, are potentially as horribly inhuman as Orwell's *1984*. [...] Luckily for humanity, the high minded tyrannies of the Utopists have existed only on paper. What would have been our fate if the philosophers of the ideal had become, as Plato hoped they might, the kings of the real world? One shudders even to think of it. ("UPN," 4)

---

[1] Revised version of a lecture held at the international conference "Excellence in Arts and Sciences: The Huxley Family" at the Hungarian Academy of Sciences in Budapest on 8 November 2019.

[2] Aldous Huxley, "Utopias, Positive and Negative (1963)," edited and with an afterword by James Sexton, *AHA*, 1 (2001), 1–5; here note 1. Hereafter, "UPN."

[3] See, e.g., Alan Wittbecker, *Eutopian Essays: Towards the Creation of Good Places through Thought Experiments and Ecological Designs* (Sarasota, FL, 2004; [1]1970).

[4] For a recent terminological discussion, see, e.g., Valery Rabinovitch, "Utopian and Anti-Utopian Thought in Aldous Huxley's Letters: His Virtual Dialogue with H. G. Wells and George Orwell," *AHA*, 17/18 (2017/2018), 271, note 2.

[5] See, e.g., Robert Nozick, "A Framework for Utopia," *Anarchy, State, and Utopia* (Oxford, 1974), ch. 10, 297–334, particularly 312: "Utopia will consist of utopias, of many different and divergent communities in which people lead different kinds of lives under different institutions. [...] Utopia is a framework for utopias, a place where people are at liberty to join together voluntarily to pursue and attempt to realize their own vision of the good life in the ideal community but where no one can *impose* his own utopian vision upon others. The utopian society is the society of utopianism. [...] [U]topia is meta-utopia: the environment in which utopian experiments may be tried out; the environment in which people are free to do their own thing; the environment which must, to a great extent, be realized first if more particular utopian visions are to be realized stably."

[6] See, e.g., Patrick Parrinder, "Utopia and Meta-Utopia,"*Shadows of the Future: H. G. Wells, Science Fiction, and Prophecy* (Syracuse, NY, 1995), ch. 7, 96–112. Parrinder speaks of "the common use of 'meta' to denote a manifest self-consciousness in discourse" (98) and then introduces a new meaning of 'meta-utopia' modelled on Hayden White's term 'metahistory,' which covers "the latent metahistorical elements—'a deep structural content which is generally poetic, and specifically linguistic, in nature, and which serves as the precritically accepted paradigm of what a distinctively "historical" explanation should be'" (98). Moreover, in a telling note he explicitly distances himself from Nozick: "This [meaning of 'meta-utopia'] should not be confused, however, with the use of the term 'meta-utopia' by some political scientists who seem quite innocent of the idea that a utopia is a particular kind of text rather than a kind of society" (98, note 3).

[7] As Lothar Fietz already convincingly argued in 2006, Huxley's anti-utopianism has to be appraised in the light of the idea of time and history, see his article "Myth, History and Utopianism," *AHA*, 6 (2006), 135–47, particularly his ten-point overview of "the implications of the key concepts of 'myth,' 'history' and 'Utopianism'" (136–37).

[8] *Brave New World* (London, 1950), 197. Hereafter, *BNW*.

[9] For Huxley's use of Berdyaev, see Irina Golovacheva, "Huxley, Blok and Berdyaev: Observations on the Nature of the Russian Revolution," *AHA*, 14 (2014), 130–34.

[10] See *BNW*, viii, and *Brave New World Revisited* (London, 1958), 12.

[11] Compare *Measure for Measure*, 2:2.146–51: "But man, proud man / Dressed in a little brief authority—/ Most ignorant of what he is most assured, / His glassy essence—like an angry ape, / Plays such fantastic tricks before high heaven /As make the angels weep."

[12] *The Perennial Philosophy* (London, 1946), 210.

[13] *Ape and Essence* (London, 1949), 54. Hereafter, *AE*.

[14] This pronouncement appears to allude to the central etching in Goya's *Caprichos* with the inscription "El sueño de la razón produce monstruos" ('The dream of reason produces monsters'), which Huxley later commented upon in detail in his "Variations on Goya," see *Themes and Variations* (London, 1950), 215–16. For an interpretation of this theme in the larger context of Huxley's critique of ideals, see Katja Reinecke, "The Order of Folly or the Folly of

Order: Aldous Huxley's Critique of Ideals Based on Goya's "El sueño," *Aldous Huxley, Man of Letters: Thinker, Critic and Artist—Proceedings of the Third International Aldous Huxley Symposium Riga 2004*, ed. Bernfried Nugel, Uwe Rasch, Gerhard Wagner, "Human Potentialities," 9 (Berlin, 2007), 205–12.

[15] See "Introduction," *Aldous Huxley and Self-Realization: His Concept of Human Potentialities, His Techniques for Actualizing Them, and His Views of Their Social Consequences*, ed. Dana Sawyer, Julian Piras and Uwe Rasch, "Human Potentialities," 12 (Berlin et al., 2019), ix-xiii, and Bernfried Nugel, "Aldous Huxley's Plea for Desirable Human Potentialities: Some Unknown Late Comments (1961–63)," *AHA*, 10/11 (2010/2011), 223–29.

[16] Aldous Huxley, *Brave New World: A Musical Comedy*, ed. Bernfried Nugel and with an afterword by Jerome Meckier, *AHA*, 3 (2003), 50–51. Hereafter, *BNWMC*.

[17] *Island* (London, 1962) [hereafter, *Island*], [6]; see *The Politics of Aristotle*, II, 6, 1265a, trans. Benjamin Jowett, I (Oxford, 1885), 39: "[In framing an ideal] we may assume what we wish, but should avoid impossibilities."

[18] In an unpublished letter to Ian Parsons of 19 January 1962, kept in the Huxley papers of Reading University Library, Huxley inserted a sketch for the cover of *Island* showing a white circle on red ground and explained it as follows: "The circle is land completely surrounded by a sinister world." (Incidentally, this sketch was used by Erwin Löhr for his original design of the poster for the Aldous Huxley Centenary Symposium Münster 1994; see <https://www.uni-muenster.de/Anglistik/Huxley/ahs_conferences.html>.)

[19] Compare Parrinder's analysis of Wells's "scientific utopia": "The problem here is that the idea of a scientific utopia is a paradox, if not an actual contradiction in terms. Science is an inherently dynamic force, relying (as Wells puts it) on 'the perpetual criticism, increase and diffusion of more knowledge and more' [...]. The effect must be to subvert any stable order. Wells's rejection of a static utopianism is one of the premises of *A Modern Utopia*" (97).

[20] Aldous Huxley, *Island*, introduced by David Bradshaw (London, 1994), [8] (in his unpaginated introduction).

Aldous Huxley Annual

A Journal of Twentieth-Century Thought and Beyond

edited by

Professor Jerome Meckier (University of Kentucky), Professor Bernfried Nugel (Universität Münster)

Bernfried Nugel; Jerome Meckier (Eds.)

Aldous Huxley Annual Volume 17/18 (2017/2018)

Volume 17/18 begins with a section containing original Huxley documents: *Below the Equator*, an unpublished film story collaboration by Isherwood and Huxley, edited by James Sexton and Bernfried Nugel, to be followed by two pieces rediscovered and edited by James Sexton, viz. *The Heroes*, William R. Cox's screenplay adaptation of a lost Huxley story, and the translation of a 1960 interview held in French by the Canadian writer Hubert Aquin. Then Huxley nephew Piero Ferrucci kindly opens his family archives of original Huxley letters and photographs and contributes a remarkable essay on his coming of age with Aldous Huxley. Rounding off this section, Peter Wood introduces an unknown 1934 letter Huxley wrote to René Schickele, a forgotten German author in the writers' community at Sanary. The second section presents a further selection of papers from the Sixth International Aldous Huxley Symposium held at Almería in April 2017 as well as other critical articles.

Bd. 17, 2019, 306 S., 39,90 €, br., ISBN 978-3-643-91080-6

Bernfried Nugel; Jerome Meckier (Eds.)

Aldous Huxley Annual

Volume 16 (2016)

Volume 16 presents a miscellany of uncollected Huxley essays, edited by James Sexton, to be followed by a first selection of papers from the Sixth International Aldous Huxley Symposium held at Almería in April 2017. This section opens with an essay that fills a blank spot on the map of Huxley criticism, James Sexton's study of Huxley and architecture. The volume continues with several articles (including one not from Almería) on *Brave New World* and its wider context and closes with essays on Huxley's lifelong struggle with his deficient eye-sight and on his view of the art of dying.

Bd. 16, 2018, 258 S., 39,90 €, br., ISBN 978-3-643-90979-4

Bernfried Nugel; Jerome Meckier (Eds.)

Aldous Huxley Annual

Volume 15 (2015)

Volume 15 is dedicated to Prof David Bradshaw (Oxford University), who died on 13 September 2016 after a long illness. His last article is published at the beginning of this issue, to be followed by Uwe Rasch's essay on Huxley's 1912 sketchbook (with over 30 unpublished images) and a new selection of unpublished Huxley letters by James Sexton. The volume continues with several articles on Huxley in the 1920s and 1930s and is rounded off with an essay on Huxley's stance as social ecologist.

N.B.: The submission deadline for volume 16 of Aldous Huxley Annual is 31 July 2017. For further details see inside front cover.

Bd. 15, 2016, 302 S., 39,90 €, br., ISBN 3-643-90845-2

Bernfried Nugel; Jerome Meckier (Eds.)

Aldous Huxley Annual

Volume 14 (2014)

Volume 14 of *Aldous Huxley Annual* begins with the presentation of Hux–ley's 1961 diary covering his trip to Europe. It continues with his role in the editing of a book by his wife Laura and the story of the Huxley Tapes, a collection of recorded lectures and readings from his late career. Further critical articles on particular aspects of Huxley's work follow, including a second selection of papers from the Oxford Symposium in 2013. The volume closes with the third Peter Edgerly Firchow Memorial Essay by Julian Piras (Belgium).

Bd. 14, 2015, 296 S., 39,90 €, br., ISBN 978-3-643-90698-4

Bernfried Nugel; Jerome Meckier (Eds.)

Aldous Huxley Annual

Volume 12/13 (2012/2013)

Bd. 12/13, 2014, 368 S., 39,90 €, br., ISBN 978-3-643-90587-1

LIT Verlag Berlin – Münster – Wien – Zürich – London

Auslieferung Deutschland / Österreich / Schweiz: siehe Impressumsseite

"Human Potentialities"

Studien zu Aldous Huxley & zeitgenössischer Kultur
Studies in Aldous Huxley & Contemporary Culture
/ edited by
Prof. Dr. Bernfried Nugel (Universität Münster) und Prof. Dr. Lothar Fietz (Universität Tübingen)

Jerome Meckier

Aldous Huxley, from Poet to Mystic

Huxley began as a poet. He perfected the voice of the modern satirical poet of ideas who used art against itself to produce a parodic poetry of breakdowns, collapses, stalemates, and dead ends best suited to the apparent pointlessness of the post-war era. His cleverest, most irreverent poems are contrapuntal; they in effect silence venerable poets and cancel traditional formats. Huxley's poetic personas either fail to preserve conventional forms or purposely sabotage them. By 1920, Huxley became the parodic equivalent of the formative intelligences (i.e., Dante, Goethe, Lucretius) who once synthesized their respective eras positively. Meckier explicates most of Huxley's poems, including "Leda" his masterpiece, an ironical modern myth. He traces Huxley's development in terms of the poets he inserted in five of his eleven novels, along with their poems. These poets mostly fail as poets, their different stances falling apart one after another. But Huxley began to detect a spiritual significance underlying the creative urge. This allowed him to rehabilitate many of the Romantic and Victorian poets he formerly ridiculed as frauds and liars. Eventually, he celebrated mystical contemplation as silent poetry, positing a utopia in which everyone is a poet to the limits of his or her potentiality. Huxley became the perennial philosopher, a neo-Brahmin: the sage-like figure he initially personified parodically. His paradigmatic career took him from a Pyrrhonic silencing of outmoded poems and poets to the advocacy of a poetry of silence.

Bd. 11, 2011, 392 S., 39,90 €, br., ISBN 978-3-643-90101-9

Katja Reinecke

Die Verarbeitung der Soziologie Vilfredo Paretos im Werk Aldous Huxleys

Aldous Huxleys herausragende Bedeutung als gesellschaftskritischer Denker und politischer Beobachter wird heutzutage kaum bestritten. Wie fundiert Huxleys Kritik an gesellschaftlichen Phänomenen ist, lässt sich an seiner Auseinandersetzung mit soziologischen Ansätzen ablesen. Bereits während seiner Studienzeit beklagte er immer wieder das Fehlen einer etablierten Soziologie in England, denn gezielte soziale Veränderungen und Reformen bedurften seiner Ansicht nach einer angemessenen wissenschaftlichen Basis. In seiner Essaysammlung Proper Studies (1927) verweist Huxley dezidiert auf Vilfredo Paretos Trattato di sociologia generale als Anregung zur Abfassung dieses Bandes. Ab 1927 befasst er sich in regelmäßigen Abständen mit Paretos Soziologie. Ergiebig sind in diesem Zusammenhang vor allem weniger bekannte Rezensionen, Essays und Artikel, in denen er sich mit soziologischen, aber auch politischen Themen befasst, sowie das Drama Now More Than Ever (1932), in dem er in Anlehnung an Paretos Charaktertypologie die Rolle und Funktion der Wirtschaftselite und des Adels analysiert und fiktional verarbeitet. Ähnlich lassen sich auch in seinen Romanen Point Counter Point (1928) und Eyeless in Gaza (1936) paretianische Vorstellungen nachweisen. Bedeutsam für Huxley wie auch Pareto ist, dass die Transformation gesellschaftlichen Lebens eng mit der Umwandlung religiöser Systeme zusammenhängt. Entsprechend sehen beide politische, ökonomische und kulturelle Phänomene als Religionssubstitute instrumentalisiert. Huxleys Auseinandersetzung mit gesellschaftstheoretischen Ansätzen unterliegt einer Entwick–lung, die sich erst anhand der chronologischen Analyse seines Werks erschließt. Vom Ideal einer streng „logisch-erfahrungsbezogenen" Wissenschaft zur Erfassung gesellschaftlicher Realität gelangt er zu der Überzeugung, dass Gesellschaftswissenschaften eines ethischen Ideals bedürfen.

Bd. 10, 2010, 512 S., 59,90 €, br., ISBN 978-3-8258-1161-7

Bernfried Nugel; Uwe Rasch; Gerhard Wagner (Eds.)

Aldous Huxley, Man of Letters: Thinker, Critic and Artist

Proceedings of the Third International Aldous Huxley Symposium Riga 2004

Bd. 9, 2008, 320 S., 39,90 €, br., ISBN 978-3-8258-9034-6

LIT Verlag Berlin – Münster – Wien – Zürich – London

Auslieferung Deutschland / Österreich / Schweiz: siehe Impressumsseite

Jerome Meckier
Aldous Huxley: Modern Satirical Novelist of Ideas
Edited by Peter Firchow and Bernfried Nugel
The essays on Aldous Huxley collected here were written between 1966 and 2005 and have been arranged by their author in such a way that they approximate a book on Huxley as a modern satirical novelist of ideas. In this capacity, Huxley assessed the intellectual condition of his era, always excoriating folly but never losing sight of human potentialities, especially his own. Huxley's ingrained skepticism persisted into his later fictions, even after his conception of the nature of things improved. The amused and highly amusing Pyrrhonic aesthete turned into a Swiftian Prospero. Detached yet totally committed to bettering the human condition, Huxley epitomized the dedicated craftsman. This lifelong aesthetician, always a philosopher, continues to command attention as thinker, critic, and artist: both satirist and sage.
Bd. 8, 2006, 408 S., 34,90 €, br., ISBN 3-8258-9668-4

Hermann Josef Real; Peter Firchow (eds.)
The Perennial Satirist
Essays in Honour of Bernfried Nugel
The present collection of essays primarily honours Bernfried Nugel the teacher and scholar, but it also pays homage to Bernfried Nugel the indefatigable worker in the cause of Aldous Huxley studies. It is due to this latter manifestation that many of the contribu- tors to this volume know each other personally, having met at one or more of the international conferences that Professor Nugel organized and either hosted or co-hosted. At Munster, his home university, he has also been instrumental in establishing and heading a Centre for admirers of Huxley's work, along with a fine library of Huxley materials, including manuscripts and numerous first editions.
Bd. 7, 2005, 400 S., 29,90 €, br., ISBN 3-8258-8339-6

Lothar Fietz
Aldous Huxley – Prätexte und Kontexte
Lothar Fietz hatte bis zu seiner Emeritierung einen Lehrstuhl für Anglistik an der Universität Tübingen inne. Schwerpunkte seiner wissenschaftlichen Publikationen sind der Strukturwandel in der englischen Literatur seit der Renaissance, die Literaturtheorie und die Theoriegeschichte.
Im 6. Band von „Human Potentialities“ sind fünfzehn Artikel versammelt, in denen er das Werk Aldous Huxleys vor dem Hintergrund literarischer und philosophischer Prätexte historisch kontextualisiert. Die Arbeiten zu Huxleys Weltanschauung und Weltanschauungskritik kreisen um Fragestellungen von Mythos und Geschichte sowie von Geschichte als Verfallsprozeß und Utopie. Der Verfasser verfolgt die Denkstruktur vom Verlust und der Rückgewinnung mythischer Ganzheit durch verschiedene Kontexte von der kontinentalen Renaissance bis ins 20. Jahrhundert. Weitere Arbeiten eruieren den Wandel der literarischen und philosophischen Fiktionsbegriffe seit dem 18. Jahrhundert, den Verhältniswandel von literarischer und szientifischer Kultur seit dem 17. Jahrhundert und strukturelle Analogien in Romanen Manns, Hesses, Brochs und Kasacks zum Spätwerk Huxleys.
Bd. 6, 2005, 256 S., 34,90 €, br., ISBN 3-8258-8497-x

James Hull
Aldous Huxley, Representative Man
Edited by Gerhard Wagner
This psychological reading of Huxley's oeuvre as a whole traces Huxley's self-transformation in his books and aims to do justice to the artist and the person who was Aldous Huxley. It is safe to regard as basic to his entire work the unfolding of the conflict we find so clearly delineated in his early short story "Farcical History of Richard Greenow" (*Limbo*, 1920), with Pearl Bellairs representing the emotional tradition that threatens the synthetic philosopher. Huxley's own story is plainly visible even in *Limbo* and *Crome Yellow* (1921), but it is in *Antic Hay* (1923) that the pattern of the future assumes a solid foundation. There we encounter in full force the tensions that follow him throughout his life: on the one hand an extreme of sensuality and on the other a longing for the "chaste pleasures," for a quiet and mystical world completely different from that in which he found himself. The question of the relations between body and mind as well as the mystery of human consciousness haunt him to the very last, but after his mid-life crisis, depicted in *Eyeless in Gaza* (1936), a strong faith in the reality of a spiritual world is obvions. In the end he even manages to reinstate the body in his scheme of things.
Bd. 5, 2004, 624 S., 49,90 €, br., ISBN 3-8258-7663-2

Philosophie – Sprache – Literatur

Prof. Dr. Hans-Ulrich Lessing (Universität Bochum)

Cornelia Eşianu

„Und so führt die Philosophie zur Poesie"

Systematische Studien zu Friedrich Schegel

Dass der heutigen Literaturwissenschaft der anthropologische wie transzendentale Akzent im Begriff der Poesie abhanden zu kommen scheint, soll weder verwundern noch alarmieren. Friedrich Schlegel bezeichnete seine Zeit als eine „entgeistete", der er vorwiegend auf den Wegen der Poesie und Philosophie und ihrer Verbindung durch das menschliche Vermögen der Einbildungskraft zu begegnen versuchte. Warum gilt die Philosophie noch immer als eine „hilfsbedürftige" Wissenschaft, die zu ihrer „Vervollkommnung" einer Ergänzung bedarf? Das Buch rekonstruiert in systematischer Weise, indem es sich sowohl in die Nähe als auch in Distanz zum theoretischen Friedrich Schlegel begibt, die Geschichte einer solchen Verbindung. Es ist jene vielversprechende Geschichte, in der sich Fantasie und Vernunft im Bewusstsein des Menschen wieder gleichermaßen einzufinden haben.

Bd. 10, 2016, 416 S., 19,90 €, br., ISBN 978-3-643-50736-5

Gaetano Chiurazzi (Ed.)

The Frontiers of the Other

Ethics and Politics of Translation

vol. 9, 2019, ca. 248 pp., ca. 29,90 €, br., ISBN-CH 978-3-643-90708-0

Miriam Rainer

Zögern / Hesitate

Versuch über das Übersetzen mit Walter Benjamin

Das Zögern, das diese Arbeit als Merkmal der Übersetzungsbewegung gegen Ideale der restlosen Aneignung und Verfremdung zu profilieren versucht, öffnet die disjunktive Übersetzungsbewegung zu einem ‚Spielraum', – in dem sich das Übersetzungsproblem, schlechthinnige Un-/Übersetzbarkeit als Form jedes sprachlichen Gebildes, in seiner reinen Potentialität entfaltet –, und hält den Raum offen. Im Übergang begriffen offenbart sich Sprache in Übersetzung – zwischen Sprachgewinn und -verlust – nicht als Mitteilung, vielmehr als Mit-Teilung, Sprache nur vermöge ihrer Teilung von sich. Ist das Labyrinth Sprache nach Walter Benjamin „die Heimat des Zögernden", bezeugt Übersetzung stets die unendlichen Intervallierungen des Kontinuums Sprache, dessen Grenzen sie unablässig neu zieht. Das Gedicht *Stimmen* von Paul Celan, dessen Übersetzungen und Reflexionen über das Übersetzen von Rosmarie Waldrop und Peter Waterhouse, sowie die Philosophie Jacques Derridas, Emmanuel Lévinas', Jean-Luc Nancys und Stanley Cavells bilden wichtige Bezüge der Arbeit.

Bd. 8, 2015, 182 S., 29,90 €, br., ISBN 978-3-643-50649-8

Esther Schröter

Erzählen, (Lebens-)Geschichte und Identität im Werk Hannah Arendts

Insgesamt lässt sich in Hannah Arendts Schriften eine Verbindung ihrer Ausführungen über Geschichte im Sinne der Historiographie, ihrer Anthropologie und der Annahme eines narrativen Selbst beobachten. Eine systematische Textinterpretation und Werkanalyse zeigt, dass diese Bereiche aufs tiefste miteinander verbunden sind, ihre Gegensätzlichkeit in der Erzählung aufgehoben und mittels der Auffassung der Welt als eine Bühne in Einklang gebracht werden können.

Bd. 6, 2014, 280 S., 24,90 €, br., ISBN 978-3-643-12531-6

Kevin Liggieri

Zur Domestikation des Menschen

Anthropotechnische und anthropoetische Optimierungsdiskurse

Nicht viele Themen werden in der aktuellen Debatte in Medien und Wissenschaft so polemisch und kontrovers diskutiert wie die facettenreiche menschliche Optimierungen. Die tiefergehende Aufgabe der vorliegenden Untersuchung liegt darin, den modern-anmutenden Topos der Optimierung historisch zu verorten. Es stellt sich die Frage, unter welchen Umständen und Verschiebungen sich der polyvalente Begriff einer Anthropotechnik über verschiedene Wissensfelder hinweg entwickelt.

Bd. 5, 2014, 152 S., 24,90 €, br., ISBN 978-3-643-12474-6

LIT Verlag Berlin – Münster – Wien – Zürich – London

Auslieferung Deutschland / Österreich / Schweiz: siehe Impressumsseite